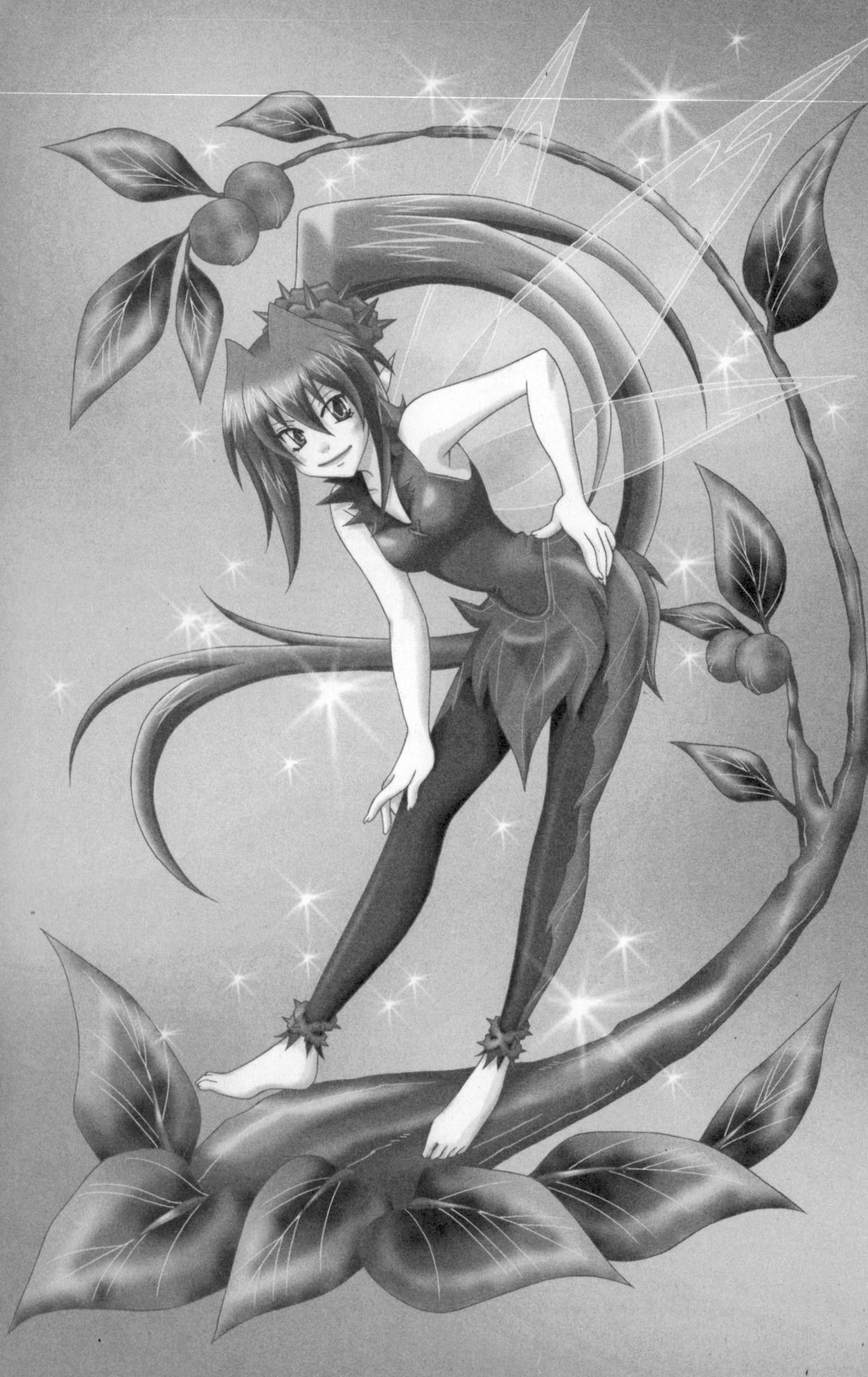

Disney Fairies: Vidia and the Fairy Crown
By Haruhi Katou

Retouch and Lettering - Star Print Brokers
Copy Editor - Shannon Watters
Production Artist - Keila N. Ramos
Graphic Designer - Monalisa De Asis

Editor - Luis Reyes
Digital Imaging Manager - Chris Buford
Pre-Production Supervisor - Vicente Rivera, Jr.
Production Specialist - Lucas Rivera
Managing Editor - Vy Nguyen
Art Director - Al-Insan Lashley
Editor-in-Chief - Rob Tokar
Publisher - Mike Kiley
President and C.O.O. - John Parker
C.E.O. and Chief Creative Officer - Stu Levy

A **TOKYOPOP** Manga

TOKYOPOP and 🐱 are trademarks or registered trademarks of TOKYOPOP Inc.

TOKYOPOP Inc.
5900 Wilshire Blvd. Suite 2000
Los Angeles, CA 90036

E-mail: info@TOKYOPOP.com
Come visit us online at www.TOKYOPOP.com

ISBN: 978-1-4278-1503-3
First TOKYOPOP printing: August 2008
10 9 8 7 6 5 4 3 2 1
Printed in the USA

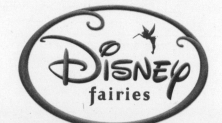

Disney
fairies

Vidia and the
Fairy Crown

By Haruhi Katou

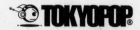

HAMBURG // LONDON // LOS ANGELES // TOKYO

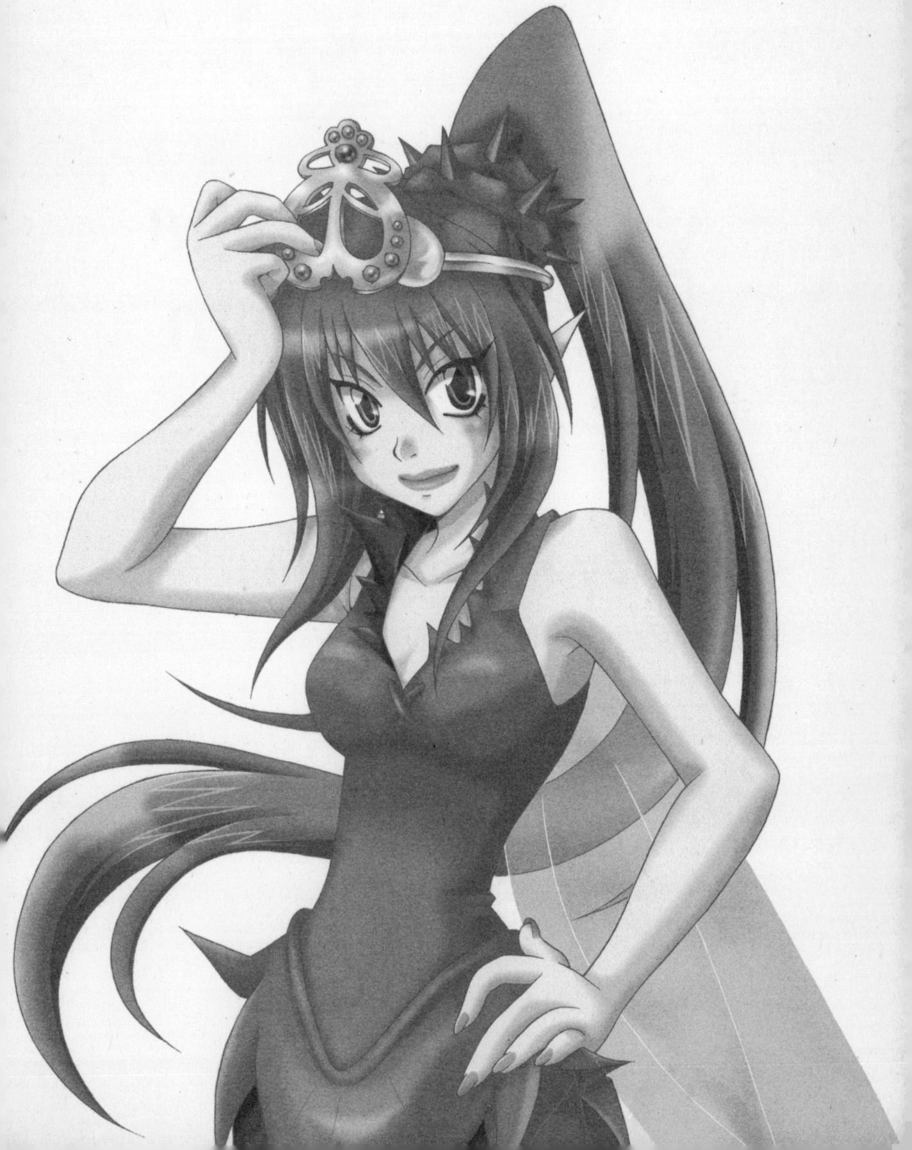

Believing is just the beginning

All About Fairies

IF YOU HEAD TOWARD THE SECOND STAR TO YOUR RIGHT AND FLY STRAIGHT ON 'TIL MORNING, YOU'LL COME TO NEVER LAND, A MAGICAL ISLAND WHERE MERMAIDS PLAY AND CHILDREN NEVER GROW UP.

WHEN YOU ARRIVE, YOU MIGHT HEAR SOMETHING LIKE THE TINKLING OF LITTLE BELLS. FOLLOW THAT SOUND AND YOU'LL FIND PIXIE HOLLOW, THE SECRET HEART OF NEVER LAND. A GREAT OLD MAPLE TREE GROWS IN PIXIE HOLLOW, AND IN IT LIVES HUNDREDS OF FAIRIES AND SPARROW MEN.

SOME OF THEM CAN DO WATER MAGIC, OTHERS CAN FLY LIKE THE WIND, AND STILL OTHERS CAN SPEAK TO ANIMALS. YOU SEE, PIXIE HOLLOW IS THE NEVER FAIRIES' KINGDOM, AND EACH FAIRY WHO LIVES THERE HAS A SPECIAL, EXTRAORDINARY TALENT.

NOT FAR FROM THE HOME TREE, NESTLED IN THE BRANCHES OF A HAWTHORN, IS MOTHER DOVE, THE MOST MAGICAL CREATURE OF ALL.

SHE SITS ON HER EGG, WATCHING OVER THE FAIRIES, WHO IN TURN WATCH OVER HER. FOR AS LONG AS MOTHER DOVE'S EGG STAYS WELL AND WHOLE, NO ONE IN NEVER LAND WILL EVER GROW OLD. ONCE, MOTHER DOVE'S EGG WAS BROKEN. BUT WE ARE NOT TELLING THE STORY OF THE EGG HERE. NOW, IT IS TIME FOR VIDIA'S TALE...

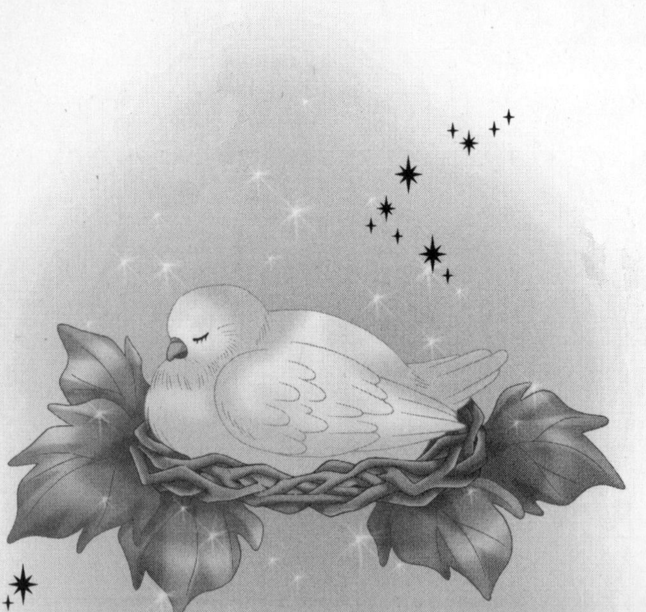

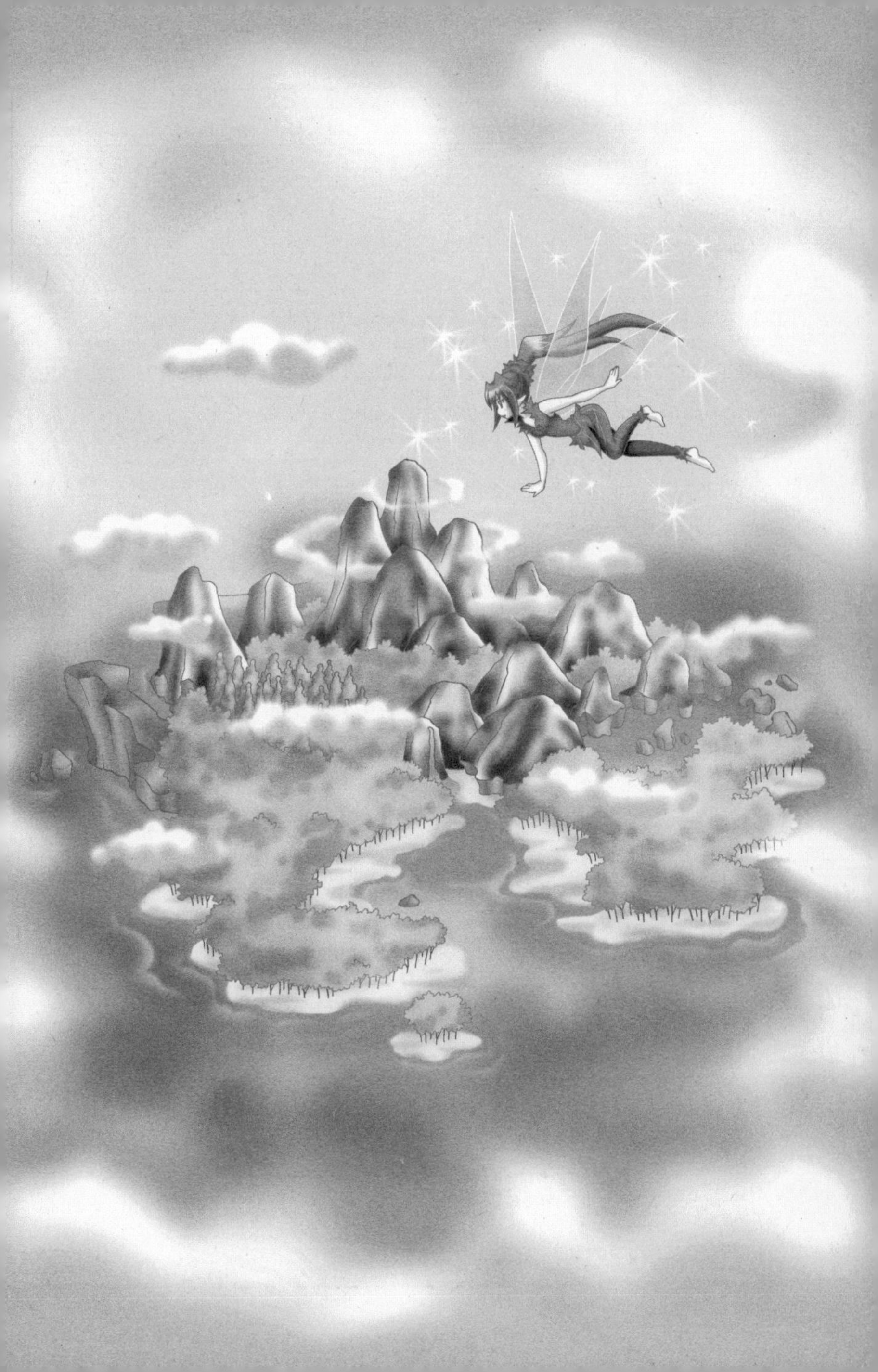

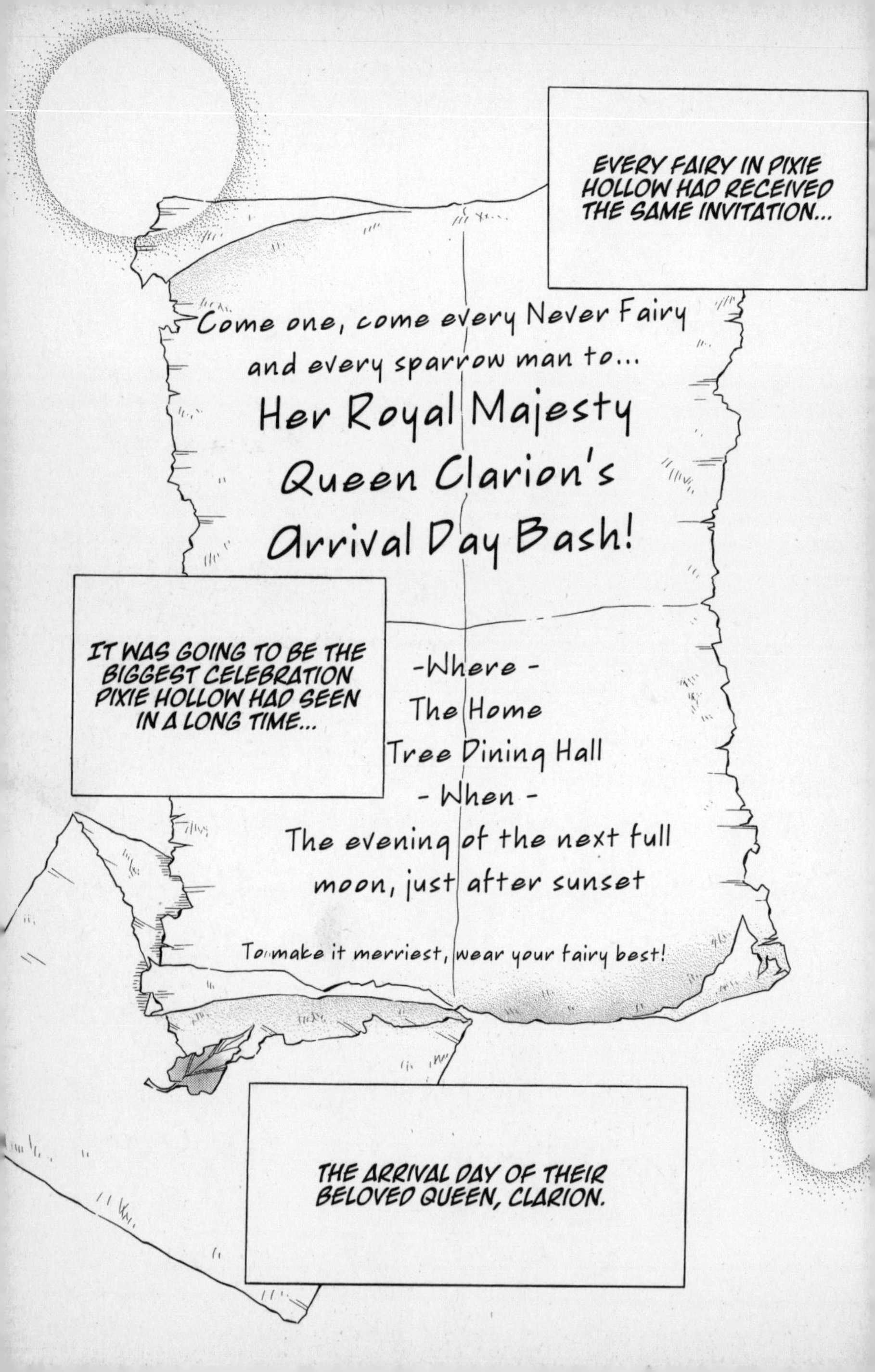
EVERY FAIRY IN PIXIE HOLLOW HAD RECEIVED THE SAME INVITATION...
Come one, come every Never Fairy and every sparrow man to...
Her Royal Majesty Queen Clarion's Arrival Day Bash!
-Where -
The Home Tree Dining Hall
- When -
The evening of the next full moon, just after sunset
To make it merriest, wear your fairy best!
IT WAS GOING TO BE THE BIGGEST CELEBRATION PIXIE HOLLOW HAD SEEN IN A LONG TIME...
THE ARRIVAL DAY OF THEIR BELOVED QUEEN, CLARION.

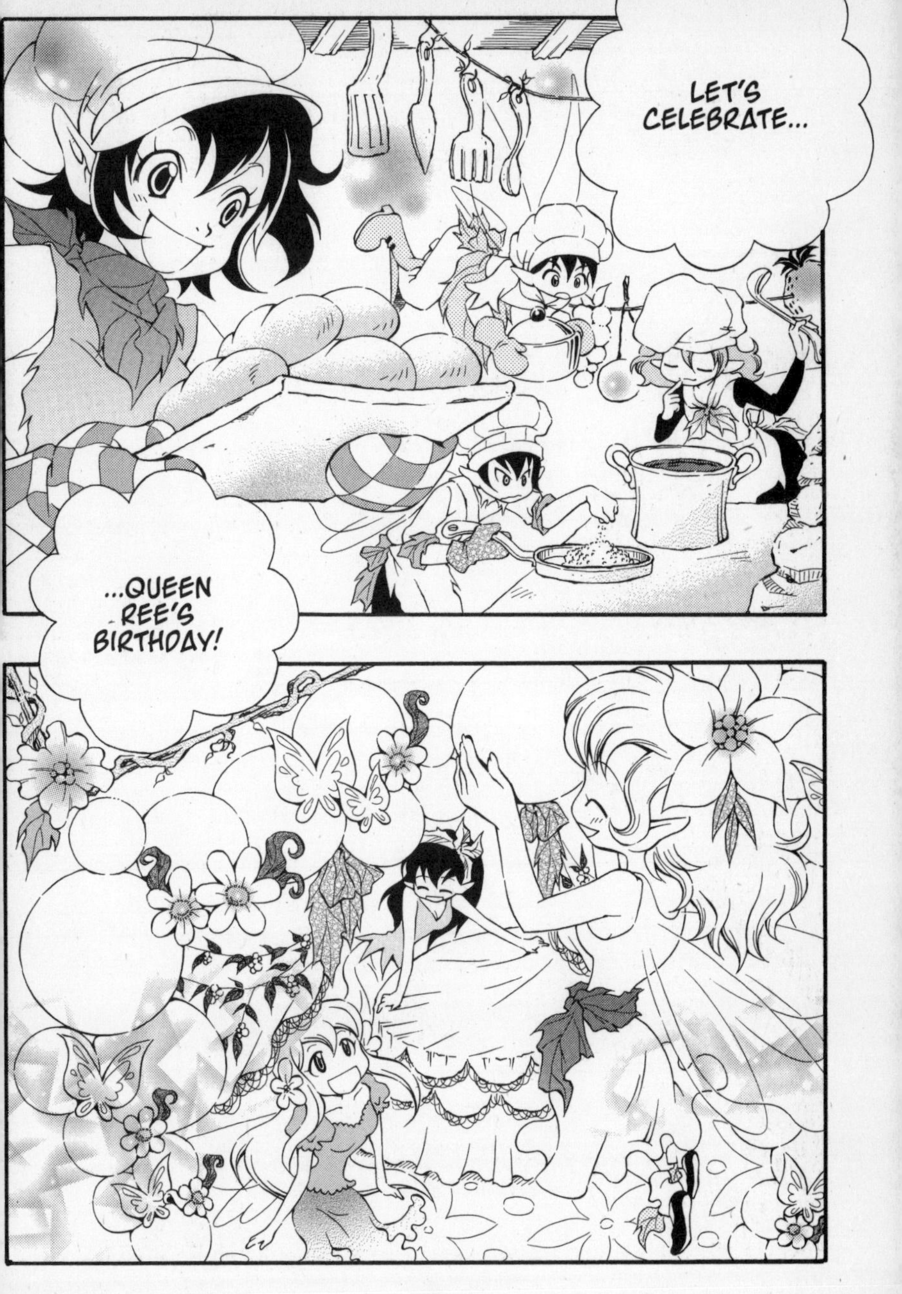
LET'S CELEBRATE...
...QUEEN REE'S BIRTHDAY!

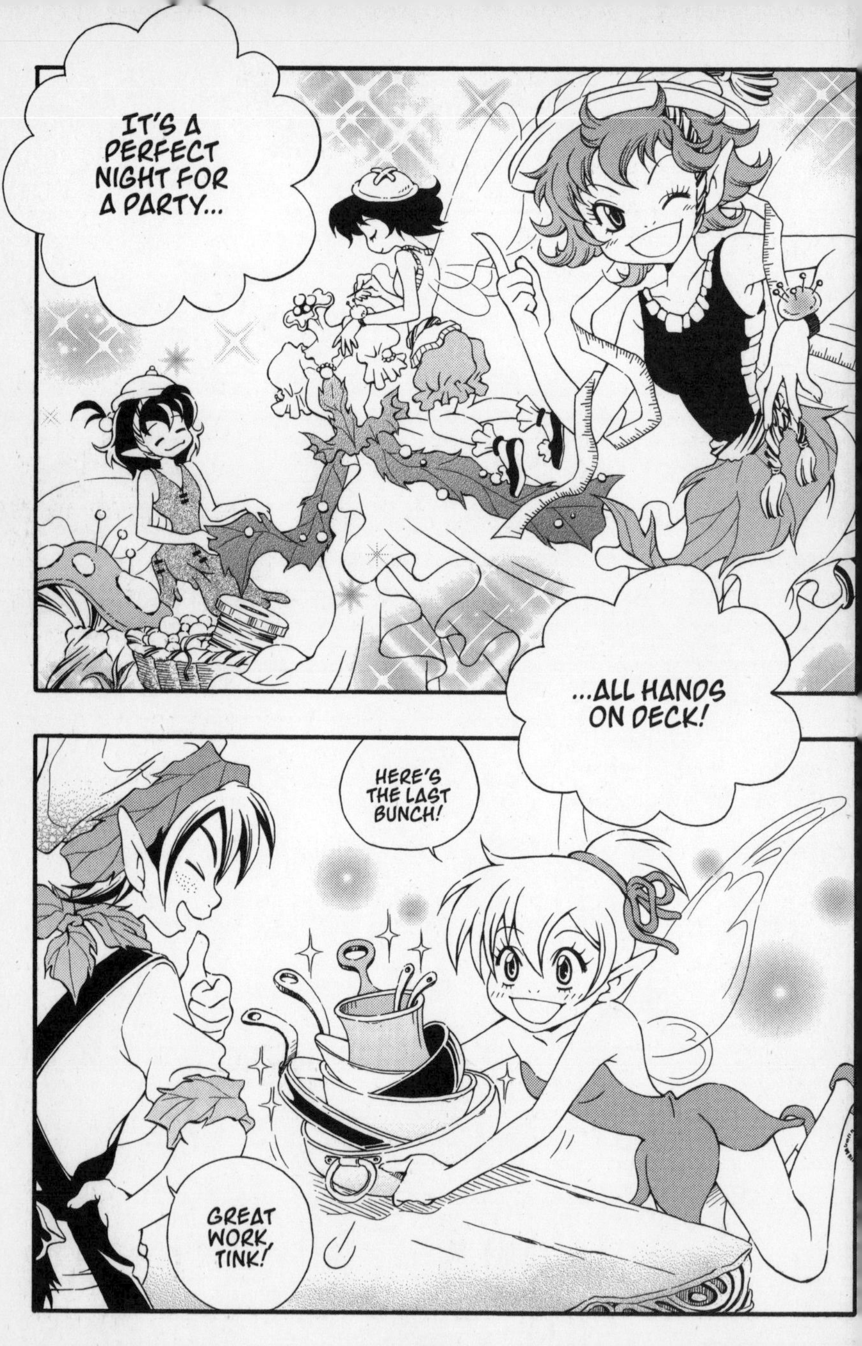
IT'S A PERFECT NIGHT FOR A PARTY...
...ALL HANDS ON DECK!
HERE'S THE LAST BUNCH!
GREAT WORK, TINK!

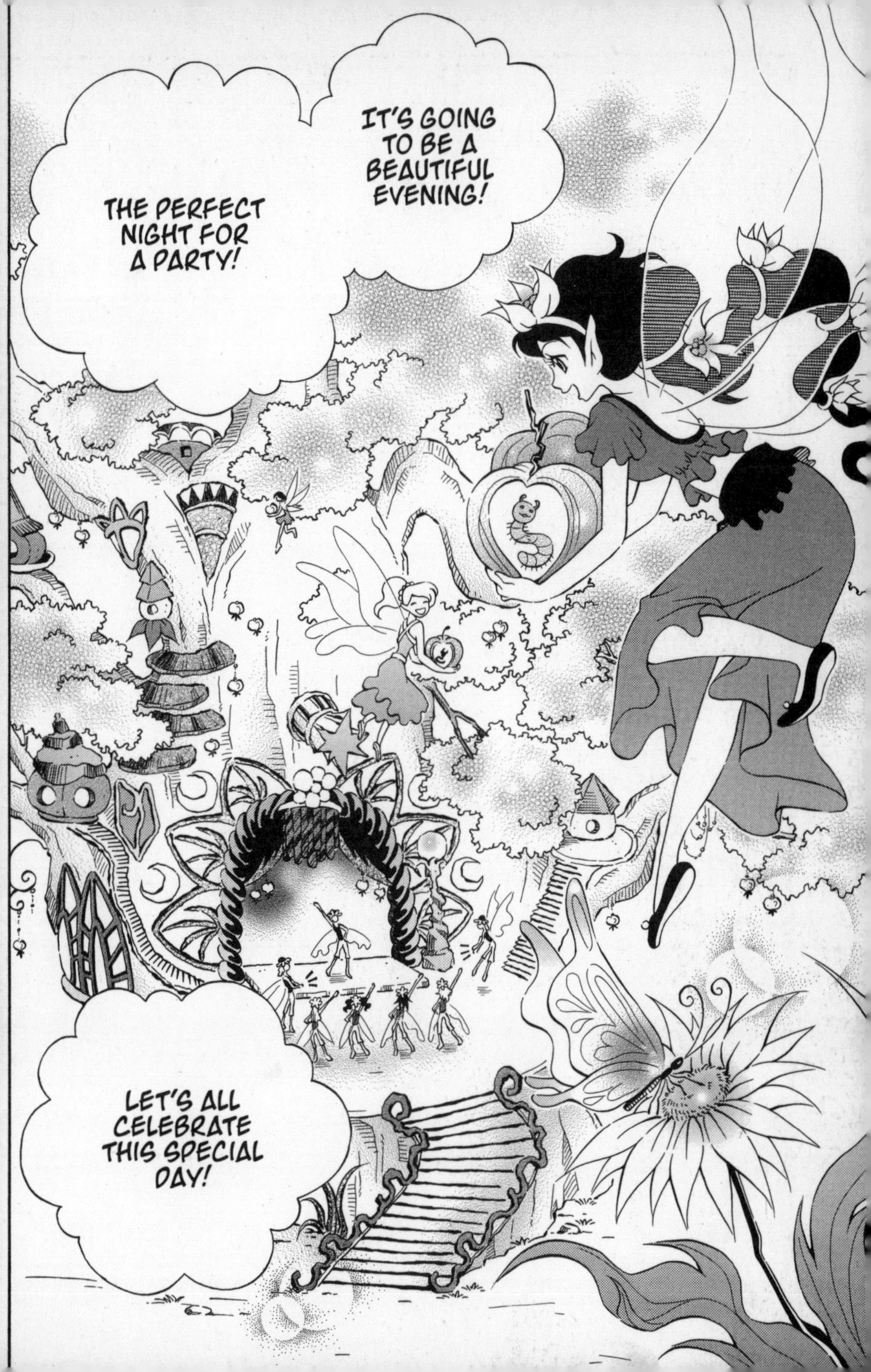
IT'S GOING TO BE A BEAUTIFUL EVENING!
THE PERFECT NIGHT FOR A PARTY!
LET'S ALL CELEBRATE THIS SPECIAL DAY!

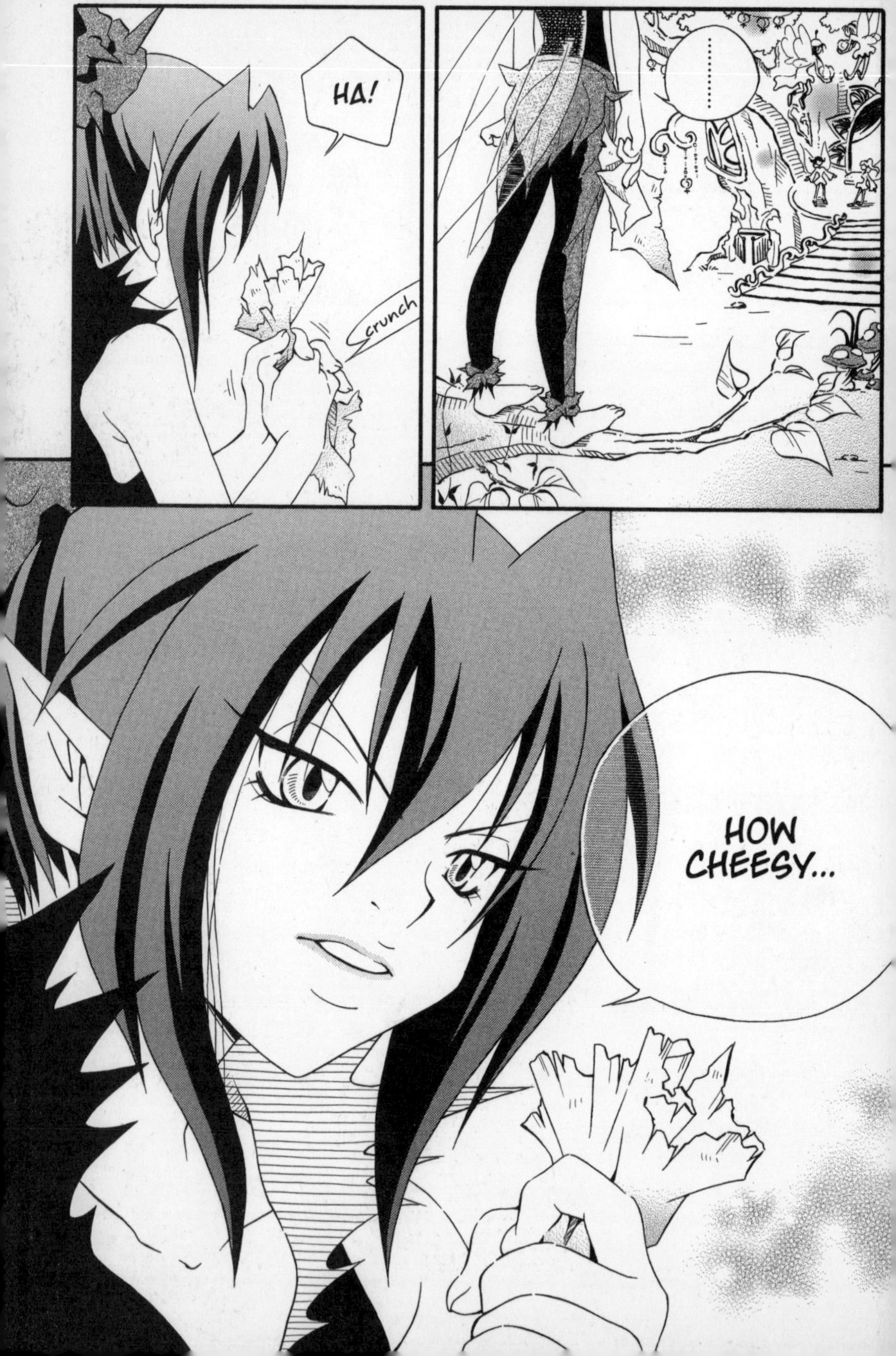

......
HA!
crunch
HOW CHEESY...

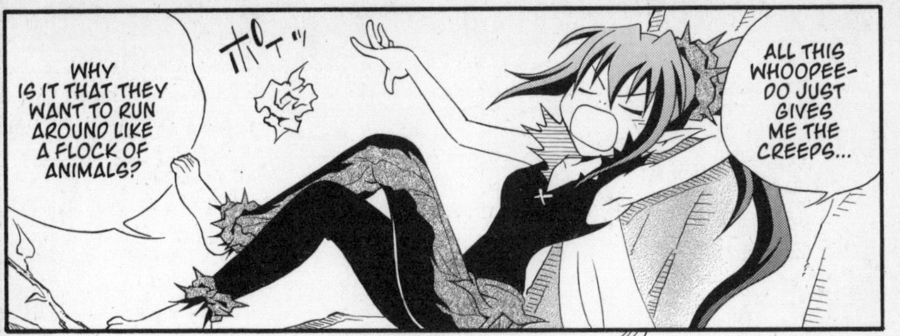
ALL THIS WHOOPEE-DO JUST GIVES ME THE CREEPS...
ポイッ
WHY IS IT THAT THEY WANT TO RUN AROUND LIKE A FLOCK OF ANIMALS?

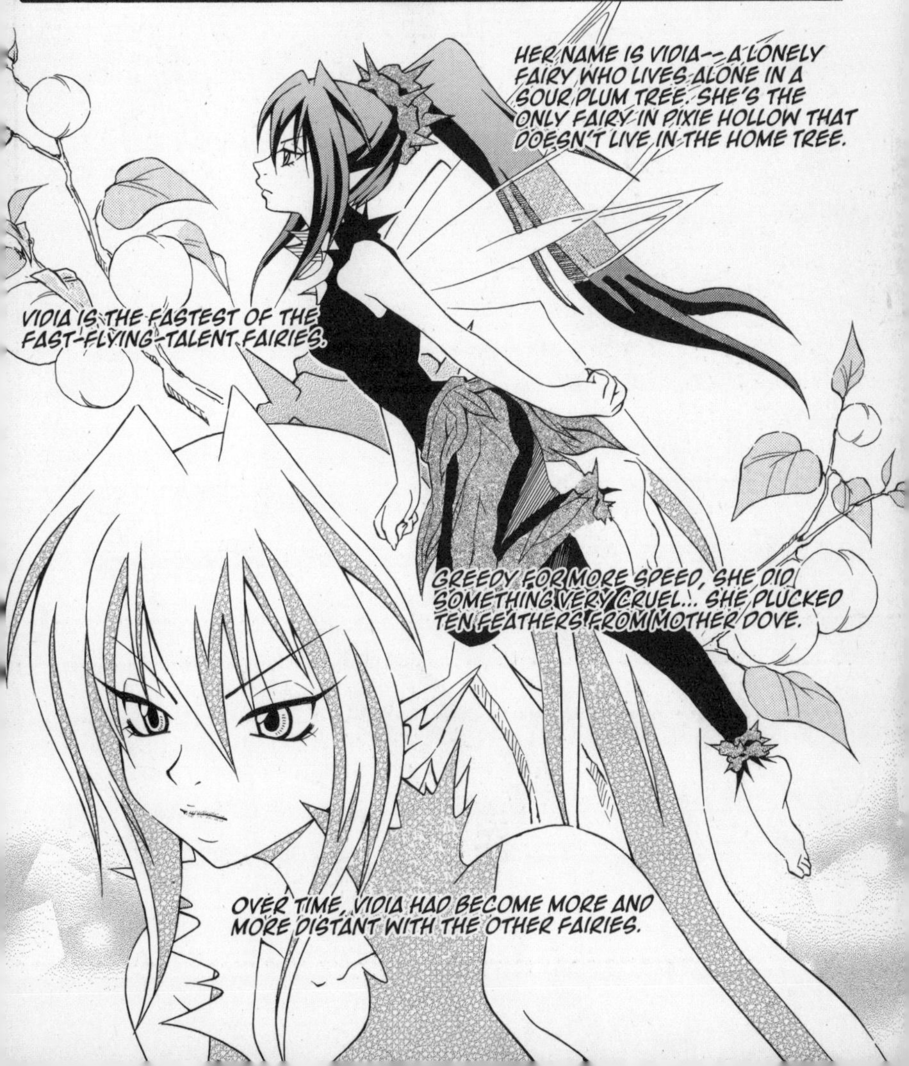
HER NAME IS VIDIA--A LONELY FAIRY WHO LIVES ALONE IN A SOUR PLUM TREE. SHE'S THE ONLY FAIRY IN PIXIE HOLLOW THAT DOESN'T LIVE IN THE HOME TREE.
VIDIA IS THE FASTEST OF THE FAST-FLYING-TALENT FAIRIES.
GREEDY FOR MORE SPEED, SHE DID SOMETHING VERY CRUEL... SHE PLUCKED TEN FEATHERS FROM MOTHER DOVE.
OVER TIME, VIDIA HAD BECOME MORE AND MORE DISTANT WITH THE OTHER FAIRIES.

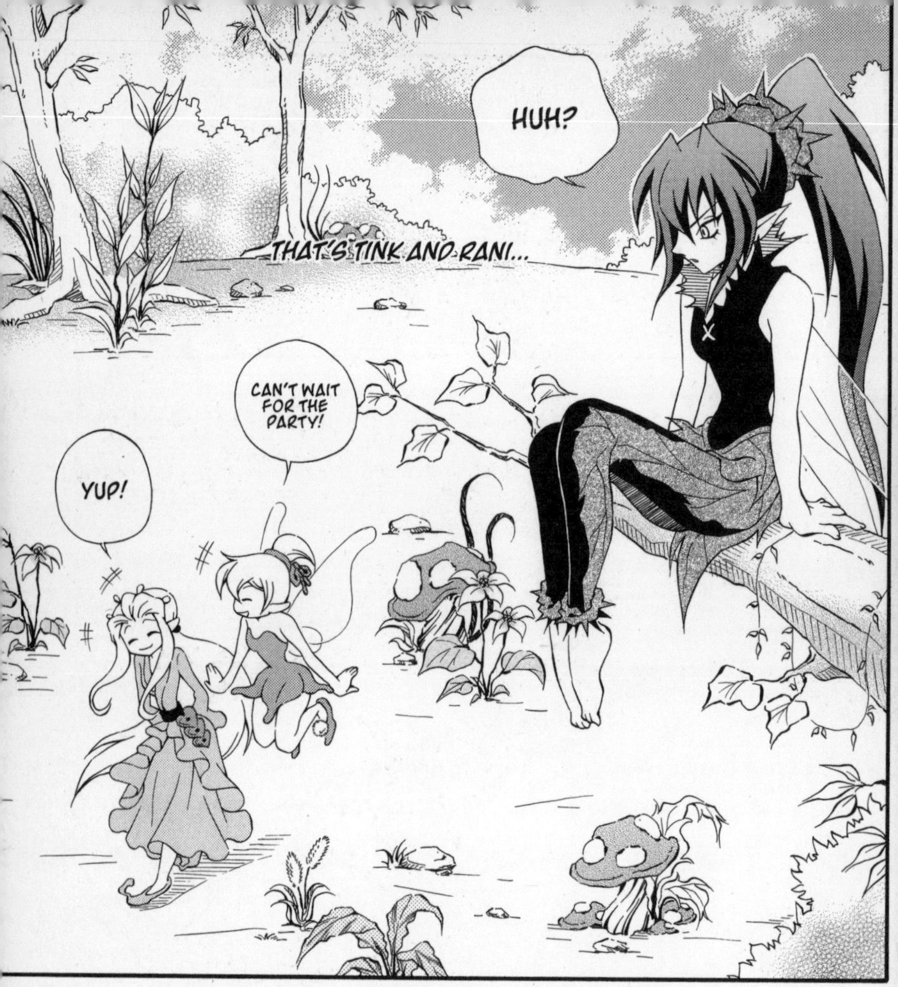
HUH?
THAT'S TINK AND RANI...
CAN'T WAIT FOR THE PARTY!
YUP!

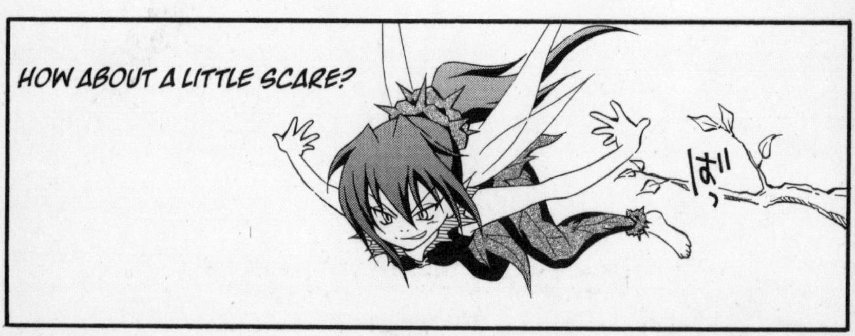
HOW ABOUT A LITTLE SCARE?
ず

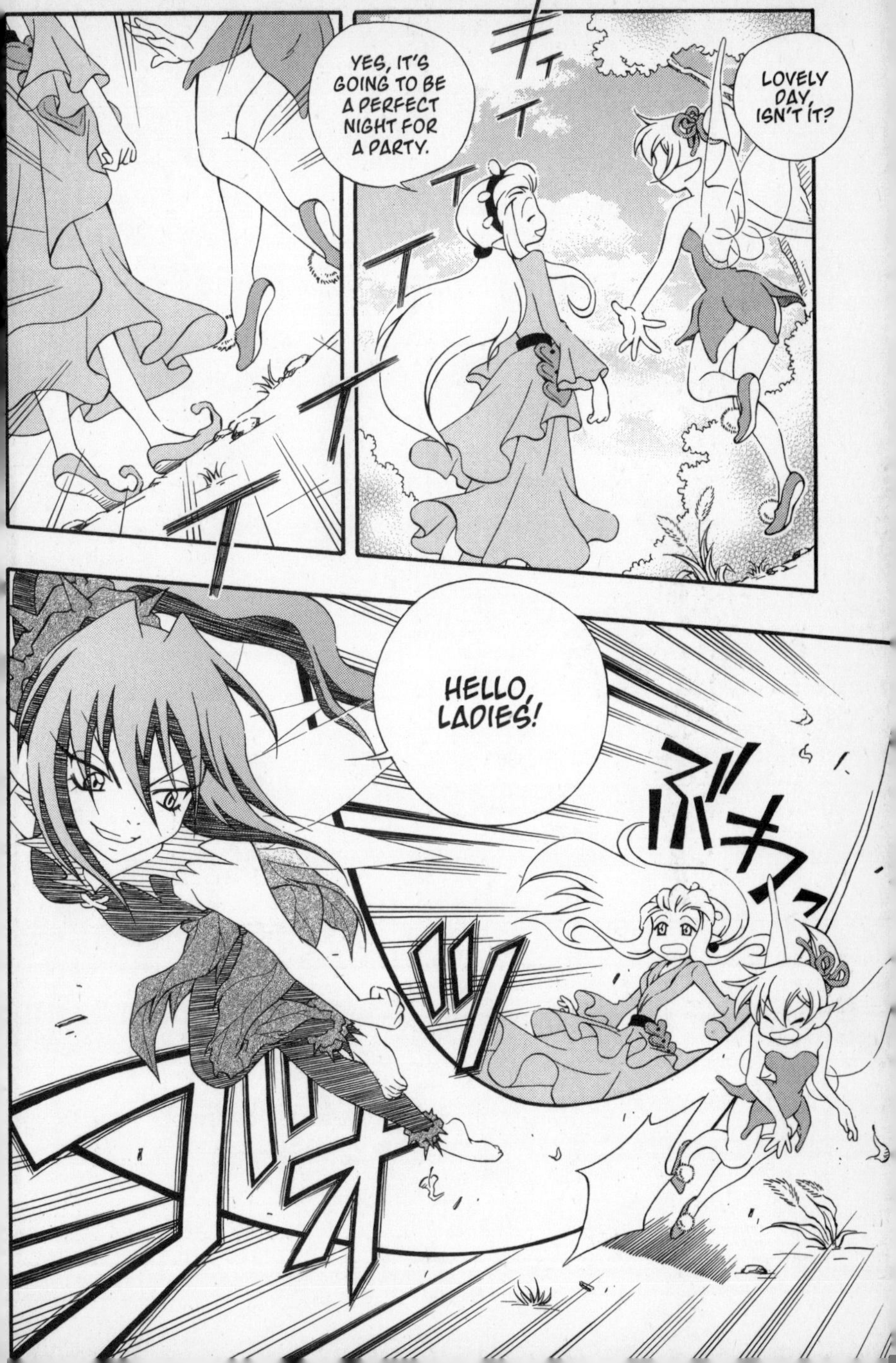
LOVELY DAY, ISN'T IT?
YES, IT'S GOING TO BE A PERFECT NIGHT FOR A PARTY.
HELLO, LADIES!

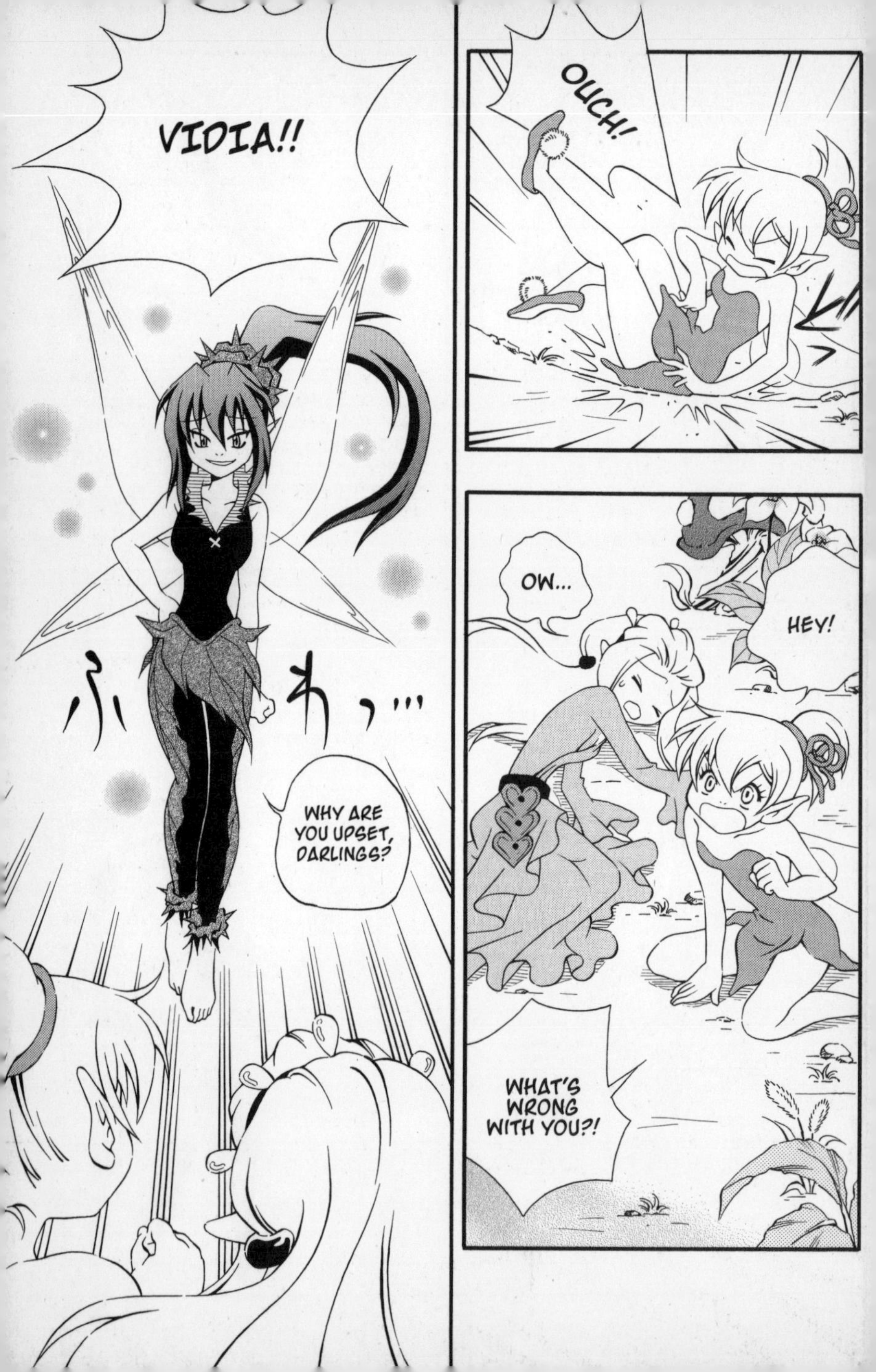
OUCH!
OW...
HEY!
WHAT'S WRONG WITH YOU?!
VIDIA!!
ふわっ…
WHY ARE YOU UPSET, DARLINGS?

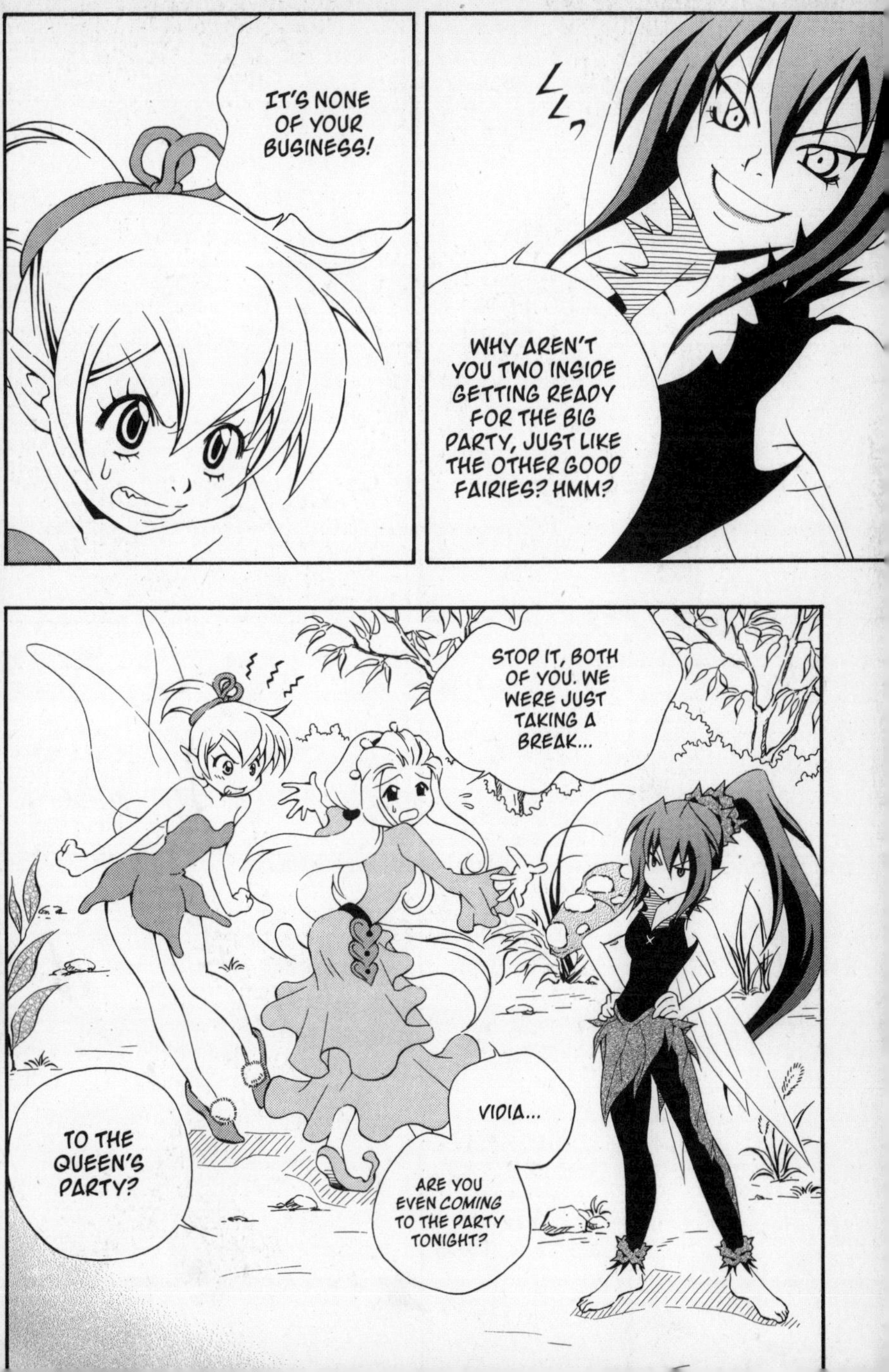
WHY AREN'T YOU TWO INSIDE GETTING READY FOR THE BIG PARTY, JUST LIKE THE OTHER GOOD FAIRIES? HMM?
IT'S NONE OF YOUR BUSINESS!
STOP IT, BOTH OF YOU. WE WERE JUST TAKING A BREAK...
VIDIA...
ARE YOU EVEN COMING TO THE PARTY TONIGHT?
TO THE QUEEN'S PARTY?

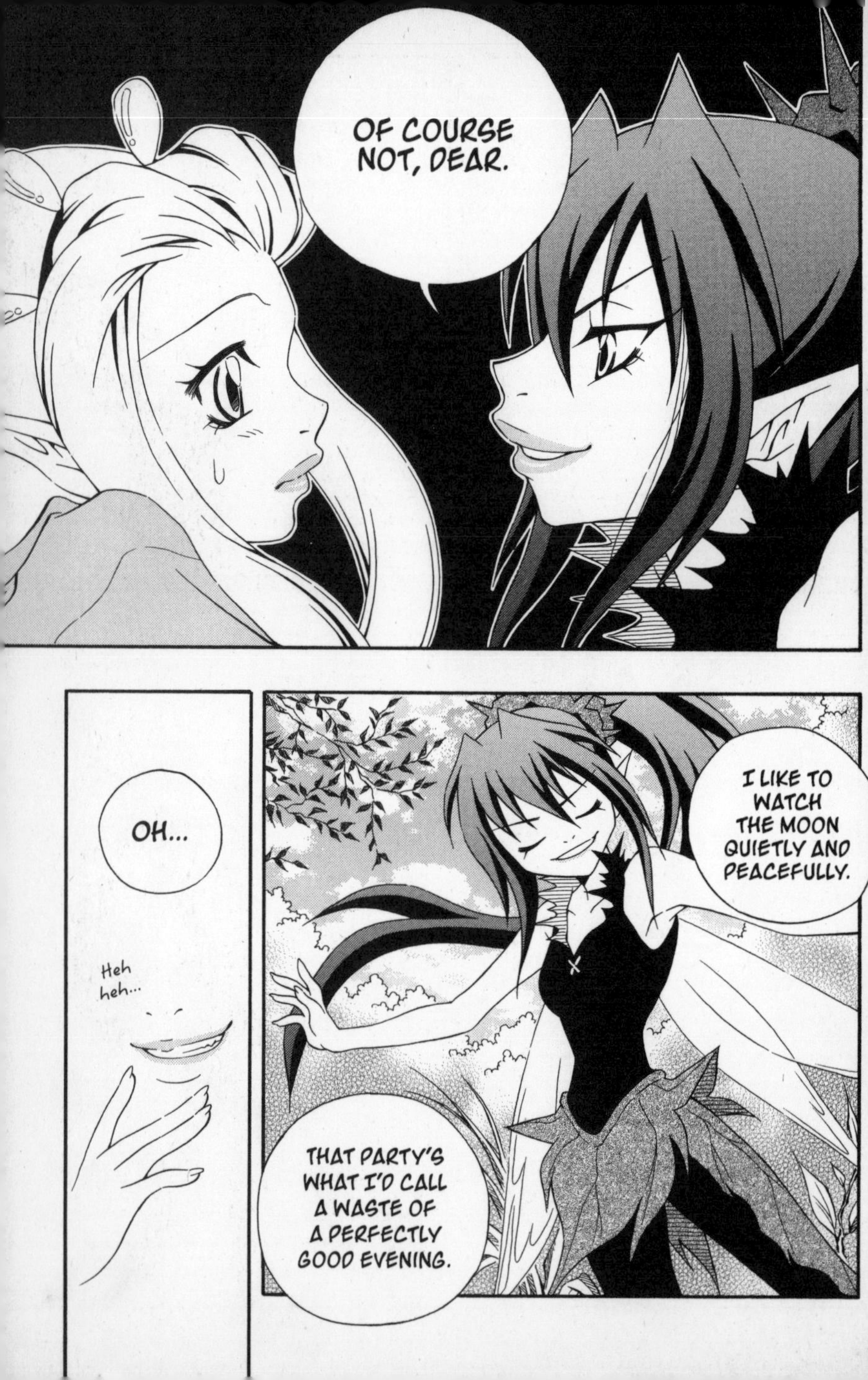
OF COURSE NOT, DEAR.
I LIKE TO WATCH THE MOON QUIETLY AND PEACEFULLY.
THAT PARTY'S WHAT I'D CALL A WASTE OF A PERFECTLY GOOD EVENING.
OH...
Heh heh...

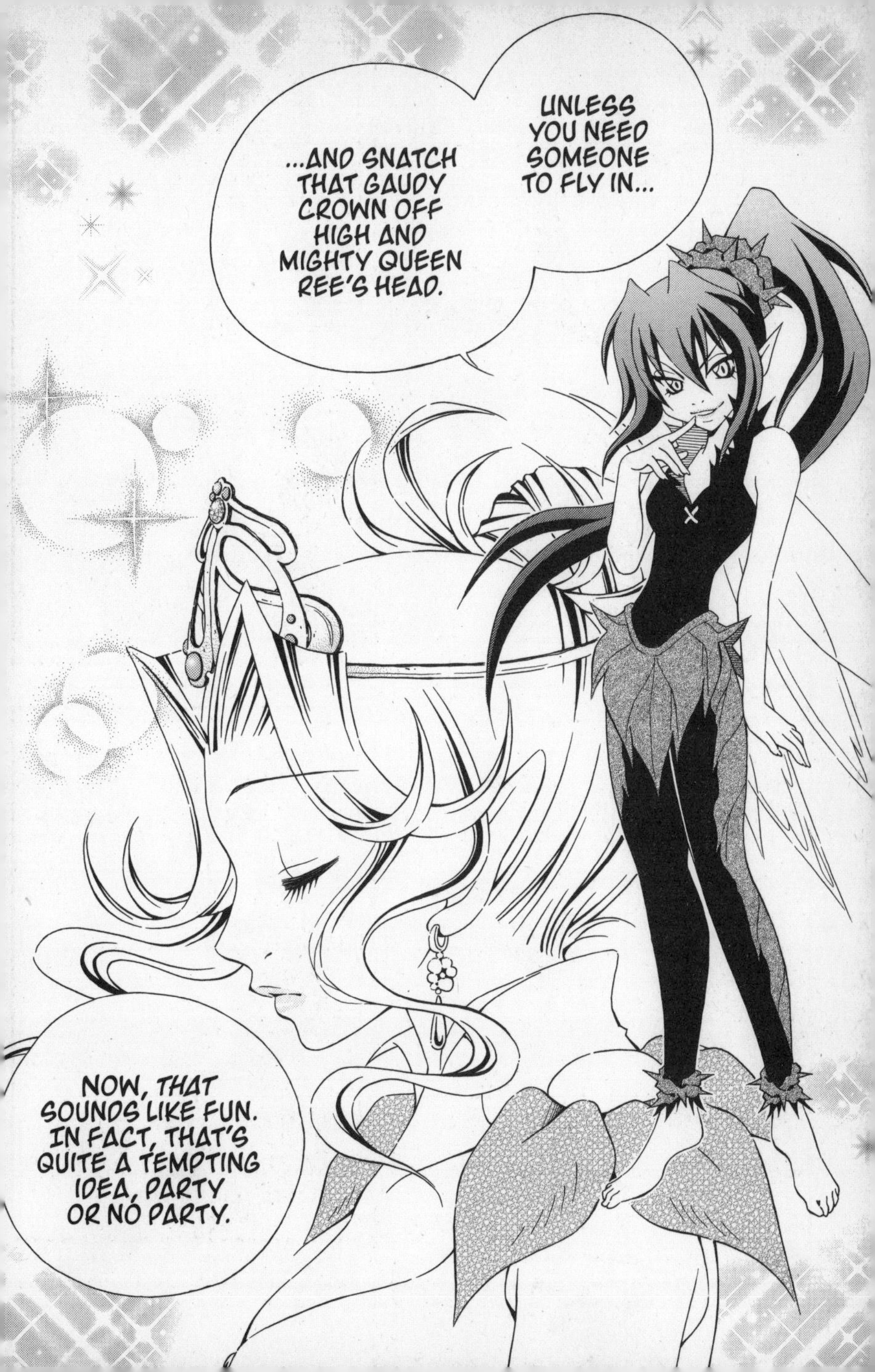
UNLESS YOU NEED SOMEONE TO FLY IN...
...AND SNATCH THAT GAUDY CROWN OFF HIGH AND MIGHTY QUEEN REE'S HEAD.
NOW, THAT SOUNDS LIKE FUN. IN FACT, THAT'S QUITE A TEMPTING IDEA, PARTY OR NO PARTY.

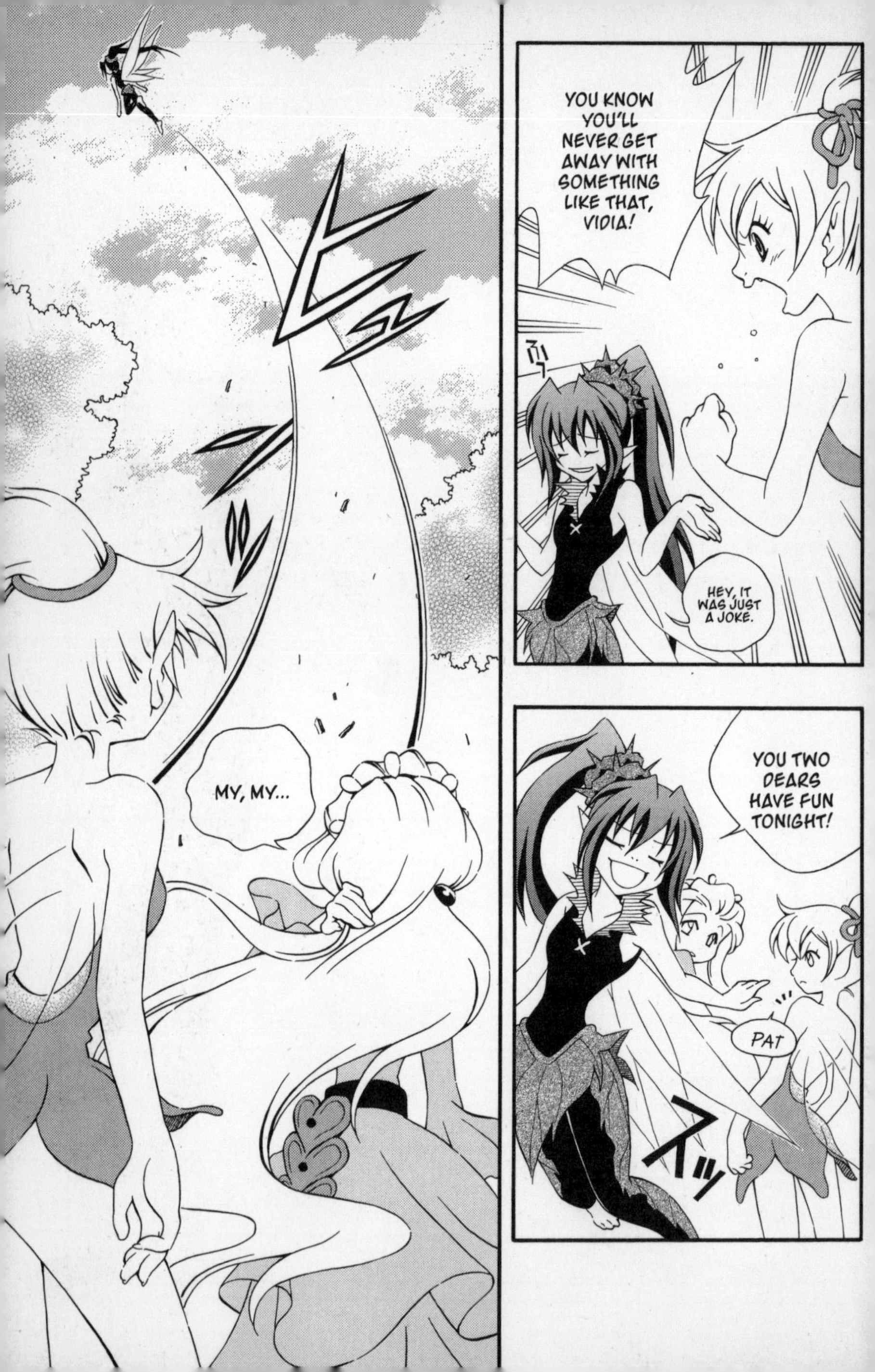
YOU KNOW YOU'LL NEVER GET AWAY WITH SOMETHING LIKE THAT, VIDIA!
HEY, IT WAS JUST A JOKE.
YOU TWO DEARS HAVE FUN TONIGHT!
PAT
MY, MY...

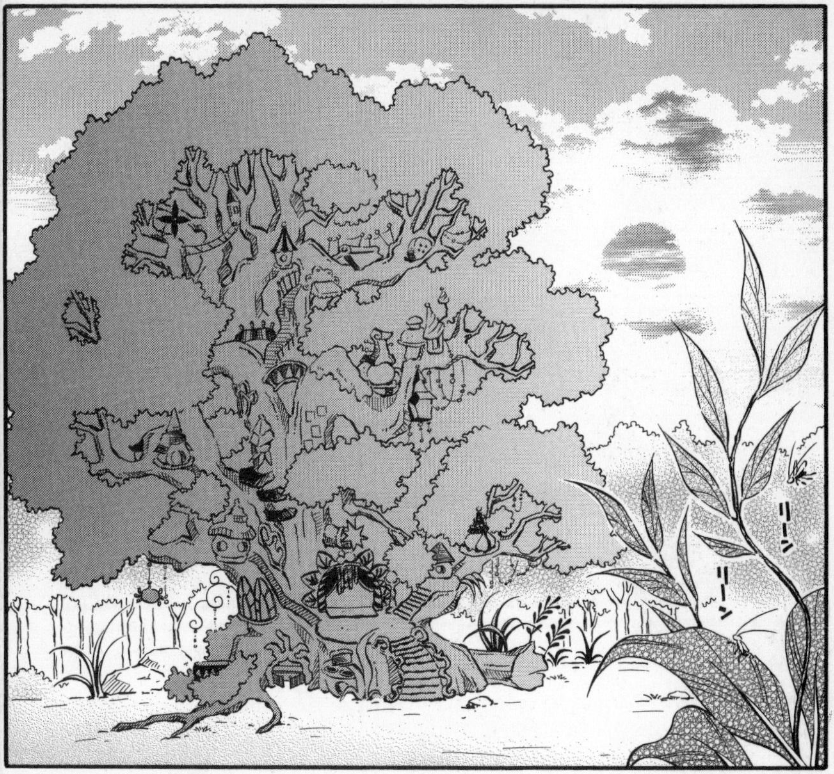
リーン
リーン

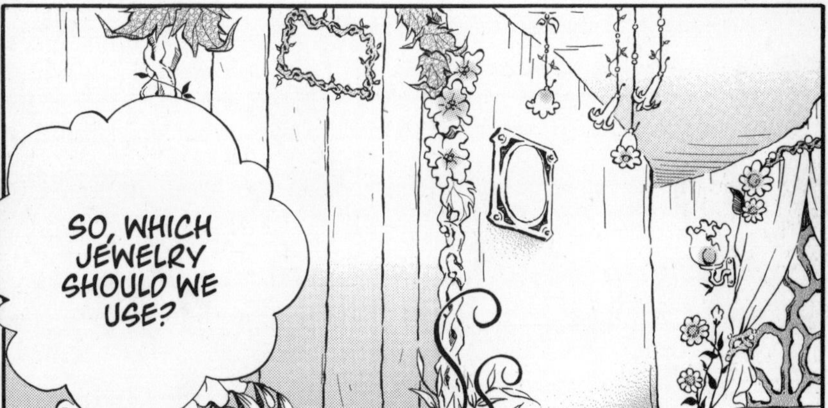
SO, WHICH JEWELRY SHOULD WE USE?

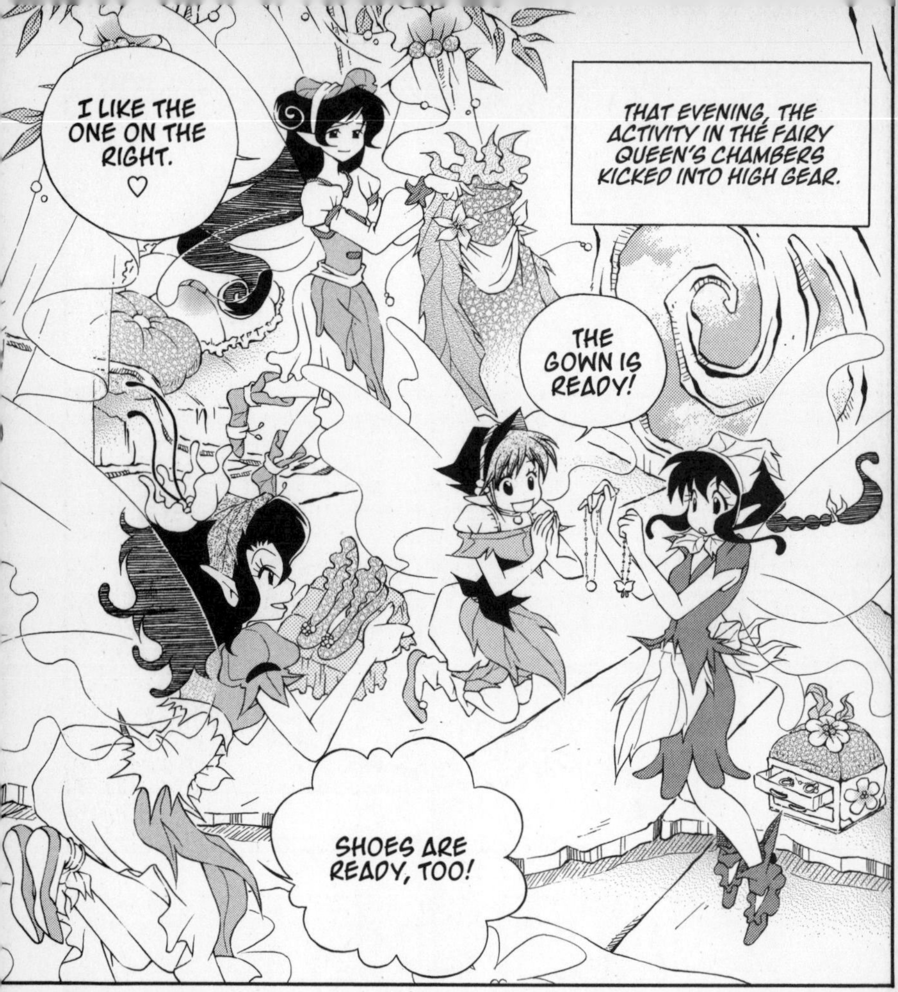
THAT EVENING, THE ACTIVITY IN THE FAIRY QUEEN'S CHAMBERS KICKED INTO HIGH GEAR.
I LIKE THE ONE ON THE RIGHT. ♡
THE GOWN IS READY!
SHOES ARE READY, TOO!

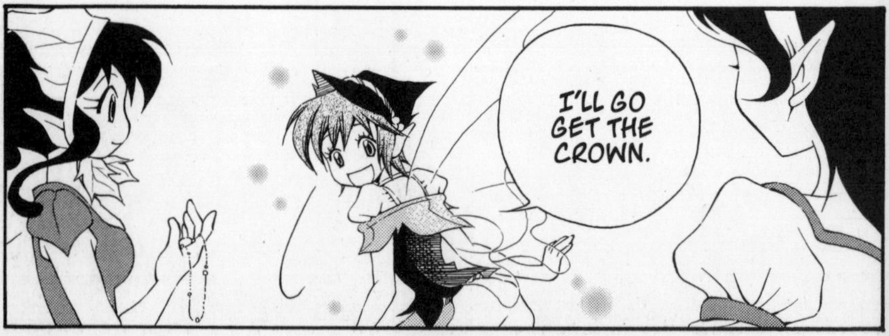
I'LL GO GET THE CROWN.

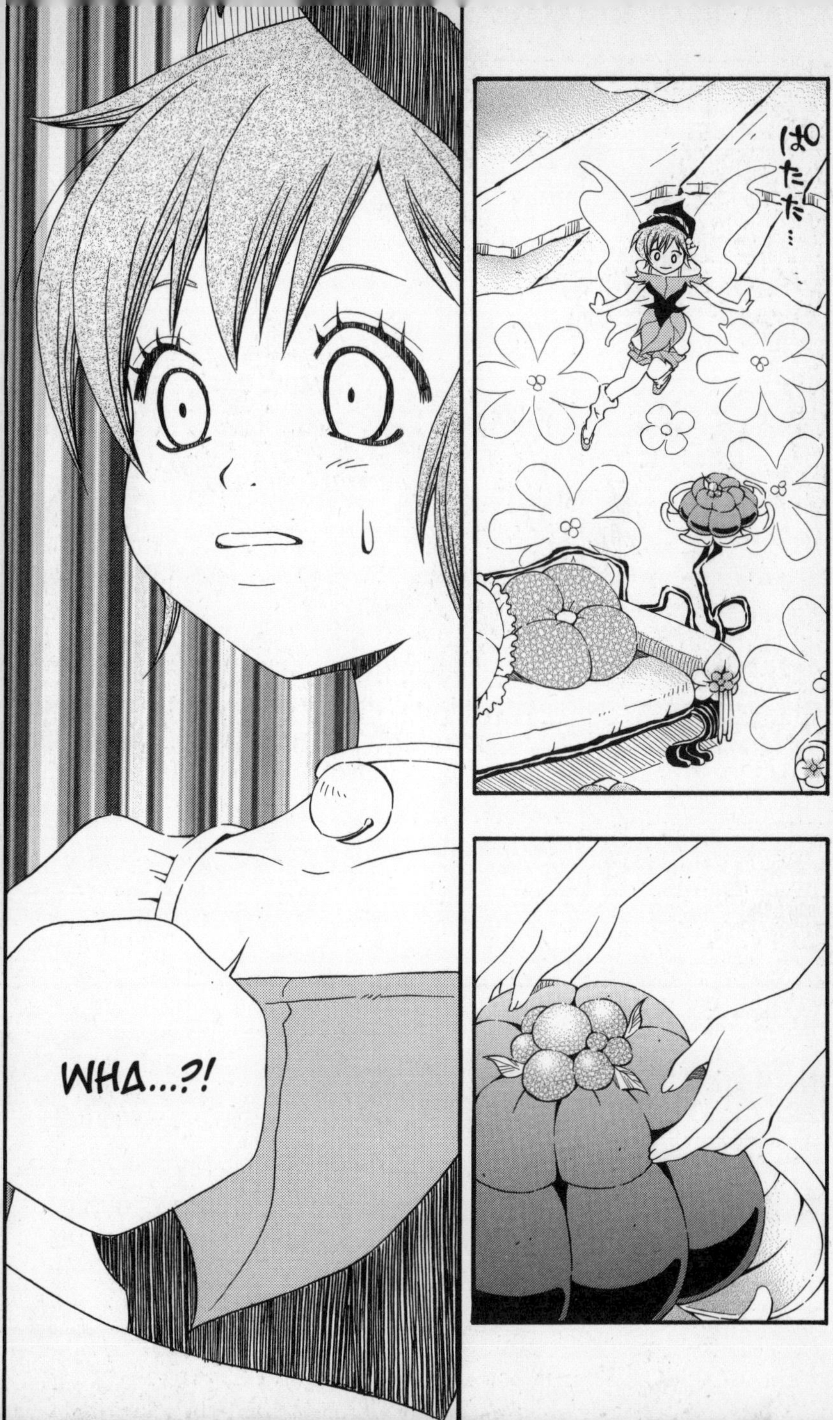
ぱたた…
WHA...?!

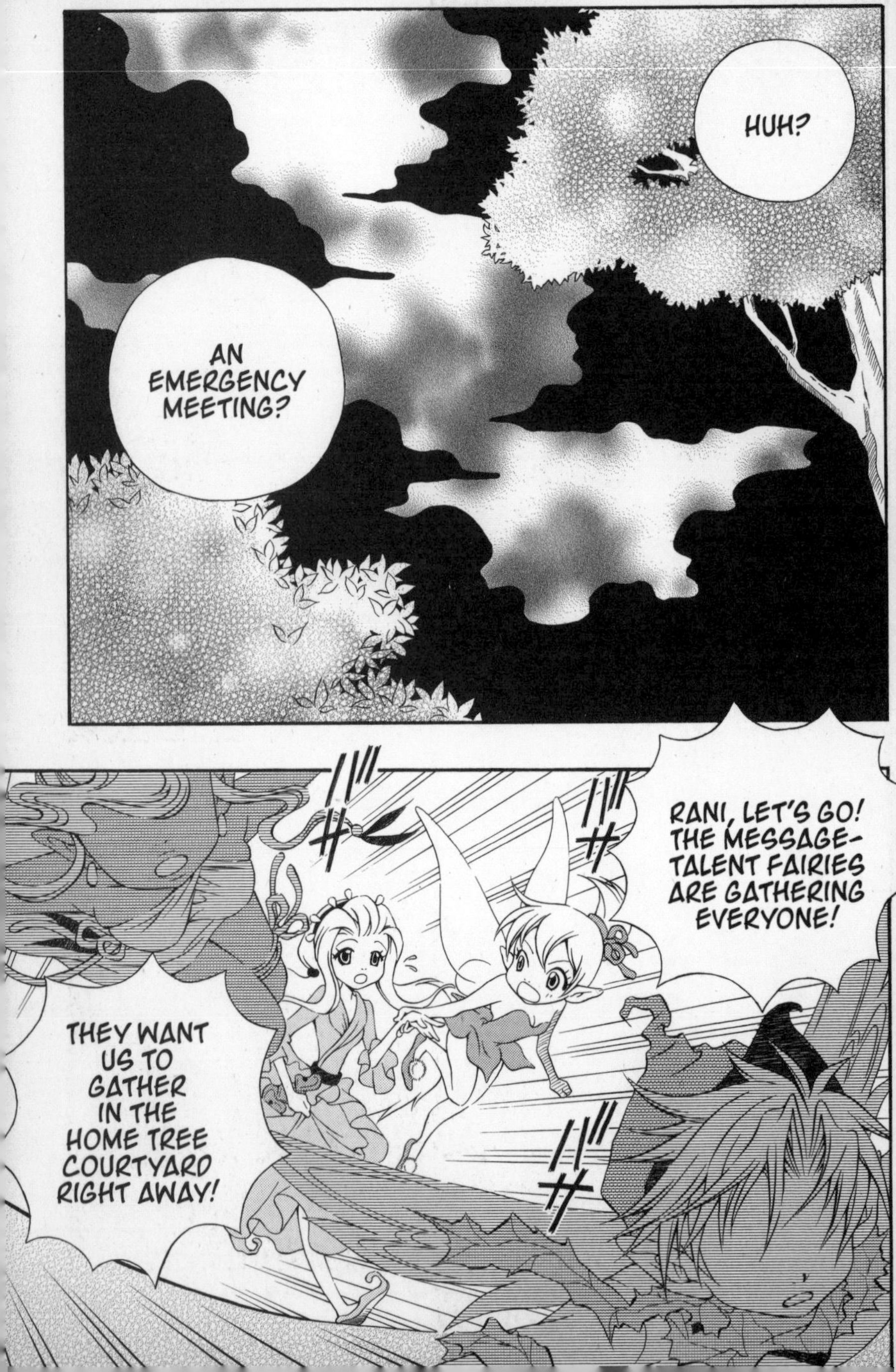
HUH?
AN EMERGENCY MEETING?
RANI, LET'S GO! THE MESSAGE-TALENT FAIRIES ARE GATHERING EVERYONE!
THEY WANT US TO GATHER IN THE HOME TREE COURTYARD RIGHT AWAY!

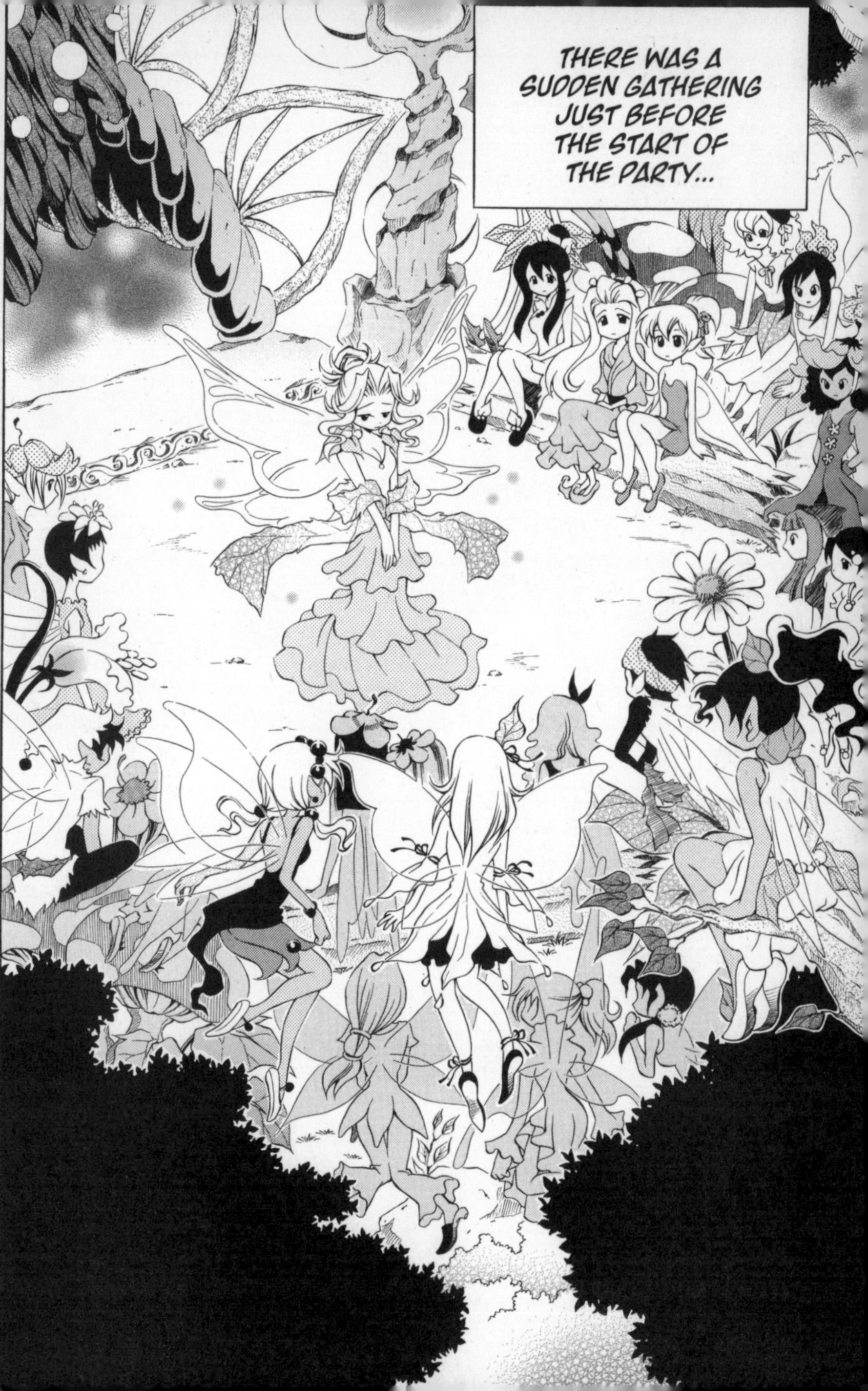
THERE WAS A SUDDEN GATHERING JUST BEFORE THE START OF THE PARTY...

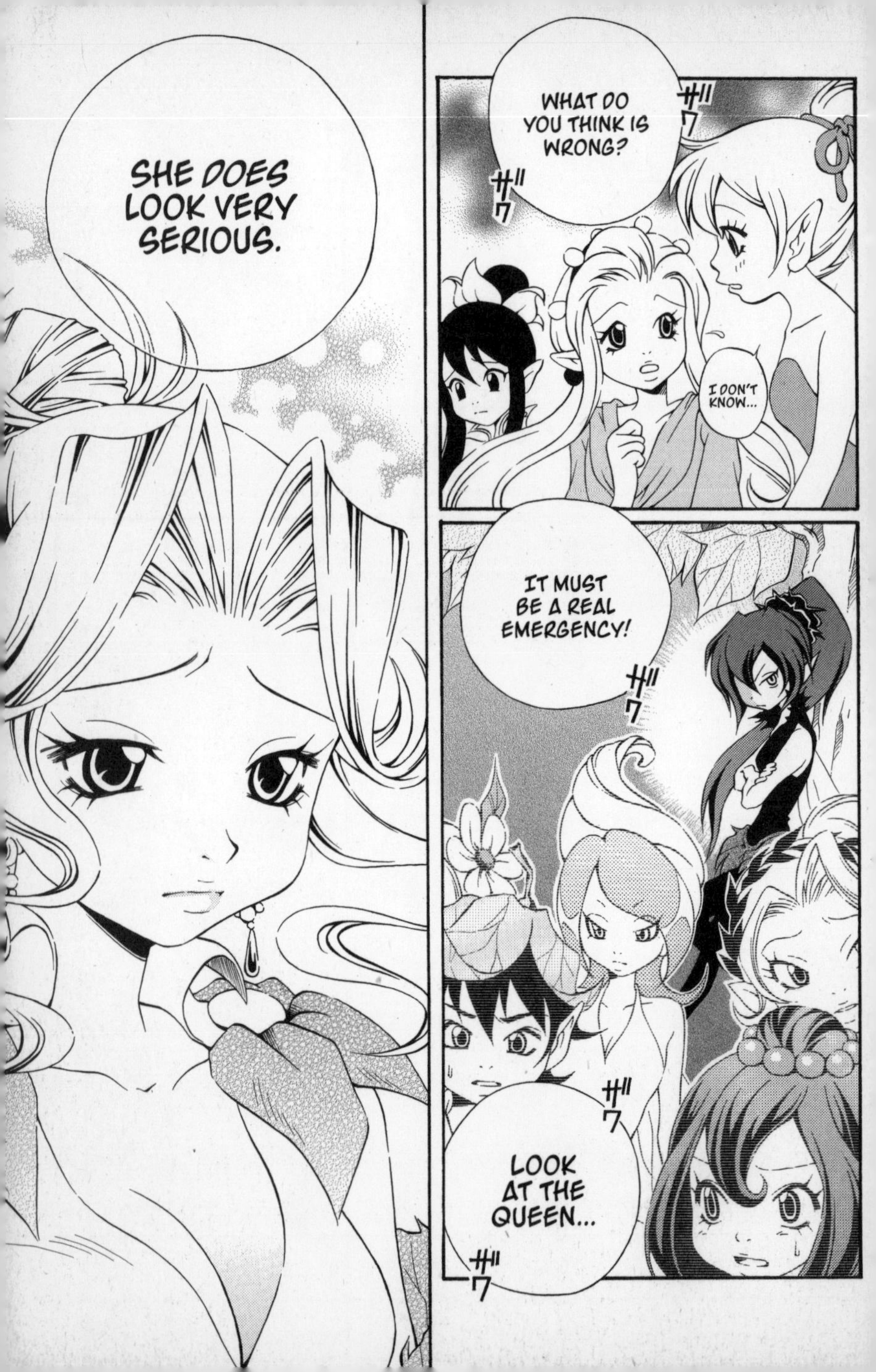
WHAT DO YOU THINK IS WRONG?
ザワ
ザワ
I DON'T KNOW...
IT MUST BE A REAL EMERGENCY!
ザワ
ザワ
LOOK AT THE QUEEN...
ザワ
SHE DOES LOOK VERY SERIOUS.

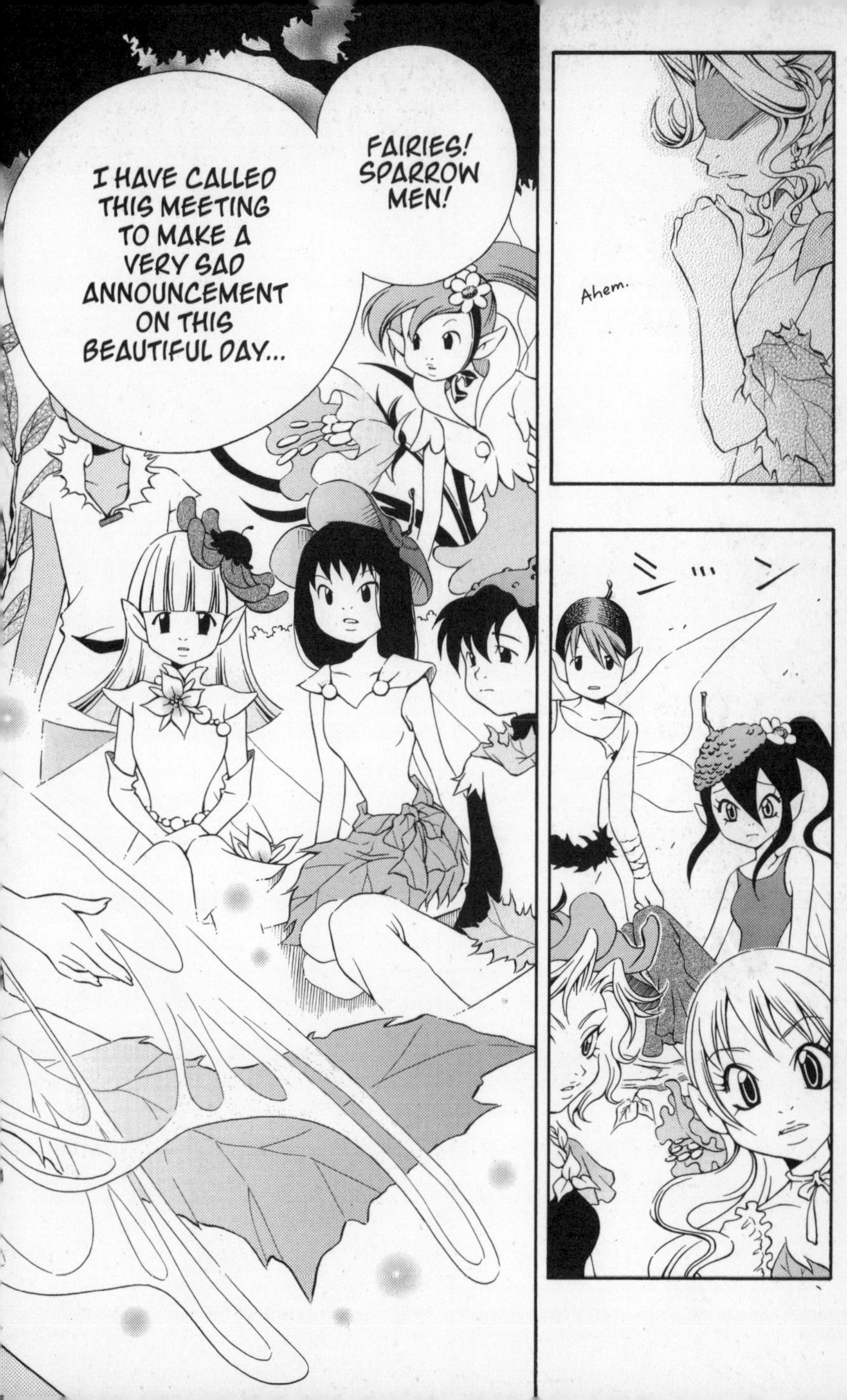
Ahem.
FAIRIES! SPARROW MEN!
I HAVE CALLED THIS MEETING TO MAKE A VERY SAD ANNOUNCEMENT ON THIS BEAUTIFUL DAY...

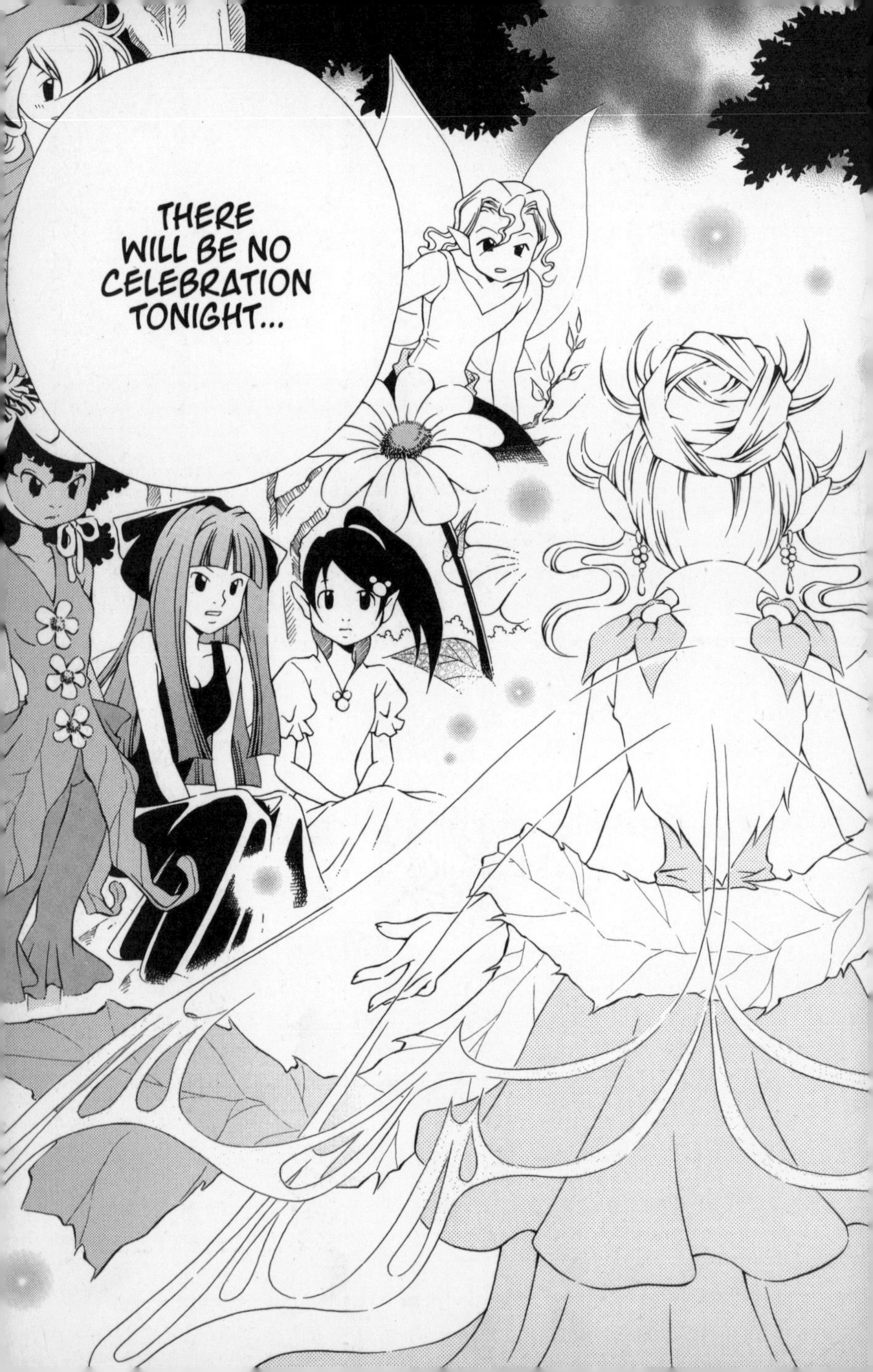
THERE WILL BE NO CELEBRATION TONIGHT...

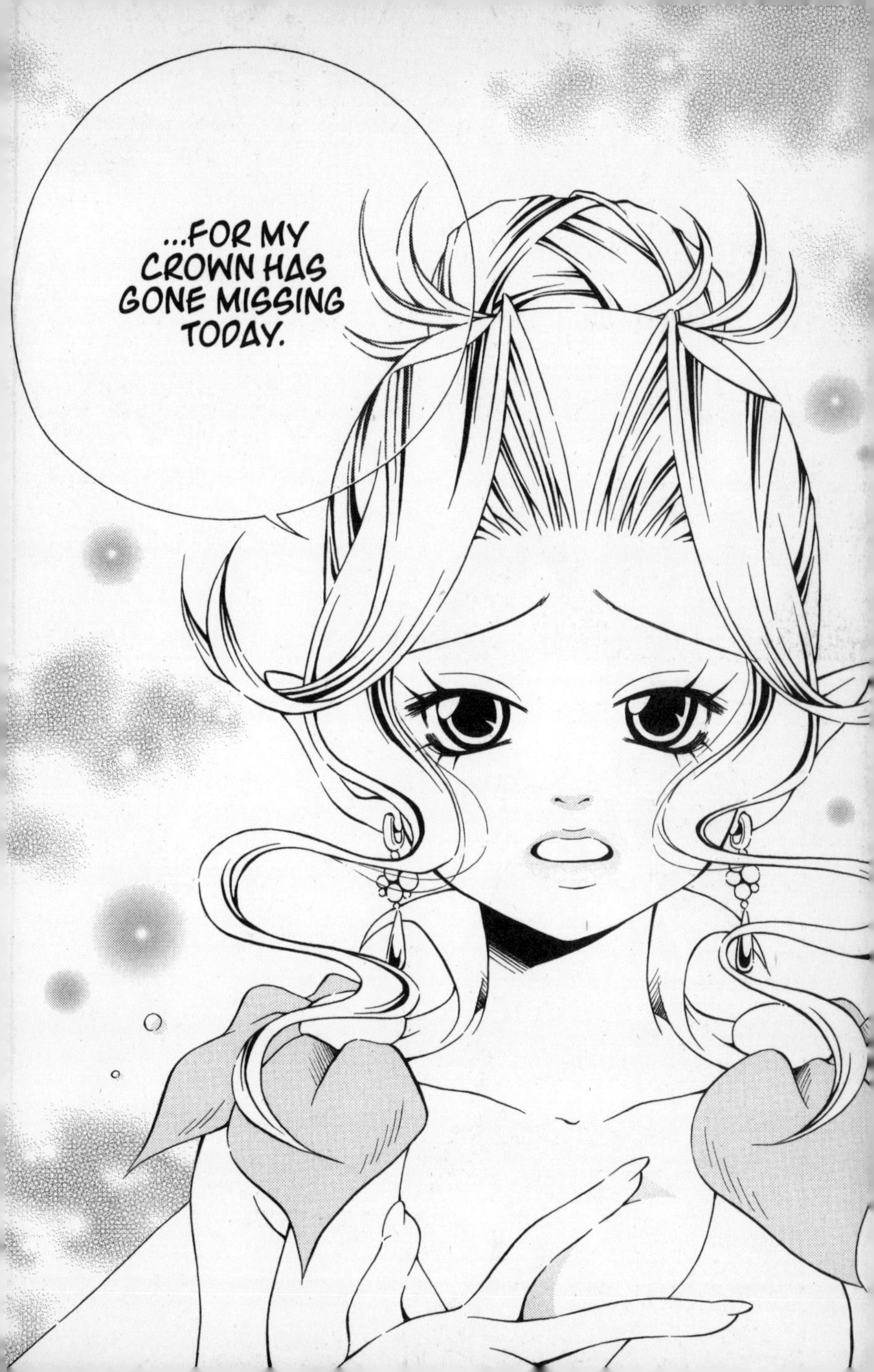
...FOR MY CROWN HAS GONE MISSING TODAY.

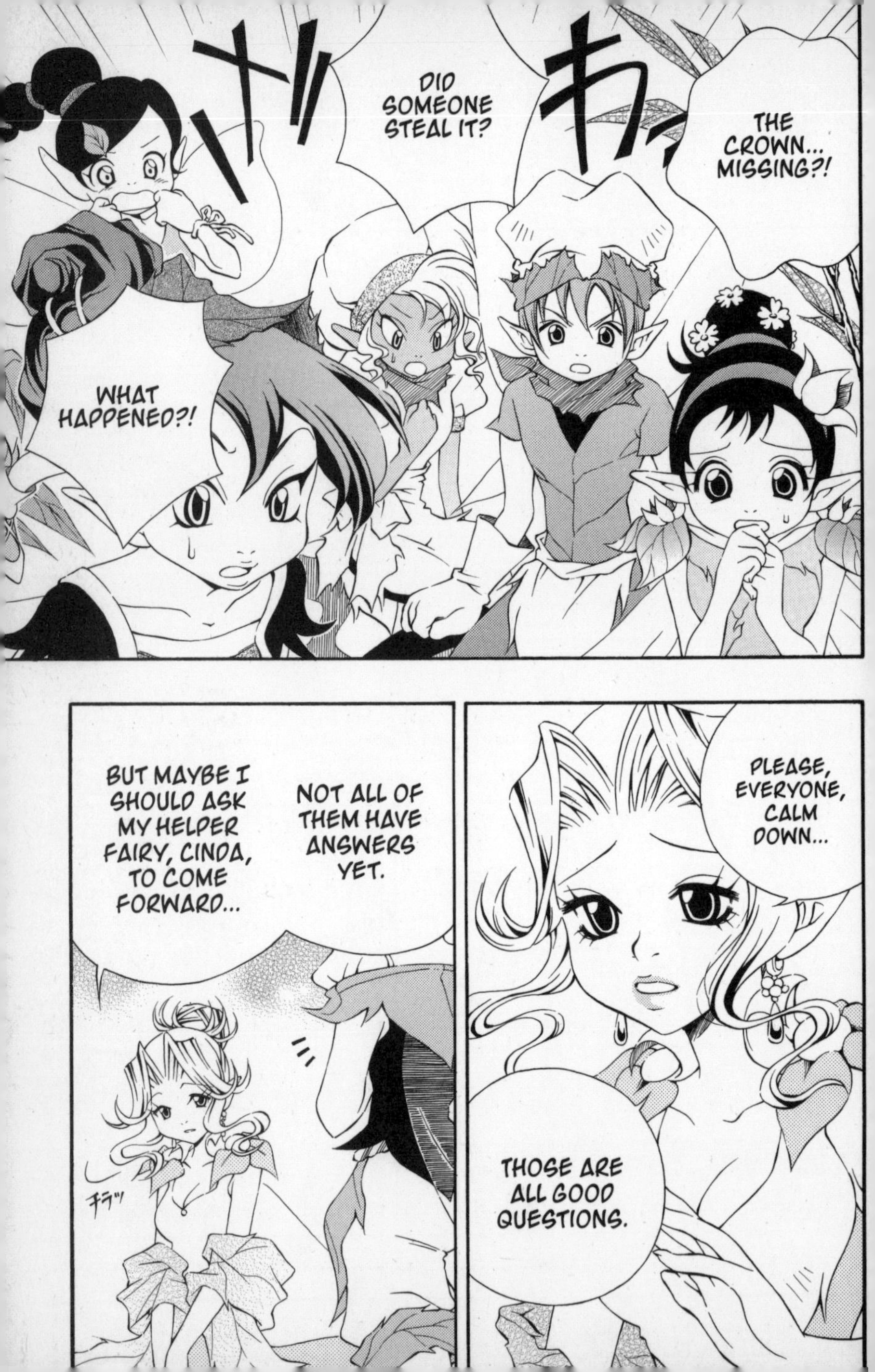
THE CROWN... MISSING?!
DID SOMEONE STEAL IT?
WHAT HAPPENED?!
PLEASE, EVERYONE, CALM DOWN...
THOSE ARE ALL GOOD QUESTIONS.
NOT ALL OF THEM HAVE ANSWERS YET.
BUT MAYBE I SHOULD ASK MY HELPER FAIRY, CINDA, TO COME FORWARD...
チラッ

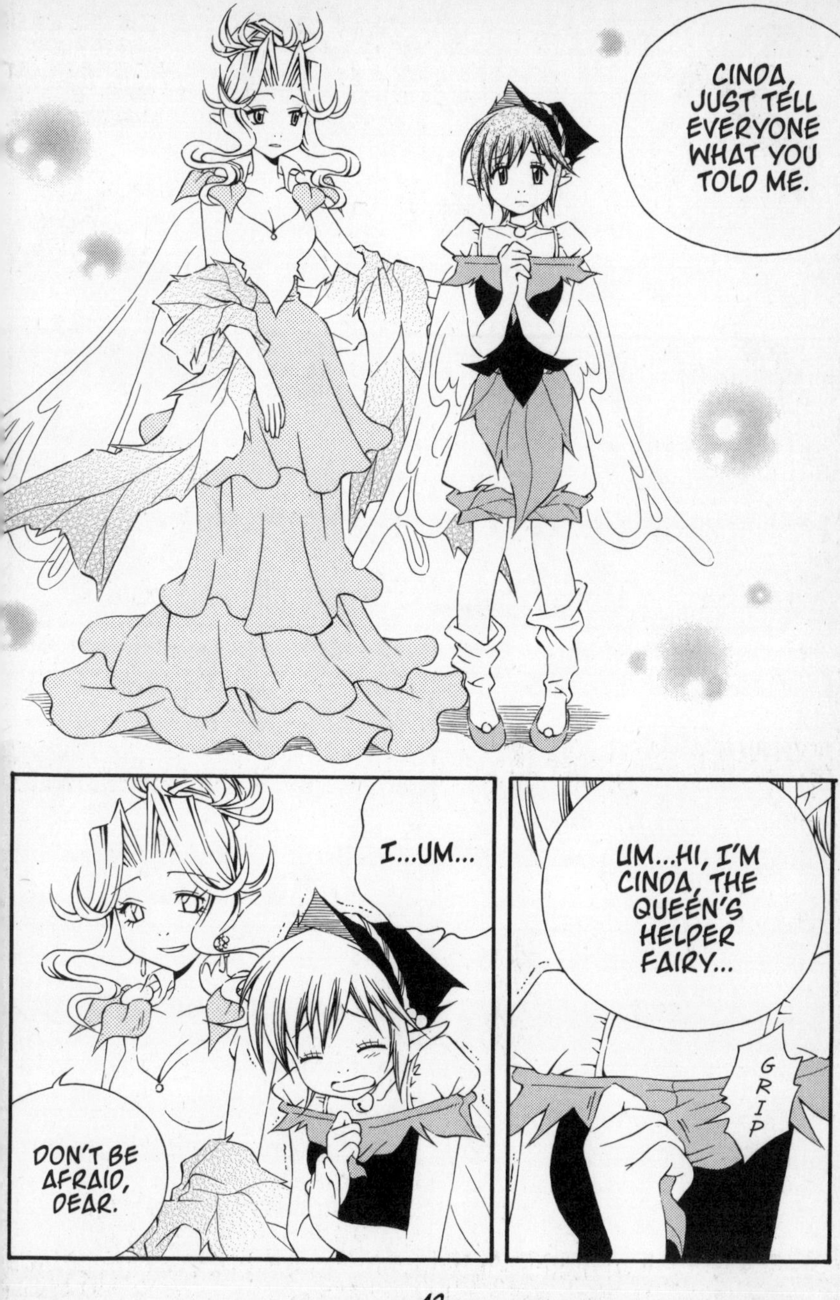
CINDA, JUST TELL EVERYONE WHAT YOU TOLD ME.
UM...HI, I'M CINDA, THE QUEEN'S HELPER FAIRY...
GRIP
I...UM...
DON'T BE AFRAID, DEAR.

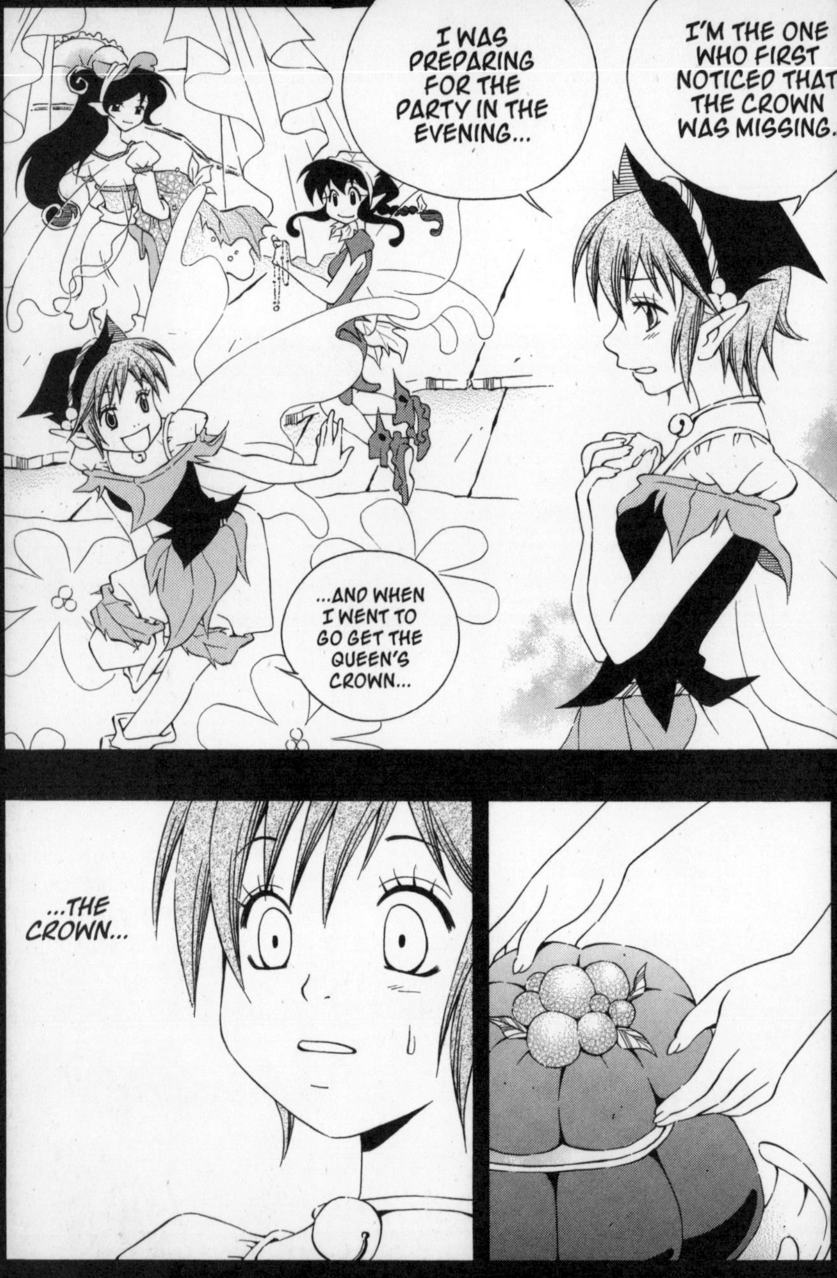
I'M THE ONE WHO FIRST NOTICED THAT THE CROWN WAS MISSING.
I WAS PREPARING FOR THE PARTY IN THE EVENING...
...AND WHEN I WENT TO GO GET THE QUEEN'S CROWN...
...THE CROWN...

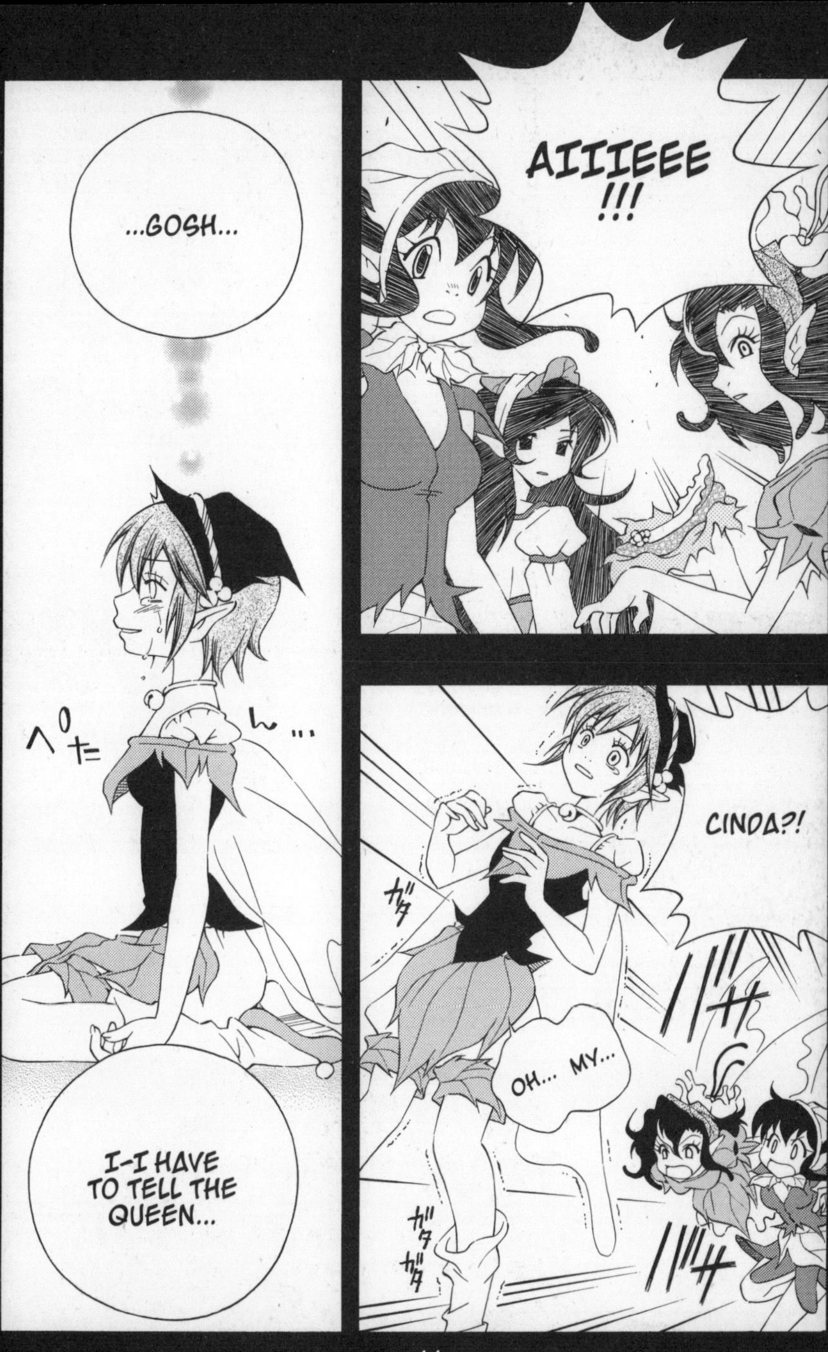
AIIIEEE !!!
CINDA?!
ダッ
OH... MY...
ガタ
ダッ
ガタガタ
...GOSH...
ぺたん...
I-I HAVE TO TELL THE QUEEN...

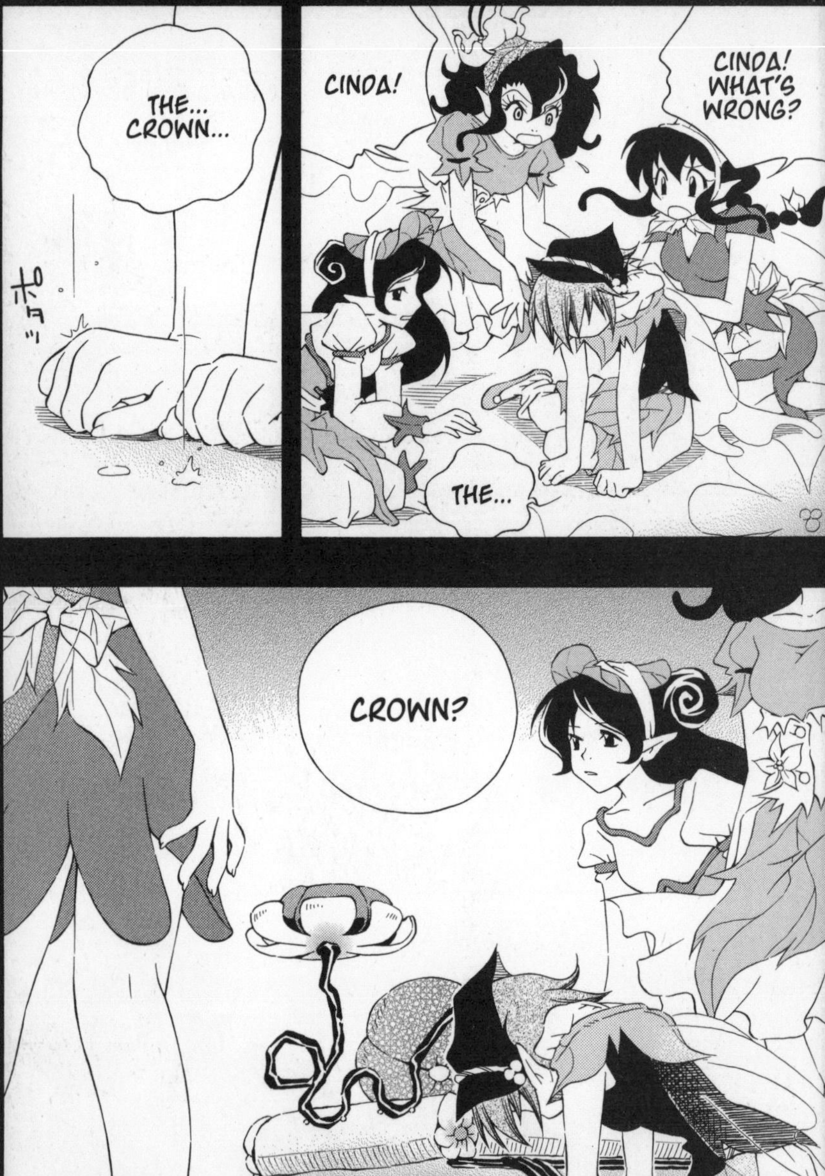
CINDA! WHAT'S WRONG?
CINDA!
THE...
THE... CROWN...
ポタッ
CROWN?

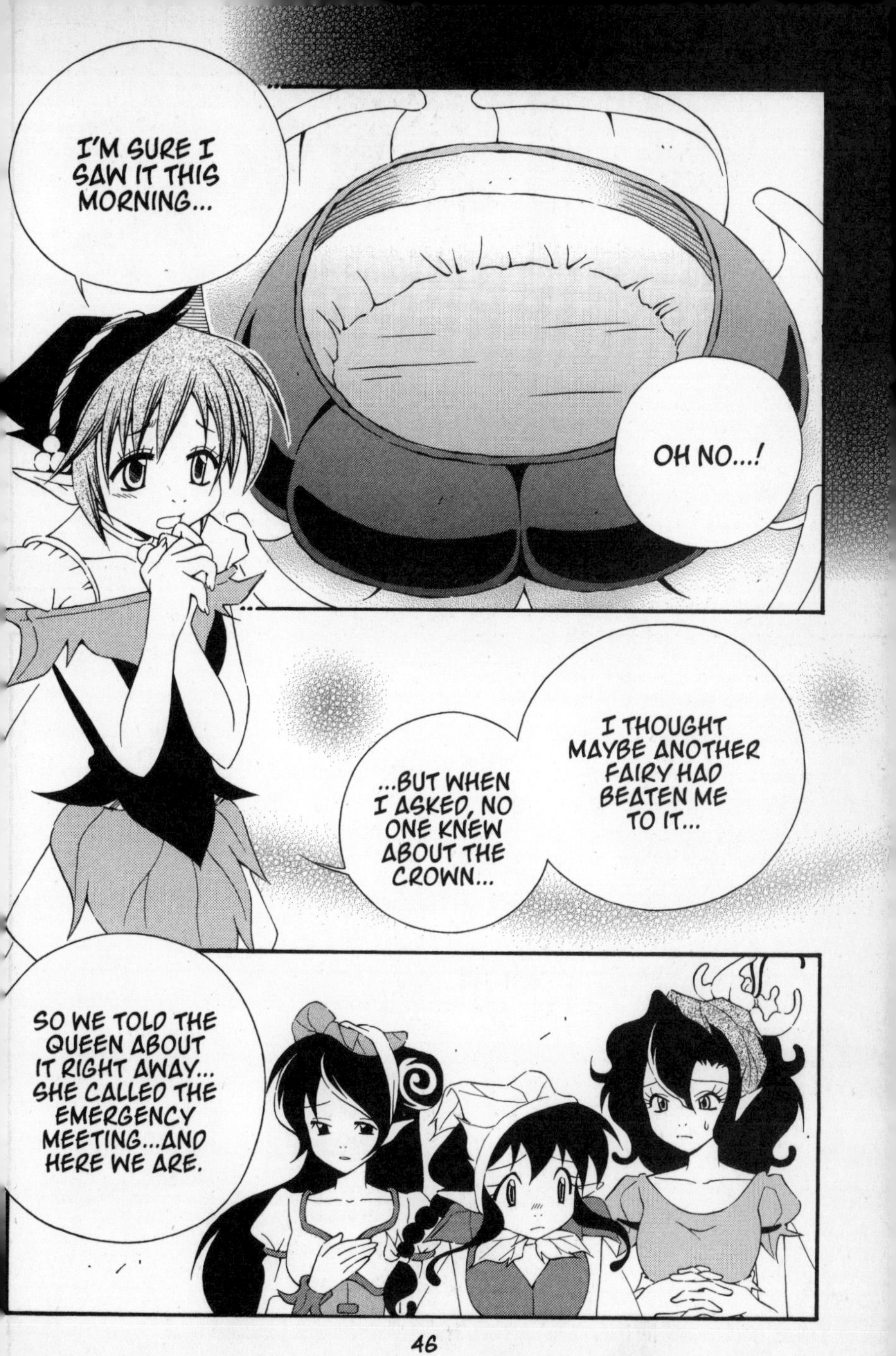
I'M SURE I SAW IT THIS MORNING...
OH NO...!
I THOUGHT MAYBE ANOTHER FAIRY HAD BEATEN ME TO IT...
...BUT WHEN I ASKED, NO ONE KNEW ABOUT THE CROWN...
SO WE TOLD THE QUEEN ABOUT IT RIGHT AWAY... SHE CALLED THE EMERGENCY MEETING...AND HERE WE ARE.

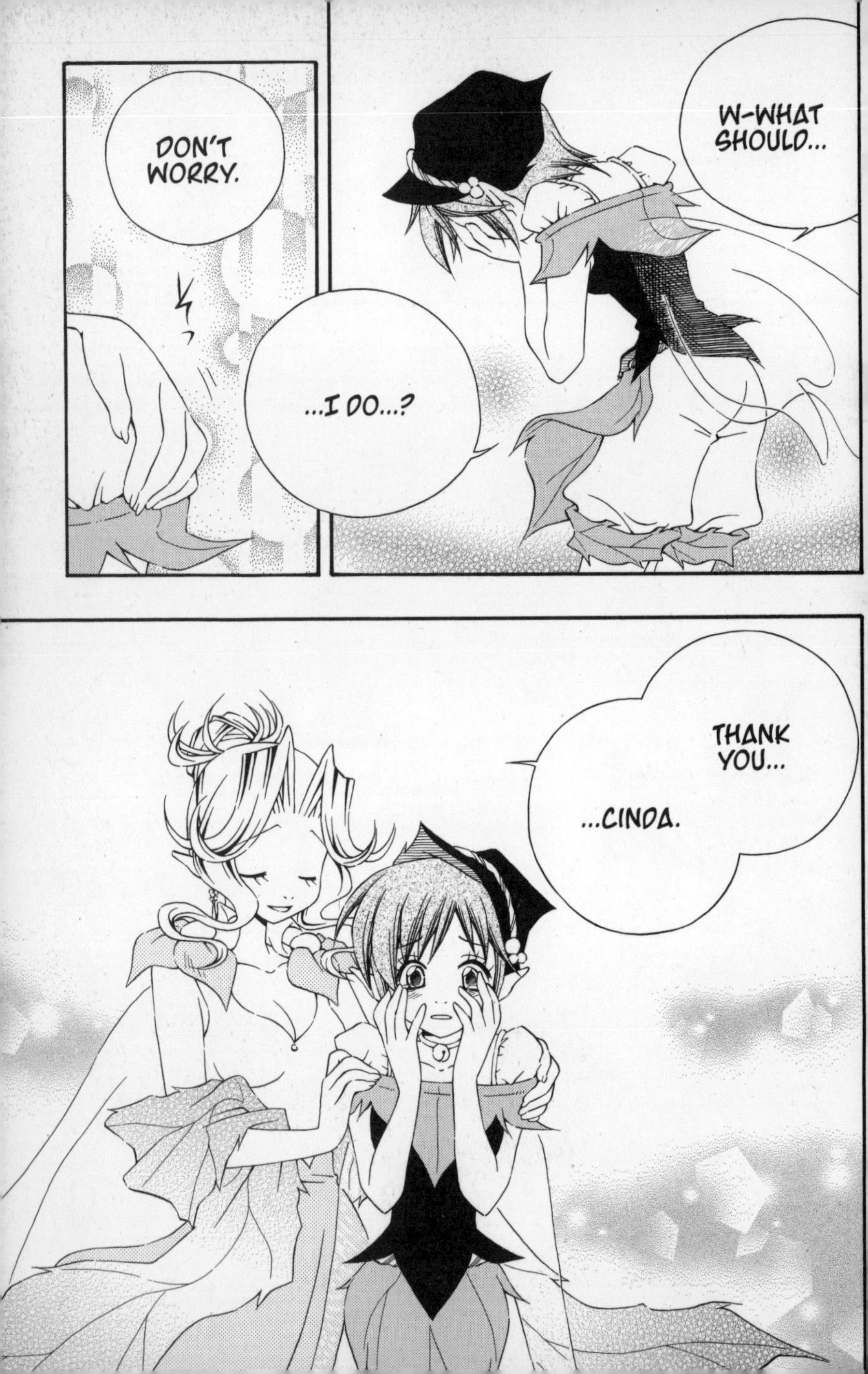
W-WHAT SHOULD...
...I DO...?
DON'T WORRY.
THANK YOU...
...CINDA.

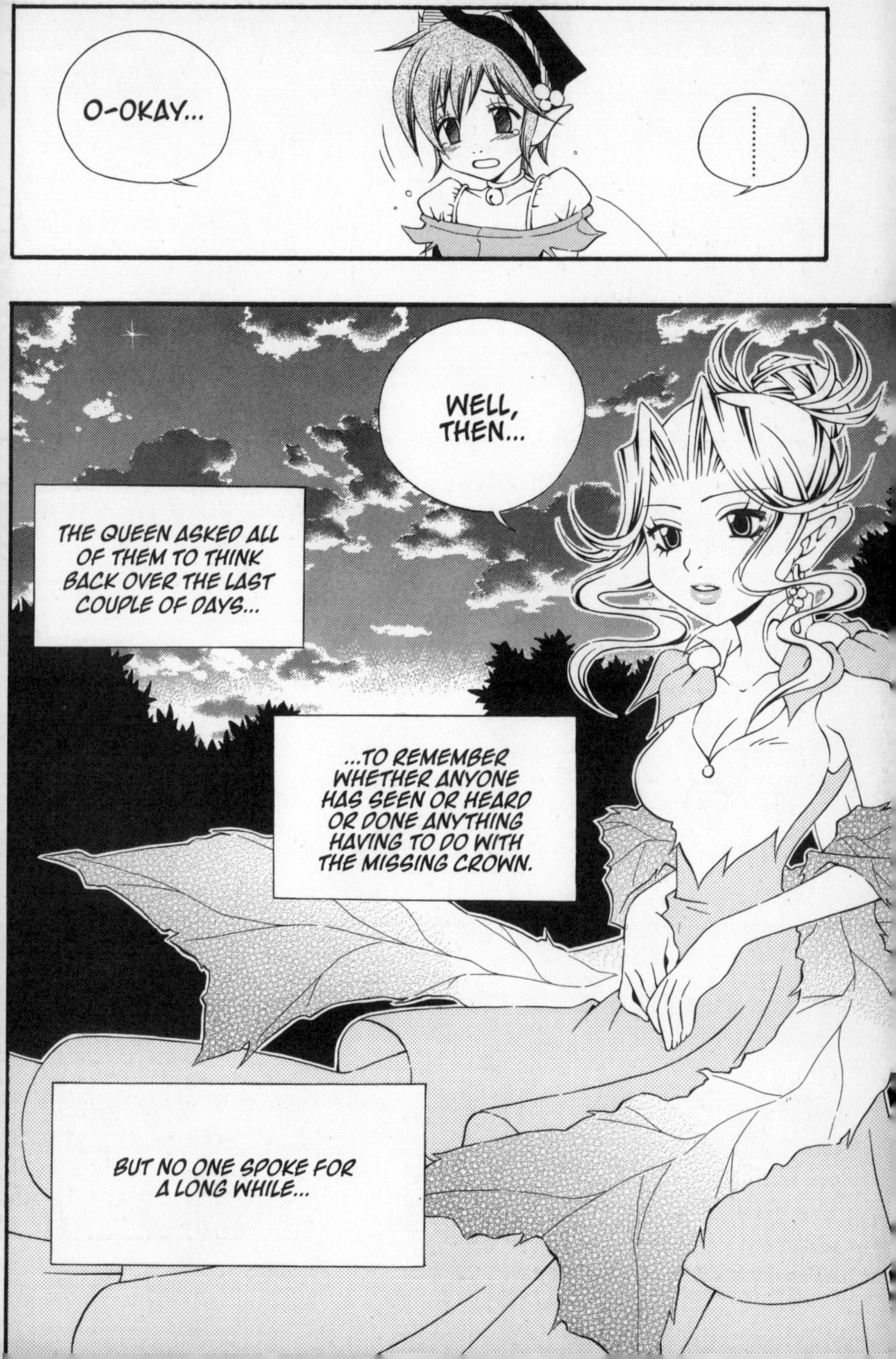
......
O-OKAY...
WELL, THEN...
THE QUEEN ASKED ALL OF THEM TO THINK BACK OVER THE LAST COUPLE OF DAYS...
...TO REMEMBER WHETHER ANYONE HAS SEEN OR HEARD OR DONE ANYTHING HAVING TO DO WITH THE MISSING CROWN.
BUT NO ONE SPOKE FOR A LONG WHILE...

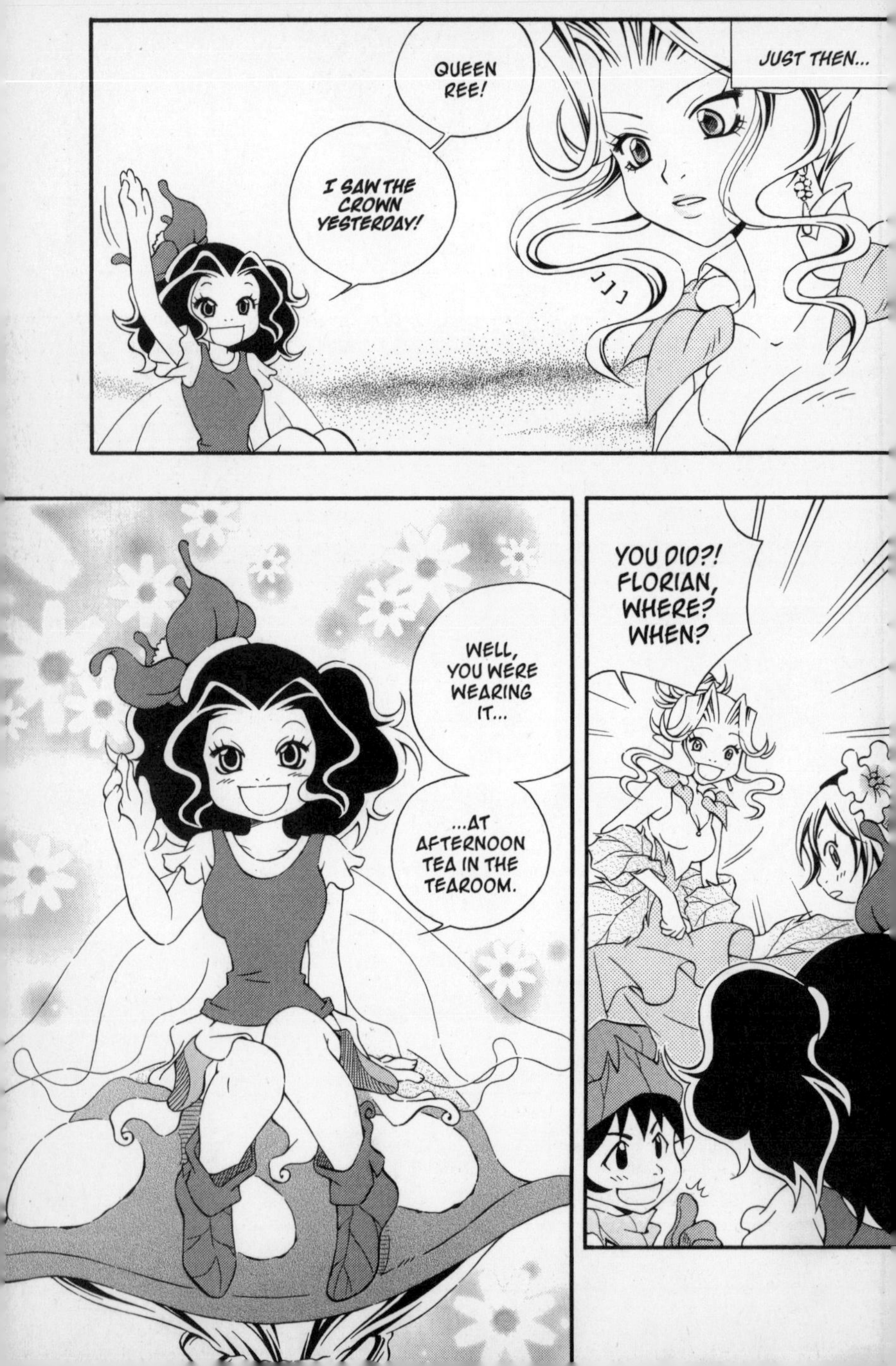
JUST THEN...
QUEEN REE!
I SAW THE CROWN YESTERDAY!
YOU DID?! FLORIAN, WHERE? WHEN?
WELL, YOU WERE WEARING IT...
...AT AFTERNOON TEA IN THE TEAROOM.

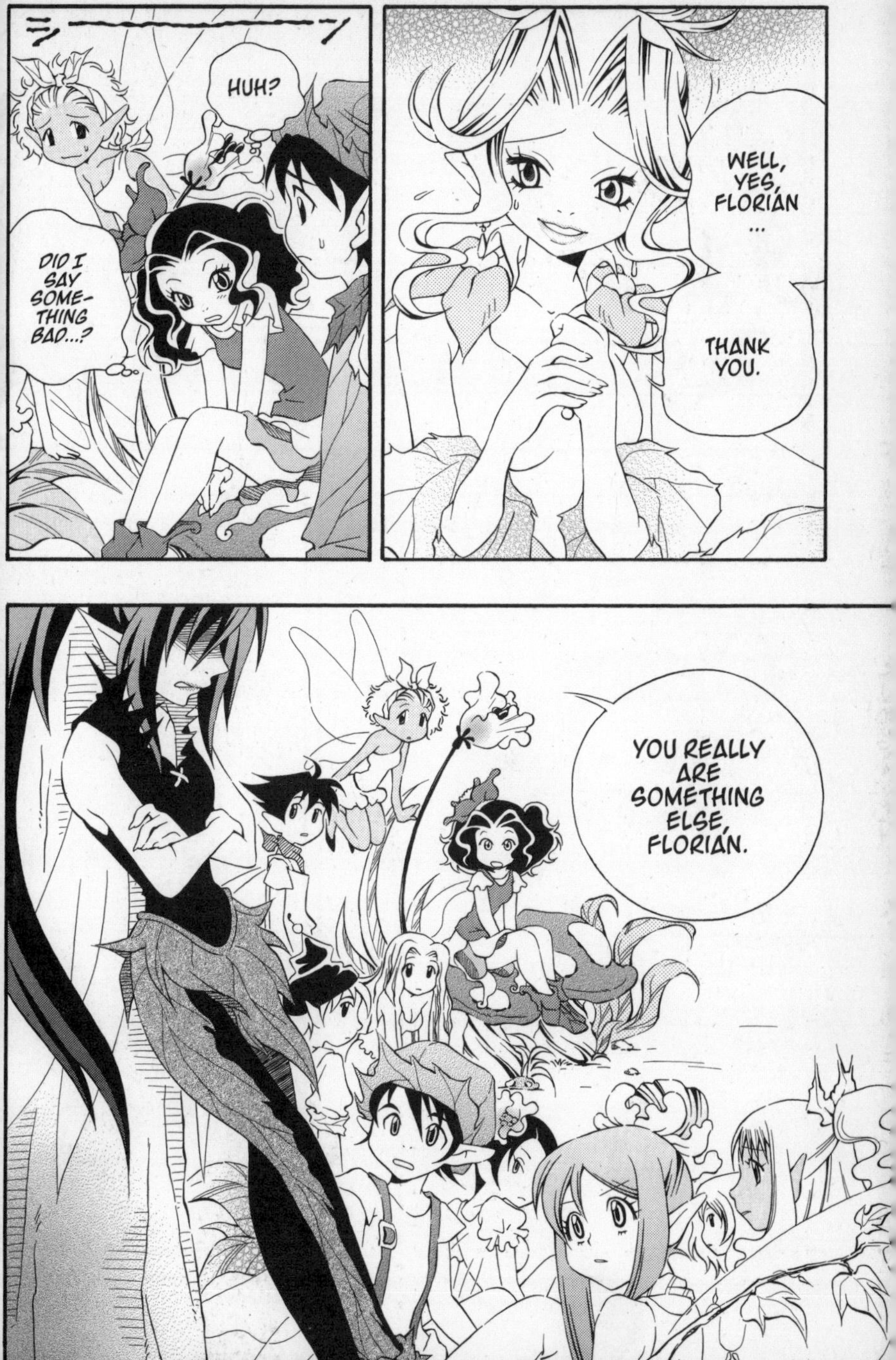
WELL, YES, FLORIÁN ...
THANK YOU.
シーン
HUH?
DID I SAY SOMETHING BAD...?
YOU REALLY ARE SOMETHING ELSE, FLORIÁN.

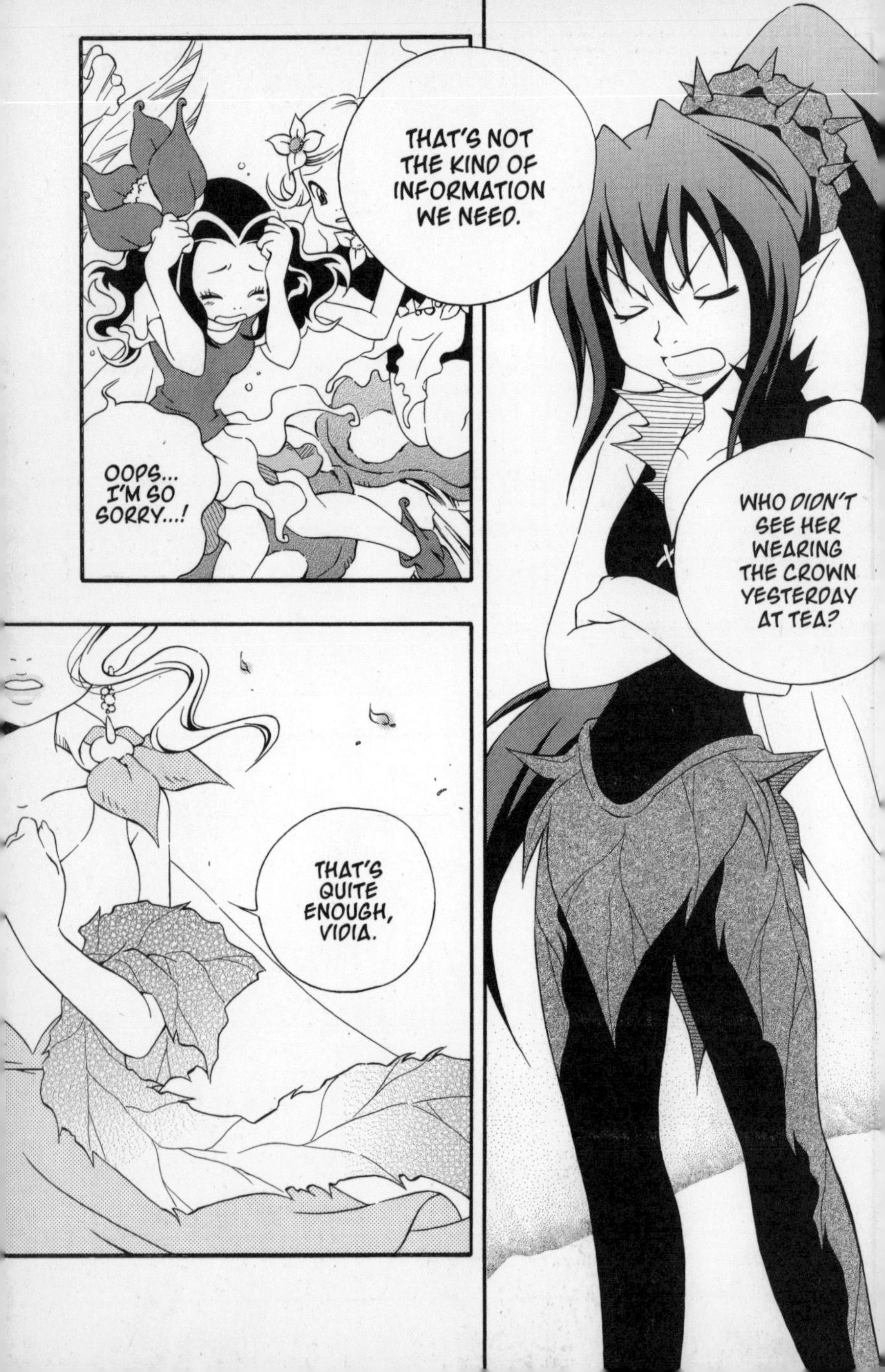
THAT'S NOT THE KIND OF INFORMATION WE NEED.
WHO *DIDN'T* SEE HER WEARING THE CROWN YESTERDAY AT TEA?
OOPS... I'M SO SORRY...!
THAT'S QUITE ENOUGH, VIDIA.

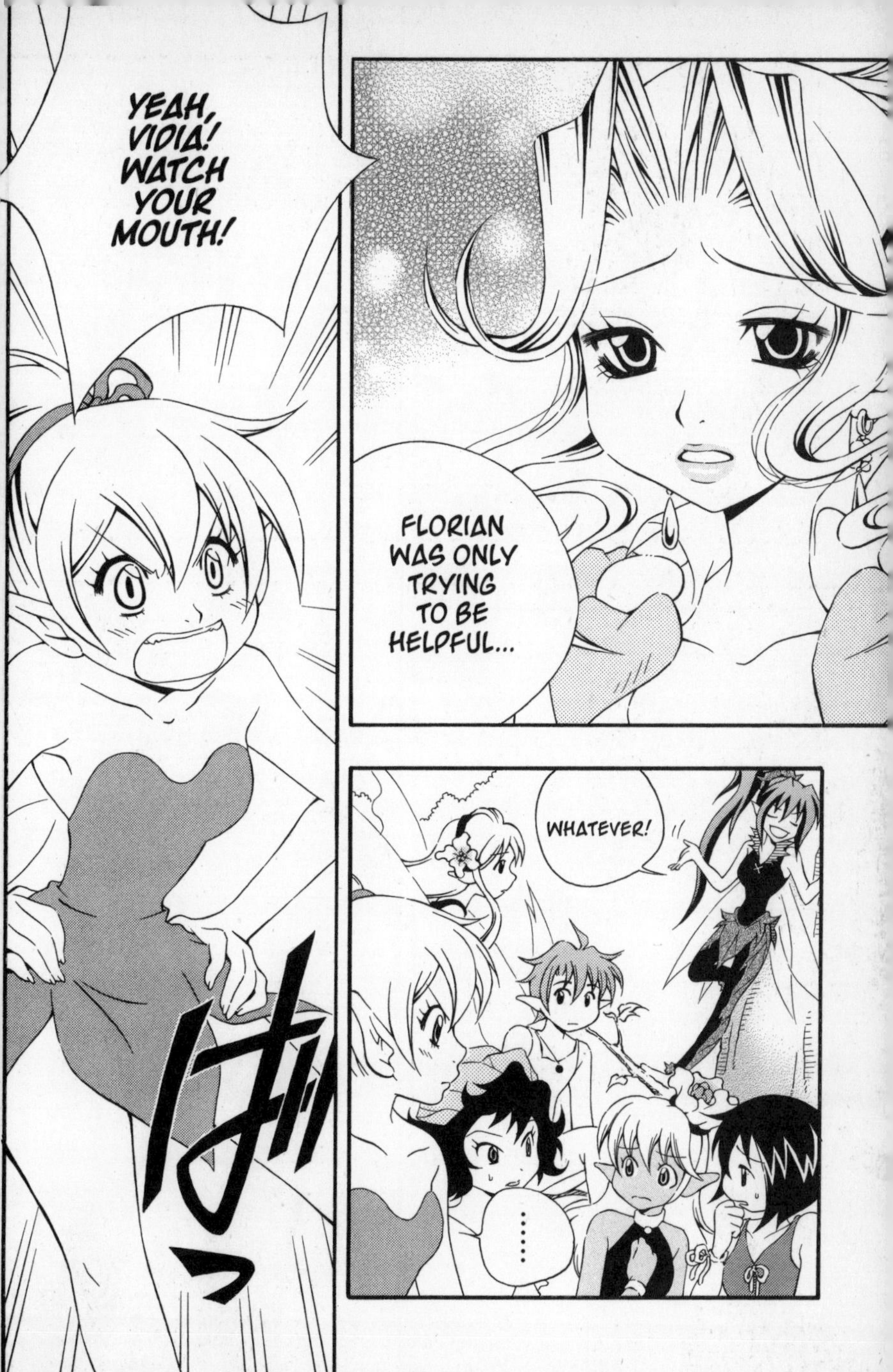
FLORIAN WAS ONLY TRYING TO BE HELPFUL...
WHATEVER!
......
YEAH, VIDIA! WATCH YOUR MOUTH!
ばっ

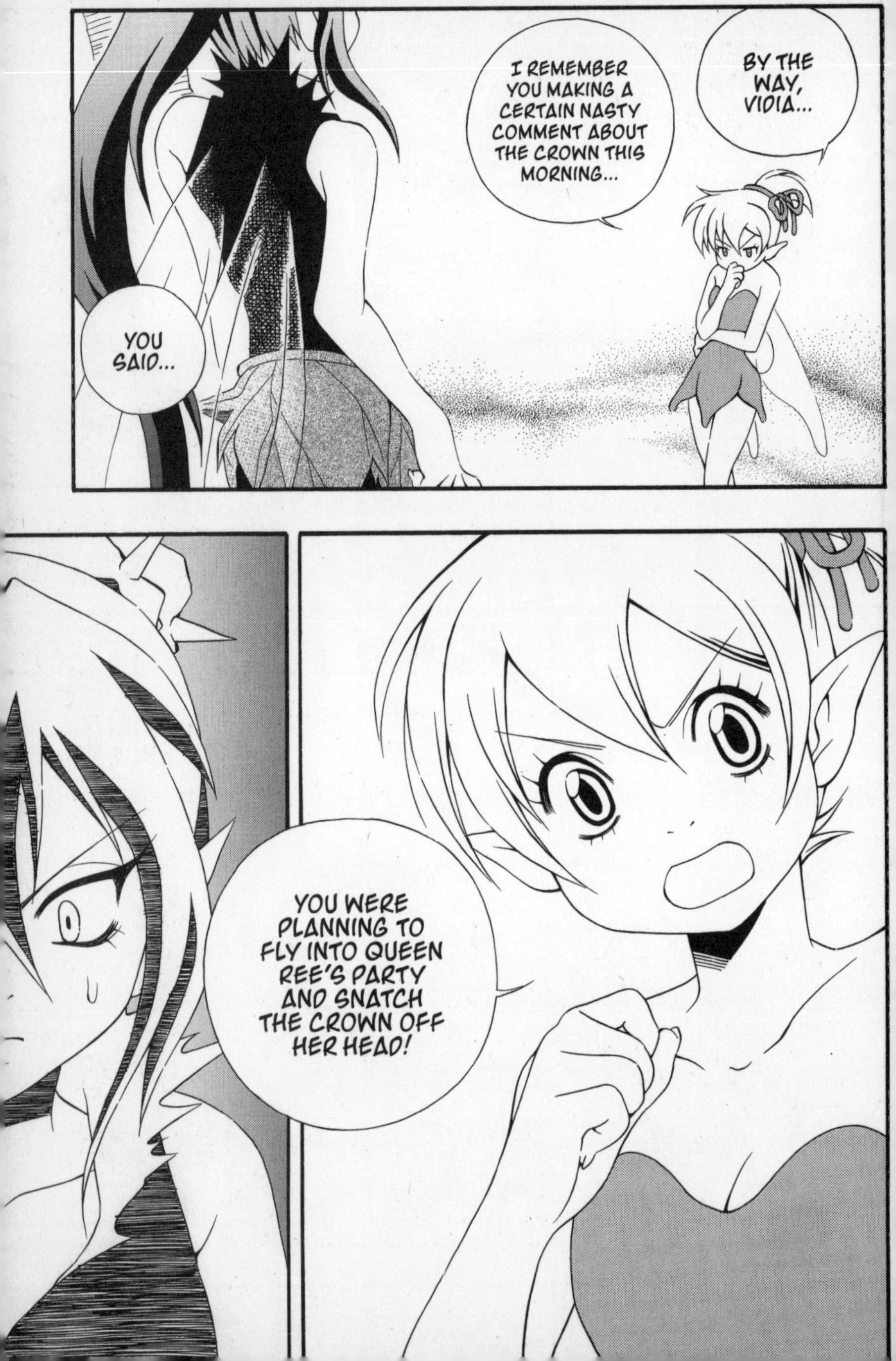
BY THE WAY, VIDIA...
I REMEMBER YOU MAKING A CERTAIN NASTY COMMENT ABOUT THE CROWN THIS MORNING...
YOU SAID...
YOU WERE PLANNING TO FLY INTO QUEEN REE'S PARTY AND SNATCH THE CROWN OFF HER HEAD!

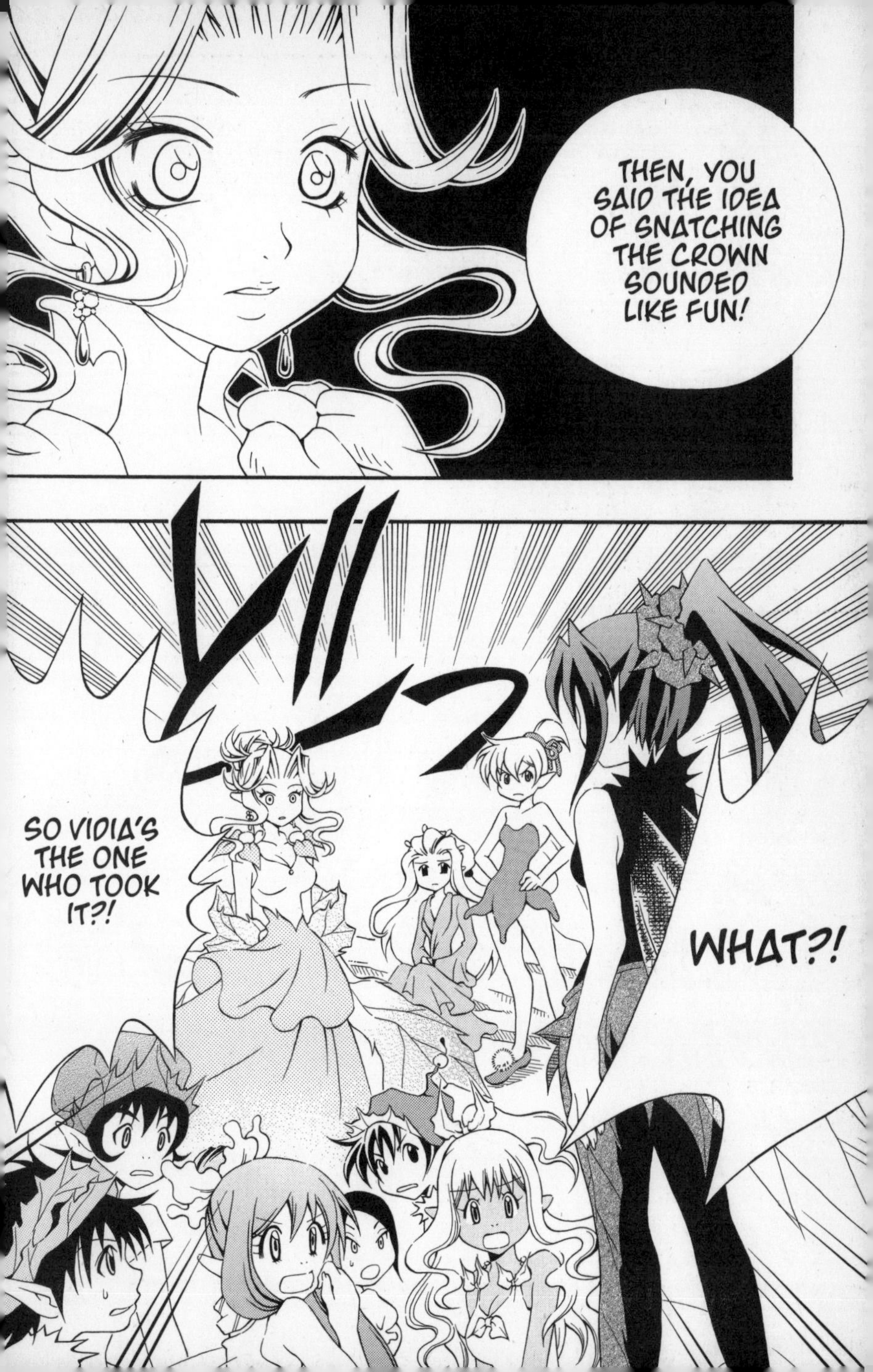
THEN, YOU SAID THE IDEA OF SNATCHING THE CROWN SOUNDED LIKE FUN!
WHAT?!
SO VIDIA'S THE ONE WHO TOOK IT?!

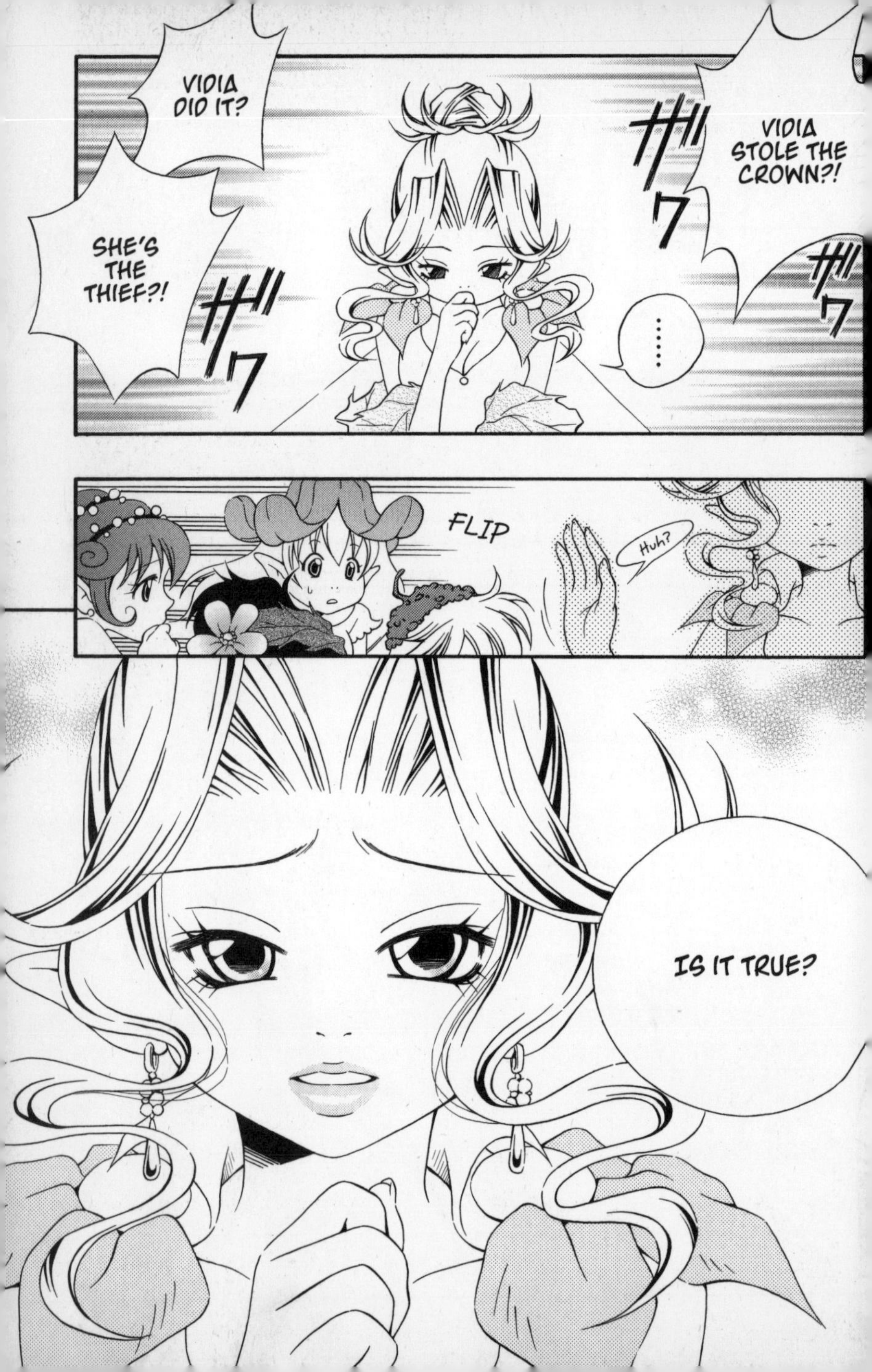
VIDIA STOLE THE CROWN?!
ザワ
ザワ
……
VIDIA DID IT?
SHE'S THE THIEF?!
ザワ
Huh?
FLIP
IS IT TRUE?

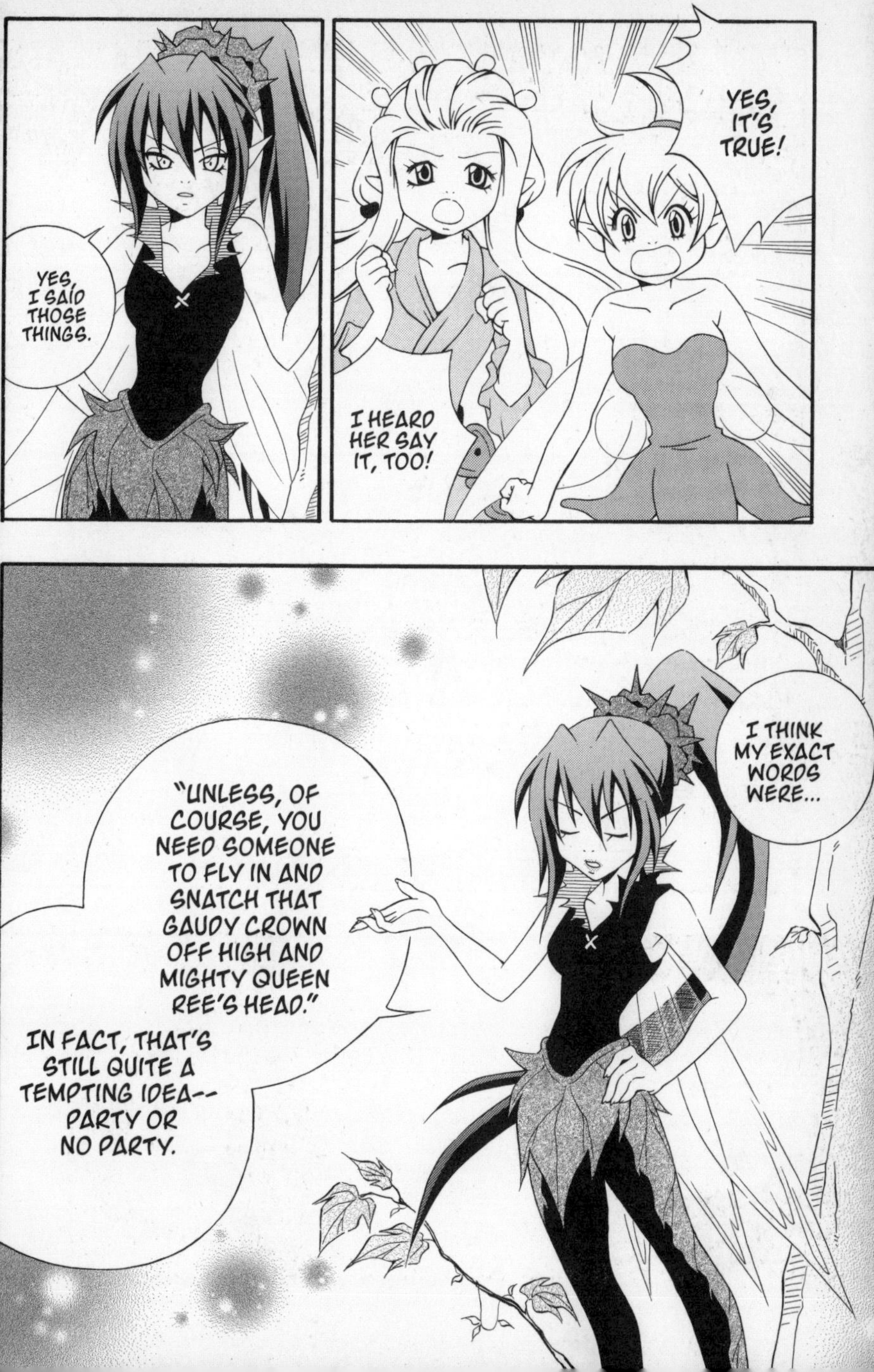
YES, IT'S TRUE!
I HEARD HER SAY IT, TOO!
YES, I SAID THOSE THINGS.
I THINK MY EXACT WORDS WERE...
"UNLESS, OF COURSE, YOU NEED SOMEONE TO FLY IN AND SNATCH THAT GAUDY CROWN OFF HIGH AND MIGHTY QUEEN REE'S HEAD."
IN FACT, THAT'S STILL QUITE A TEMPTING IDEA--PARTY OR NO PARTY.

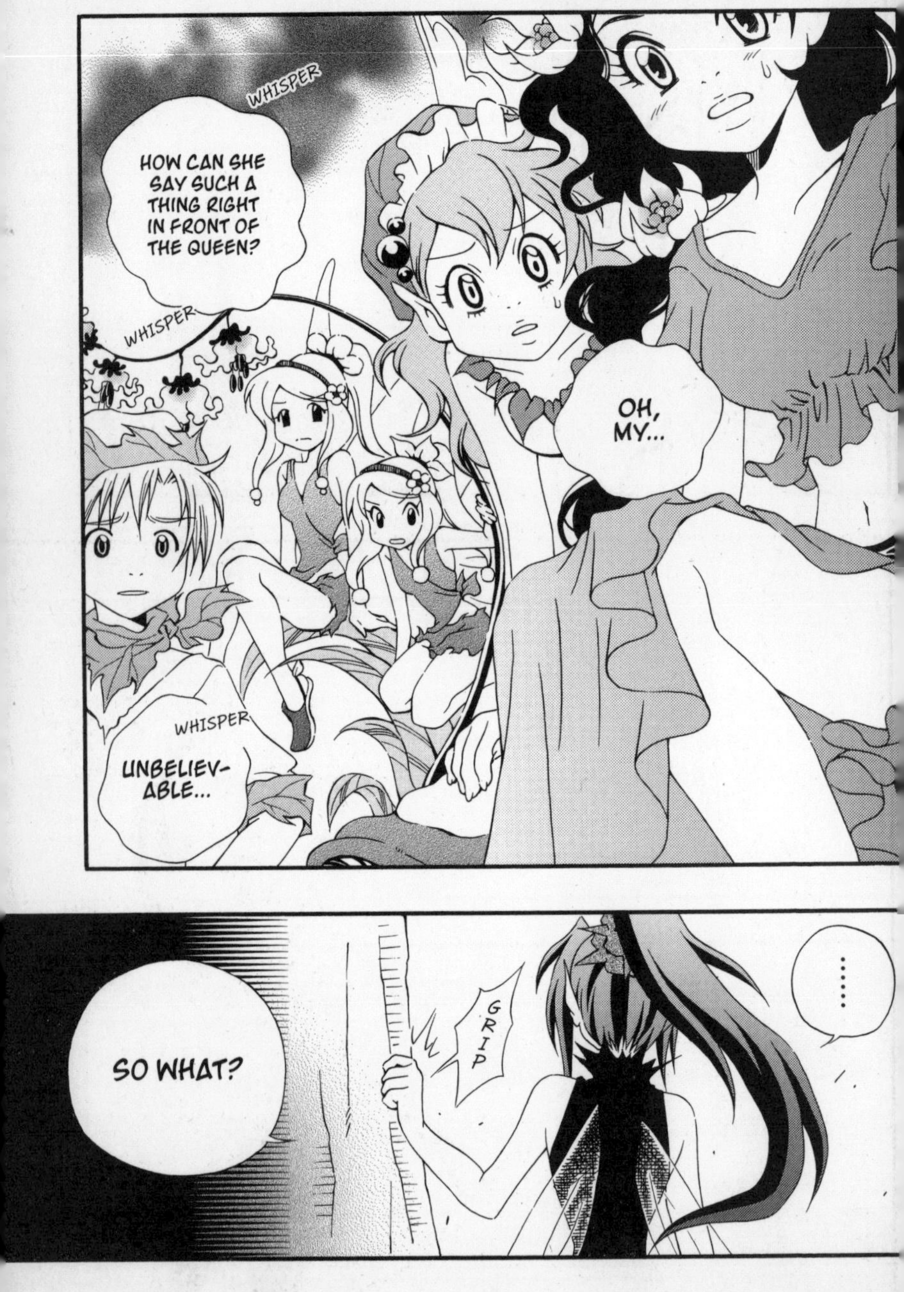
OH, MY...
WHISPER
HOW CAN SHE SAY SUCH A THING RIGHT IN FRONT OF THE QUEEN?
WHISPER
WHISPER
UNBELIEV-ABLE...
......
GRIP
SO WHAT?

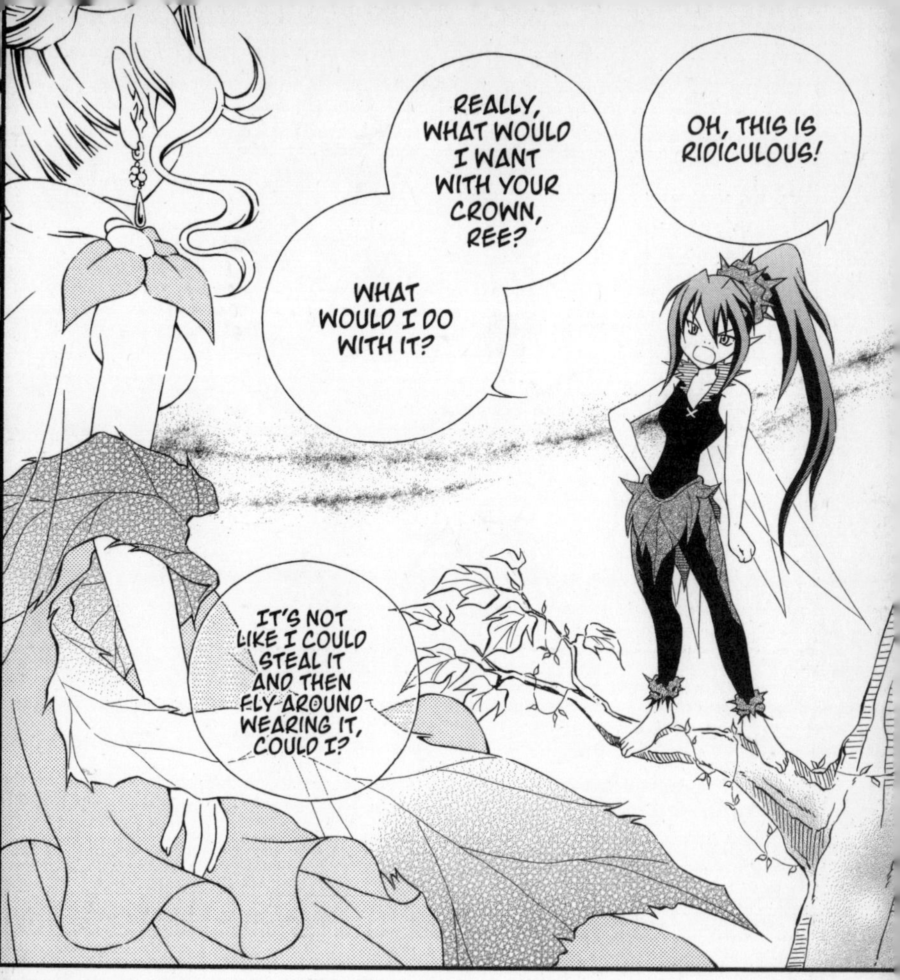
OH, THIS IS RIDICULOUS!
REALLY, WHAT WOULD I WANT WITH YOUR CROWN, REE?
WHAT WOULD I DO WITH IT?
IT'S NOT LIKE I COULD STEAL IT AND THEN FLY AROUND WEARING IT, COULD I?

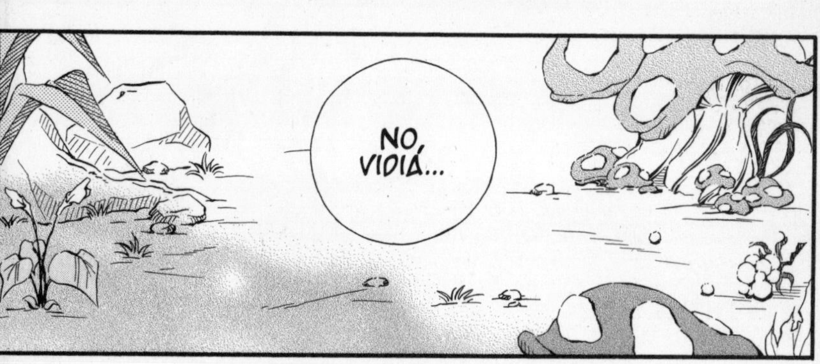
NO, VIDIA...

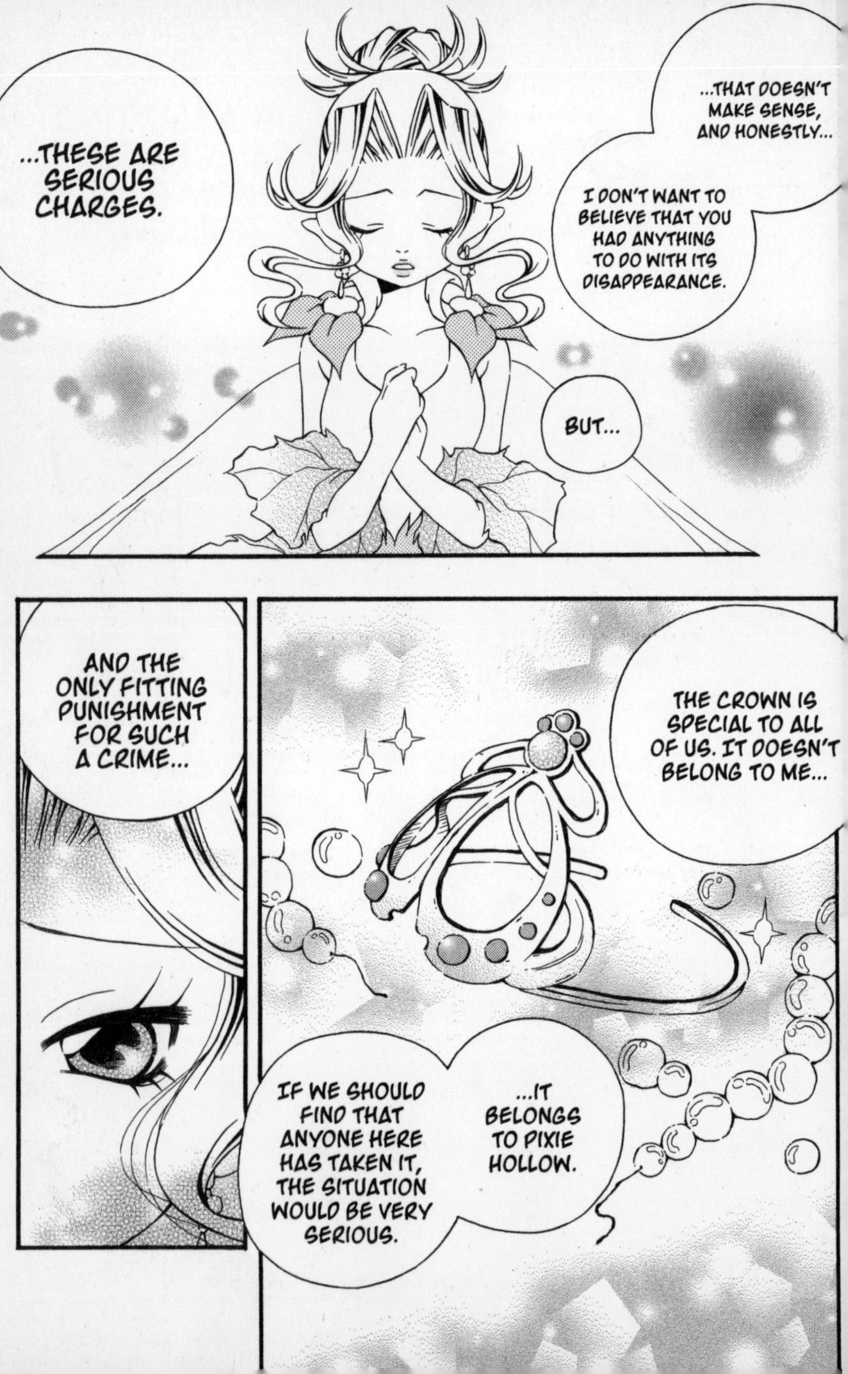
...THAT DOESN'T MAKE SENSE, AND HONESTLY...
I DON'T WANT TO BELIEVE THAT YOU HAD ANYTHING TO DO WITH ITS DISAPPEARANCE.
BUT...
...THESE ARE SERIOUS CHARGES.
THE CROWN IS SPECIAL TO ALL OF US. IT DOESN'T BELONG TO ME...
...IT BELONGS TO PIXIE HOLLOW.
IF WE SHOULD FIND THAT ANYONE HERE HAS TAKEN IT, THE SITUATION WOULD BE VERY SERIOUS.
AND THE ONLY FITTING PUNISHMENT FOR SUCH A CRIME...

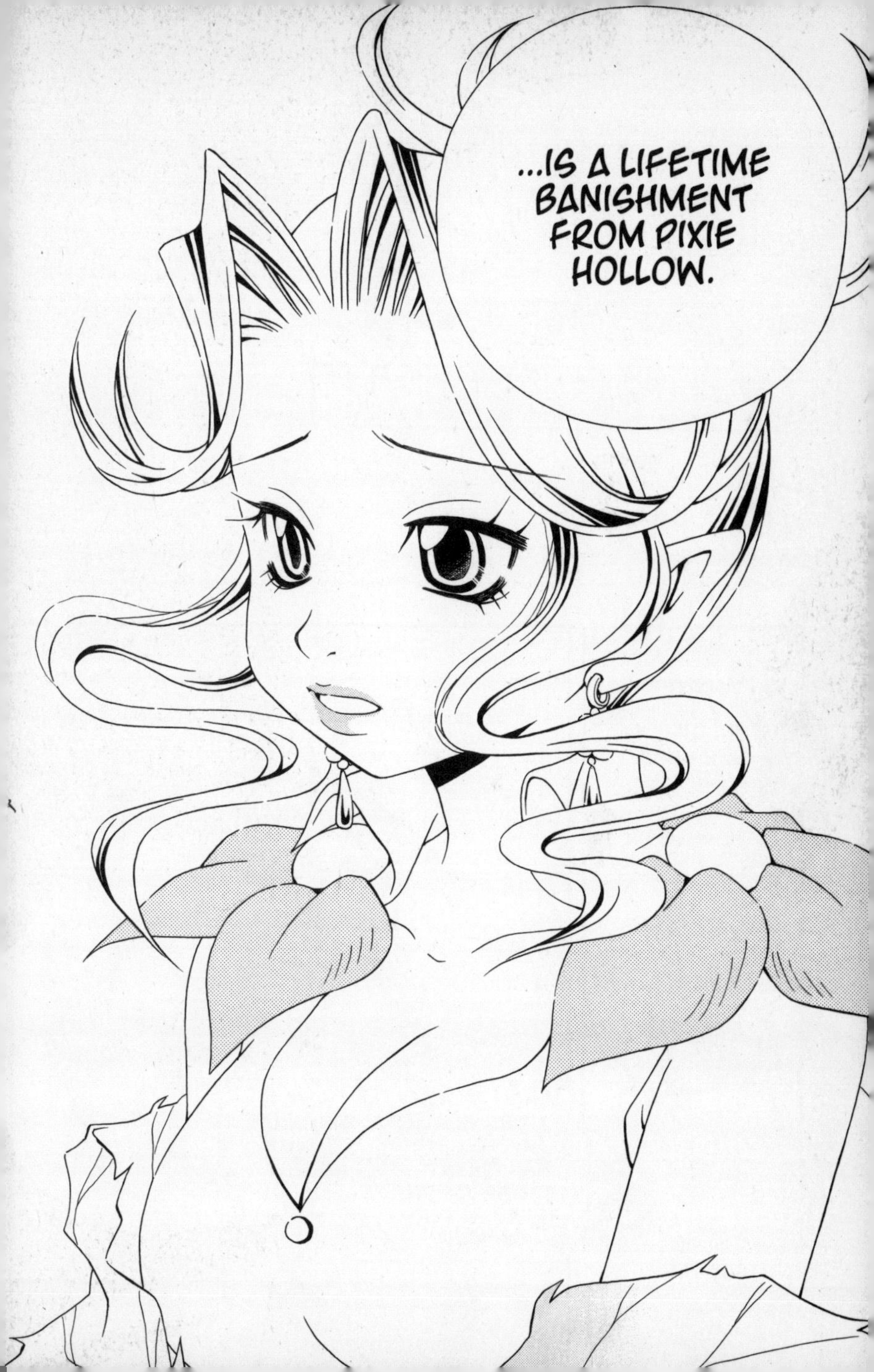
...IS A LIFETIME BANISHMENT FROM PIXIE HOLLOW.

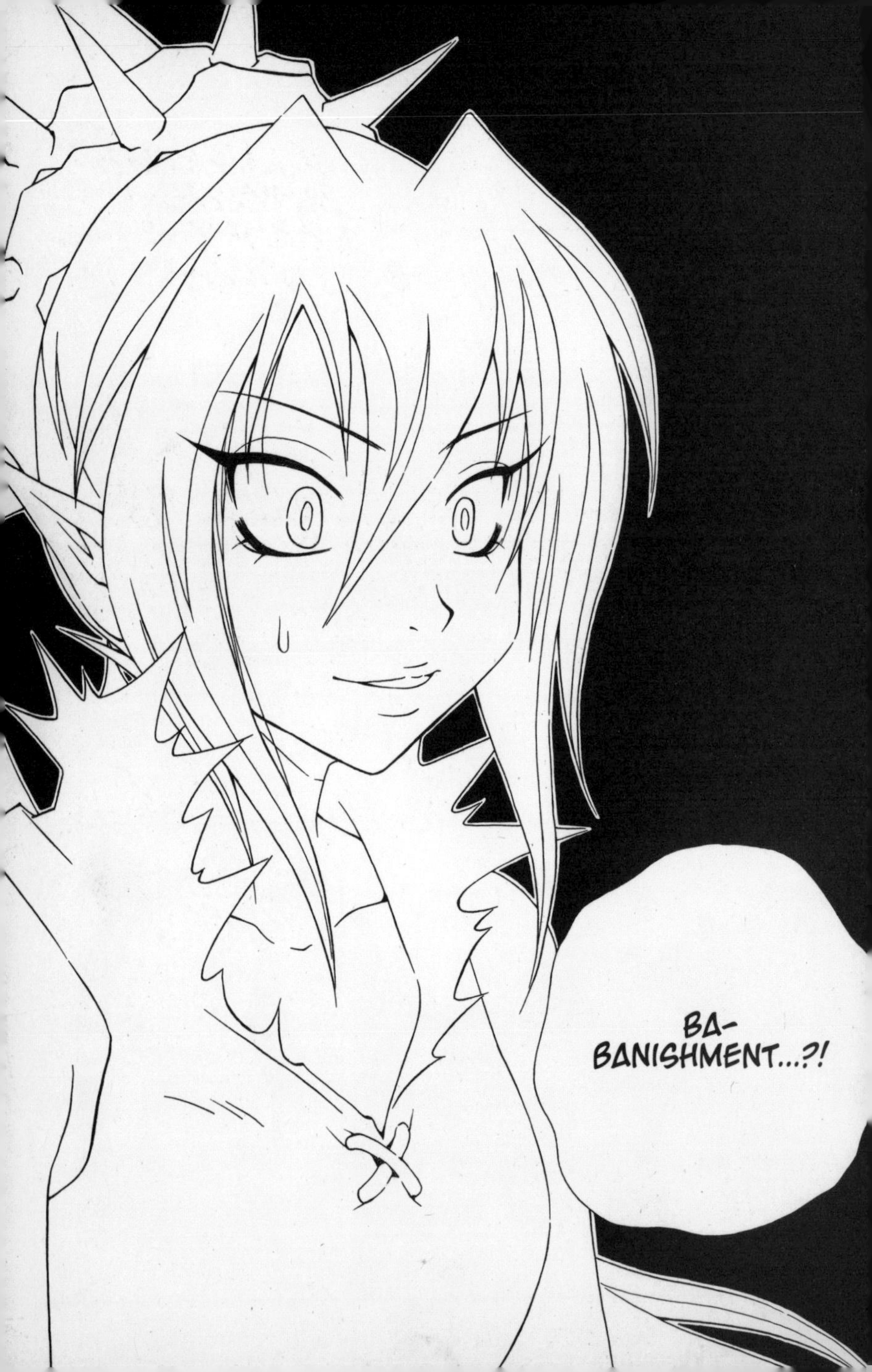
BA-
BANISHMENT...?!

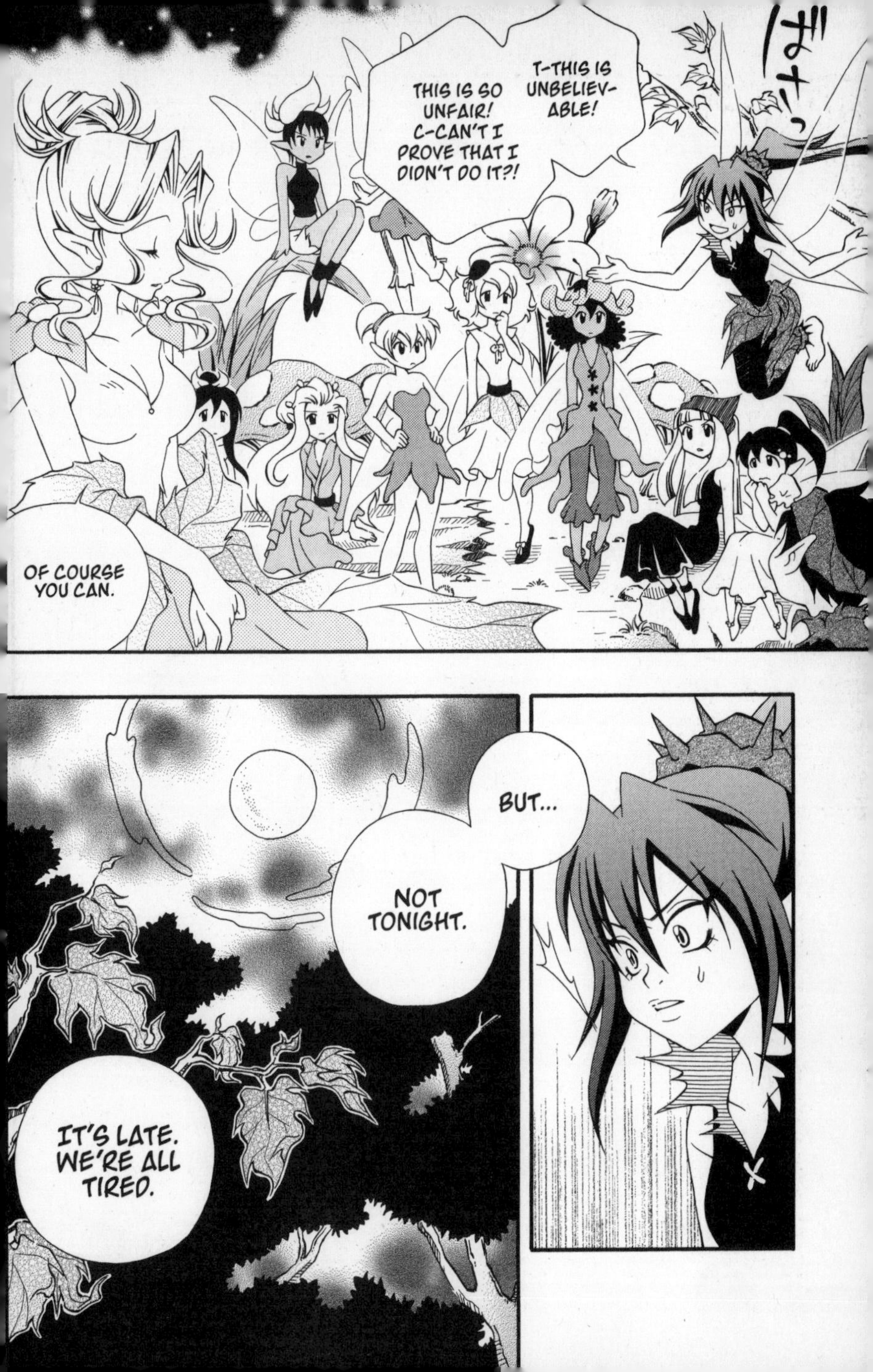
ばさっ
T-THIS IS UNBELIEV-ABLE!
THIS IS SO UNFAIR! C-CAN'T I PROVE THAT I DIDN'T DO IT?!
OF COURSE YOU CAN.
BUT...
NOT TONIGHT.
IT'S LATE. WE'RE ALL TIRED.

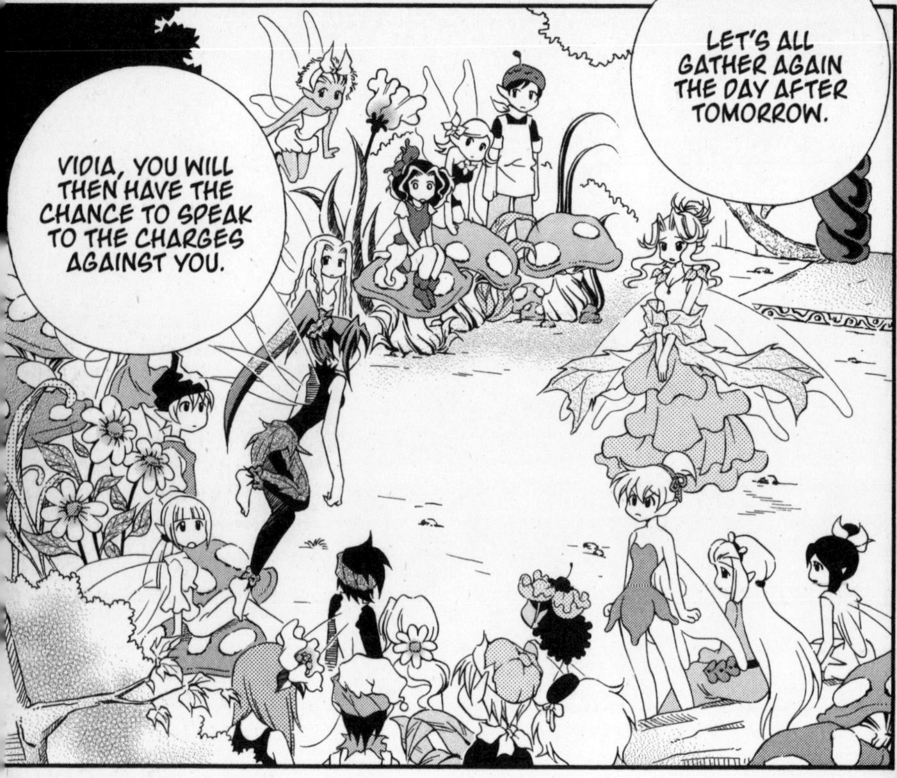
LET'S ALL GATHER AGAIN THE DAY AFTER TOMORROW.
VIDIA, YOU WILL THEN HAVE THE CHANCE TO SPEAK TO THE CHARGES AGAINST YOU.

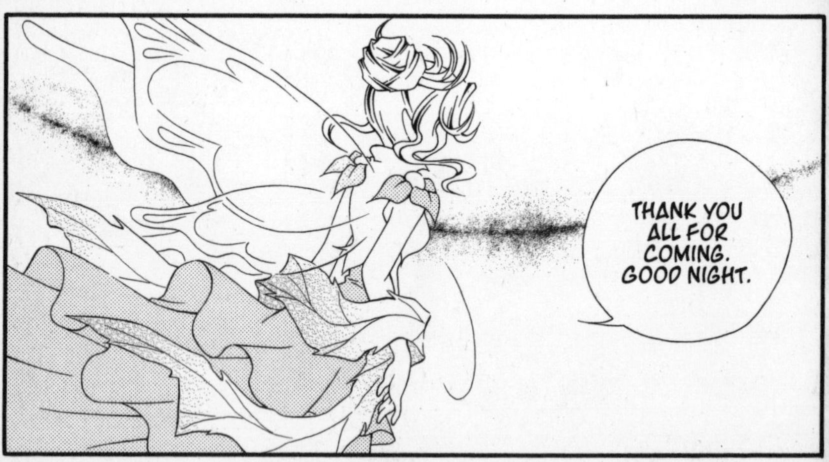
THANK YOU ALL FOR COMING. GOOD NIGHT.

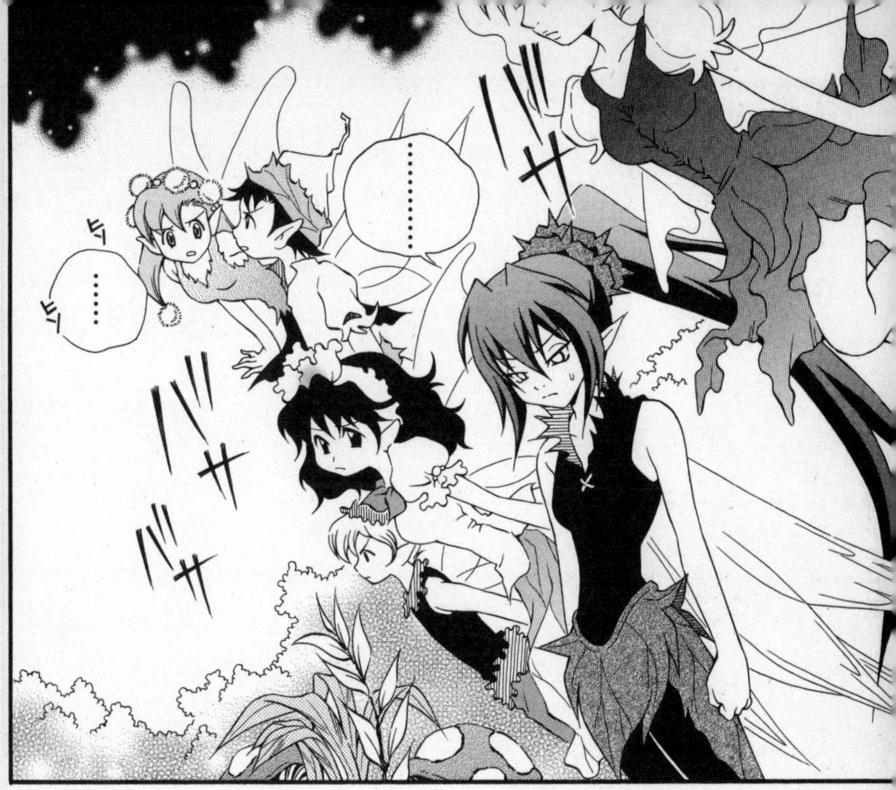
バサ
バサ
……
ビク
ビク
……
バサ
バサ
バサ
バサ
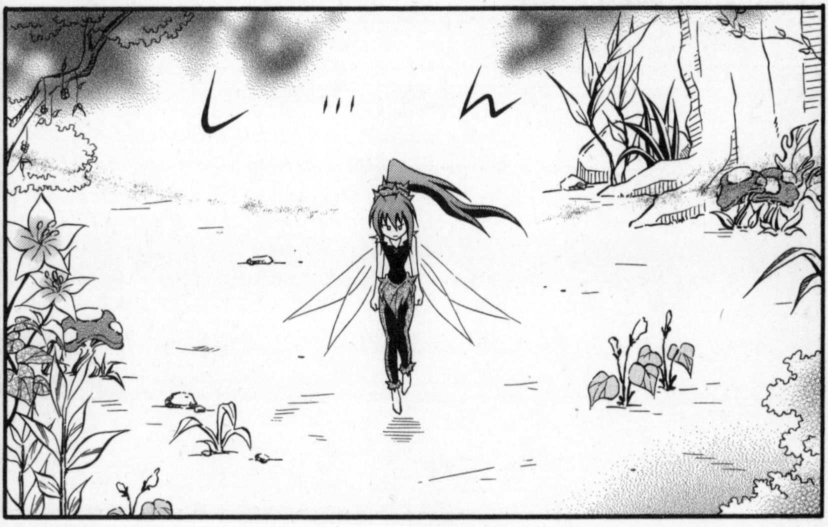
し〃ん

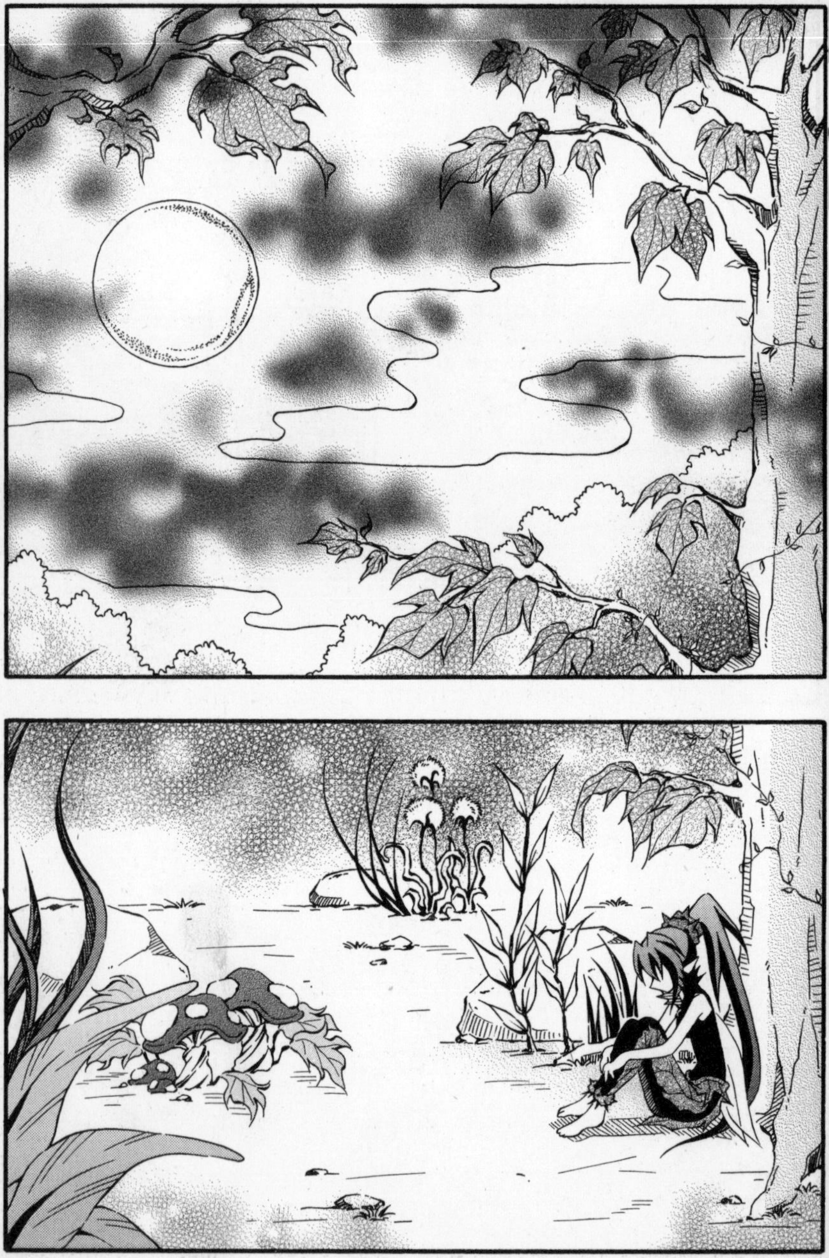

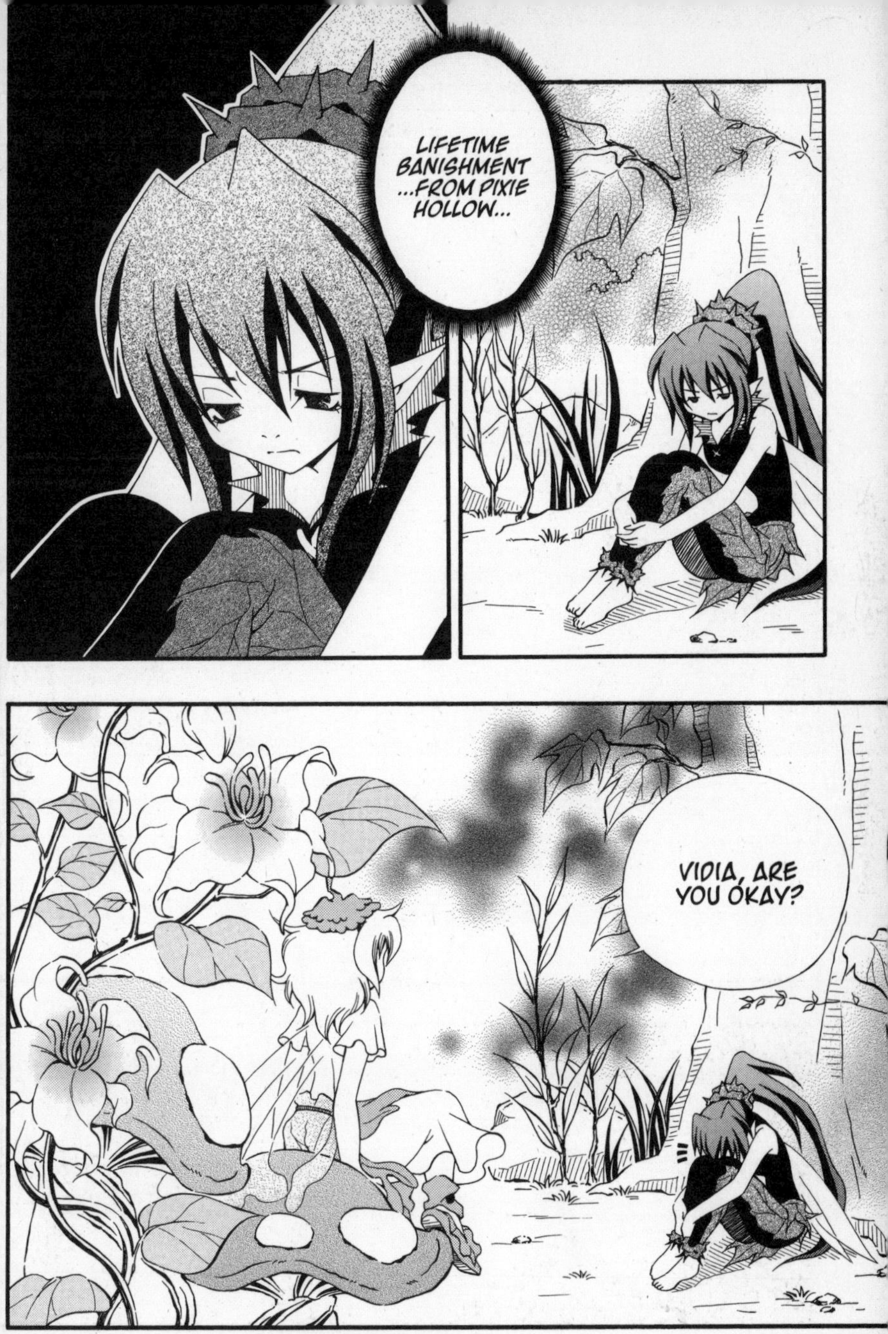
LIFETIME BANISHMENT ...FROM PIXIE HOLLOW...
VIDIA, ARE YOU OKAY?

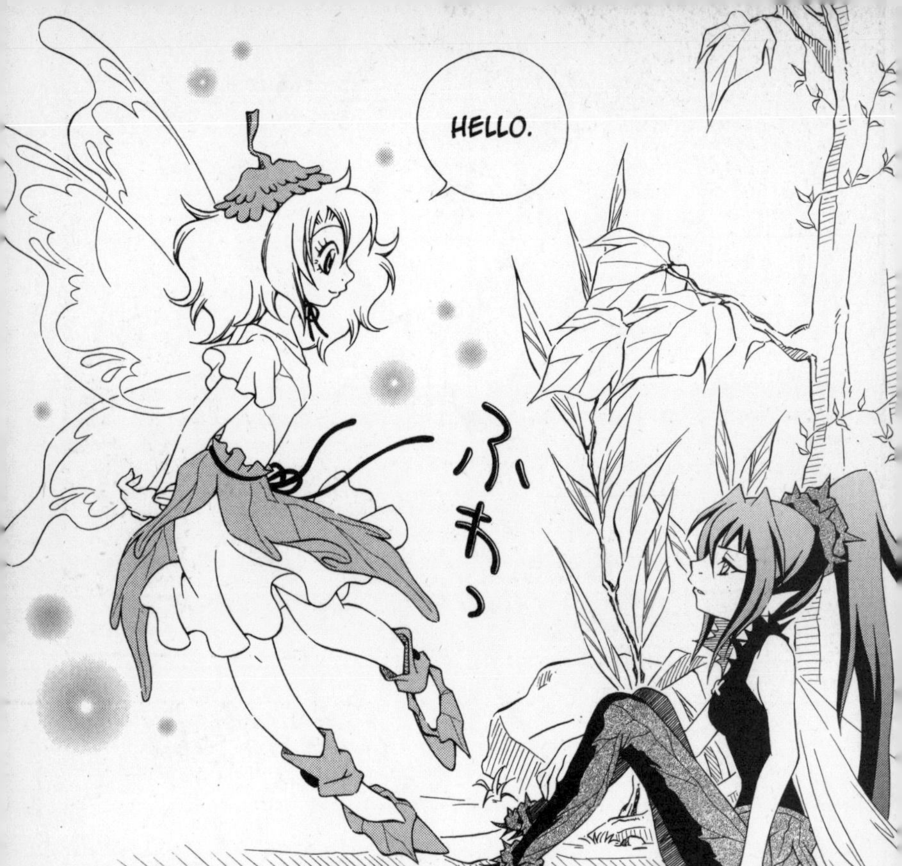
HELLO.
ふわっ

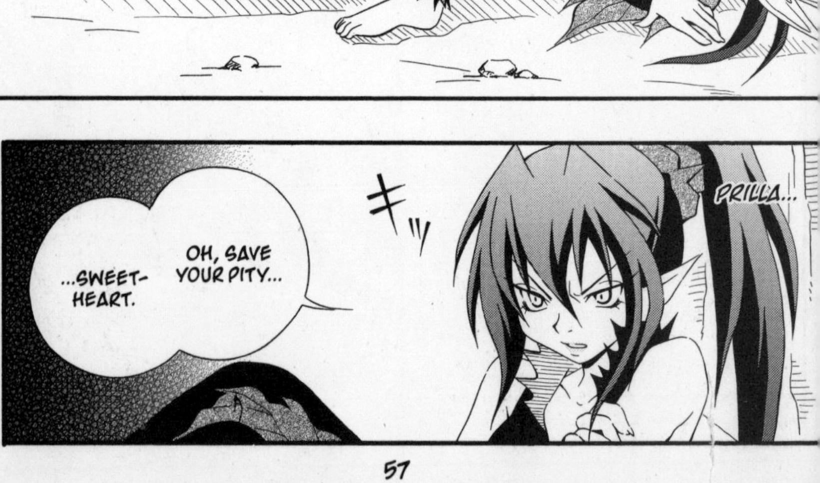
PRILLA...
キッ
OH, SAVE YOUR PITY...
...SWEET-HEART.

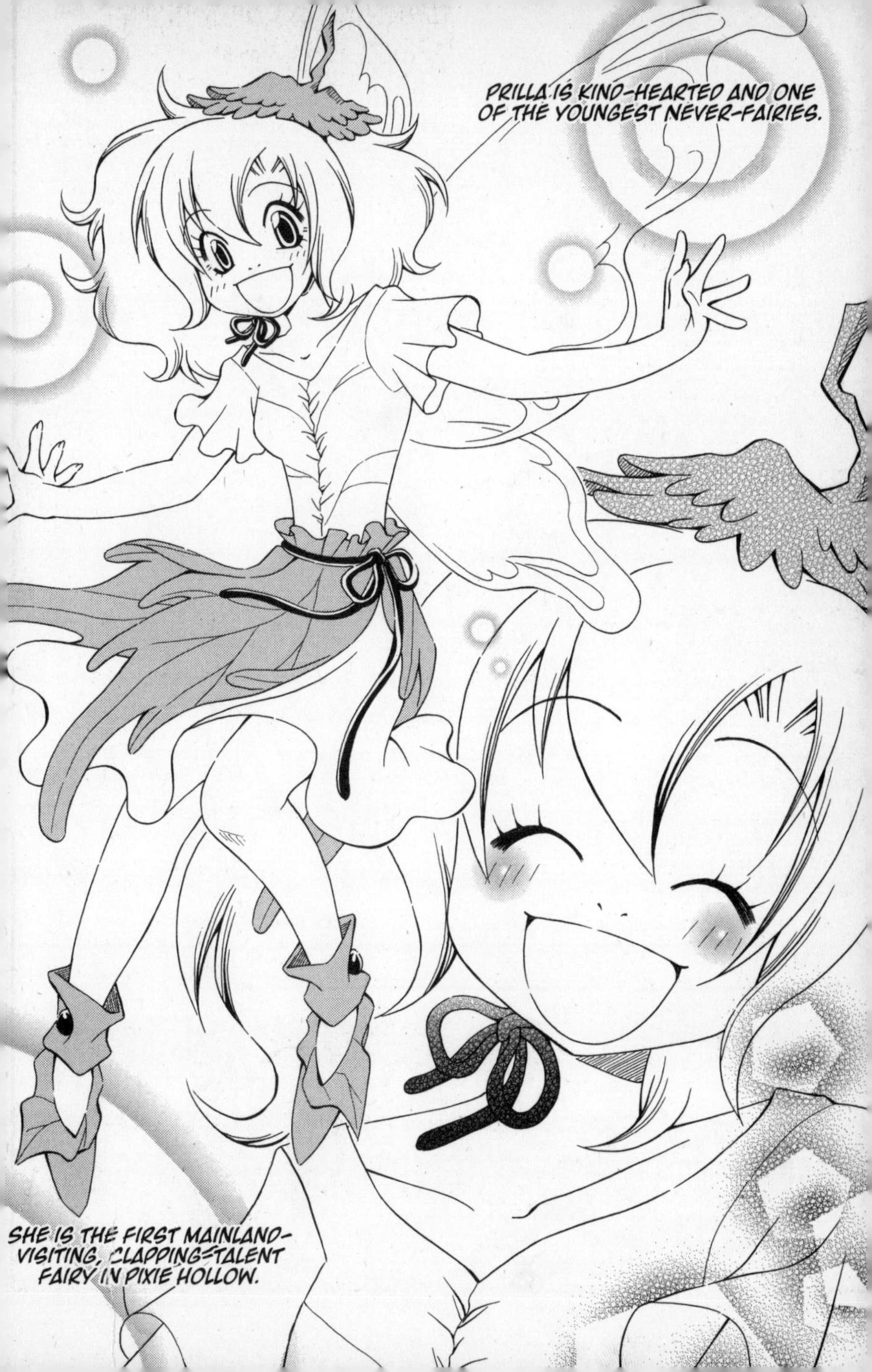
PRILLA IS KIND-HEARTED AND ONE OF THE YOUNGEST NEVER-FAIRIES.
SHE IS THE FIRST MAINLAND-VISITING, CLAPPING-TALENT FAIRY IN PIXIE HOLLOW.

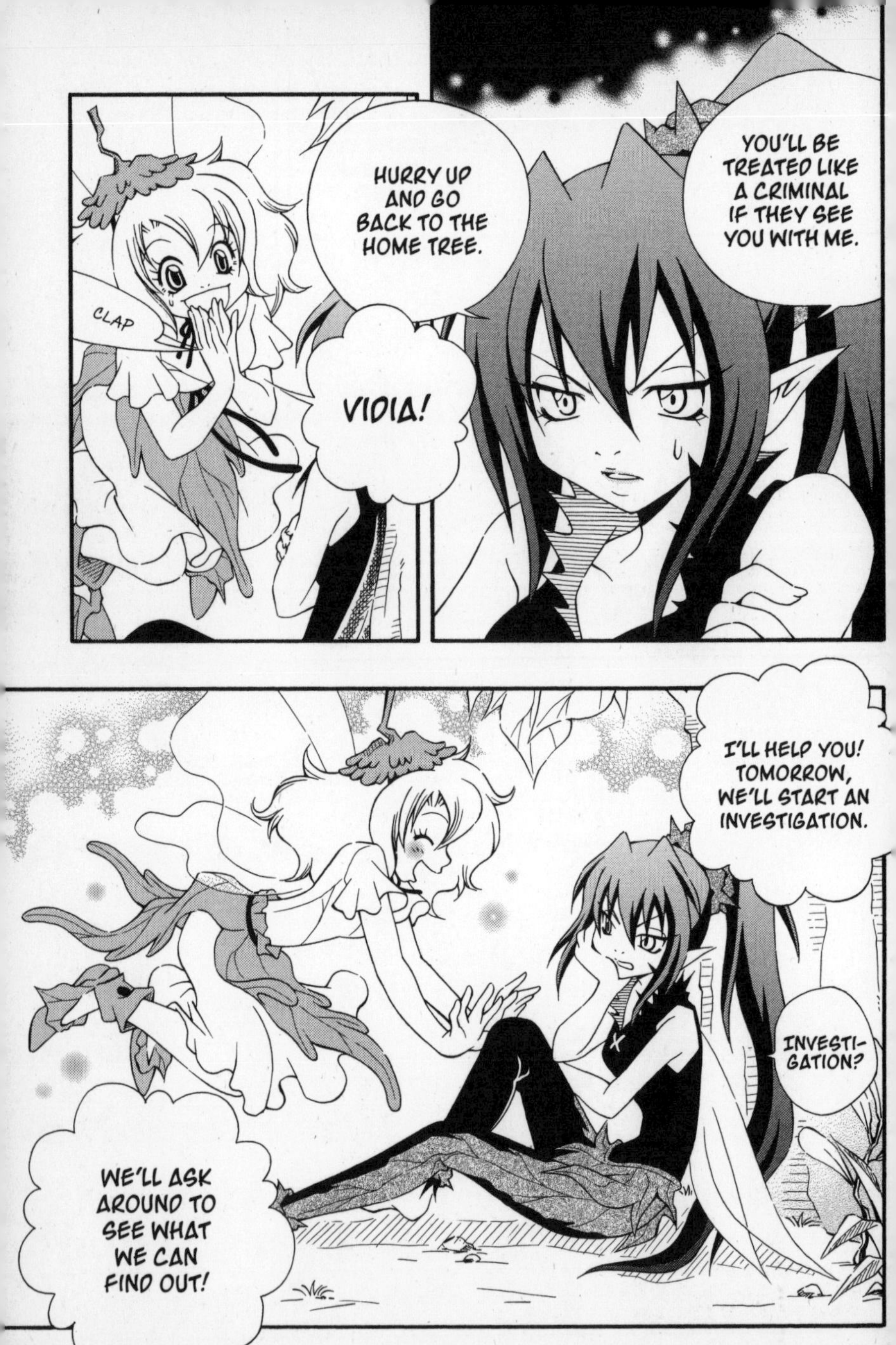
YOU'LL BE TREATED LIKE A CRIMINAL IF THEY SEE YOU WITH ME.
HURRY UP AND GO BACK TO THE HOME TREE.
VIDIA!
CLAP
I'LL HELP YOU! TOMORROW, WE'LL START AN INVESTIGATION.
INVESTI-GATION?
WE'LL ASK AROUND TO SEE WHAT WE CAN FIND OUT!

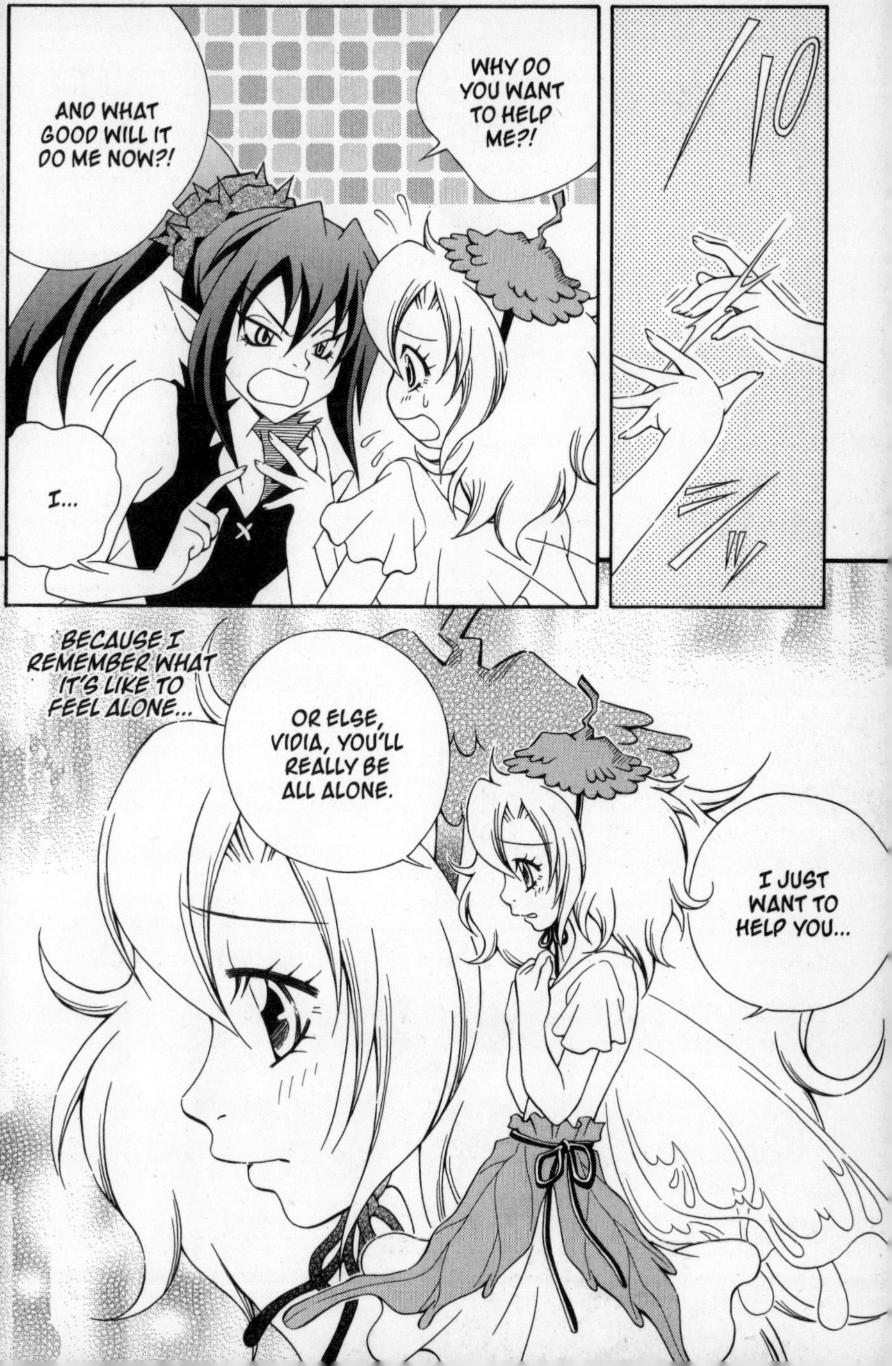
WHY DO YOU WANT TO HELP ME?!
AND WHAT GOOD WILL IT DO ME NOW?!
I...
I JUST WANT TO HELP YOU...
OR ELSE, VIDIA, YOU'LL REALLY BE ALL ALONE.
BECAUSE I REMEMBER WHAT IT'S LIKE TO FEEL ALONE...

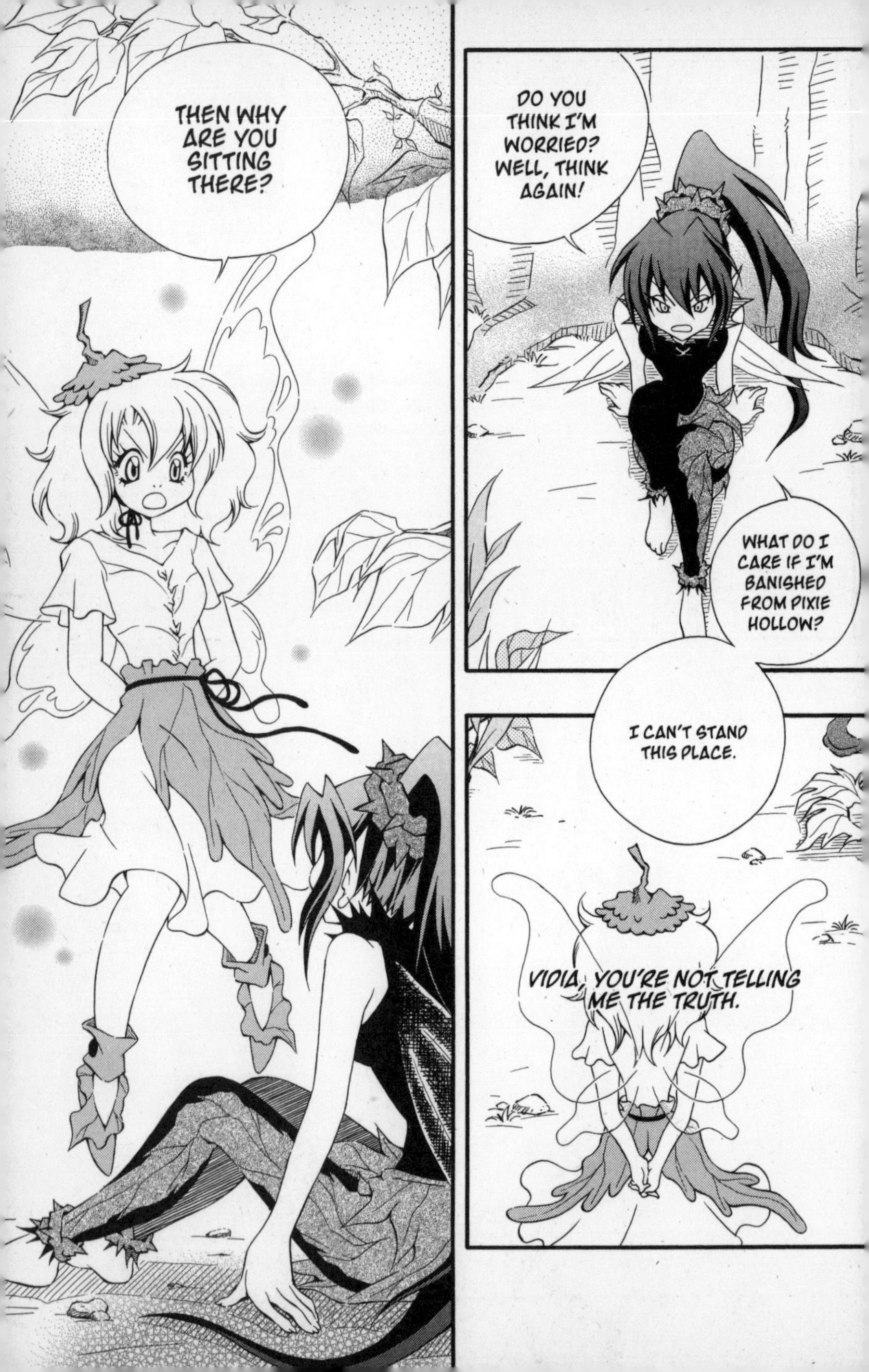
DO YOU THINK I'M WORRIED? WELL, THINK AGAIN!
WHAT DO I CARE IF I'M BANISHED FROM PIXIE HOLLOW?
I CAN'T STAND THIS PLACE.
VIDIA, YOU'RE NOT TELLING ME THE TRUTH.
THEN WHY ARE YOU SITTING THERE?

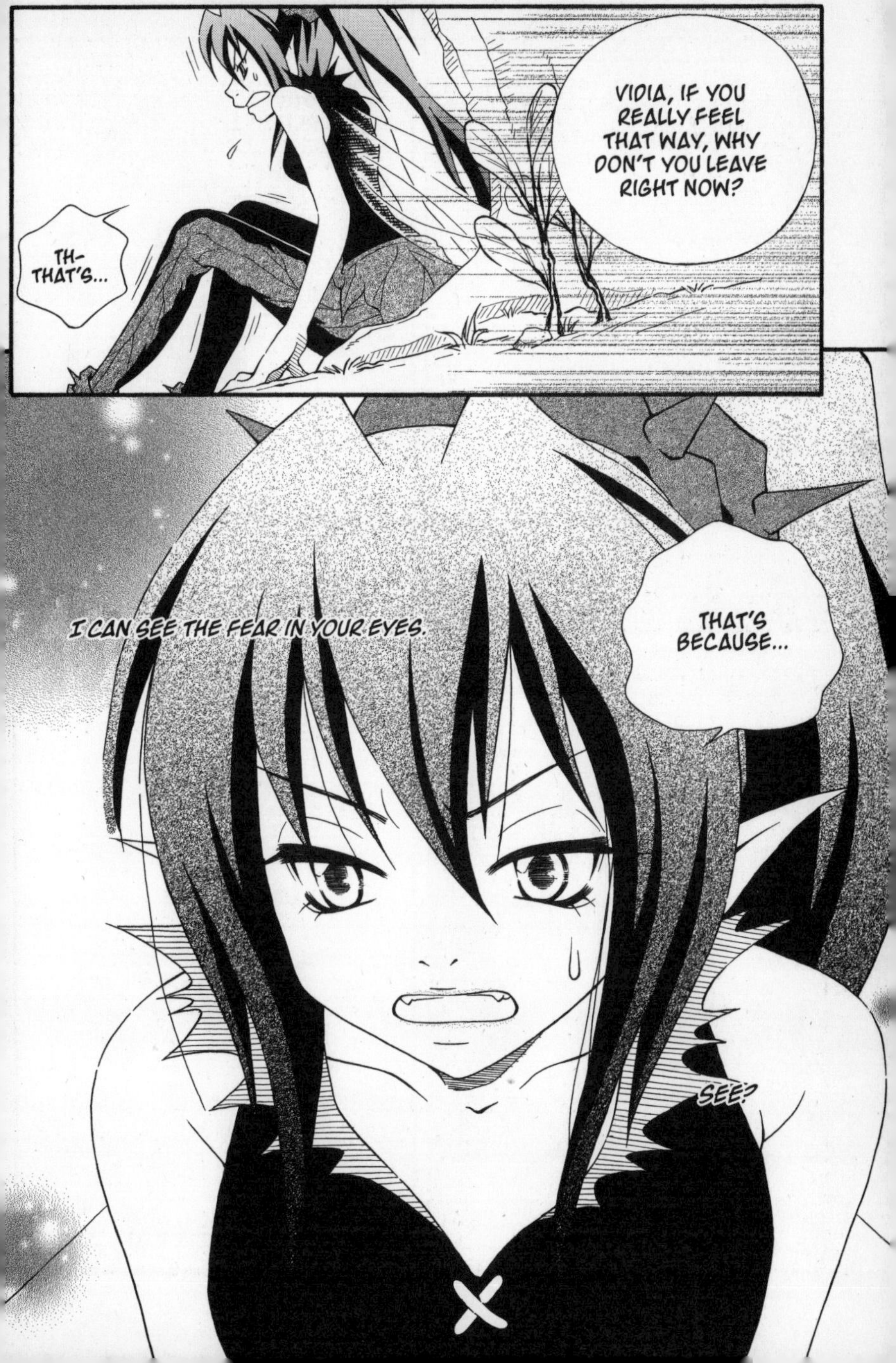
VIDIA, IF YOU REALLY FEEL THAT WAY, WHY DON'T YOU LEAVE RIGHT NOW?
TH- THAT'S...
THAT'S BECAUSE...
I CAN SEE THE FEAR IN YOUR EYES.
SEE?

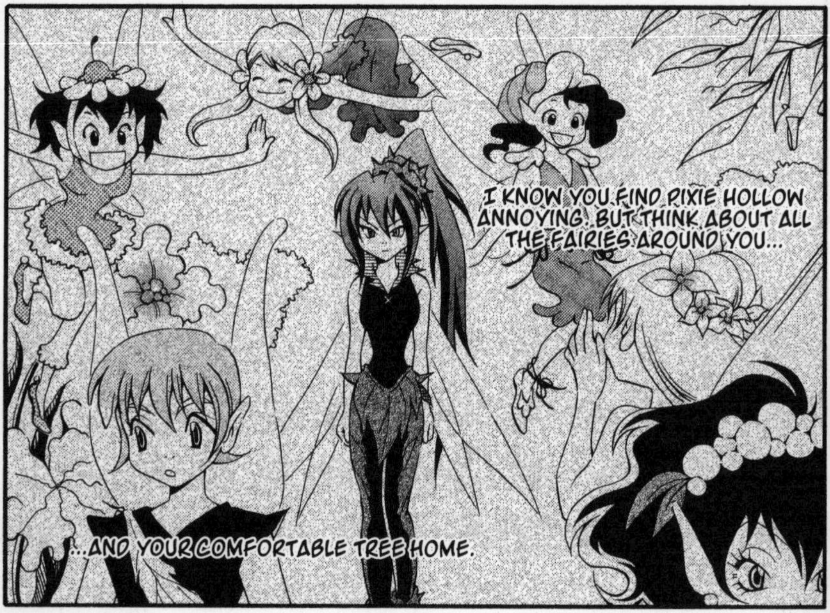
I KNOW YOU FIND PIXIE HOLLOW ANNOYING, BUT THINK ABOUT ALL THE FAIRIES AROUND YOU...
...AND YOUR COMFORTABLE TREE HOME.

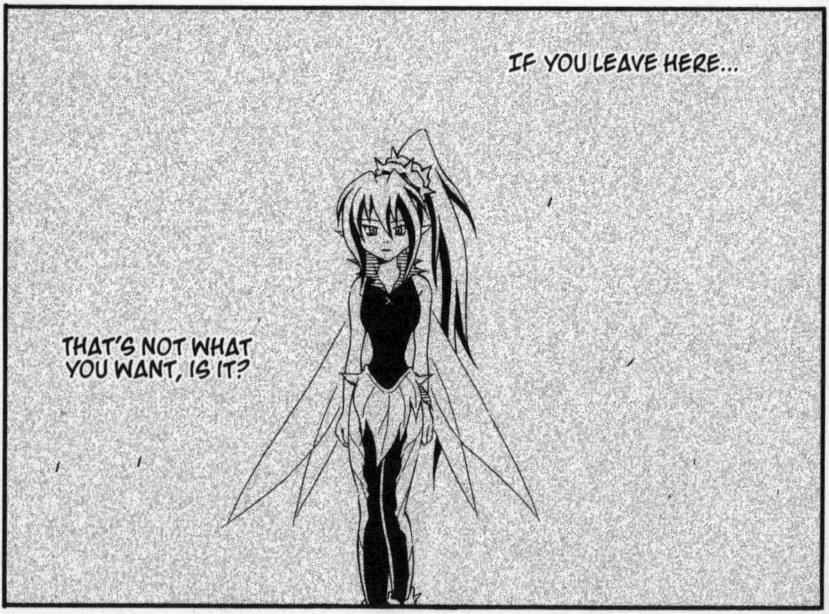
IF YOU LEAVE HERE...
THAT'S NOT WHAT YOU WANT, IS IT?

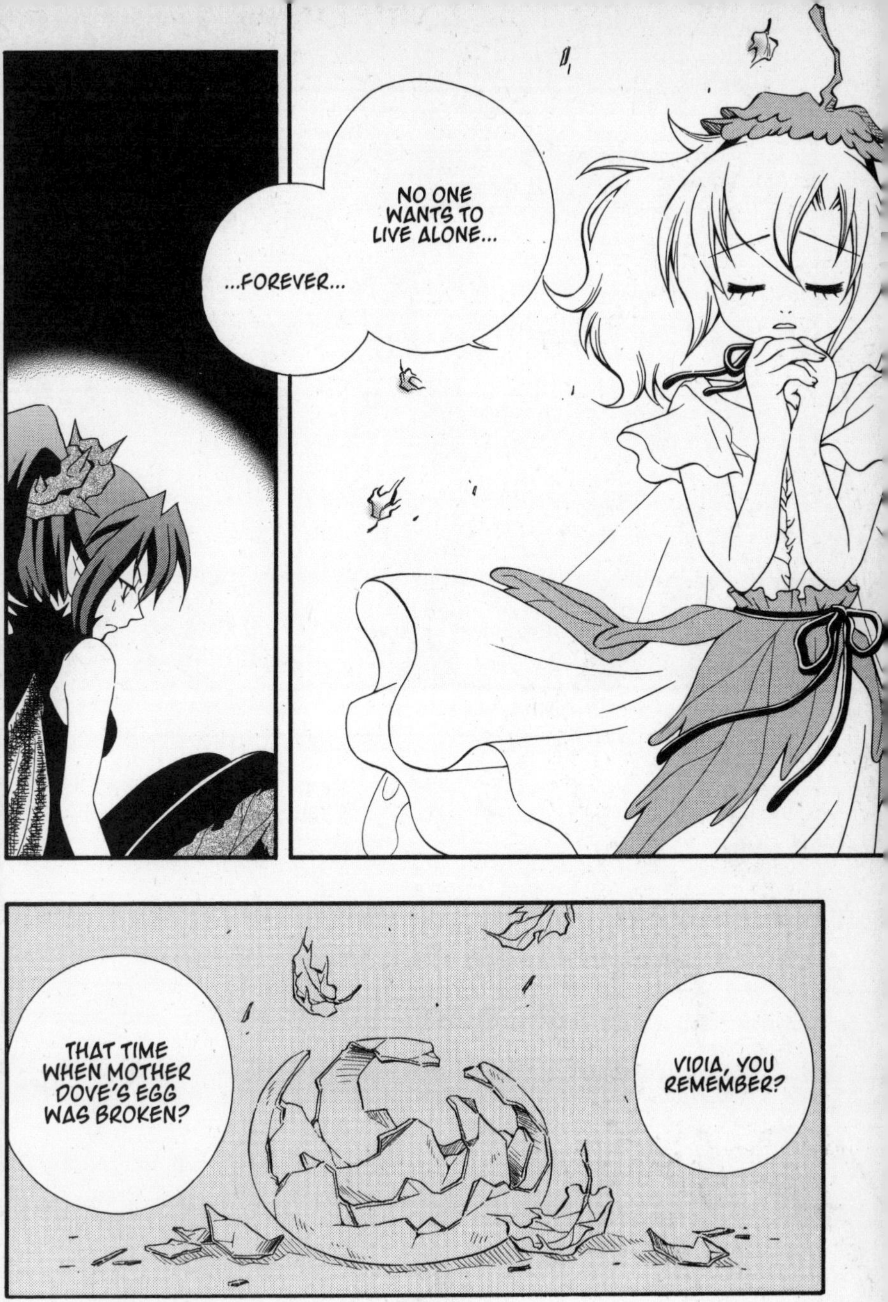
NO ONE WANTS TO LIVE ALONE...
...FOREVER...
VIDIA, YOU REMEMBER?
THAT TIME WHEN MOTHER DOVE'S EGG WAS BROKEN?

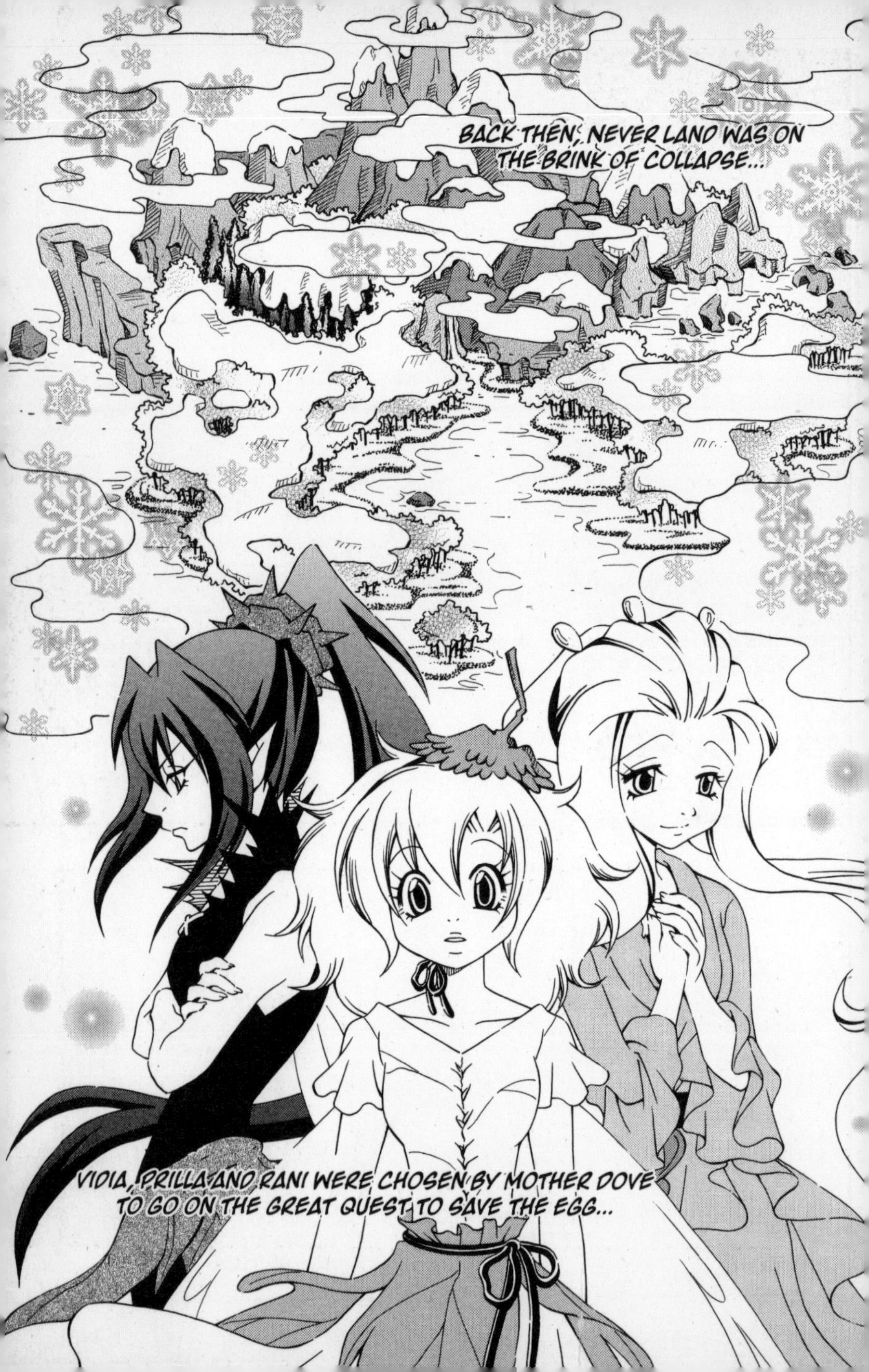
BACK THEN, NEVER LAND WAS ON THE BRINK OF COLLAPSE...
VIDIA, PRILLA AND RANI WERE CHOSEN BY MOTHER DOVE TO GO ON THE GREAT QUEST TO SAVE THE EGG...

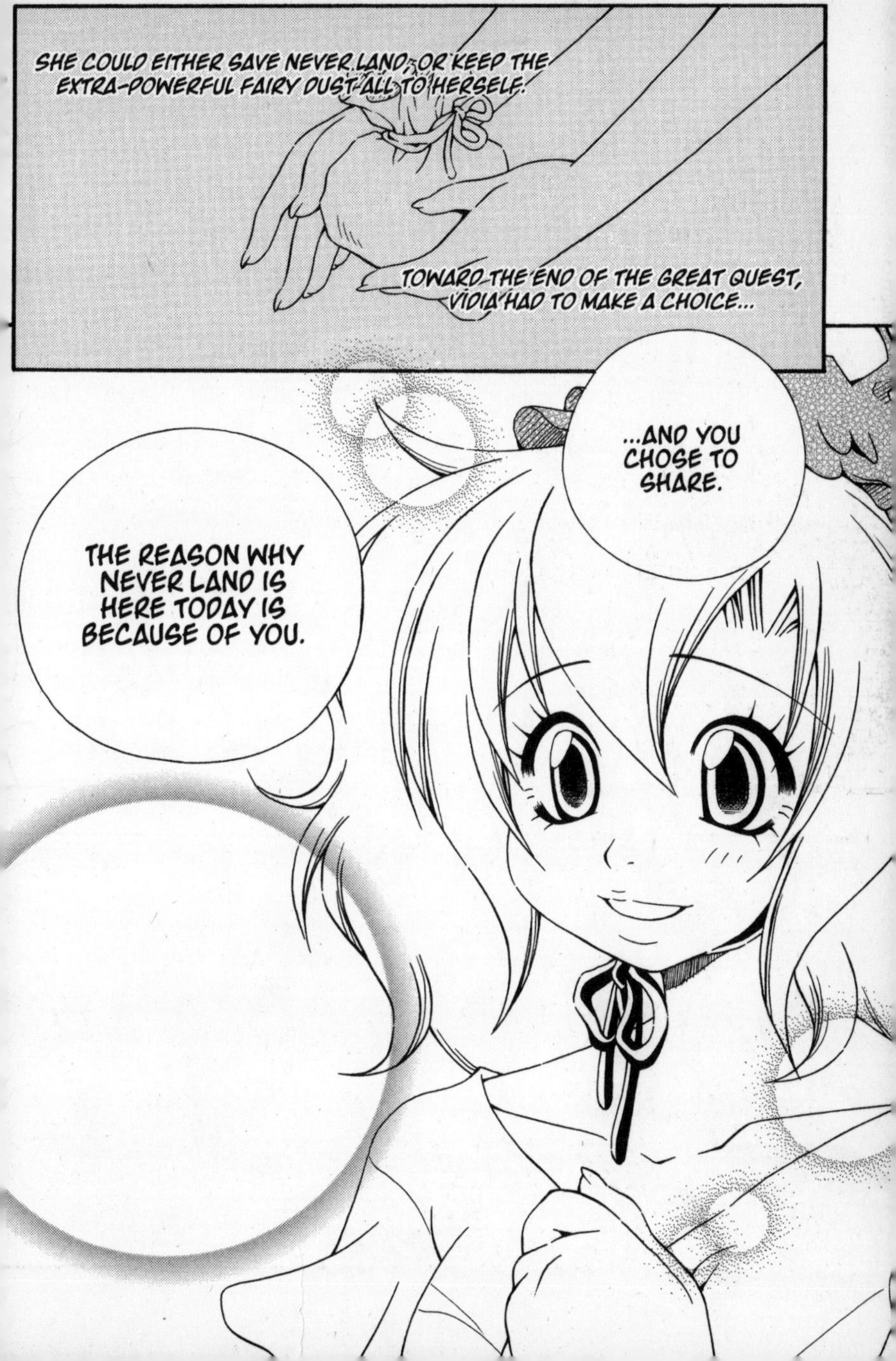
TOWARD THE END OF THE GREAT QUEST, VIDIA HAD TO MAKE A CHOICE...
SHE COULD EITHER SAVE NEVER LAND, OR KEEP THE EXTRA-POWERFUL FAIRY DUST ALL TO HERSELF.
...AND YOU CHOSE TO SHARE.
THE REASON WHY NEVER LAND IS HERE TODAY IS BECAUSE OF YOU.

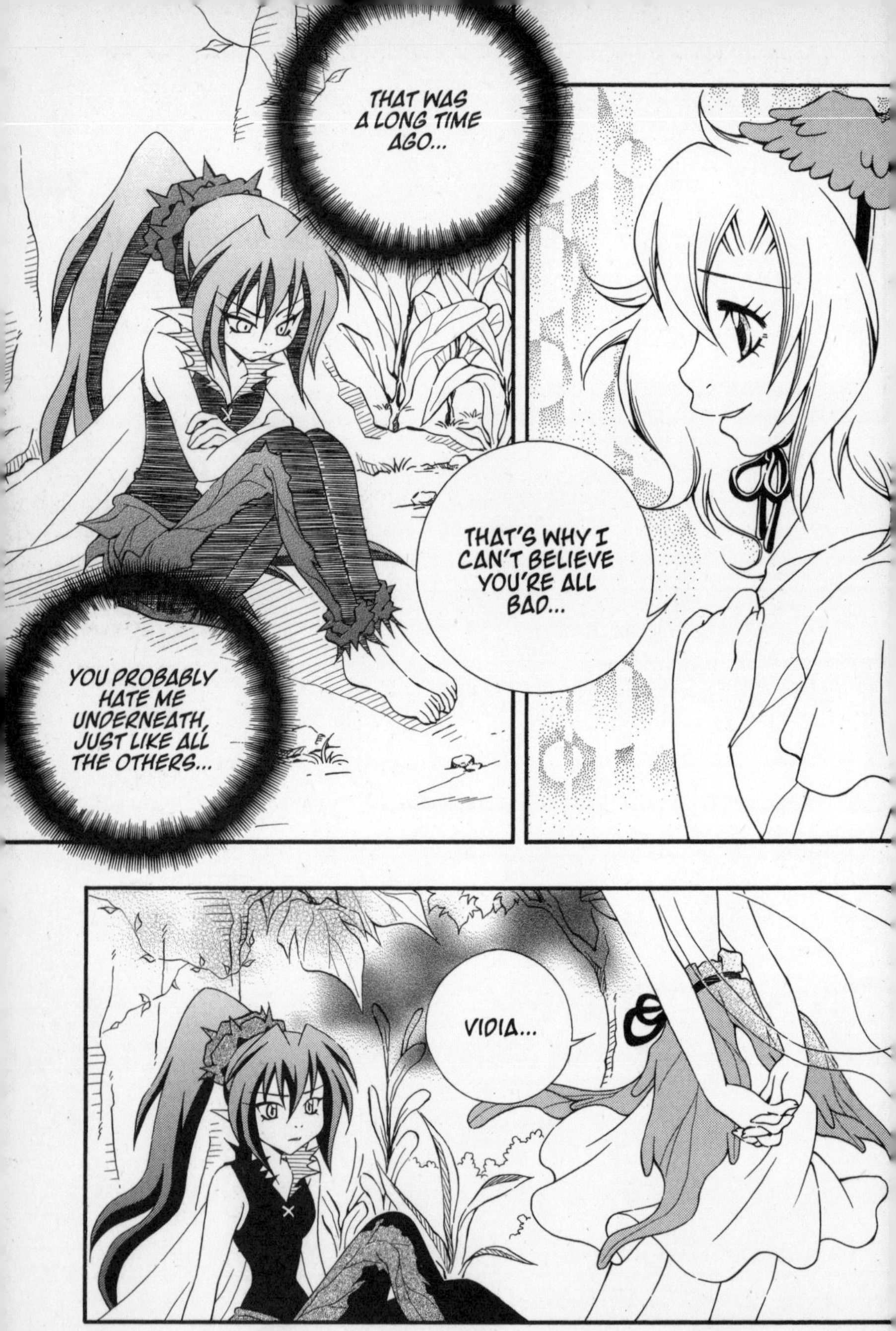
THAT WAS A LONG TIME AGO...
THAT'S WHY I CAN'T BELIEVE YOU'RE ALL BAD...
YOU PROBABLY HATE ME UNDERNEATH, JUST LIKE ALL THE OTHERS...
VIDIA...

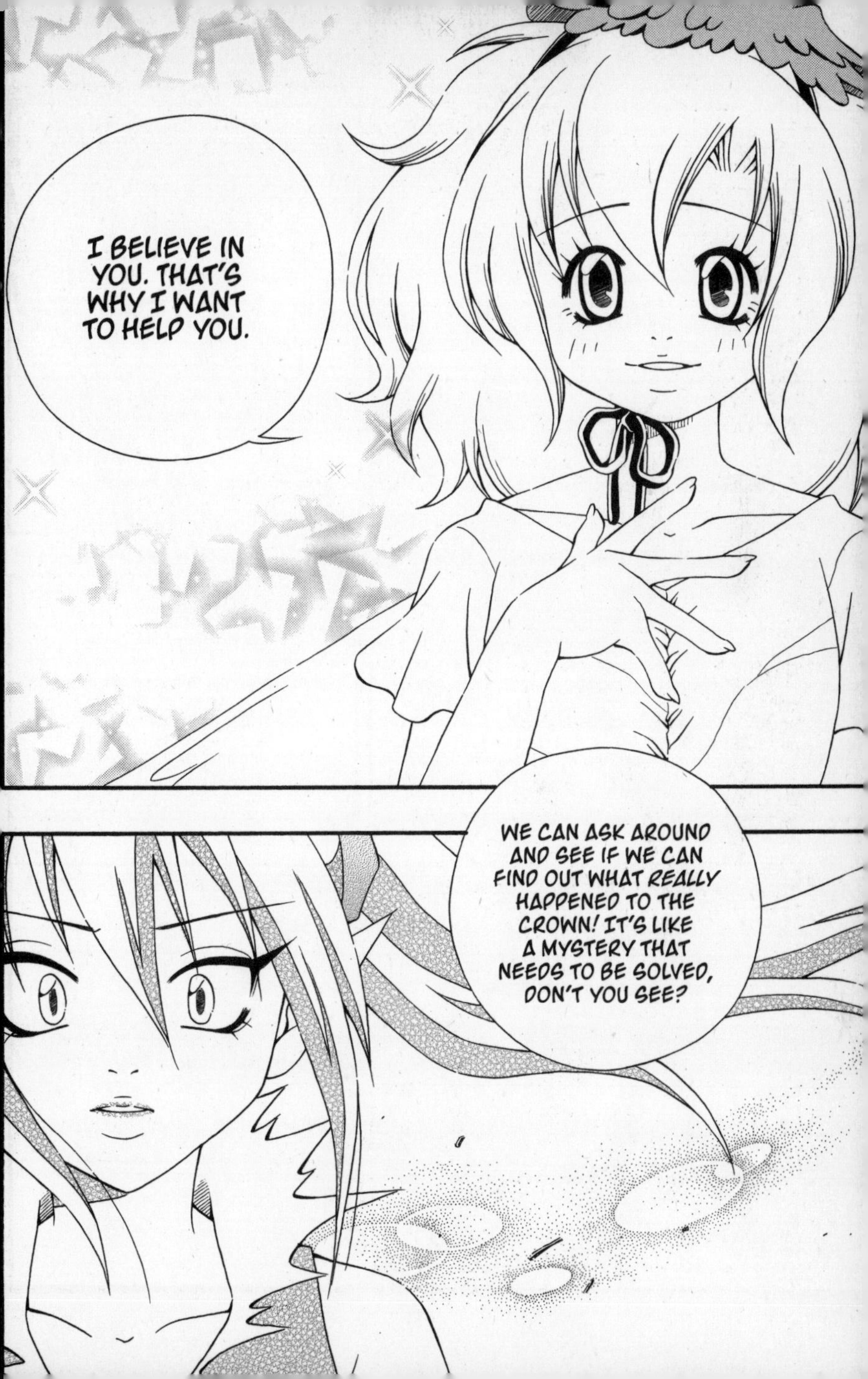
I BELIEVE IN YOU. THAT'S WHY I WANT TO HELP YOU.
WE CAN ASK AROUND AND SEE IF WE CAN FIND OUT WHAT REALLY HAPPENED TO THE CROWN! IT'S LIKE A MYSTERY THAT NEEDS TO BE SOLVED, DON'T YOU SEE?

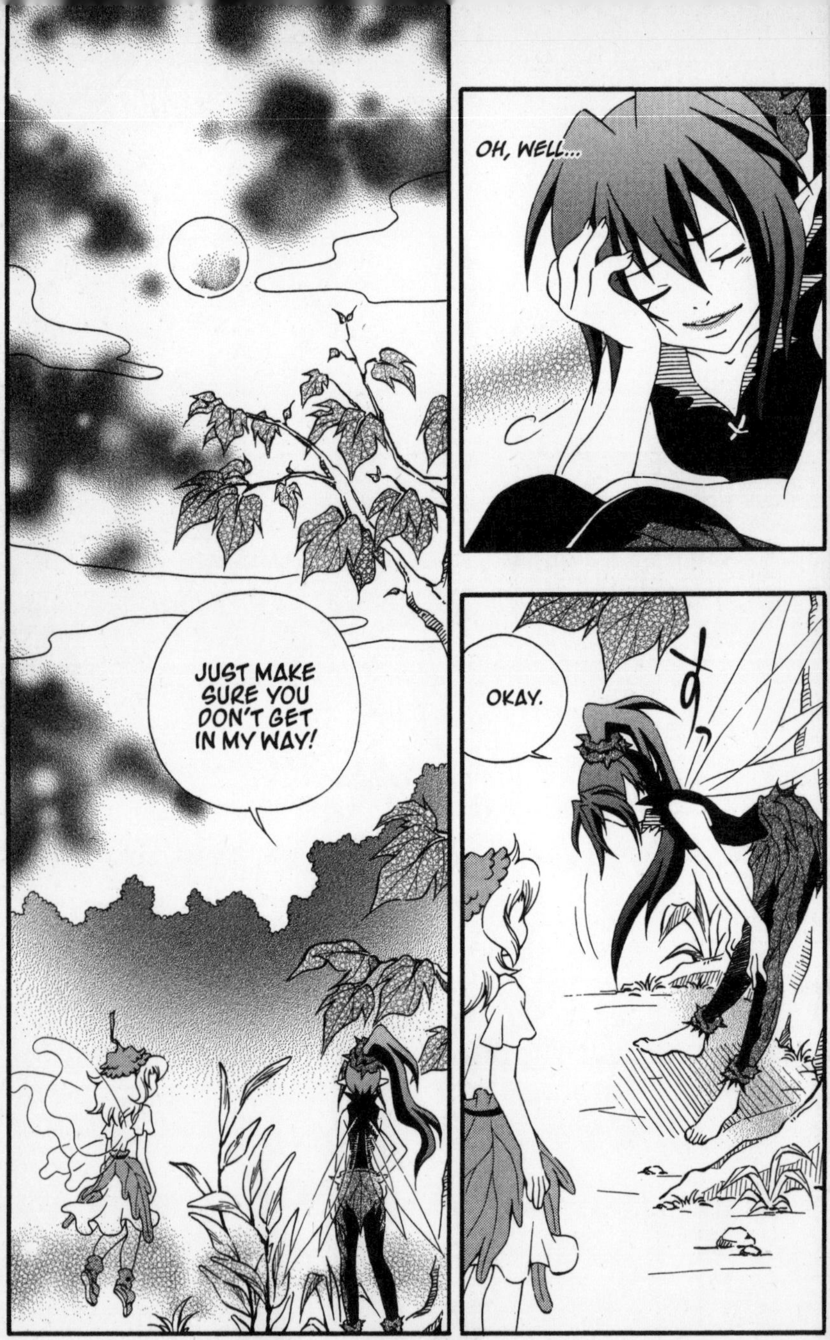
OH, WELL...
OKAY.
すっ
JUST MAKE SURE YOU DON'T GET IN MY WAY!

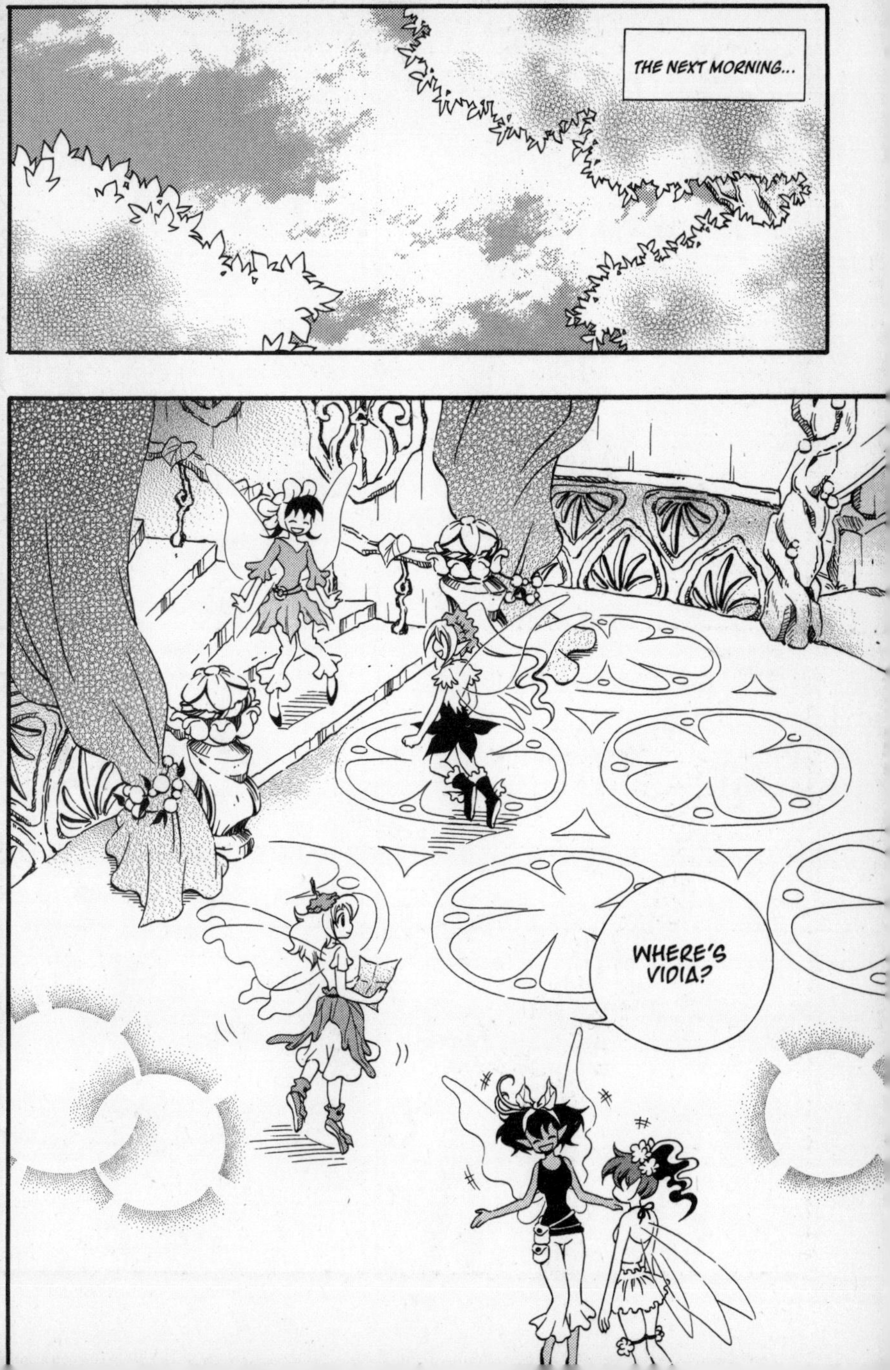
THE NEXT MORNING...
WHERE'S VIDIA?

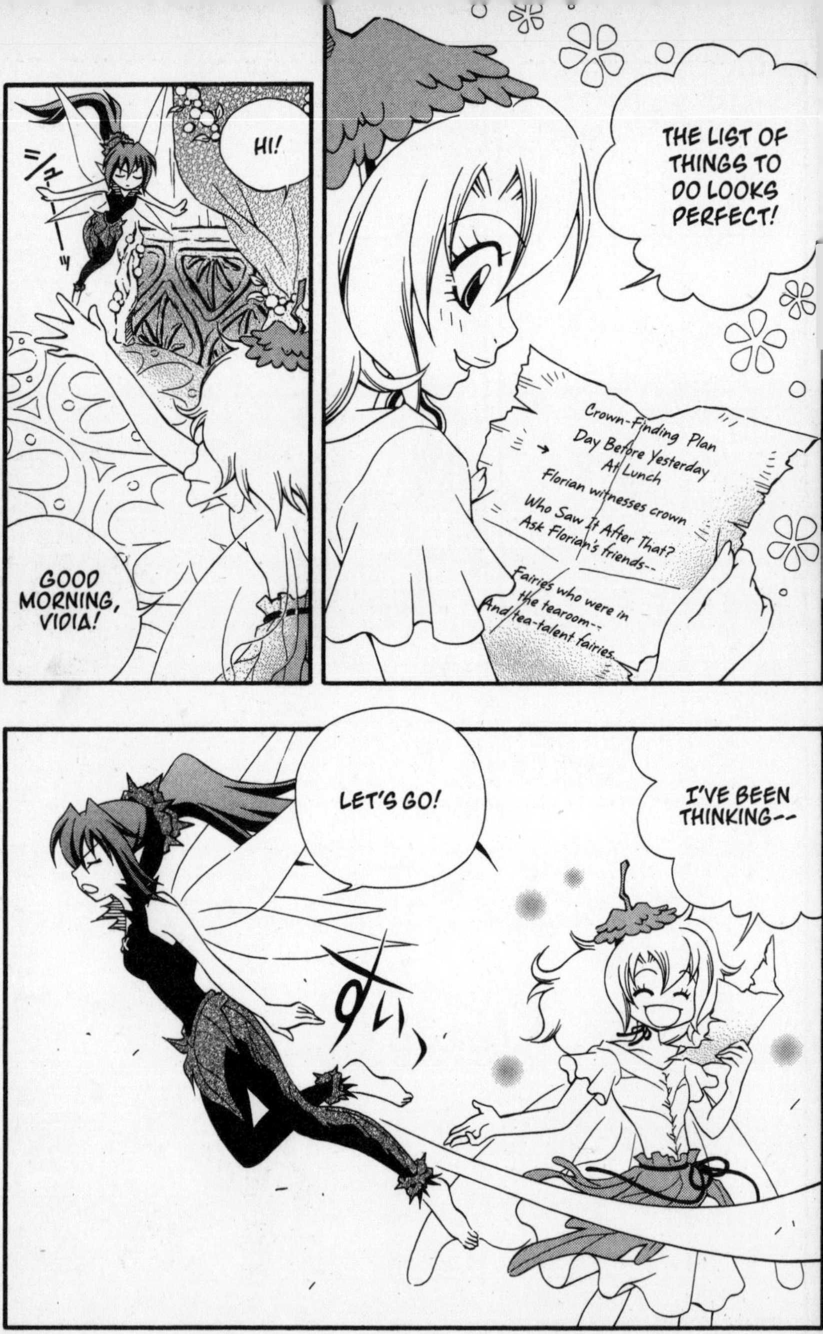
THE LIST OF THINGS TO DO LOOKS PERFECT!
Crown-Finding Plan
Day Before Yesterday At Lunch
Florian witnesses crown
Who Saw It After That? Ask Florian's friends--
Fairies who were in the tearoom-- And tea-talent fairies.
HI!
GOOD MORNING, VIDIA!
I'VE BEEN THINKING--
LET'S GO!

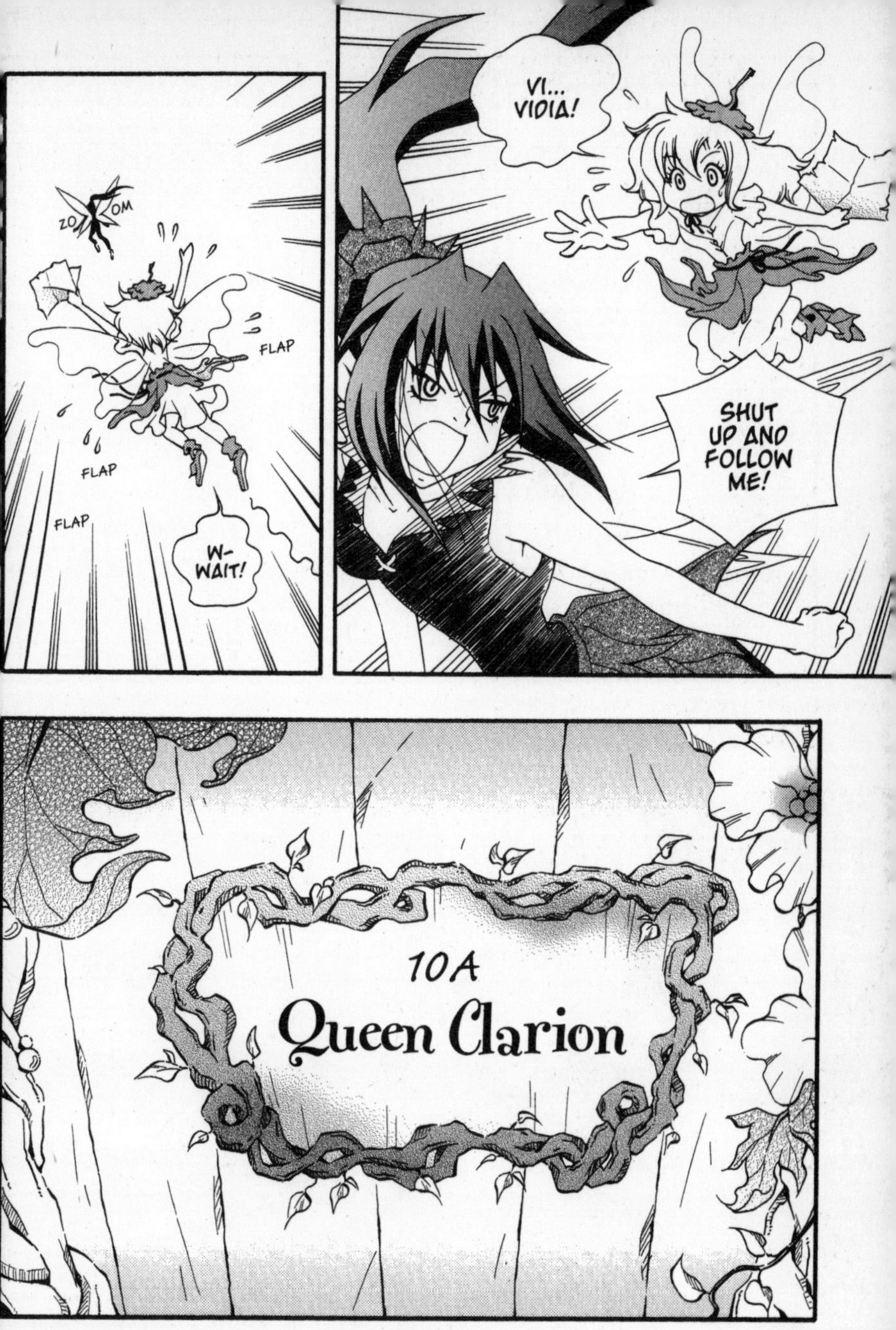
VI... VIDIA!
SHUT UP AND FOLLOW ME!
ZOOM
FLAP
FLAP
FLAP
W-WAIT!
10A
Queen Clarion

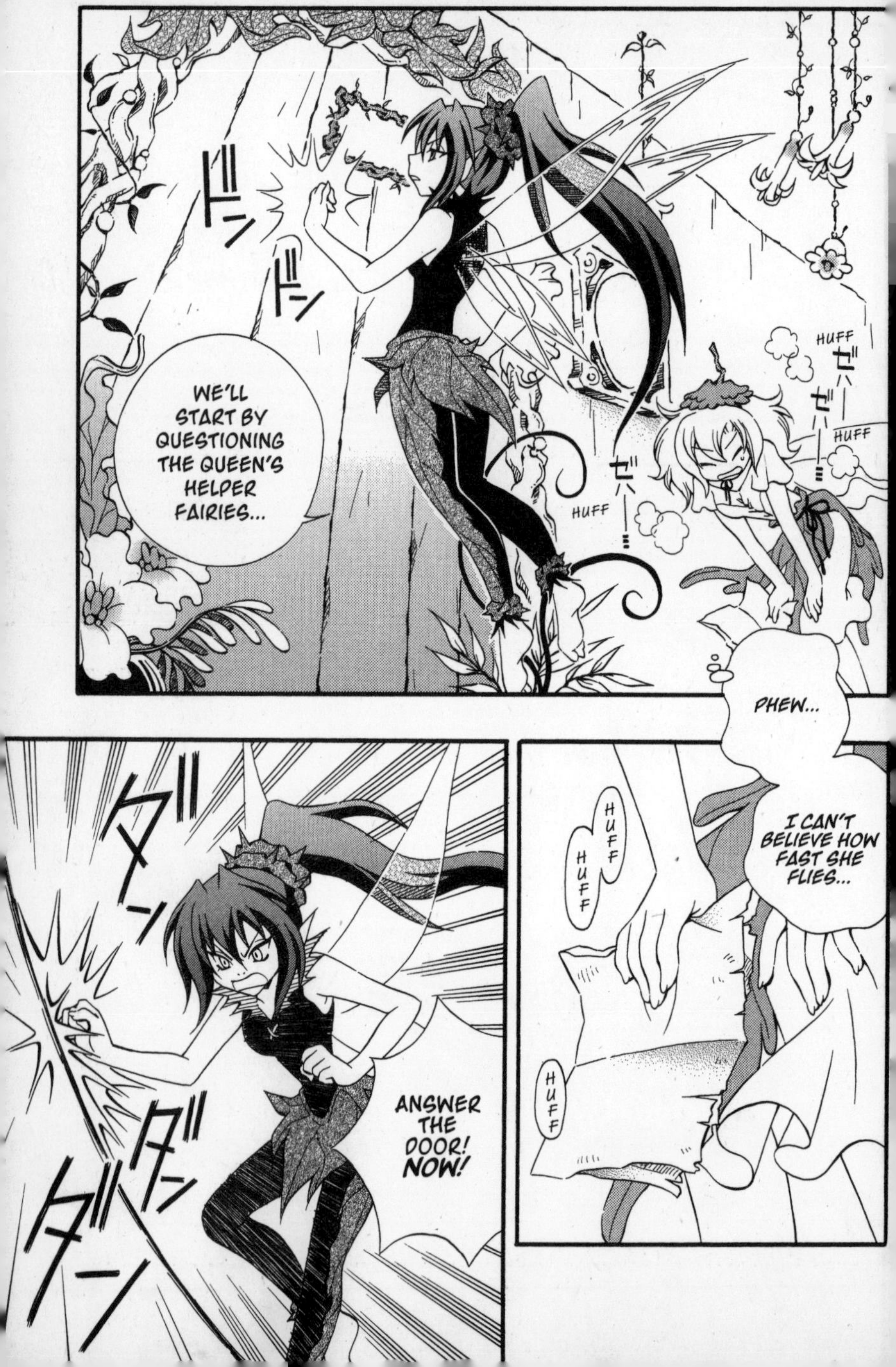
HUFF
ゼハー
ゼハー
HUFF
ゼハー
HUFF
ドン
ドン
WE'LL START BY QUESTIONING THE QUEEN'S HELPER FAIRIES...
PHEW...
I CAN'T BELIEVE HOW FAST SHE FLIES...
HUFF
HUFF
HUFF
ダーン
ANSWER THE DOOR! NOW!
ダン
ダーン

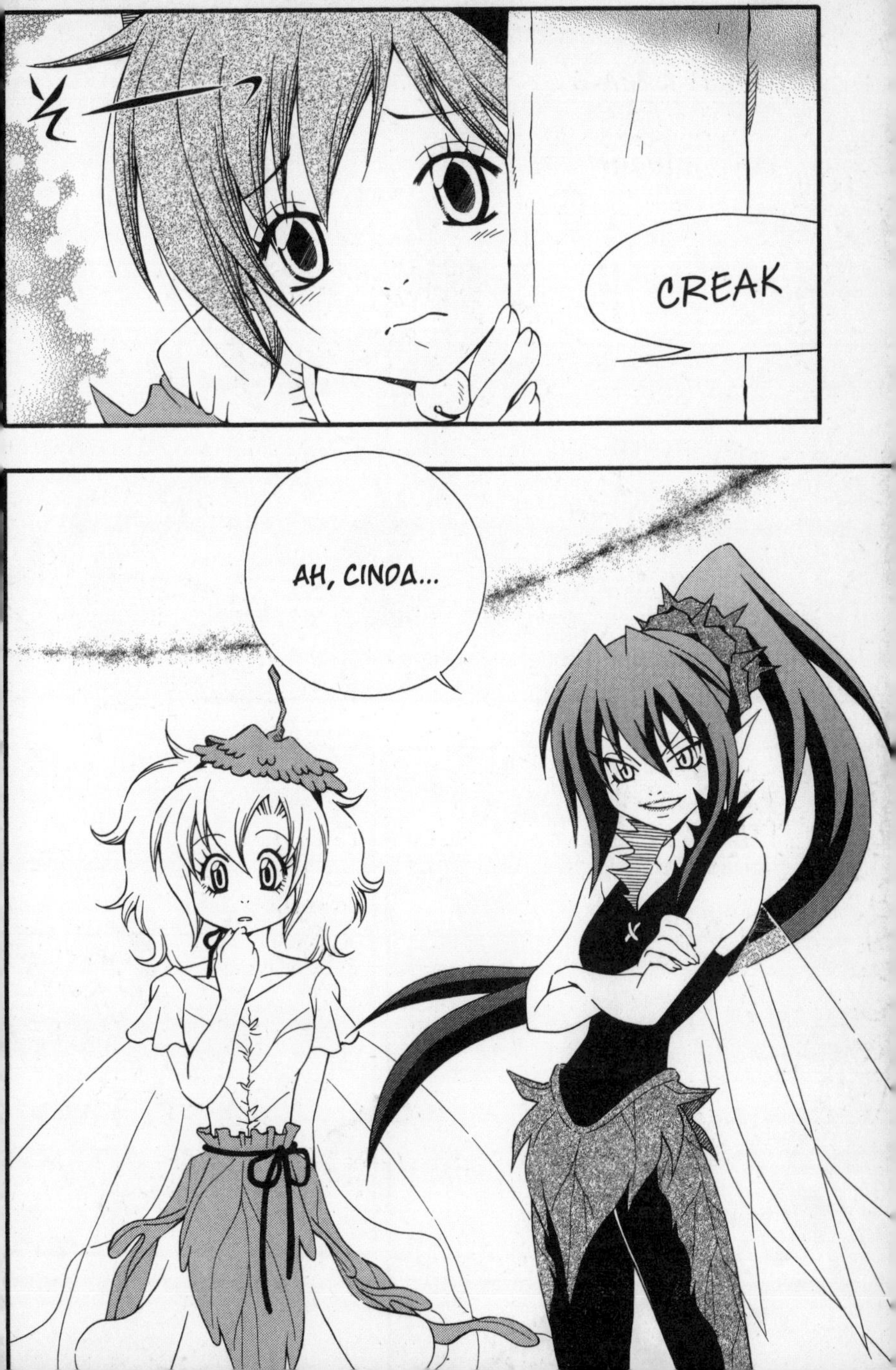
CREAK
AH, CINDA...

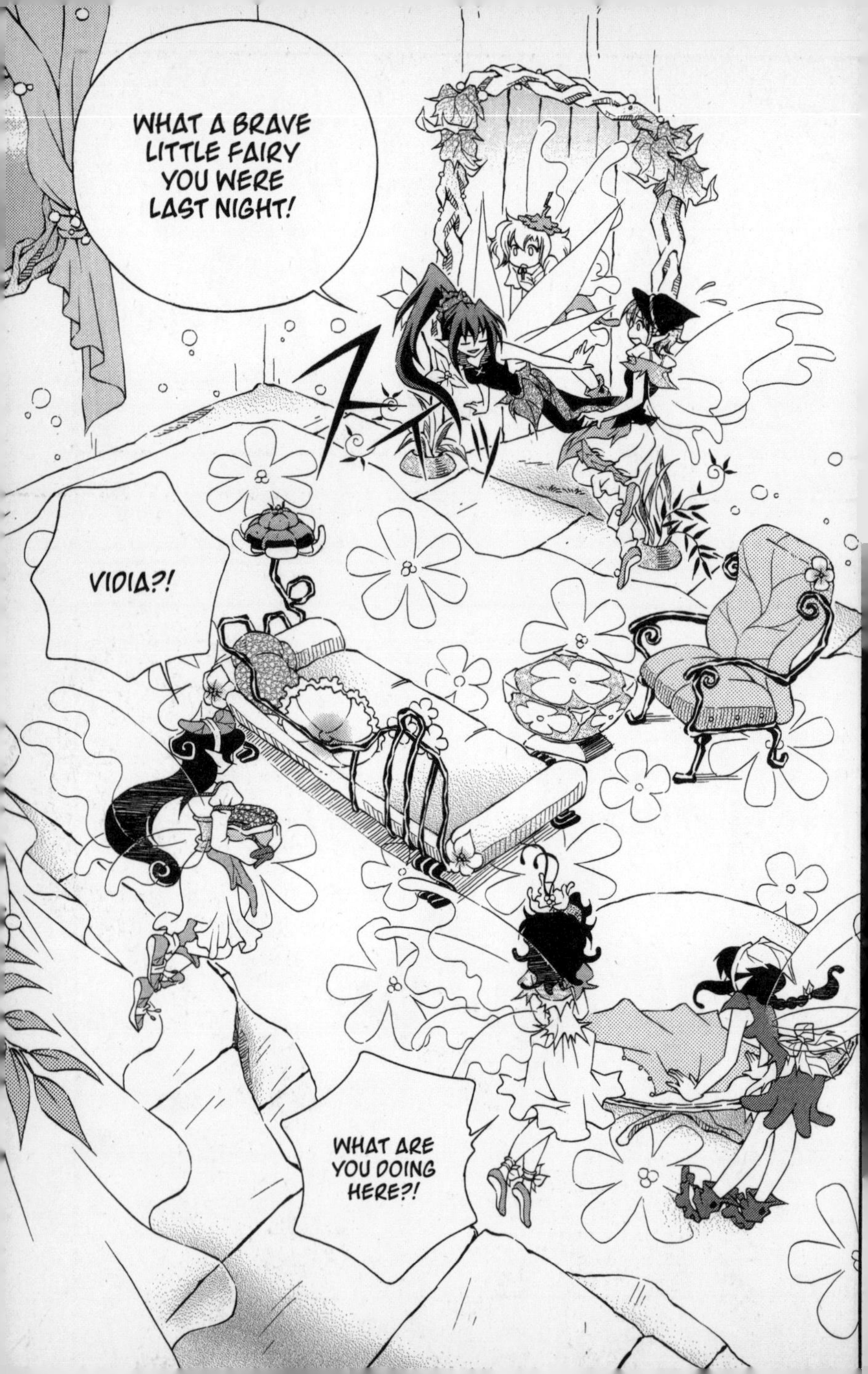
WHAT A BRAVE LITTLE FAIRY YOU WERE LAST NIGHT!
VIDIA?!
WHAT ARE YOU DOING HERE?!

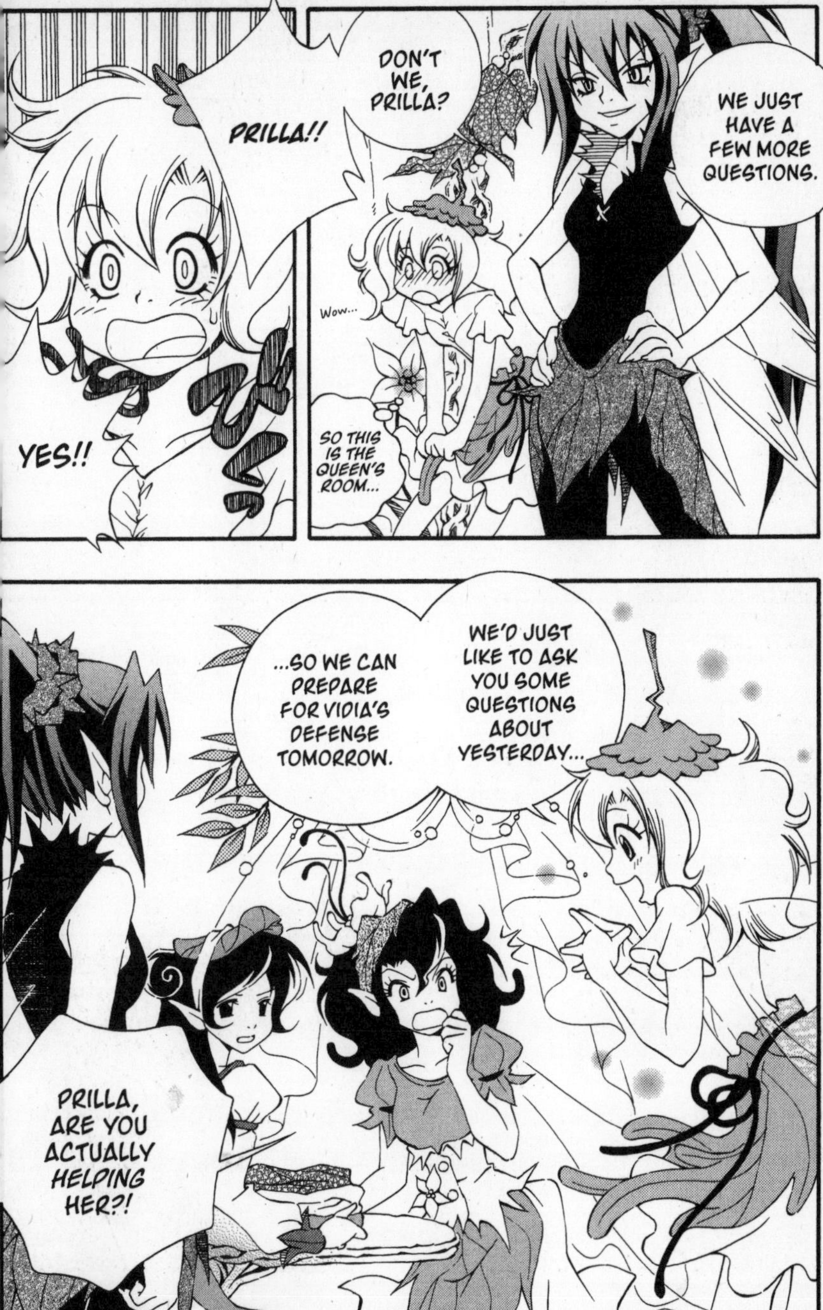
WE JUST HAVE A FEW MORE QUESTIONS.
DON'T WE, PRILLA?
SO THIS IS THE QUEEN'S ROOM...
Wow...
PRILLA!!
YES!!
WE'D JUST LIKE TO ASK YOU SOME QUESTIONS ABOUT YESTERDAY...
...SO WE CAN PREPARE FOR VIDIA'S DEFENSE TOMORROW.
PRILLA, ARE YOU ACTUALLY HELPING HER?!

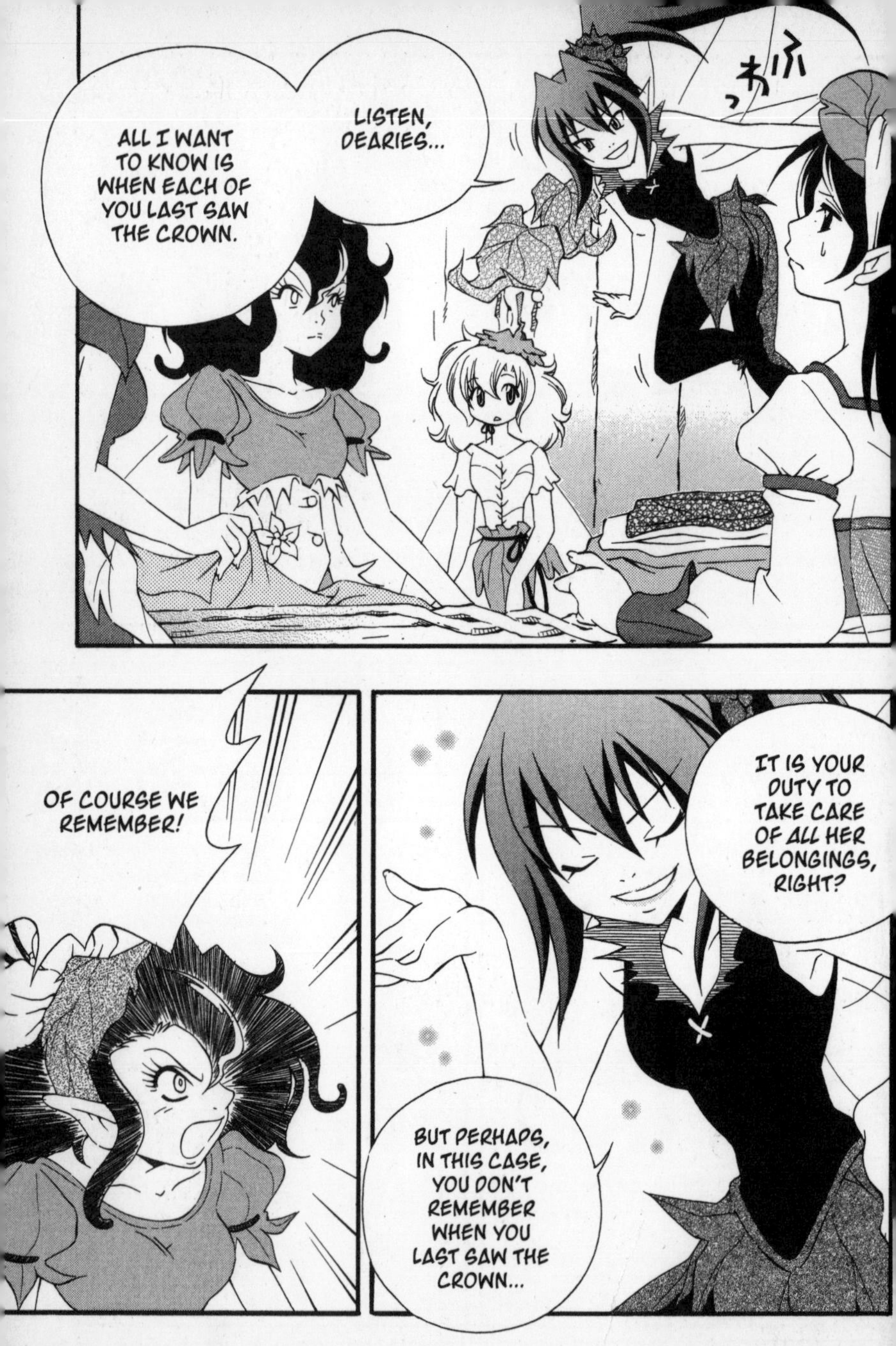
ふわっ
LISTEN, DEARIES...
ALL I WANT TO KNOW IS WHEN EACH OF YOU LAST SAW THE CROWN.
IT IS YOUR DUTY TO TAKE CARE OF ALL HER BELONGINGS, RIGHT?
BUT PERHAPS, IN THIS CASE, YOU DON'T REMEMBER WHEN YOU LAST SAW THE CROWN...
OF COURSE WE REMEMBER!

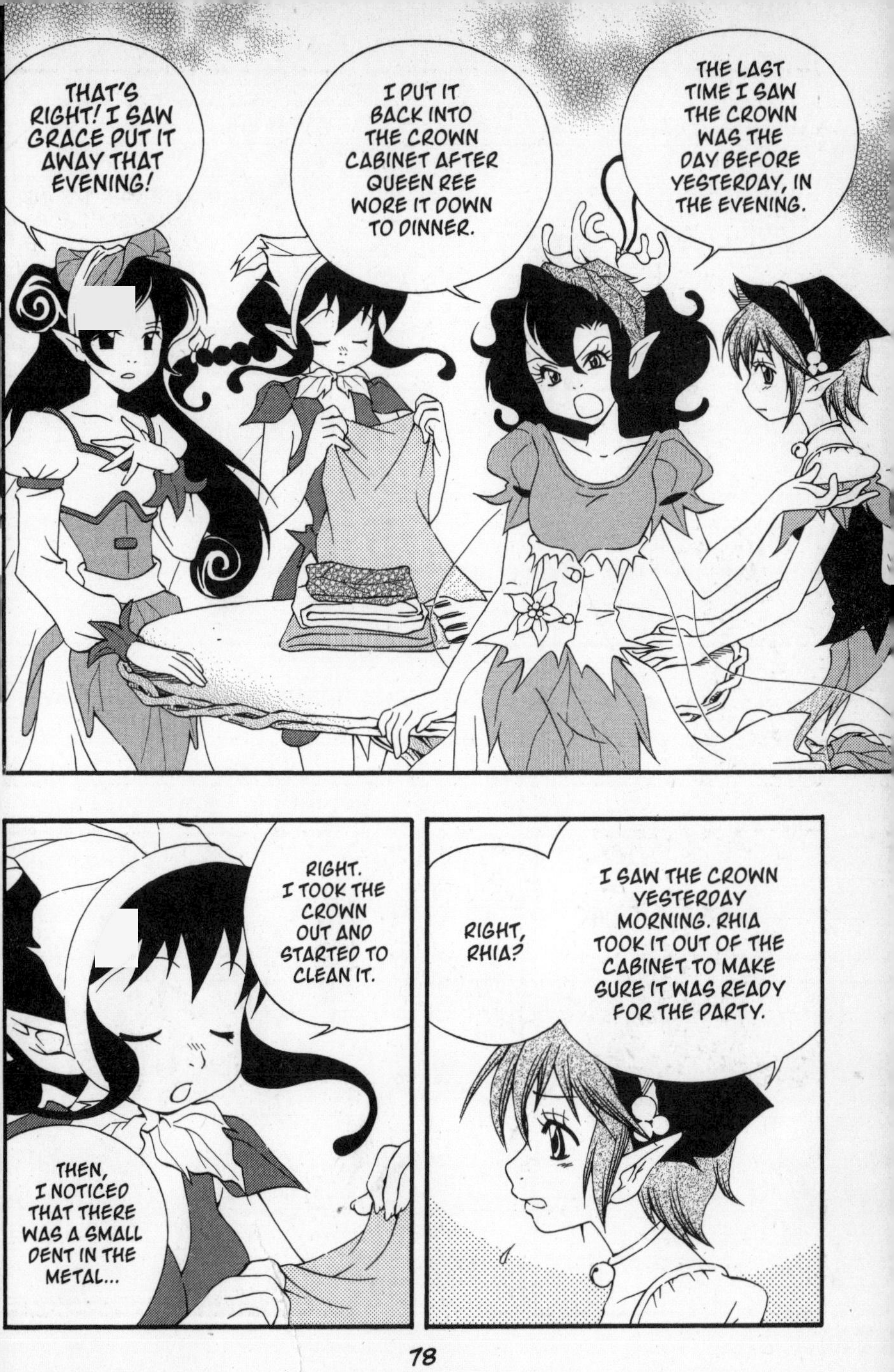
THE LAST TIME I SAW THE CROWN WAS THE DAY BEFORE YESTERDAY, IN THE EVENING.
I PUT IT BACK INTO THE CROWN CABINET AFTER QUEEN REE WORE IT DOWN TO DINNER.
THAT'S RIGHT! I SAW GRACE PUT IT AWAY THAT EVENING!
I SAW THE CROWN YESTERDAY MORNING. RHIA TOOK IT OUT OF THE CABINET TO MAKE SURE IT WAS READY FOR THE PARTY.
RIGHT, RHIA?
RIGHT. I TOOK THE CROWN OUT AND STARTED TO CLEAN IT.
THEN, I NOTICED THAT THERE WAS A SMALL DENT IN THE METAL...

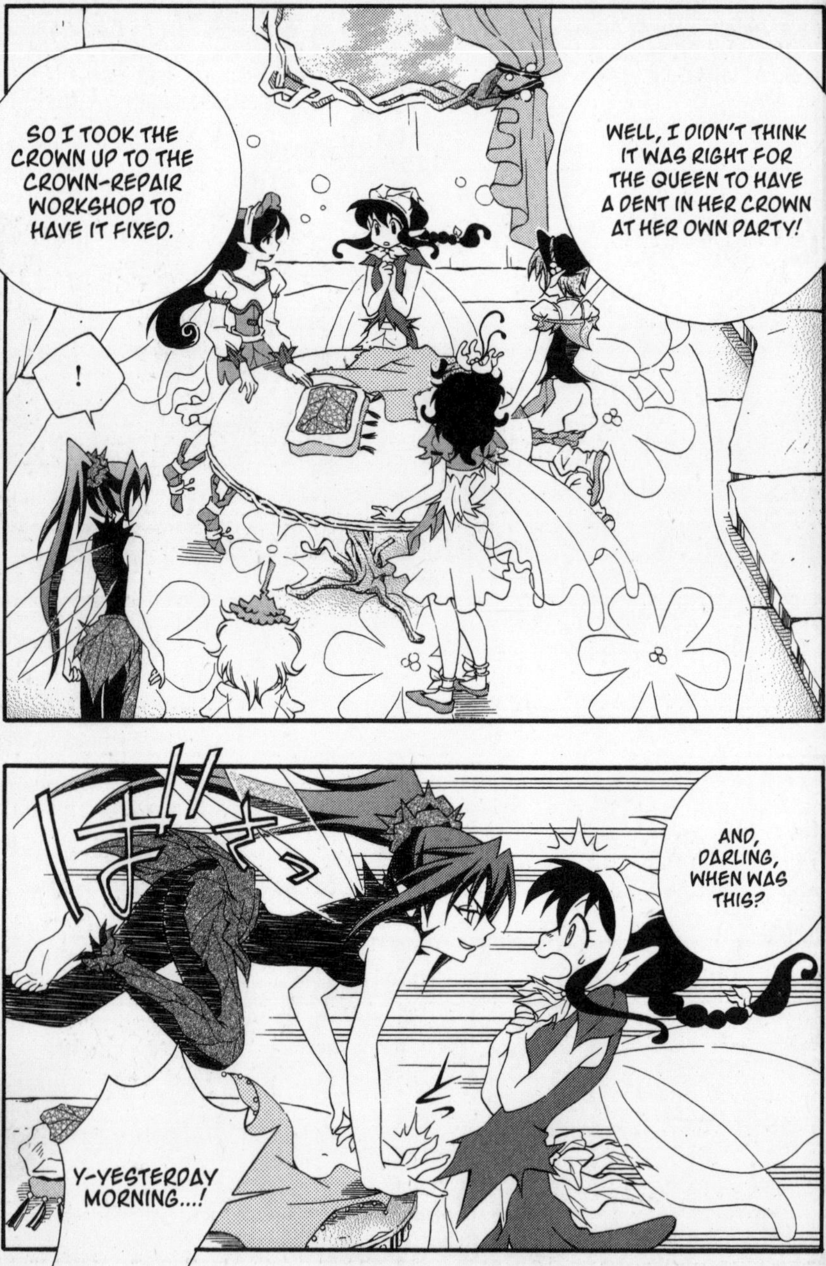
WELL, I DIDN'T THINK IT WAS RIGHT FOR THE QUEEN TO HAVE A DENT IN HER CROWN AT HER OWN PARTY!
SO I TOOK THE CROWN UP TO THE CROWN-REPAIR WORKSHOP TO HAVE IT FIXED.
!
AND, DARLING, WHEN WAS THIS?
Y-YESTERDAY MORNING...!

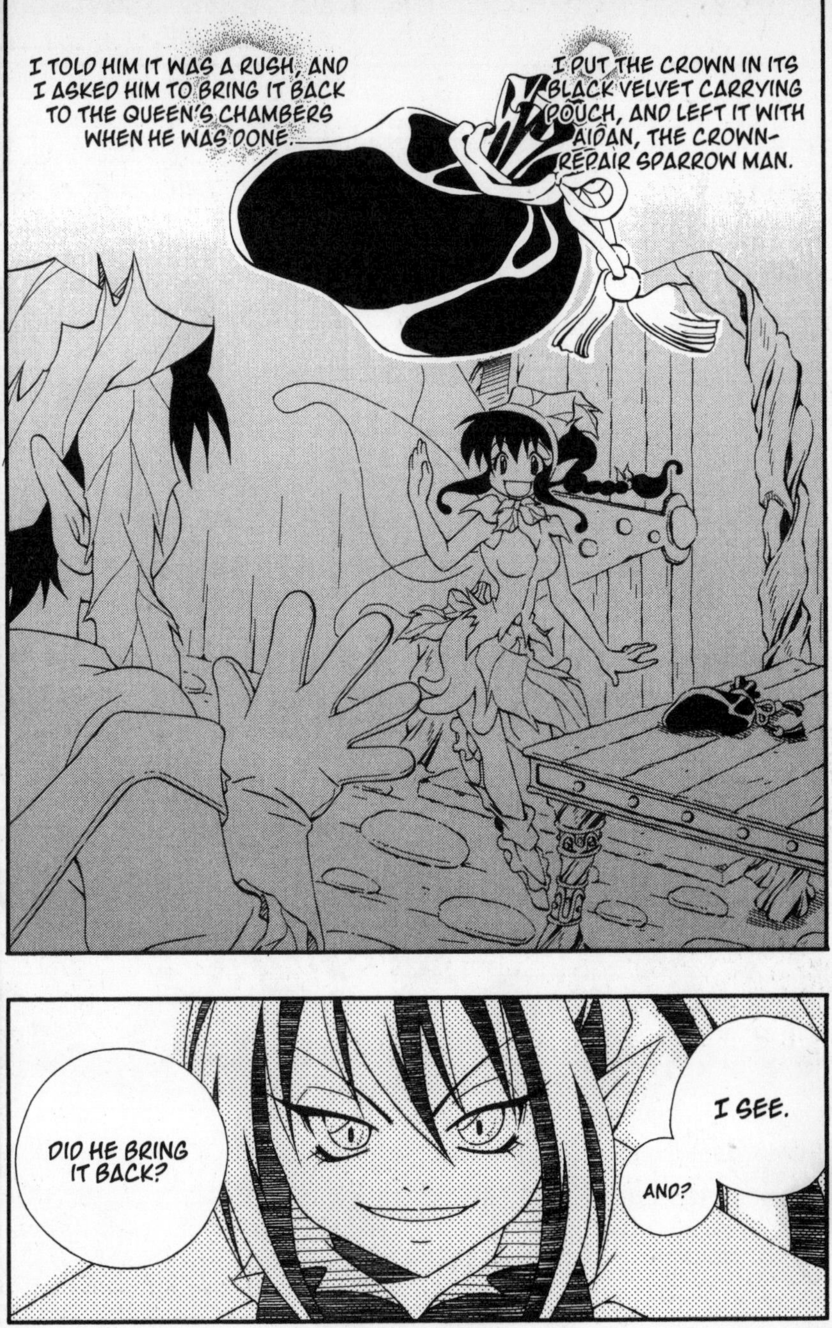
I PUT THE CROWN IN ITS BLACK VELVET CARRYING POUCH, AND LEFT IT WITH AIDAN, THE CROWN-REPAIR SPARROW MAN.
I TOLD HIM IT WAS A RUSH, AND I ASKED HIM TO BRING IT BACK TO THE QUEEN'S CHAMBERS WHEN HE WAS DONE.
I SEE.
AND?
DID HE BRING IT BACK?

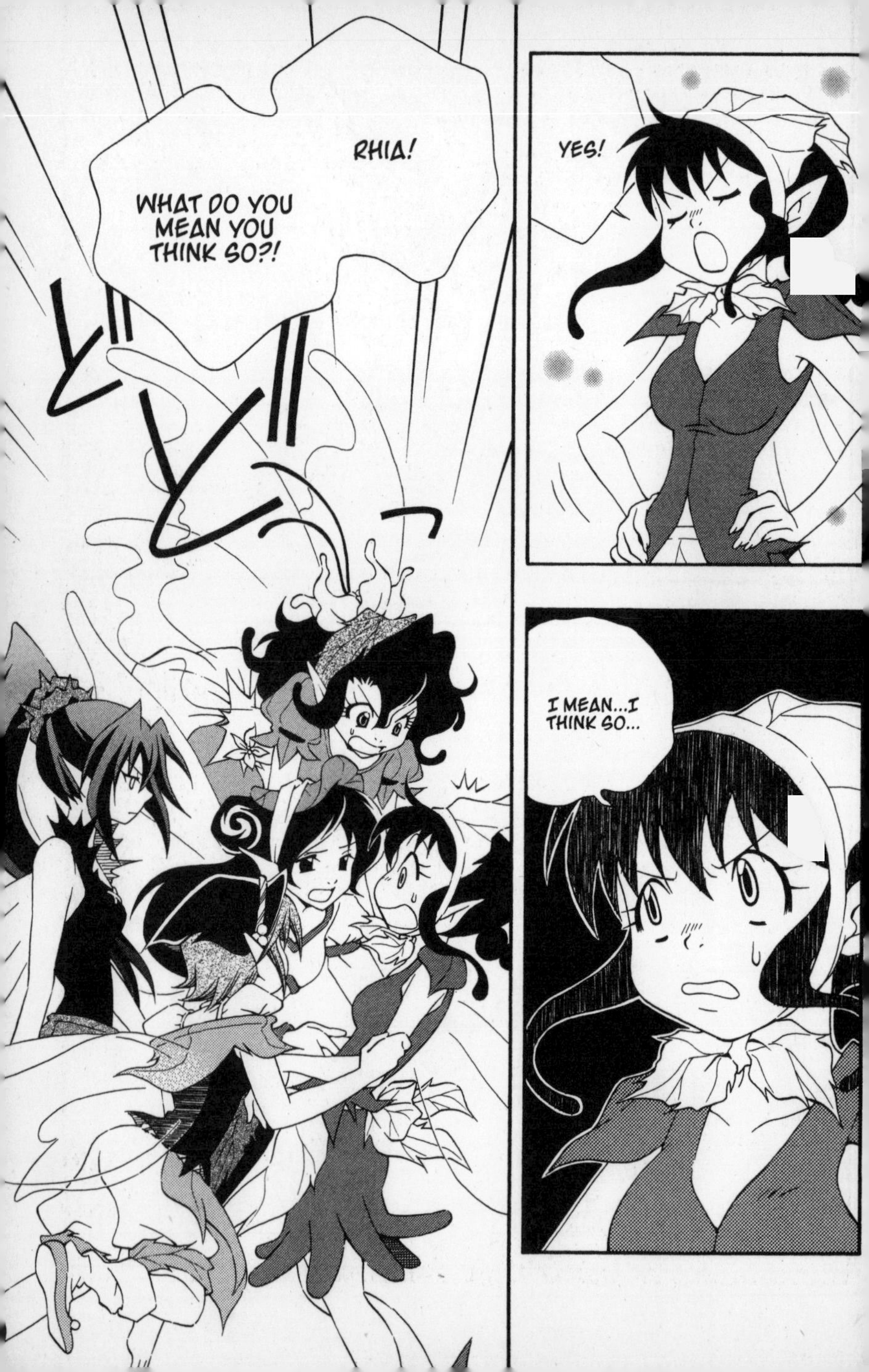
YES!
I MEAN...I THINK SO...
RHIA!
WHAT DO YOU MEAN YOU THINK SO?!

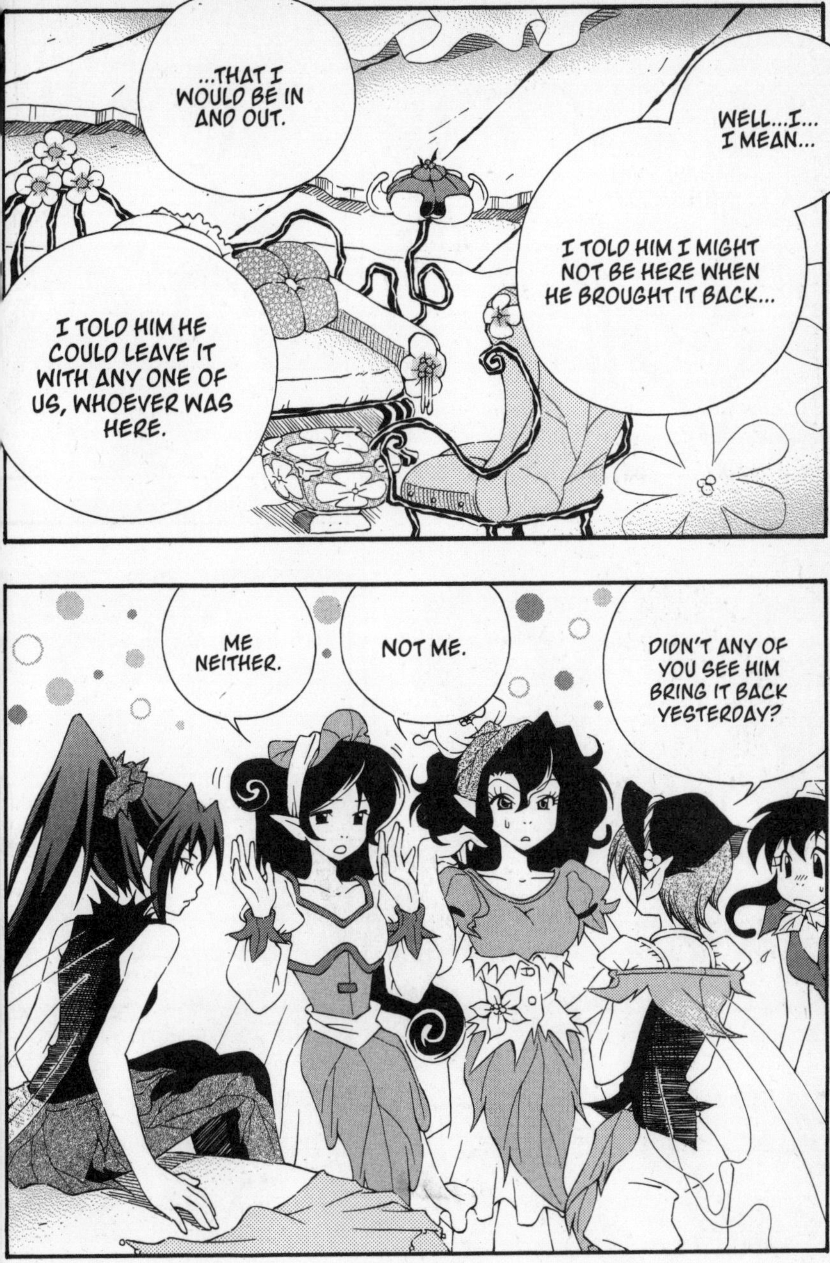
WELL...I...
I MEAN...
I TOLD HIM I MIGHT NOT BE HERE WHEN HE BROUGHT IT BACK...
...THAT I WOULD BE IN AND OUT.
I TOLD HIM HE COULD LEAVE IT WITH ANY ONE OF US, WHOEVER WAS HERE.
DIDN'T ANY OF YOU SEE HIM BRING IT BACK YESTERDAY?
NOT ME.
ME NEITHER.

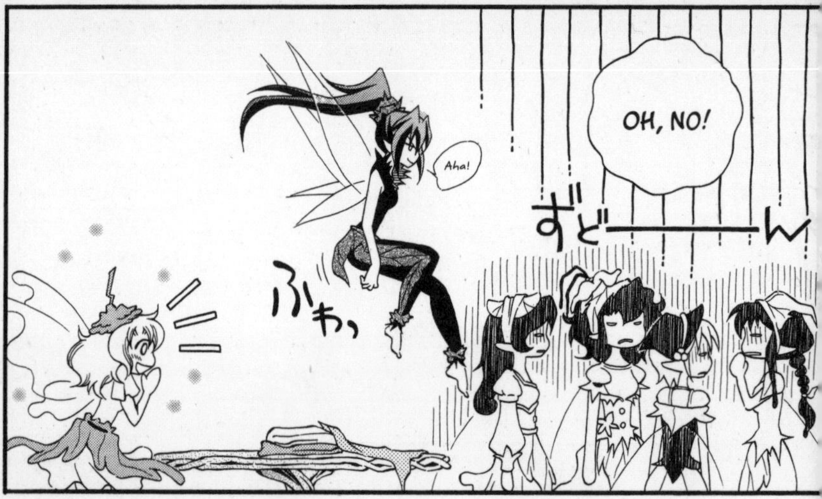
OH, NO!
ずど――ん
Aha!
ふわっ
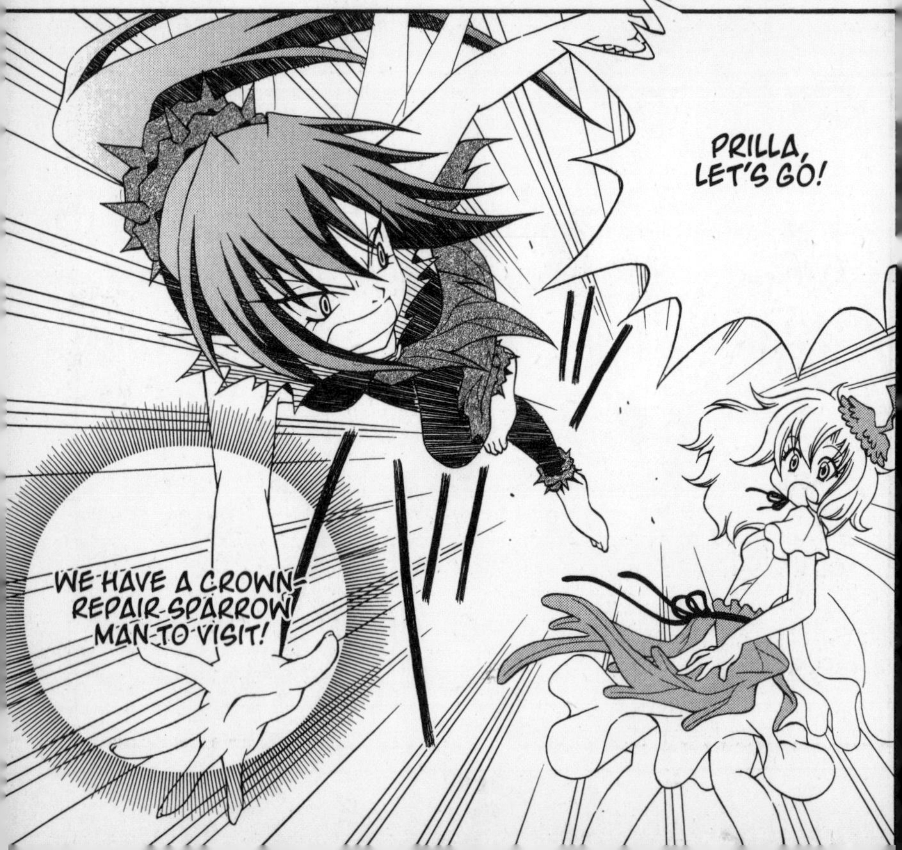
PRILLA, LET'S GO!
WE HAVE A CROWN-REPAIR-SPARROW MAN TO VISIT!

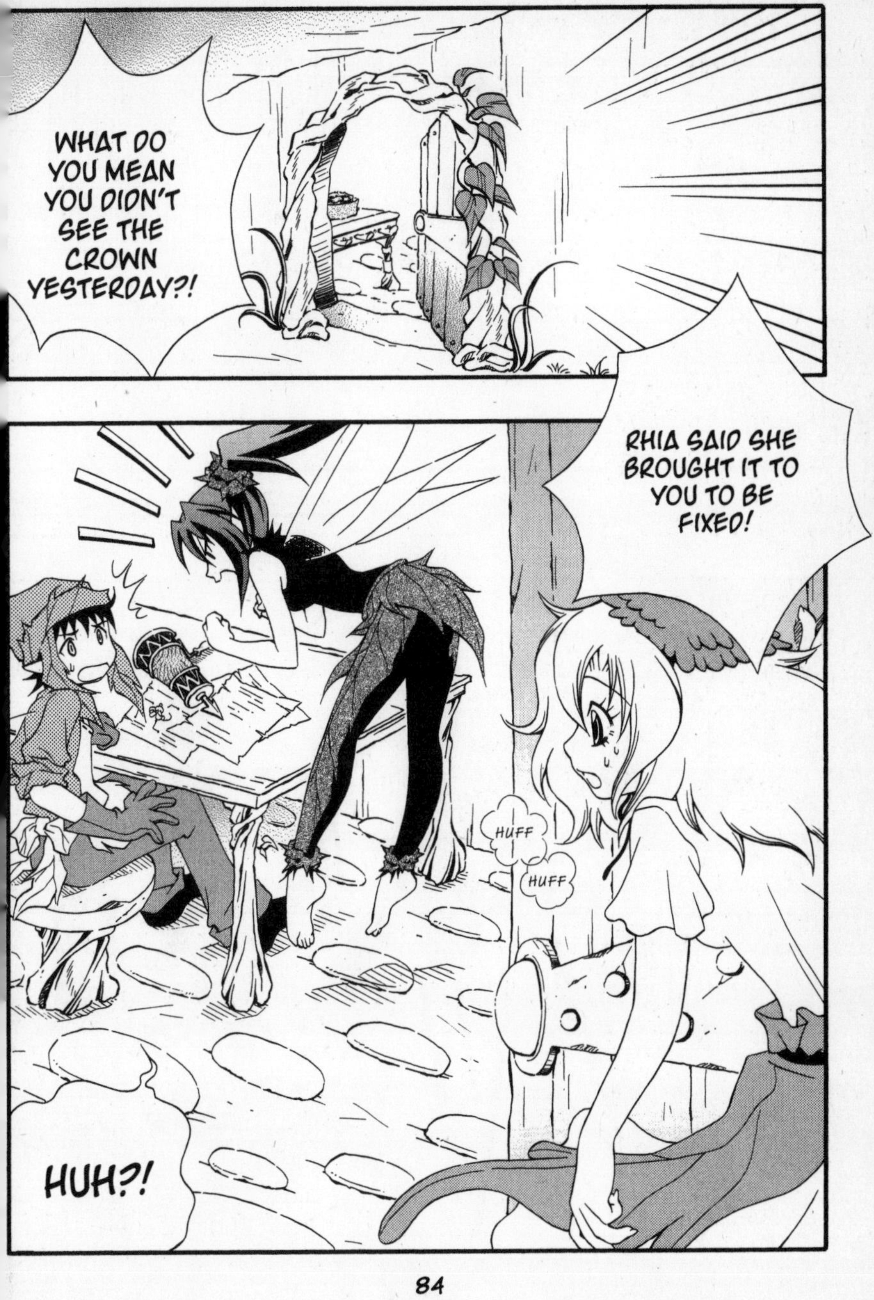
WHAT DO YOU MEAN YOU DIDN'T SEE THE CROWN YESTERDAY?!
RHIA SAID SHE BROUGHT IT TO YOU TO BE FIXED!
HUFF
HUFF
HUH?!

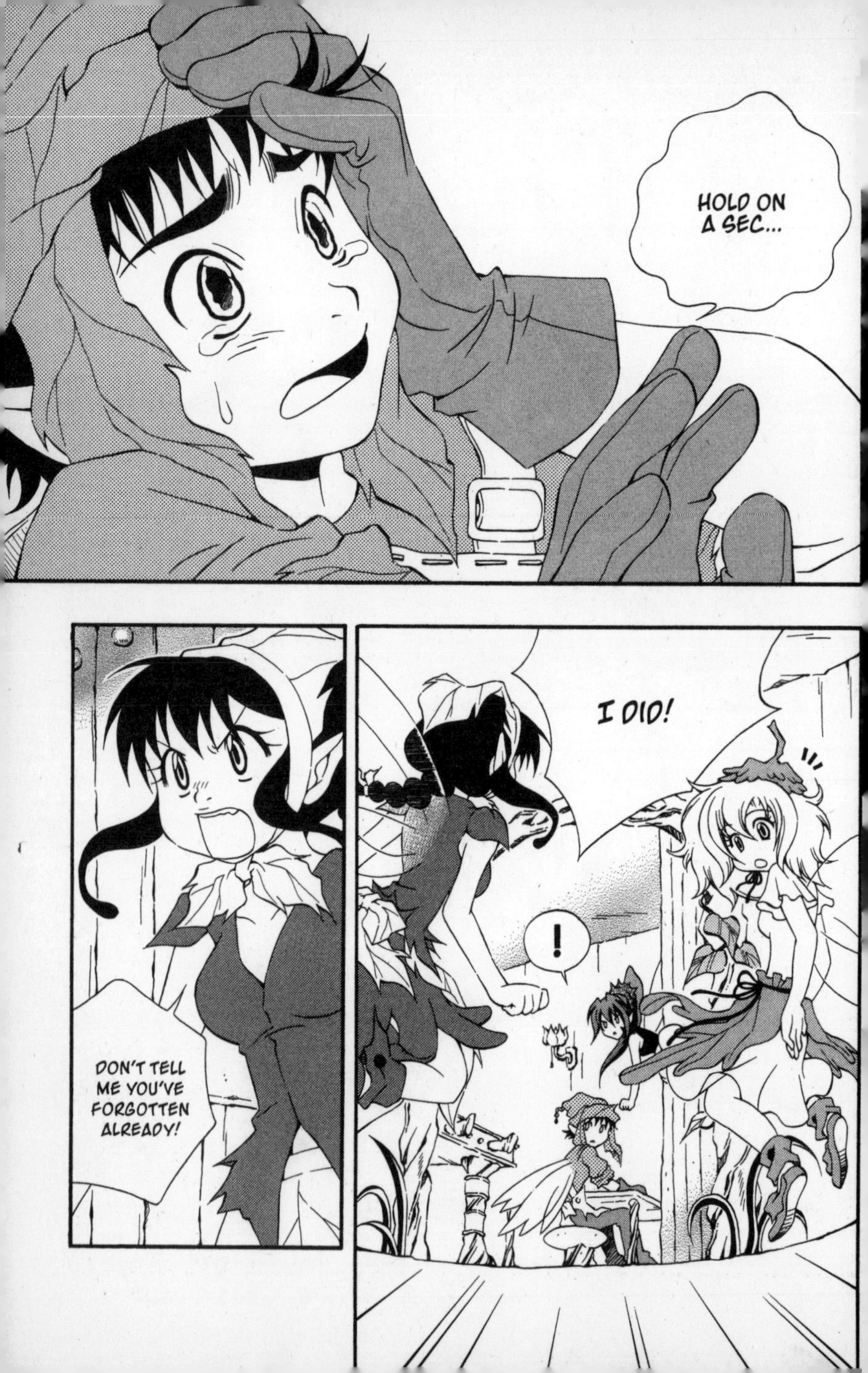
HOLD ON A SEC...
I DID!
!
DON'T TELL ME YOU'VE FORGOTTEN ALREADY!

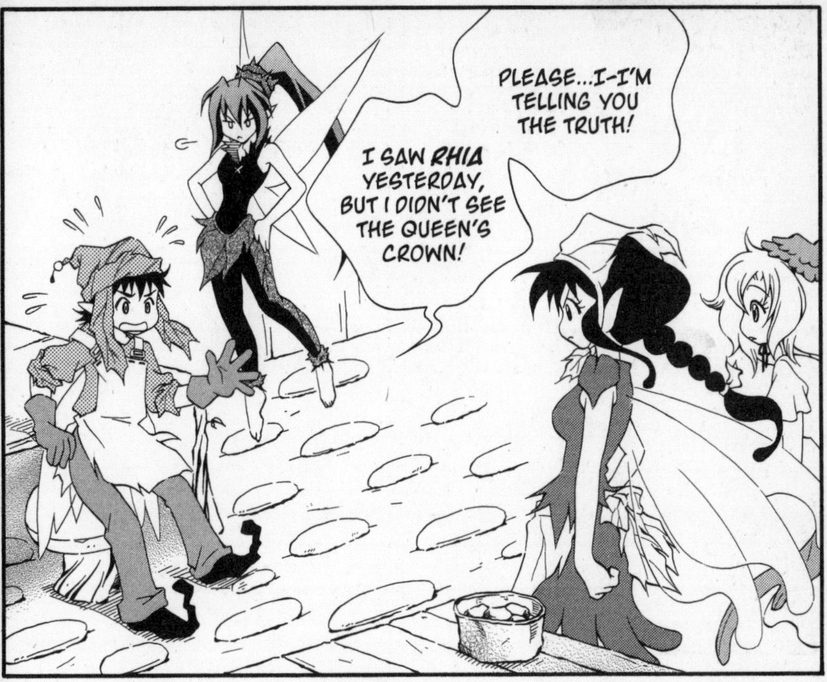
PLEASE...I-I'M TELLING YOU THE TRUTH!
I SAW *RHIA* YESTERDAY, BUT I DIDN'T SEE THE QUEEN'S CROWN!

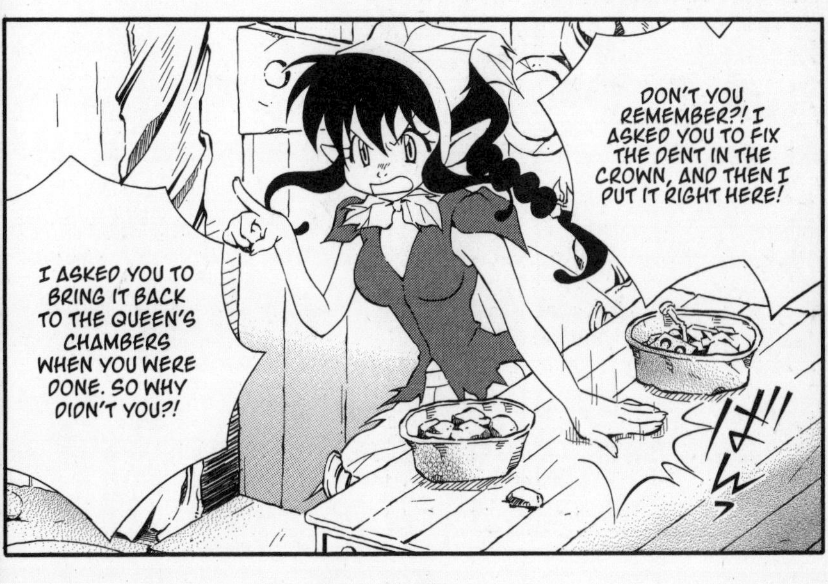
DON'T YOU REMEMBER?! I ASKED YOU TO FIX THE DENT IN THE CROWN, AND THEN I PUT IT RIGHT HERE!
ばんっ
I ASKED YOU TO BRING IT BACK TO THE QUEEN'S CHAMBERS WHEN YOU WERE DONE. SO WHY DIDN'T YOU?!

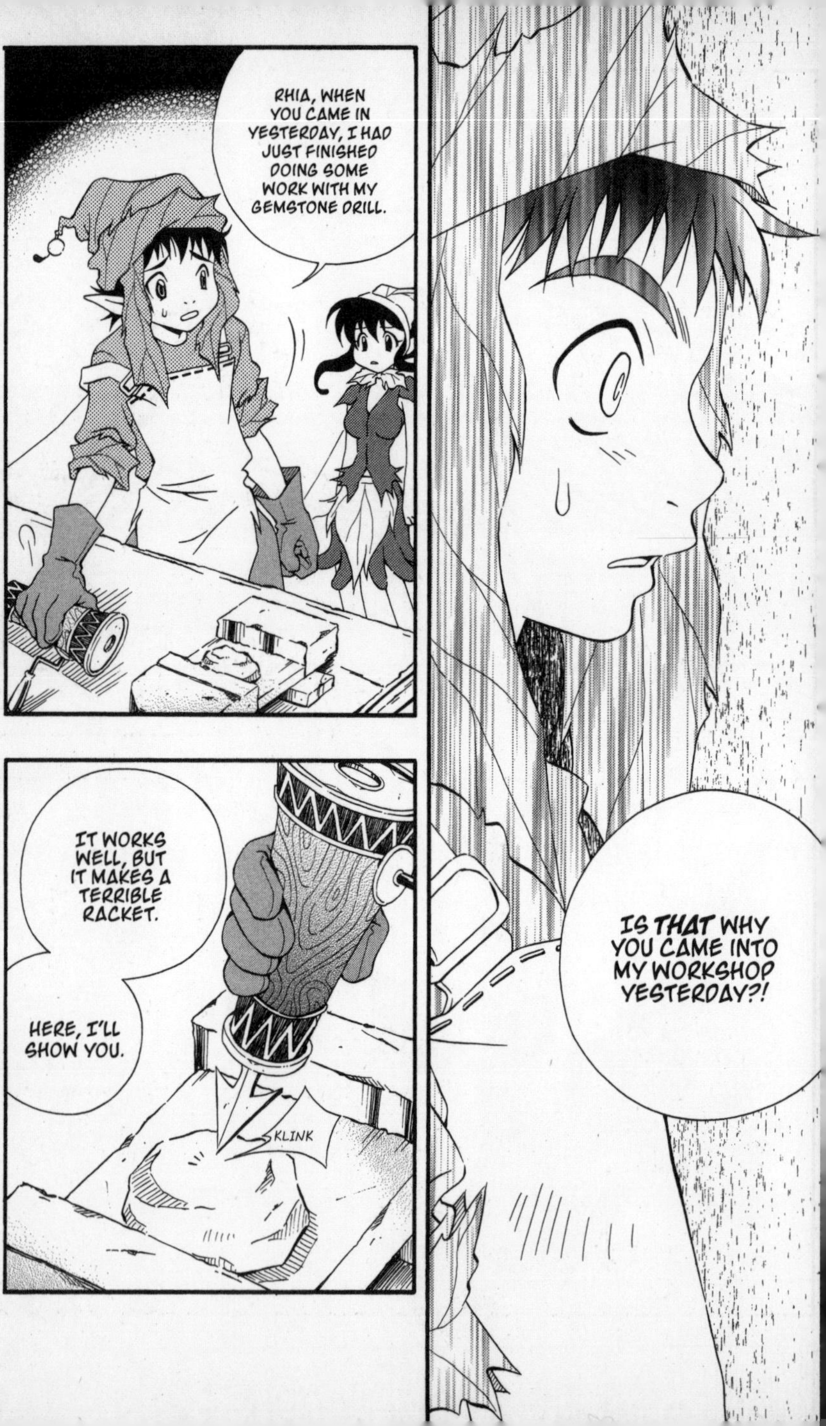
IS THAT WHY YOU CAME INTO MY WORKSHOP YESTERDAY?!
RHIA, WHEN YOU CAME IN YESTERDAY, I HAD JUST FINISHED DOING SOME WORK WITH MY GEMSTONE DRILL.
IT WORKS WELL, BUT IT MAKES A TERRIBLE RACKET.
HERE, I'LL SHOW YOU.
KLINK

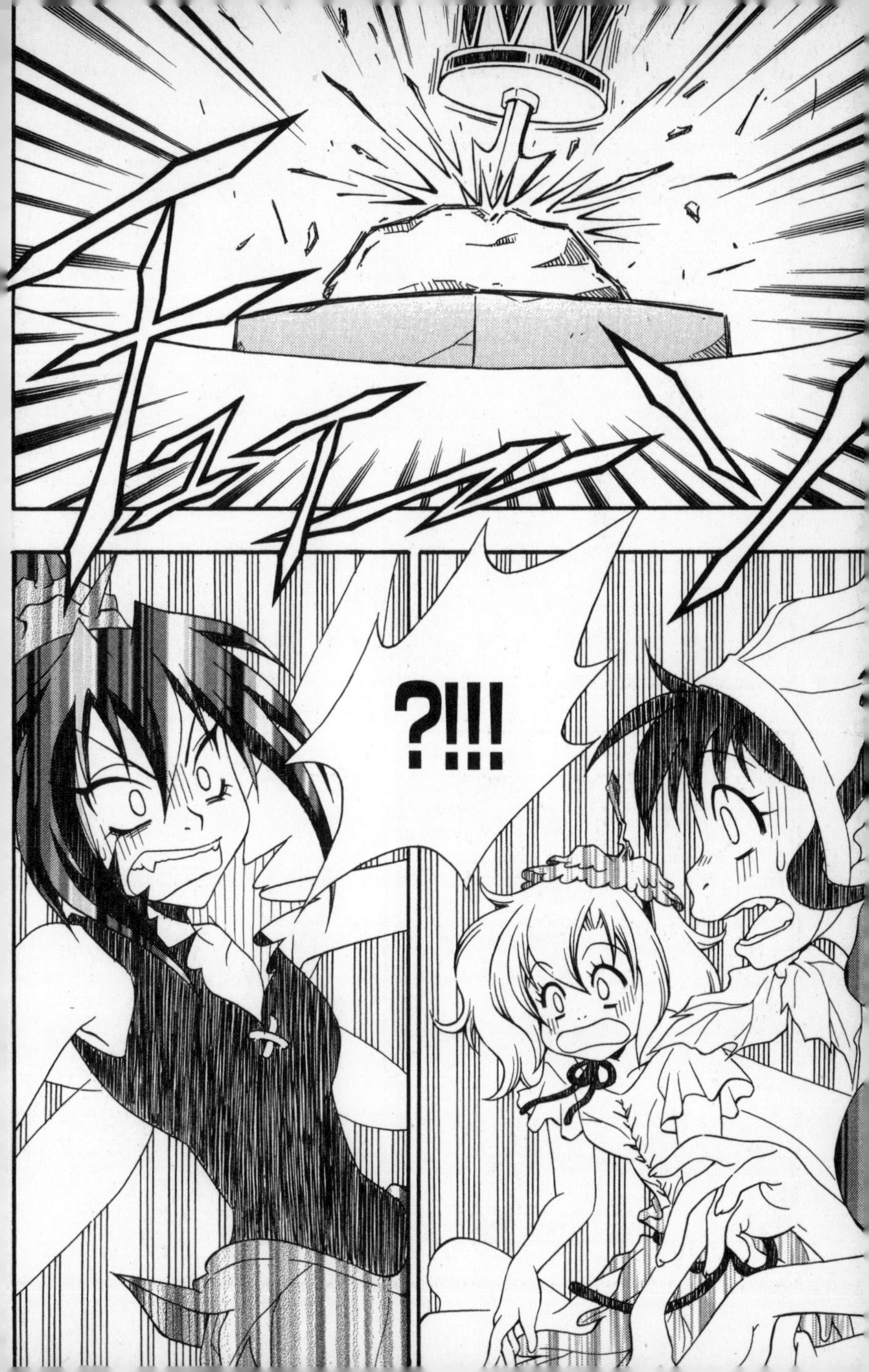
?!!!

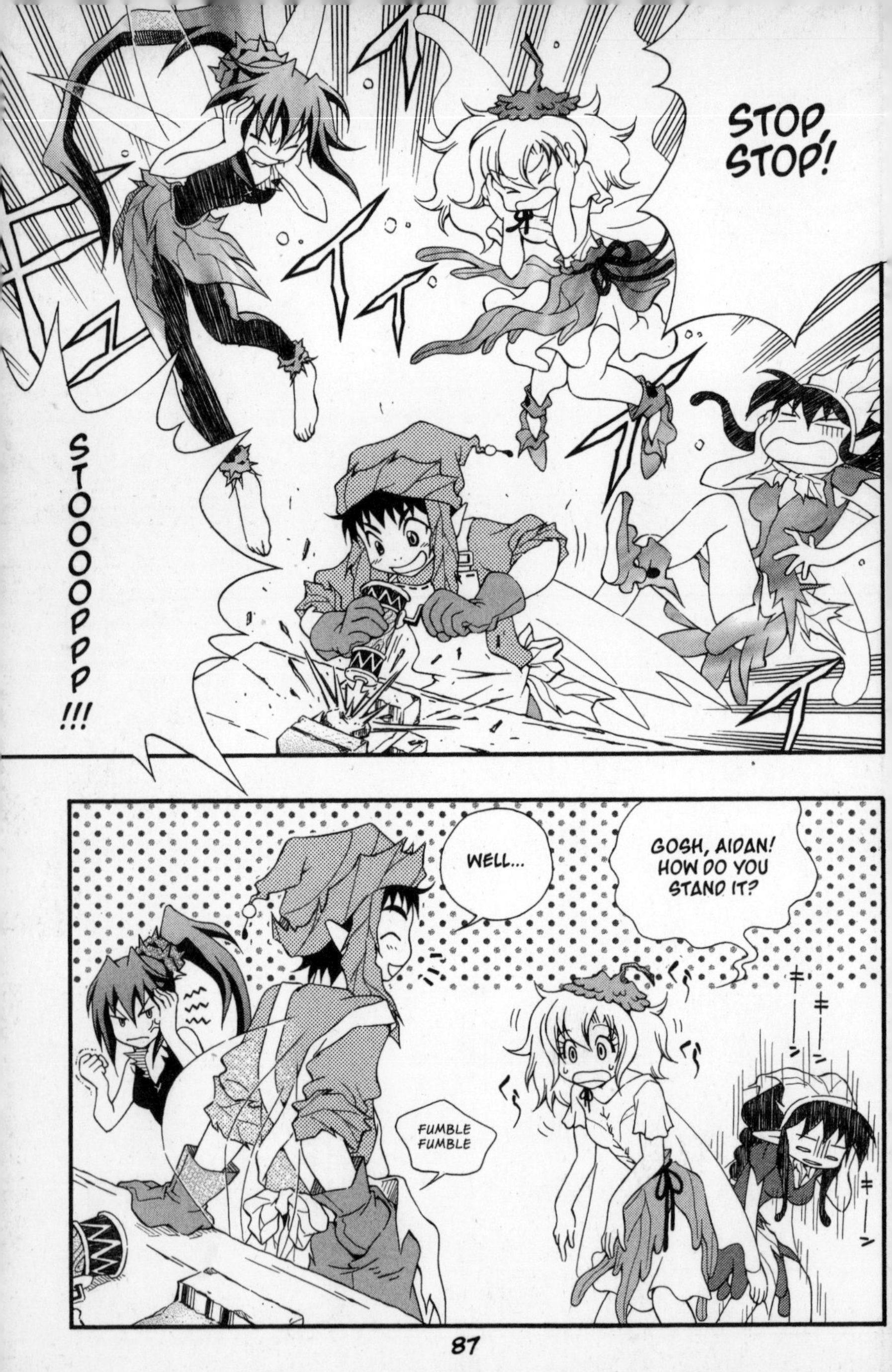
STOP, STOP!
STOOOOOPPP!!!
GOSH, AIDAN! HOW DO YOU STAND IT?
WELL...
FUMBLE FUMBLE

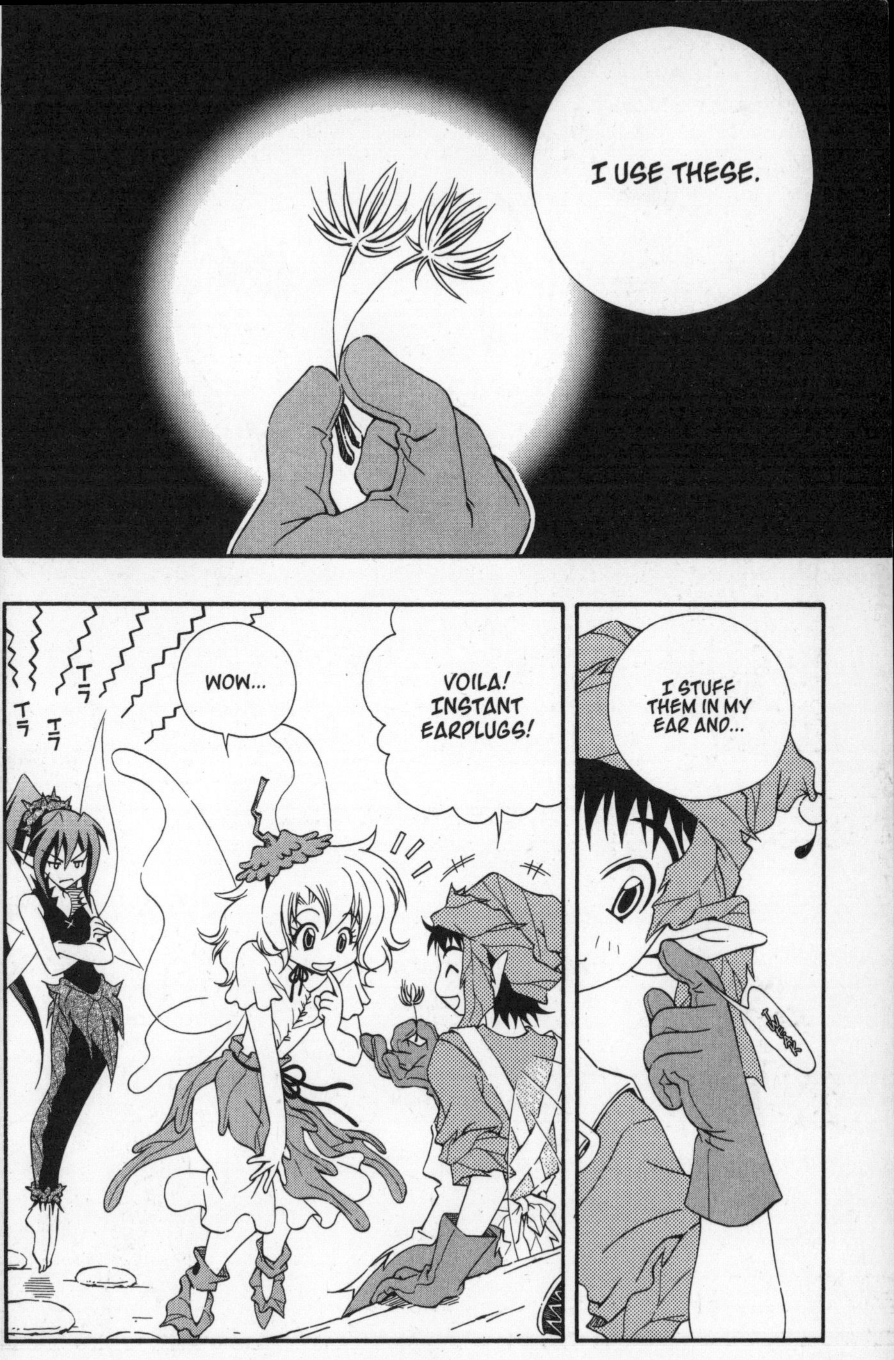
I USE THESE.
I STUFF THEM IN MY EAR AND...
VOILA! INSTANT EARPLUGS!
WOW...

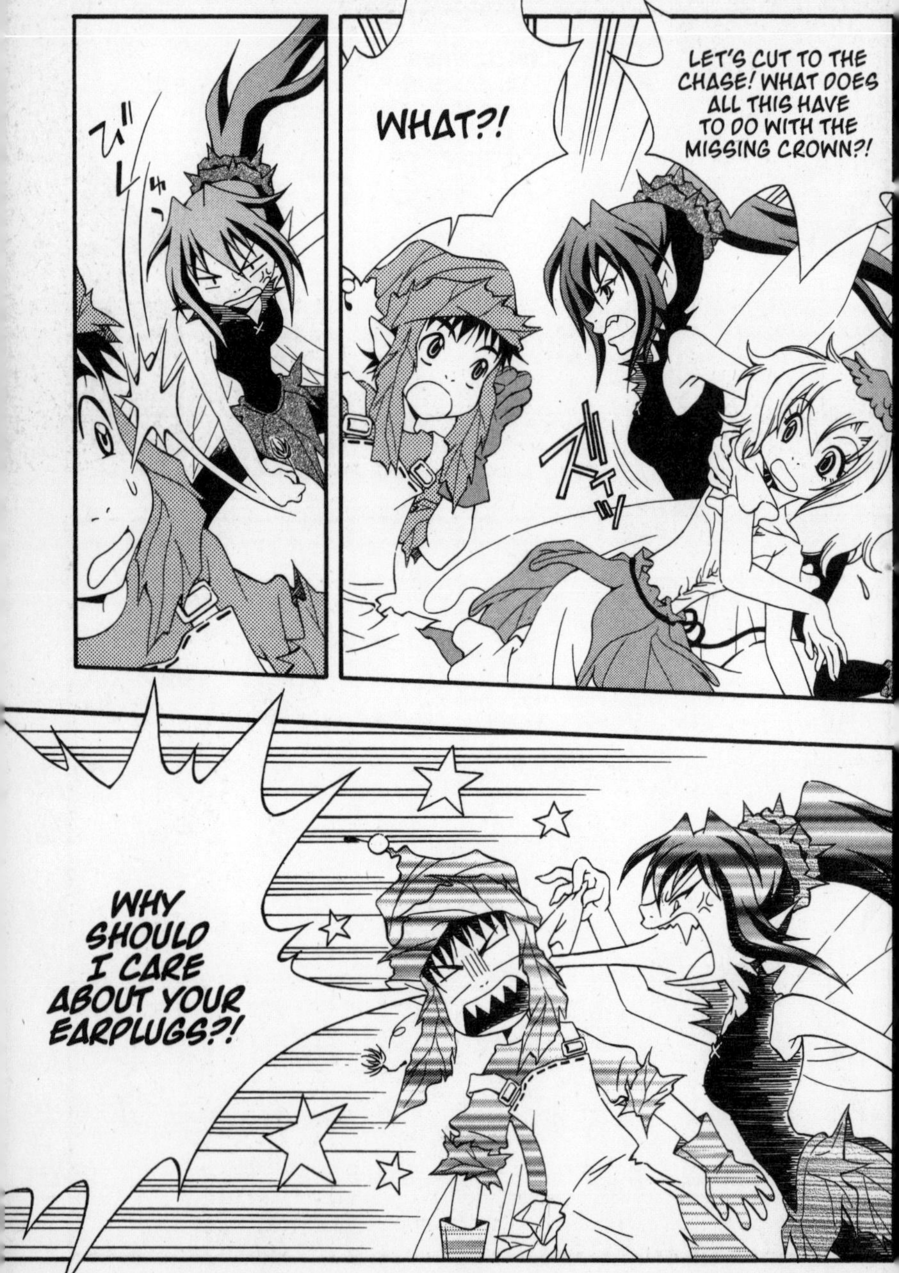
LET'S CUT TO THE CHASE! WHAT DOES ALL THIS HAVE TO DO WITH THE MISSING CROWN?!
WHAT?!
WHY SHOULD I CARE ABOUT YOUR EARPLUGS?!

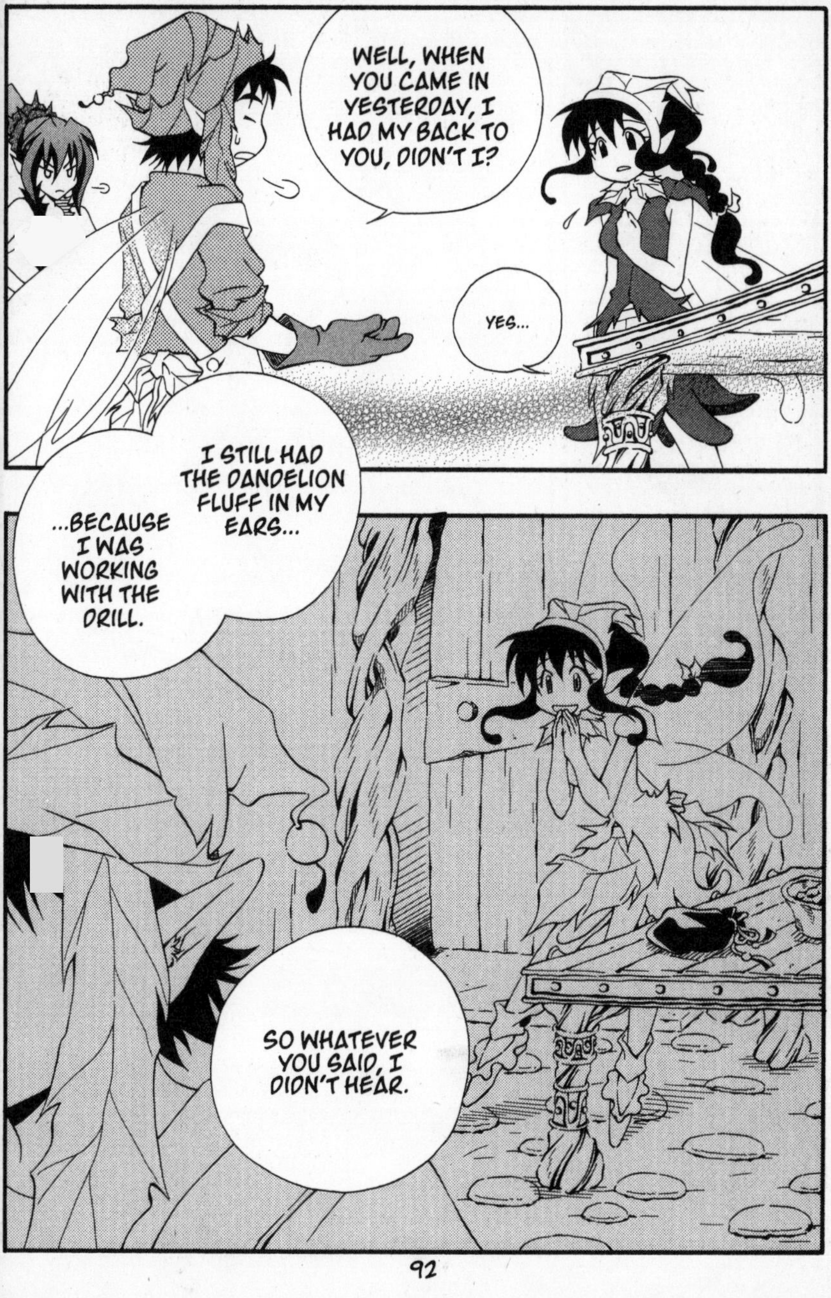
WELL, WHEN YOU CAME IN YESTERDAY, I HAD MY BACK TO YOU, DIDN'T I?
YES...
I STILL HAD THE DANDELION FLUFF IN MY EARS...
...BECAUSE I WAS WORKING WITH THE DRILL.
SO WHATEVER YOU SAID, I DIDN'T HEAR.

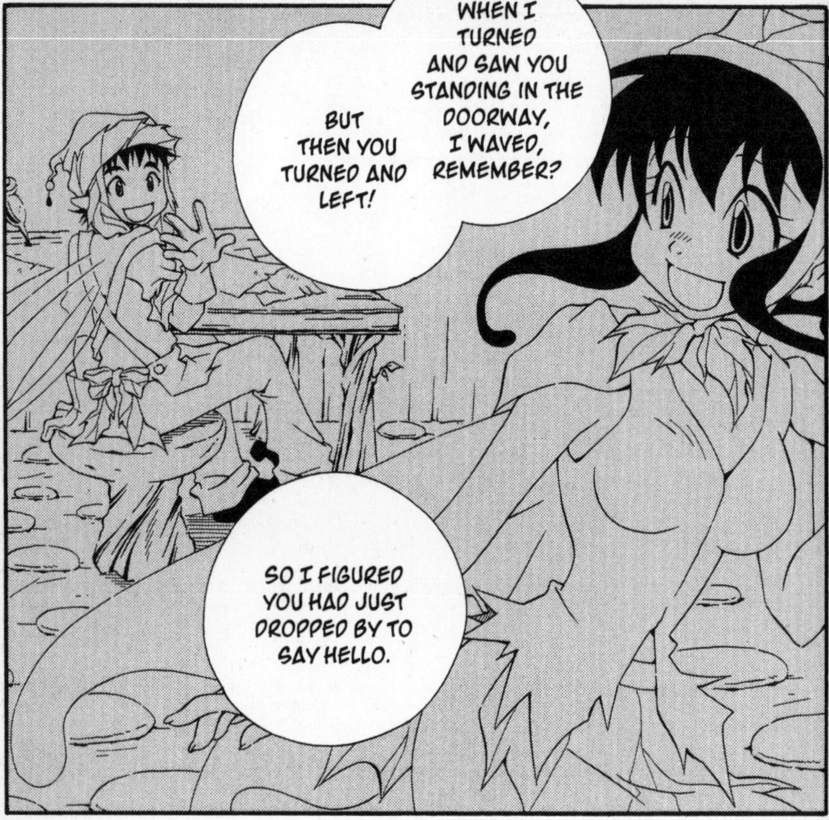
WHEN I TURNED AND SAW YOU STANDING IN THE DOORWAY, I WAVED, REMEMBER?
BUT THEN YOU TURNED AND LEFT!
SO I FIGURED YOU HAD JUST DROPPED BY TO SAY HELLO.

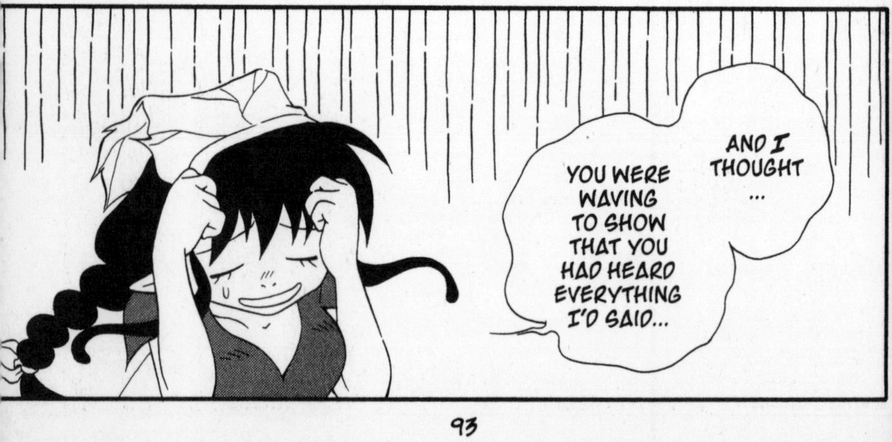
AND I THOUGHT ...
YOU WERE WAVING TO SHOW THAT YOU HAD HEARD EVERYTHING I'D SAID...

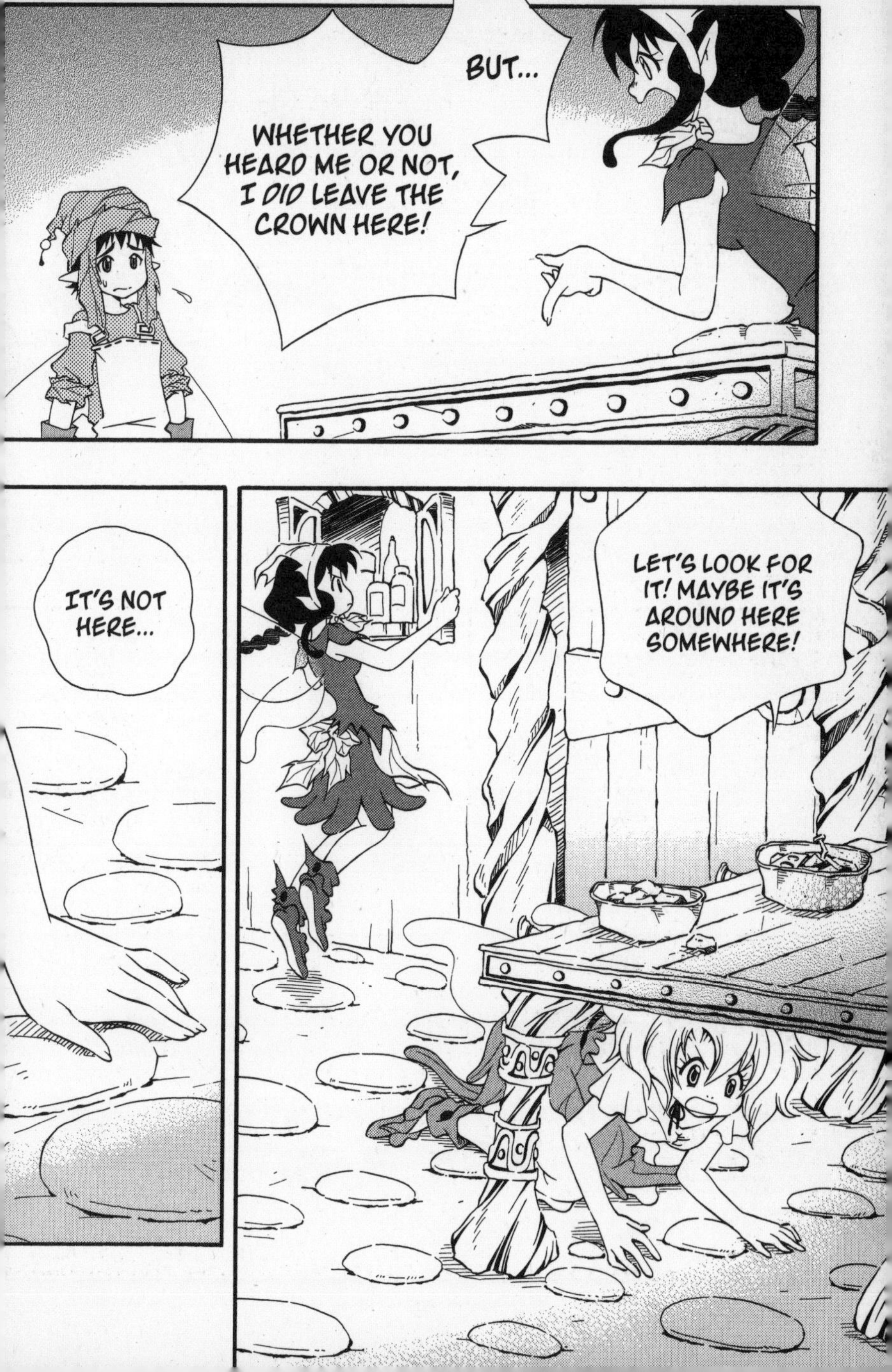
BUT...
WHETHER YOU HEARD ME OR NOT, I *DID* LEAVE THE CROWN HERE!
LET'S LOOK FOR IT! MAYBE IT'S AROUND HERE SOMEWHERE!
IT'S NOT HERE...

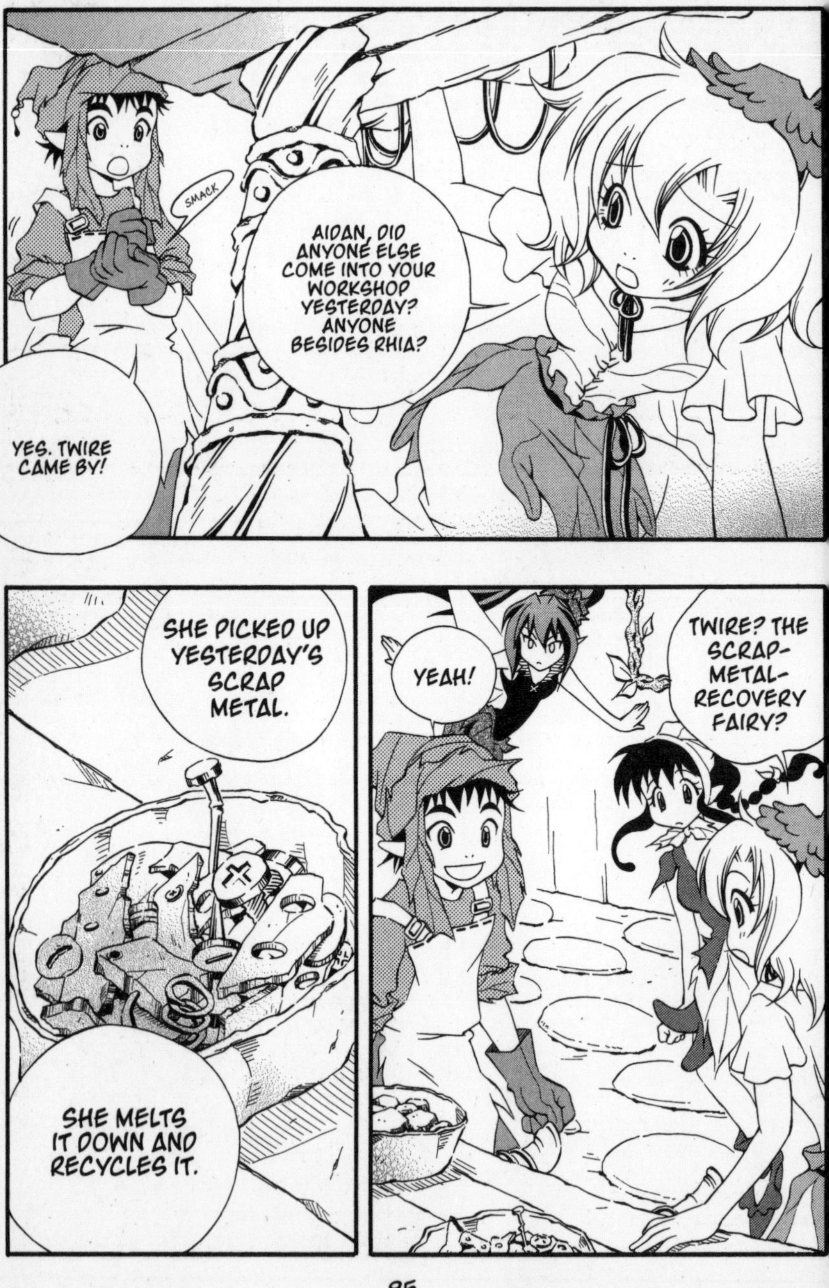
AIDAN, DID ANYONE ELSE COME INTO YOUR WORKSHOP YESTERDAY? ANYONE BESIDES RHIA?
SMACK
YES. TWIRE CAME BY!
TWIRE? THE SCRAP-METAL-RECOVERY FAIRY?
YEAH!
SHE PICKED UP YESTERDAY'S SCRAP METAL.
SHE MELTS IT DOWN AND RECYCLES IT.

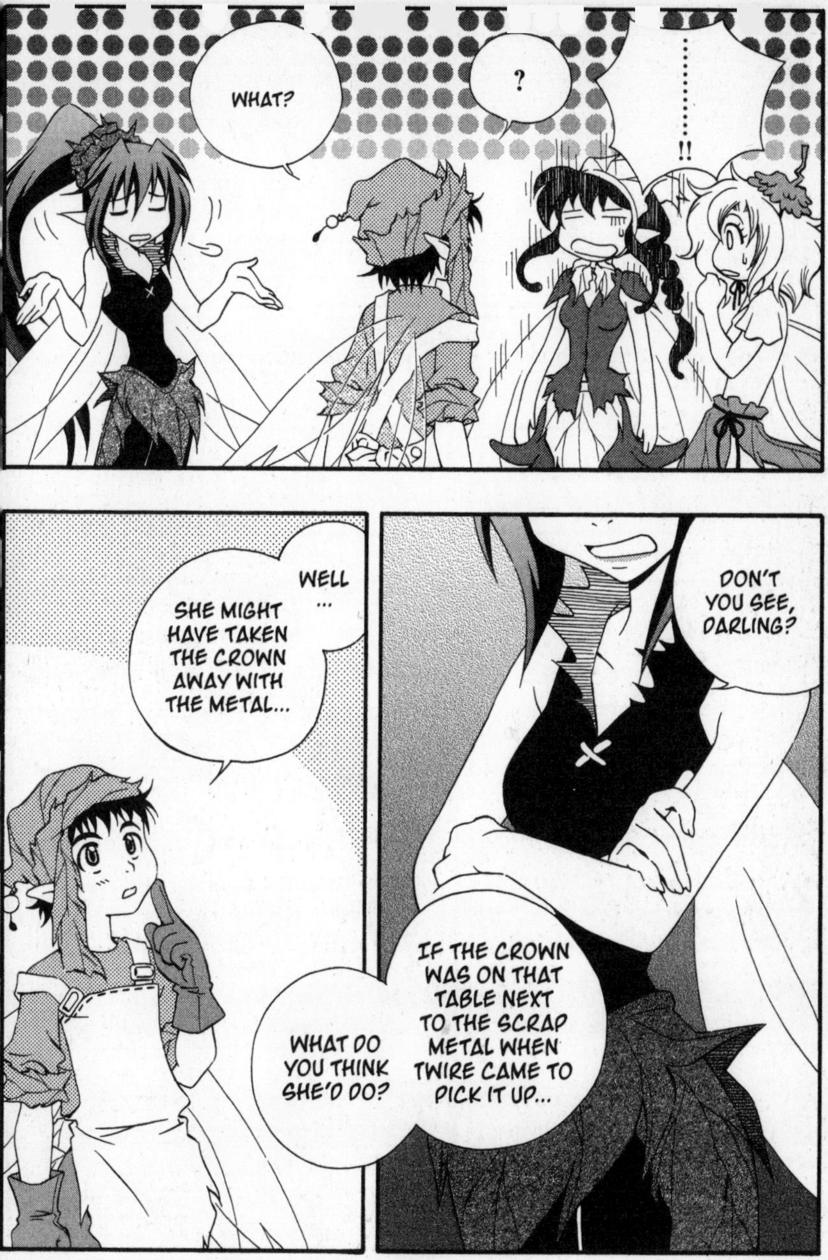
......!!
?
WHAT?
DON'T YOU SEE, DARLING?
IF THE CROWN WAS ON THAT TABLE NEXT TO THE SCRAP METAL WHEN TWIRE CAME TO PICK IT UP...
WHAT DO YOU THINK SHE'D DO?
WELL ...
SHE MIGHT HAVE TAKEN THE CROWN AWAY WITH THE METAL...

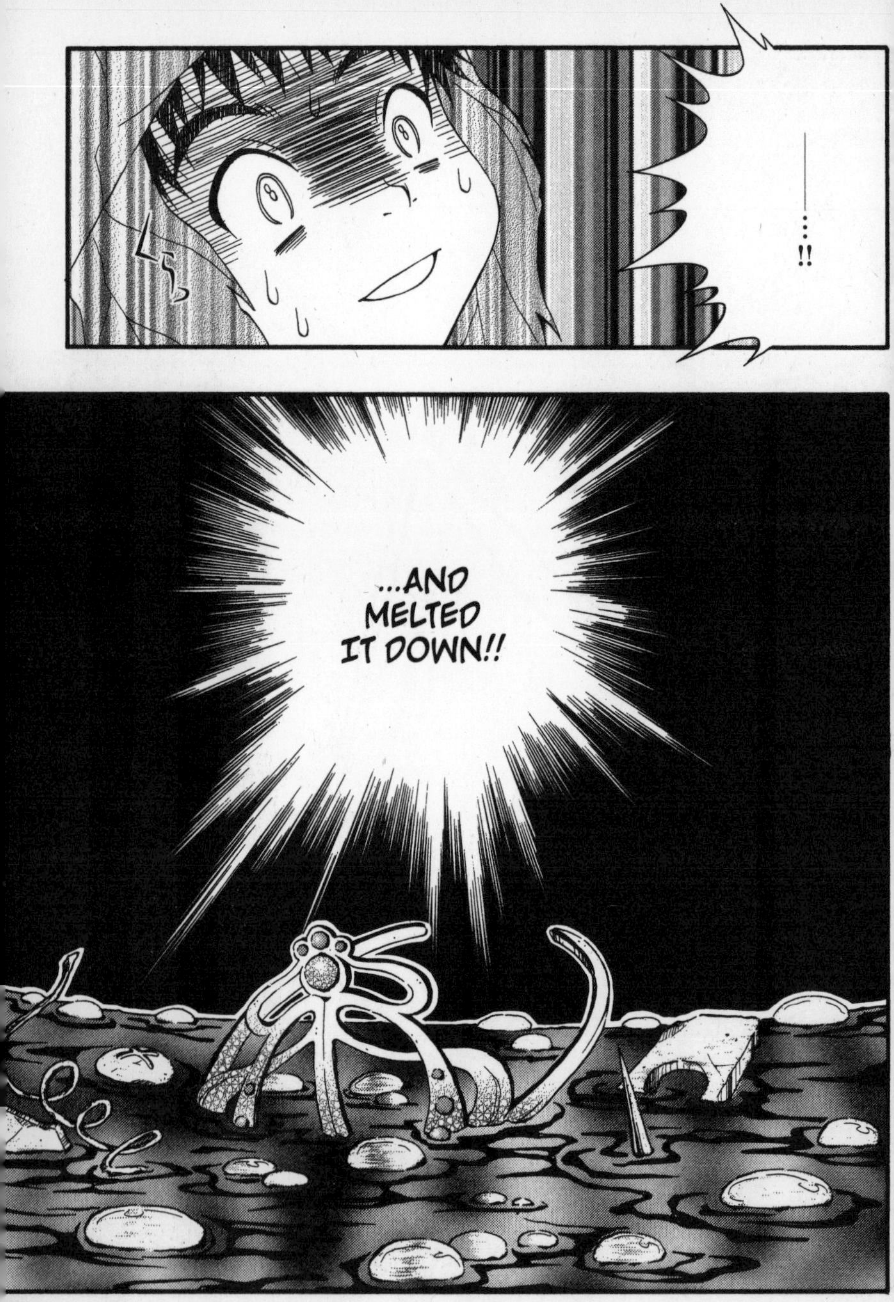
…!!
...AND MELTED IT DOWN!!

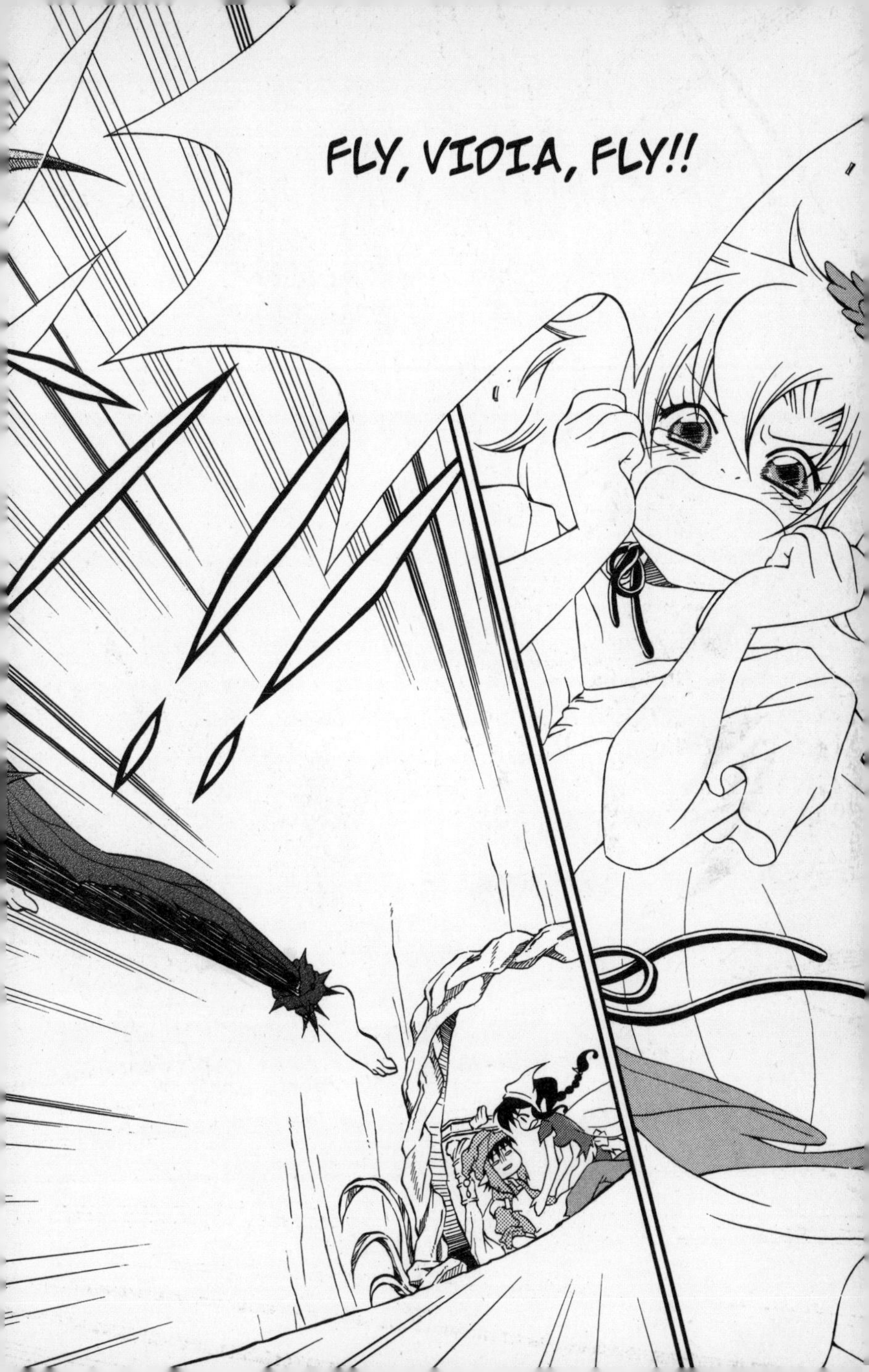
FLY, VIDIA, FLY!!

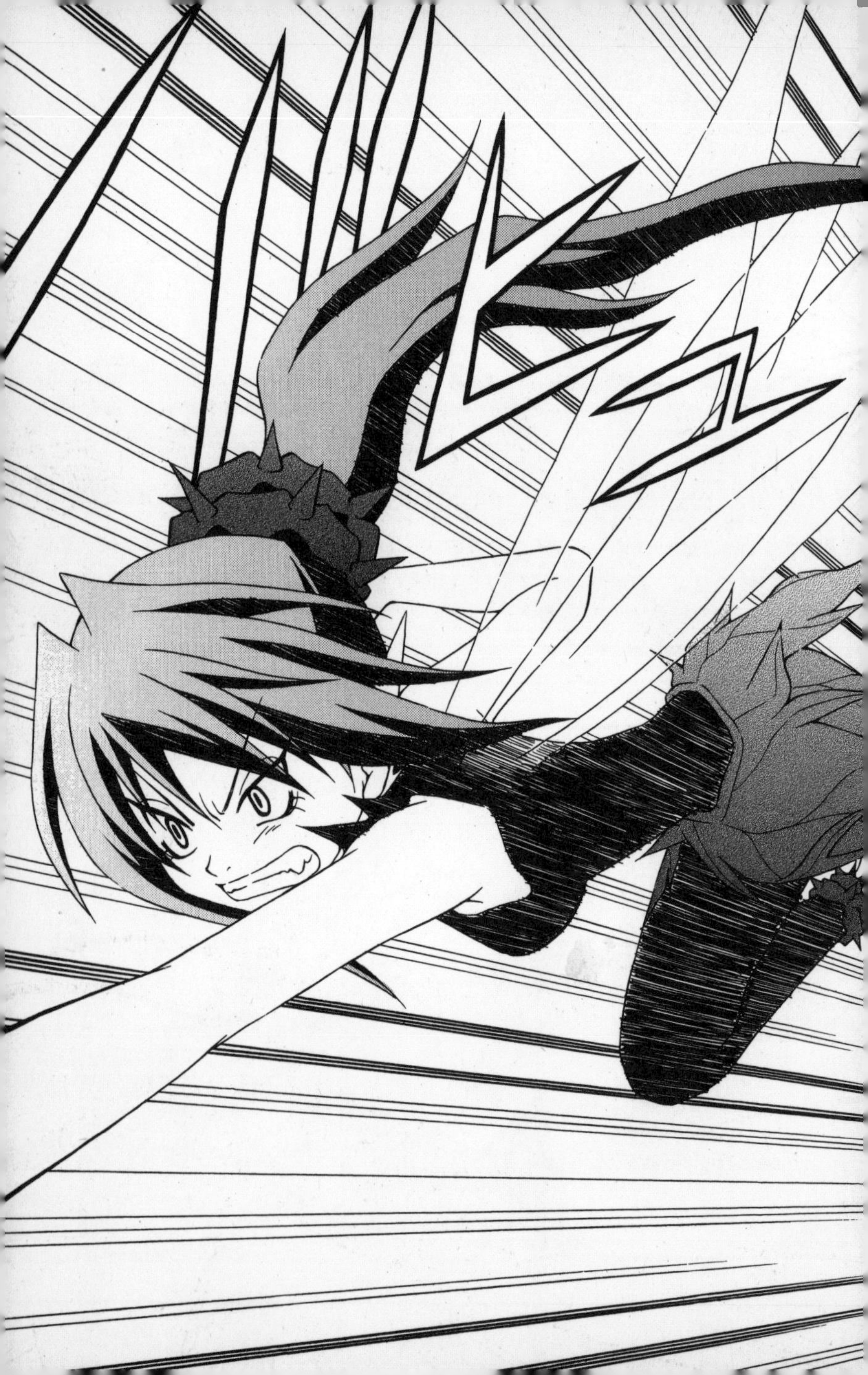

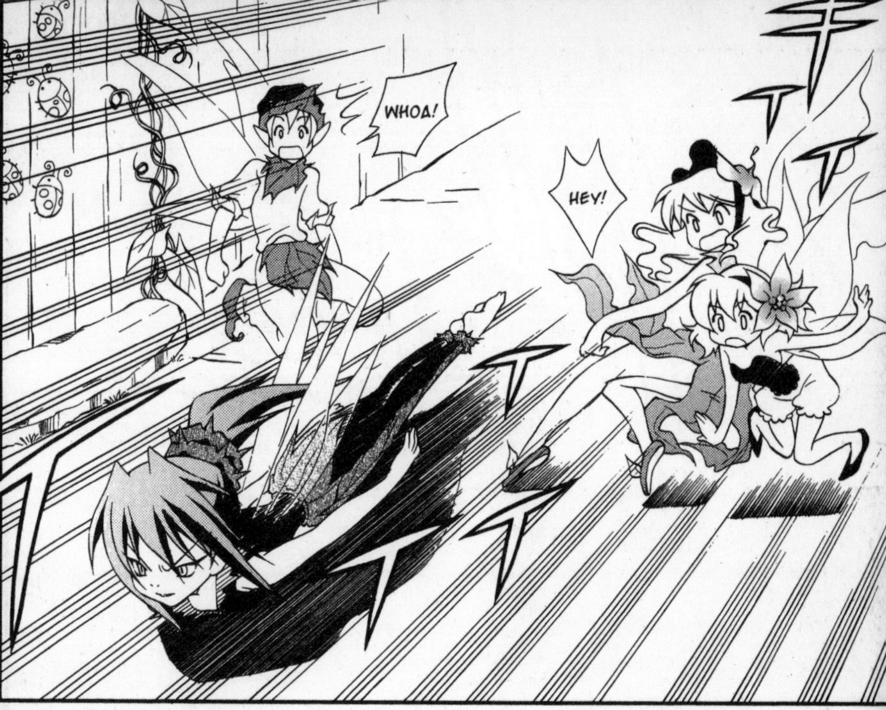
HEY!
WHOA!

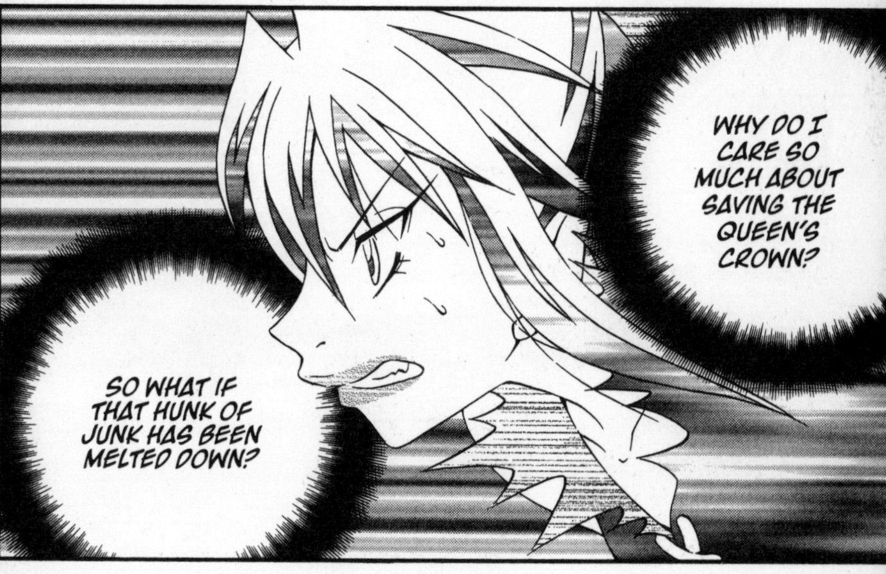
WHY DO I CARE SO MUCH ABOUT SAVING THE QUEEN'S CROWN?
SO WHAT IF THAT HUNK OF JUNK HAS BEEN MELTED DOWN?

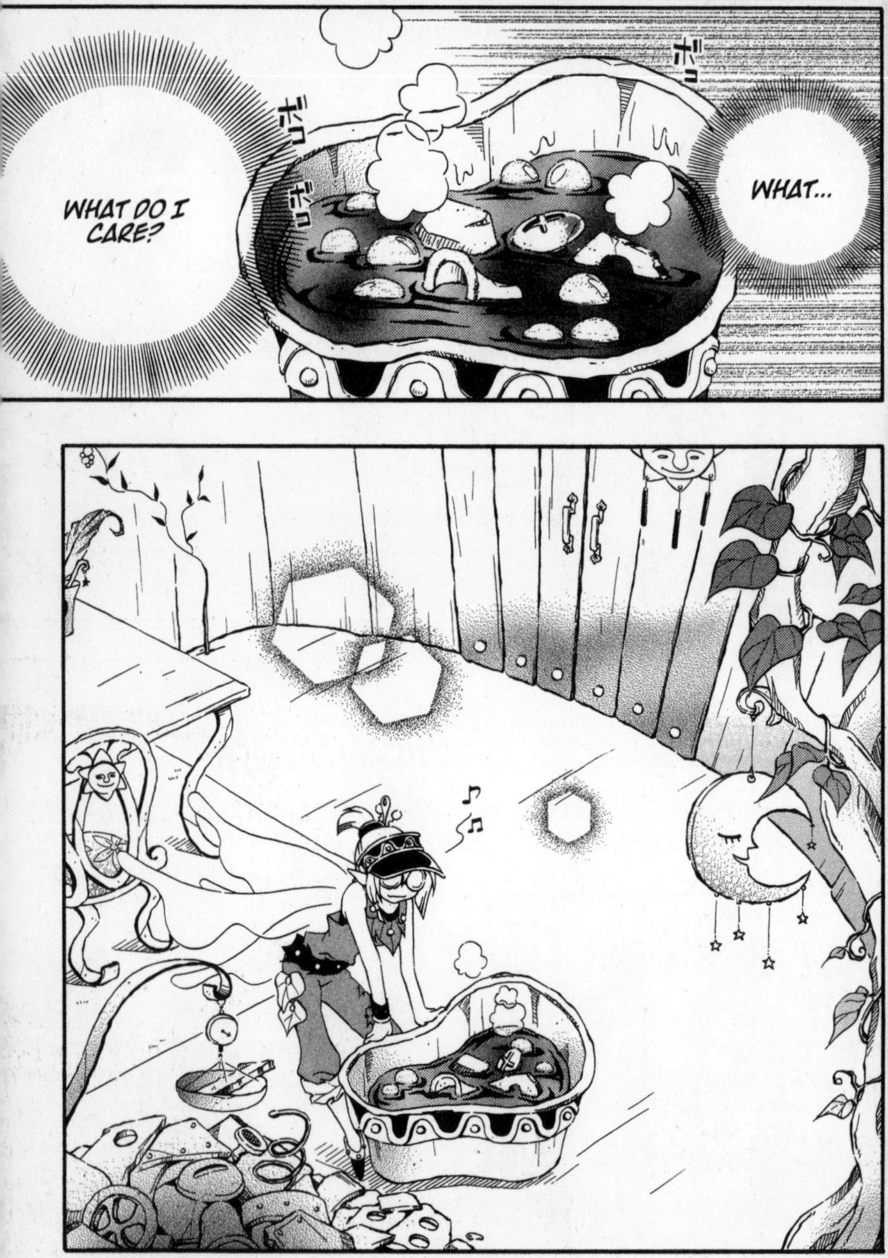
WHAT...
WHAT DO I CARE?

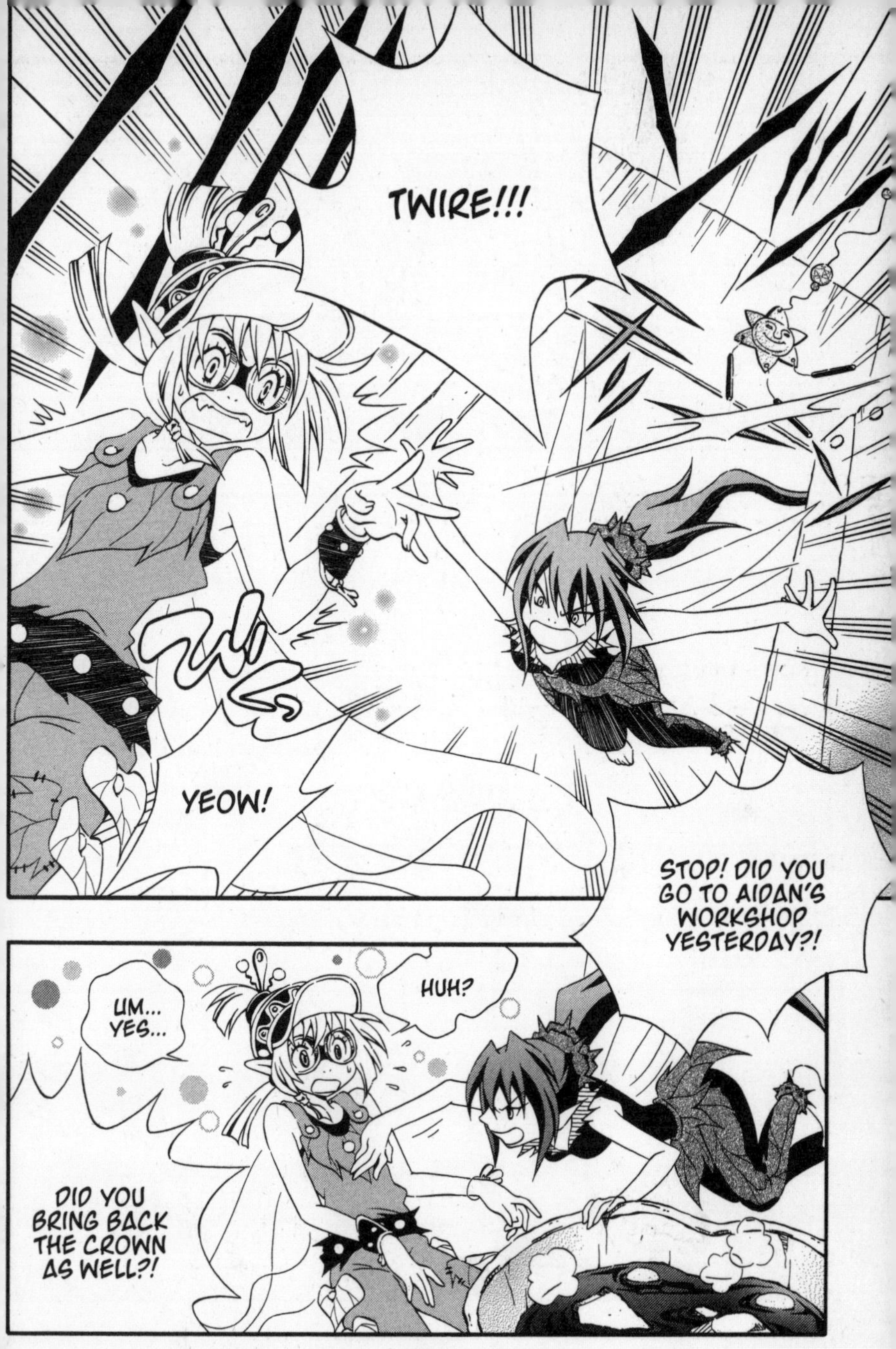
TWIRE!!!
YEOW!
STOP! DID YOU GO TO AIDAN'S WORKSHOP YESTERDAY?!
HUH?
UM... YES...
DID YOU BRING BACK THE CROWN AS WELL?!

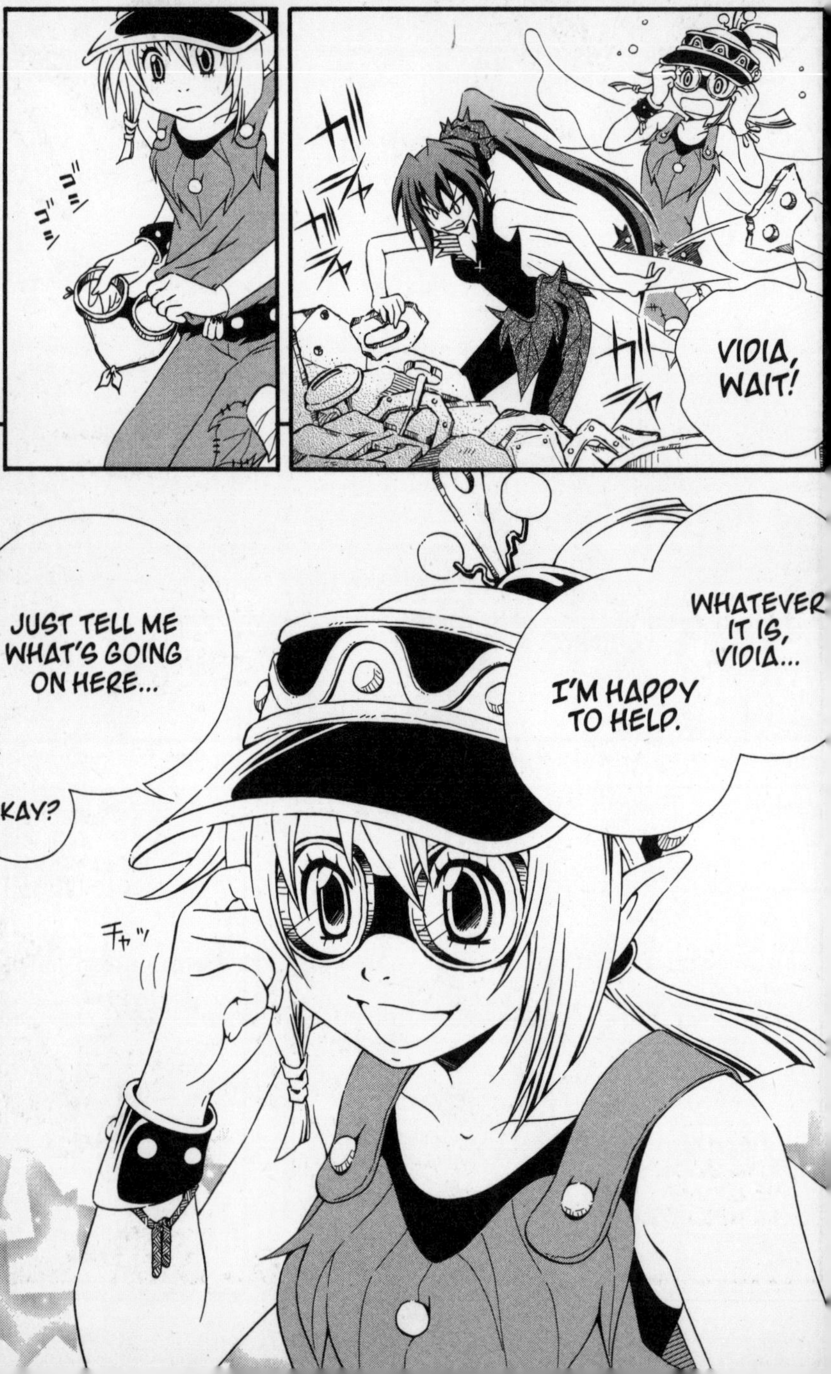
VIDIA, WAIT!
WHATEVER IT IS, VIDIA...
I'M HAPPY TO HELP.
JUST TELL ME WHAT'S GOING ON HERE...
OKAY?

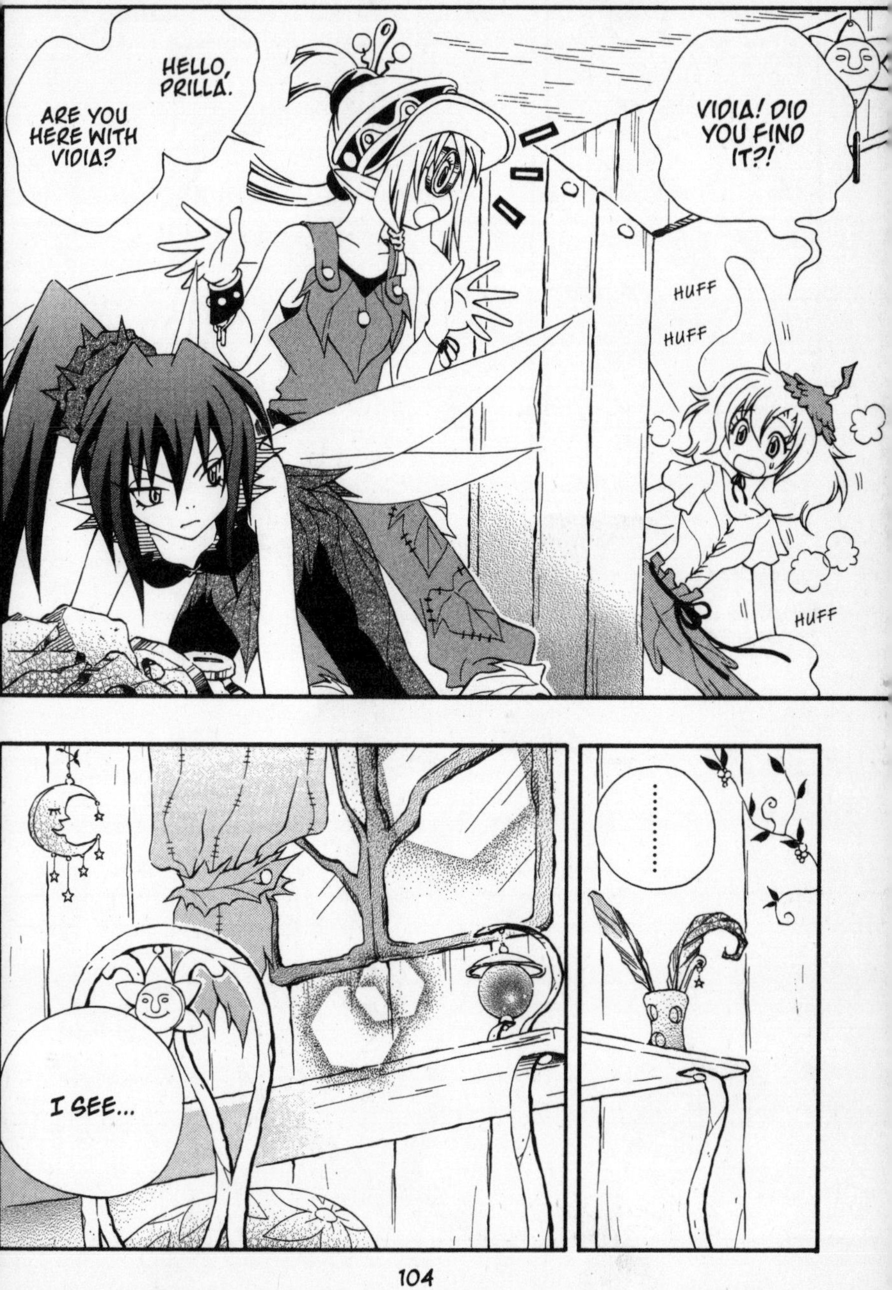
VIDIA! DID YOU FIND IT?!
HUFF
HUFF
HUFF
HELLO, PRILLA.
ARE YOU HERE WITH VIDIA?
......
I SEE...

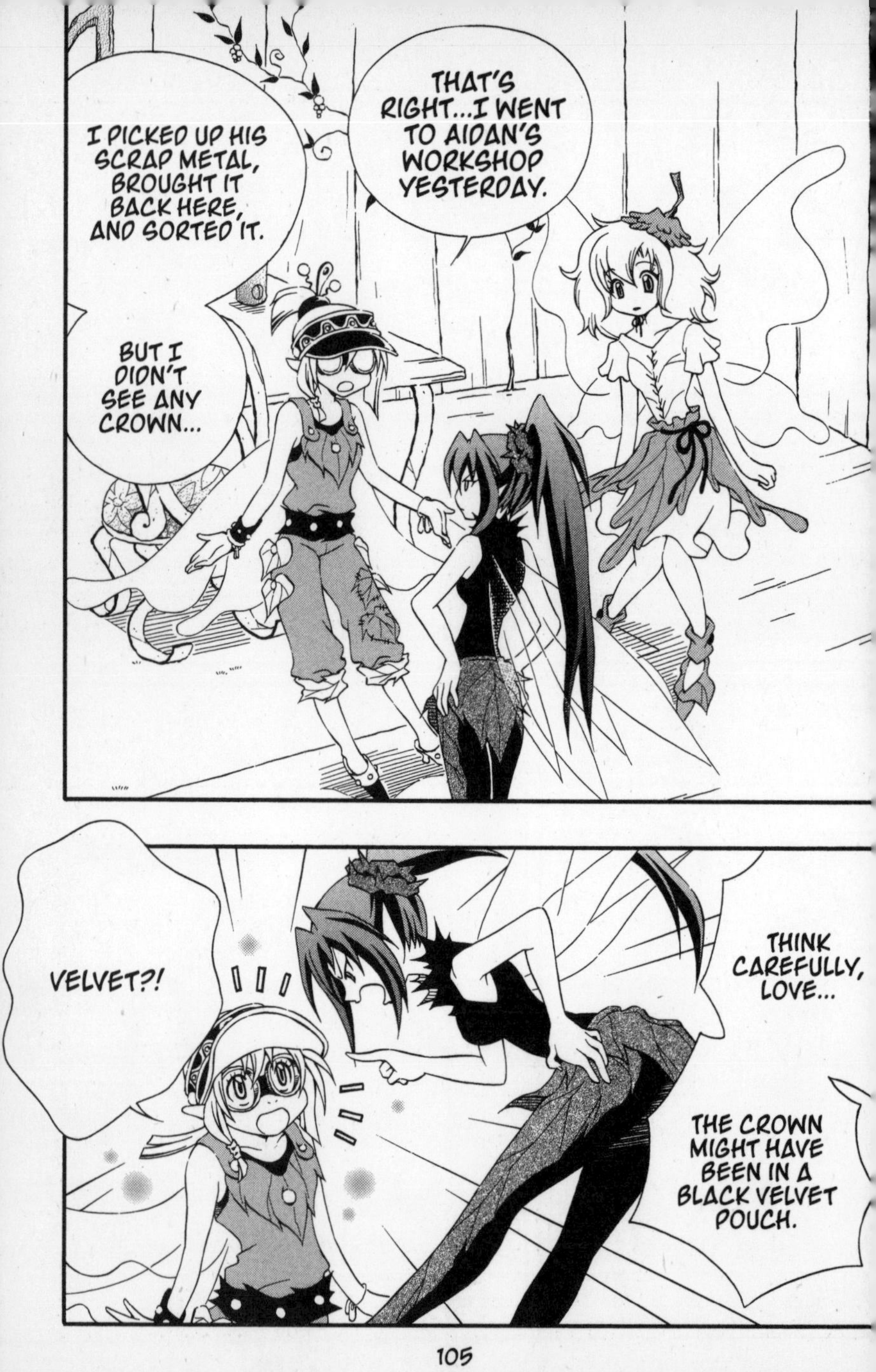
THAT'S RIGHT...I WENT TO AIDAN'S WORKSHOP YESTERDAY.
I PICKED UP HIS SCRAP METAL, BROUGHT IT BACK HERE, AND SORTED IT.
BUT I DIDN'T SEE ANY CROWN...
THINK CAREFULLY, LOVE...
THE CROWN MIGHT HAVE BEEN IN A BLACK VELVET POUCH.
VELVET?!

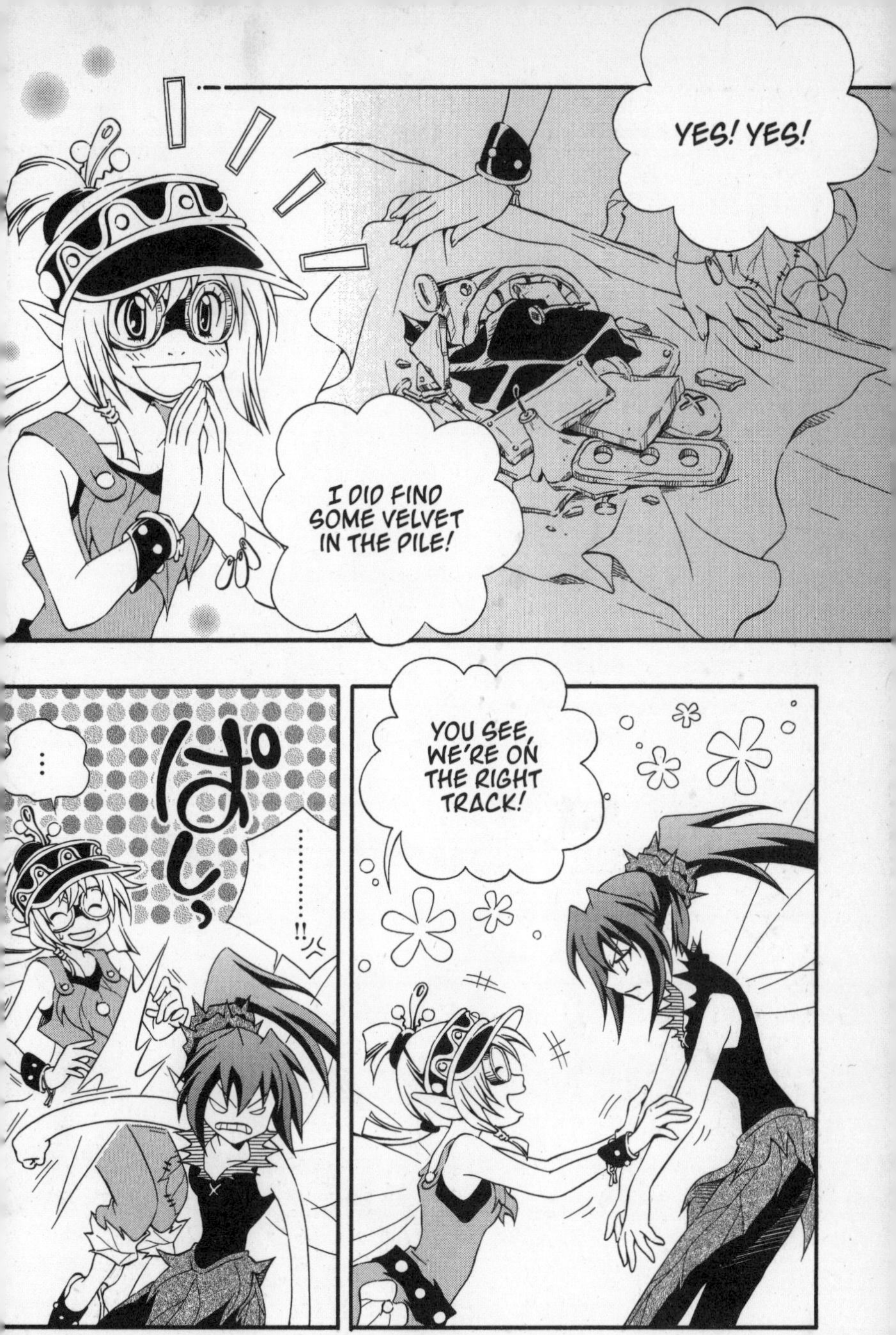

YES! YES!
I DID FIND SOME VELVET IN THE PILE!
YOU SEE, WE'RE ON THE RIGHT TRACK!
ぱし
...
........!!

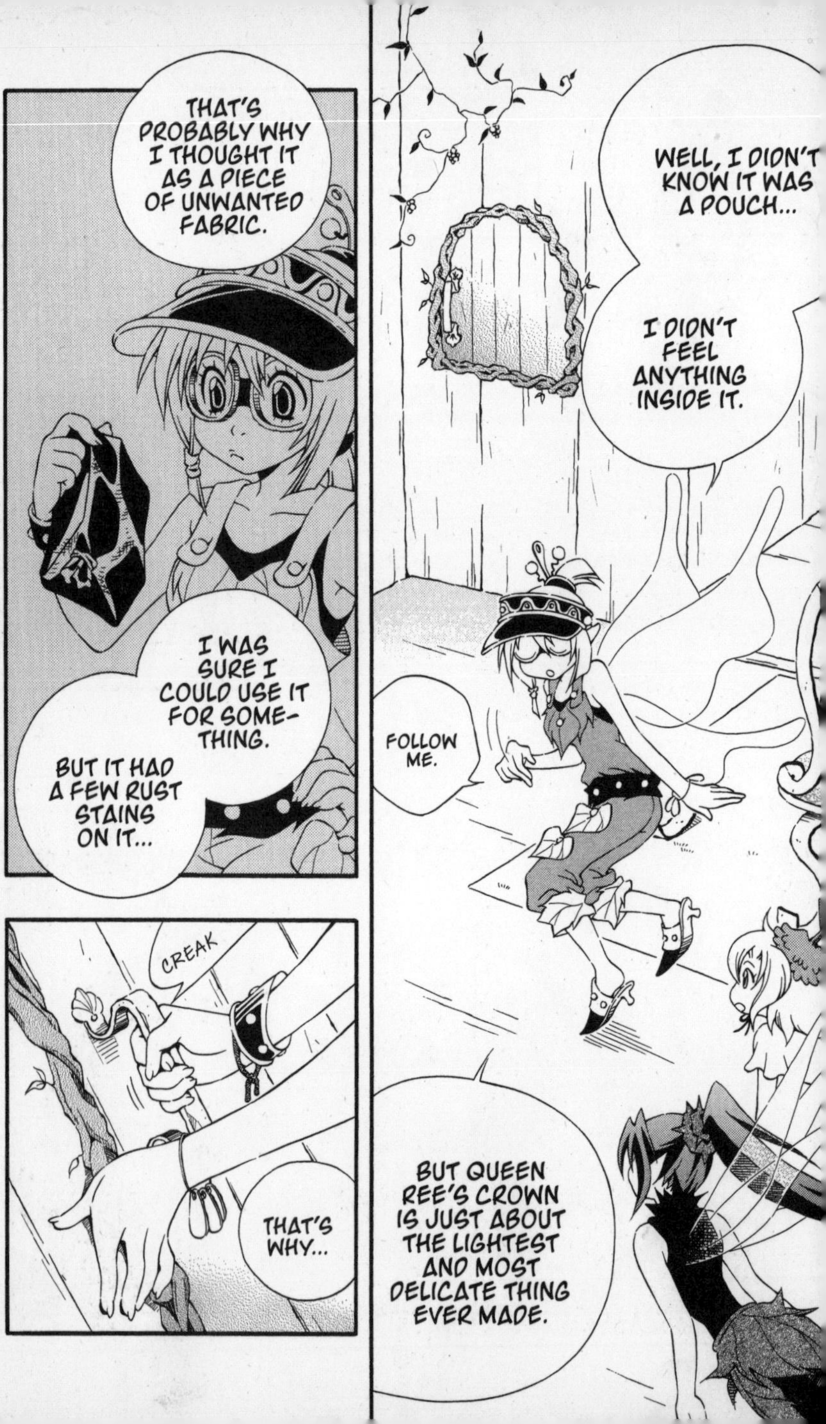
WELL, I DIDN'T KNOW IT WAS A POUCH...
I DIDN'T FEEL ANYTHING INSIDE IT.
FOLLOW ME.
BUT QUEEN REE'S CROWN IS JUST ABOUT THE LIGHTEST AND MOST DELICATE THING EVER MADE.
THAT'S PROBABLY WHY I THOUGHT IT AS A PIECE OF UNWANTED FABRIC.
I WAS SURE I COULD USE IT FOR SOME-THING.
BUT IT HAD A FEW RUST STAINS ON IT...
CREAK
THAT'S WHY...

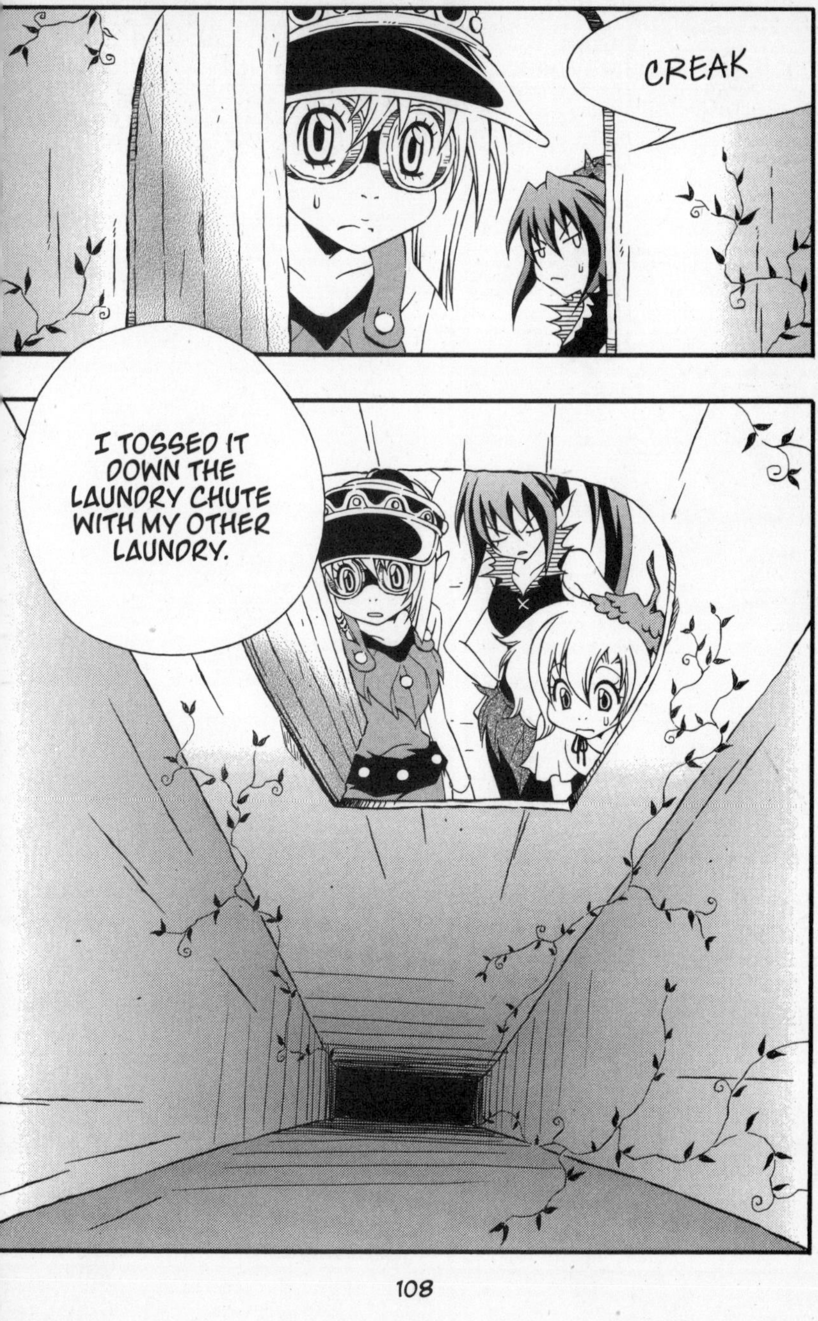
CREAK
I TOSSED IT DOWN THE LAUNDRY CHUTE WITH MY OTHER LAUNDRY.

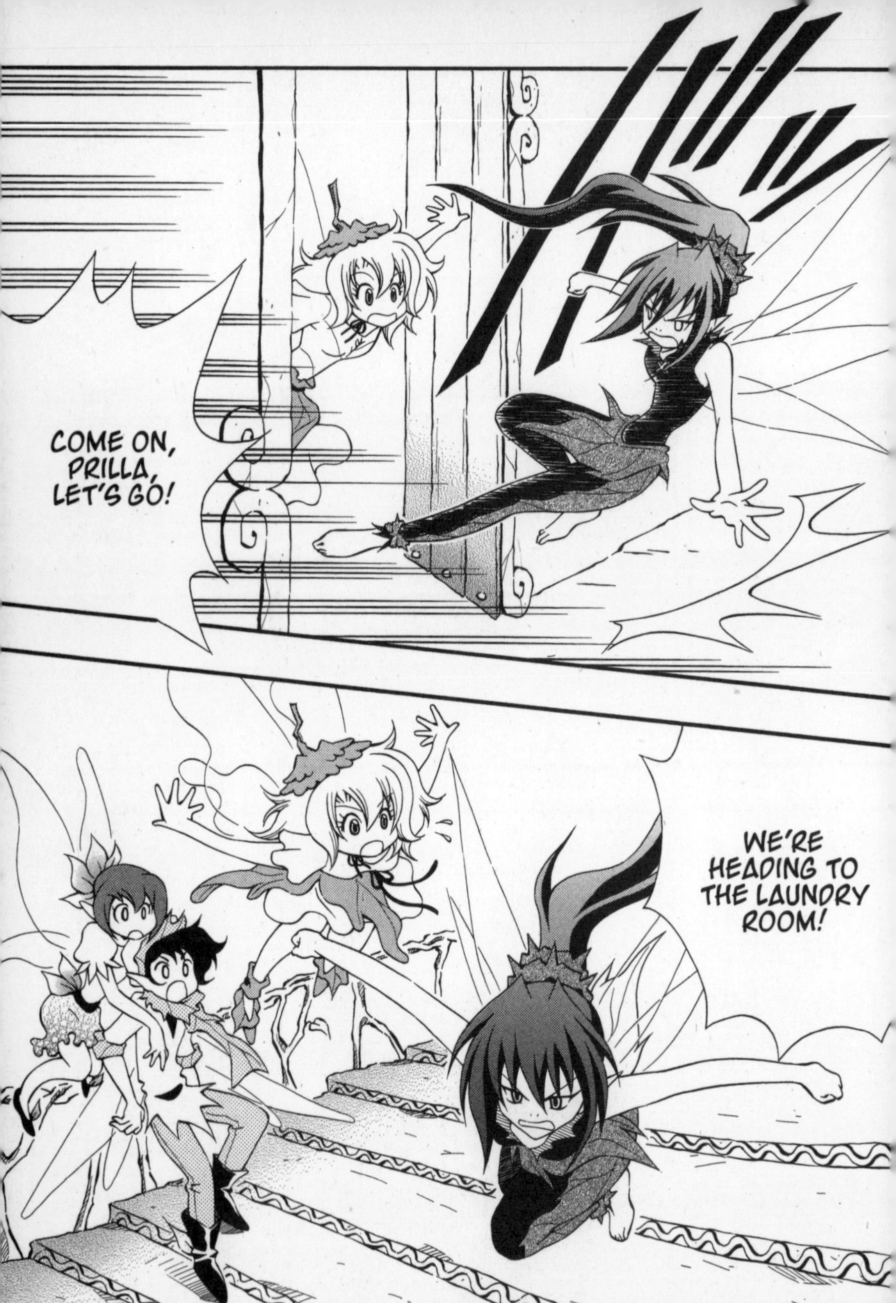
COME ON, PRILLA, LET'S GO!
WE'RE HEADING TO THE LAUNDRY ROOM!

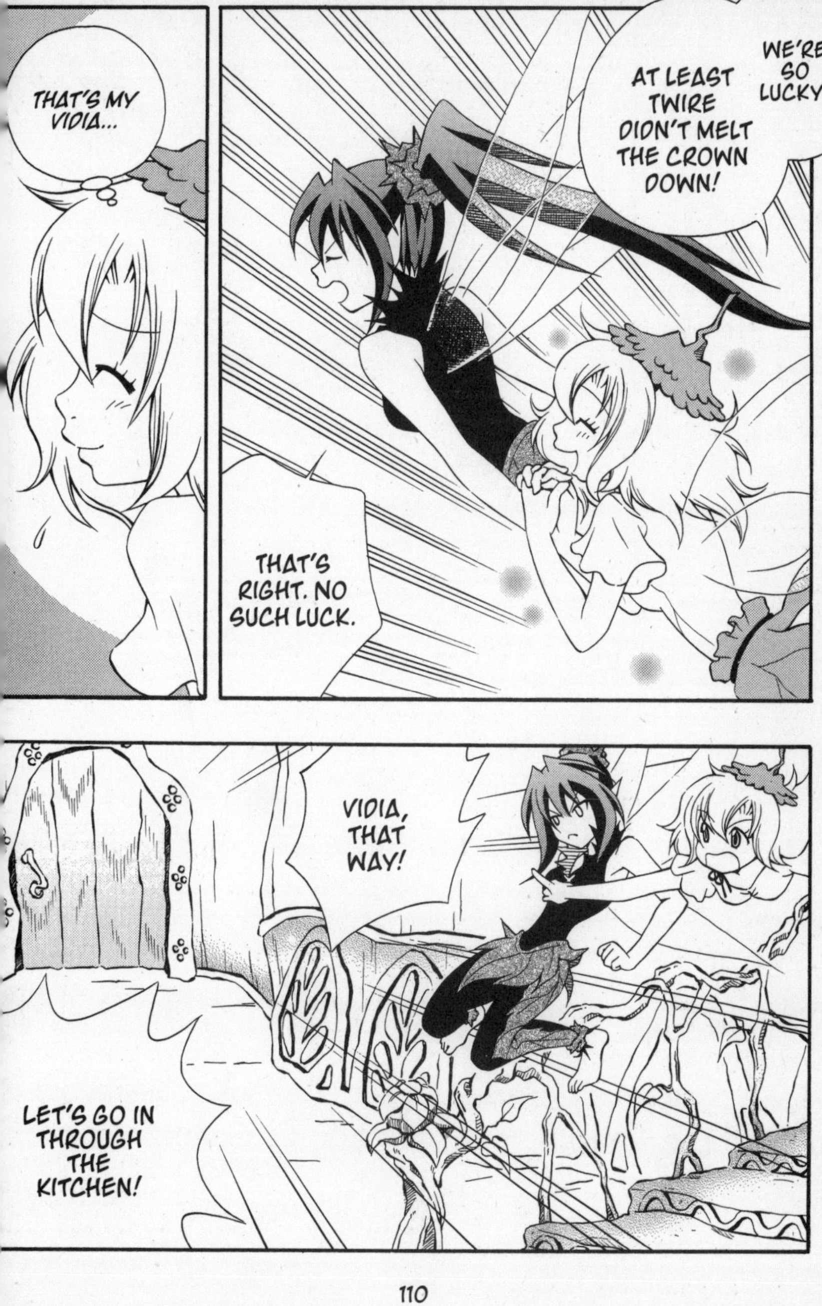
WE'RE SO LUCKY!
AT LEAST TWIRE DIDN'T MELT THE CROWN DOWN!
THAT'S RIGHT. NO SUCH LUCK.
THAT'S MY VIDIA...
VIDIA, THAT WAY!
LET'S GO IN THROUGH THE KITCHEN!

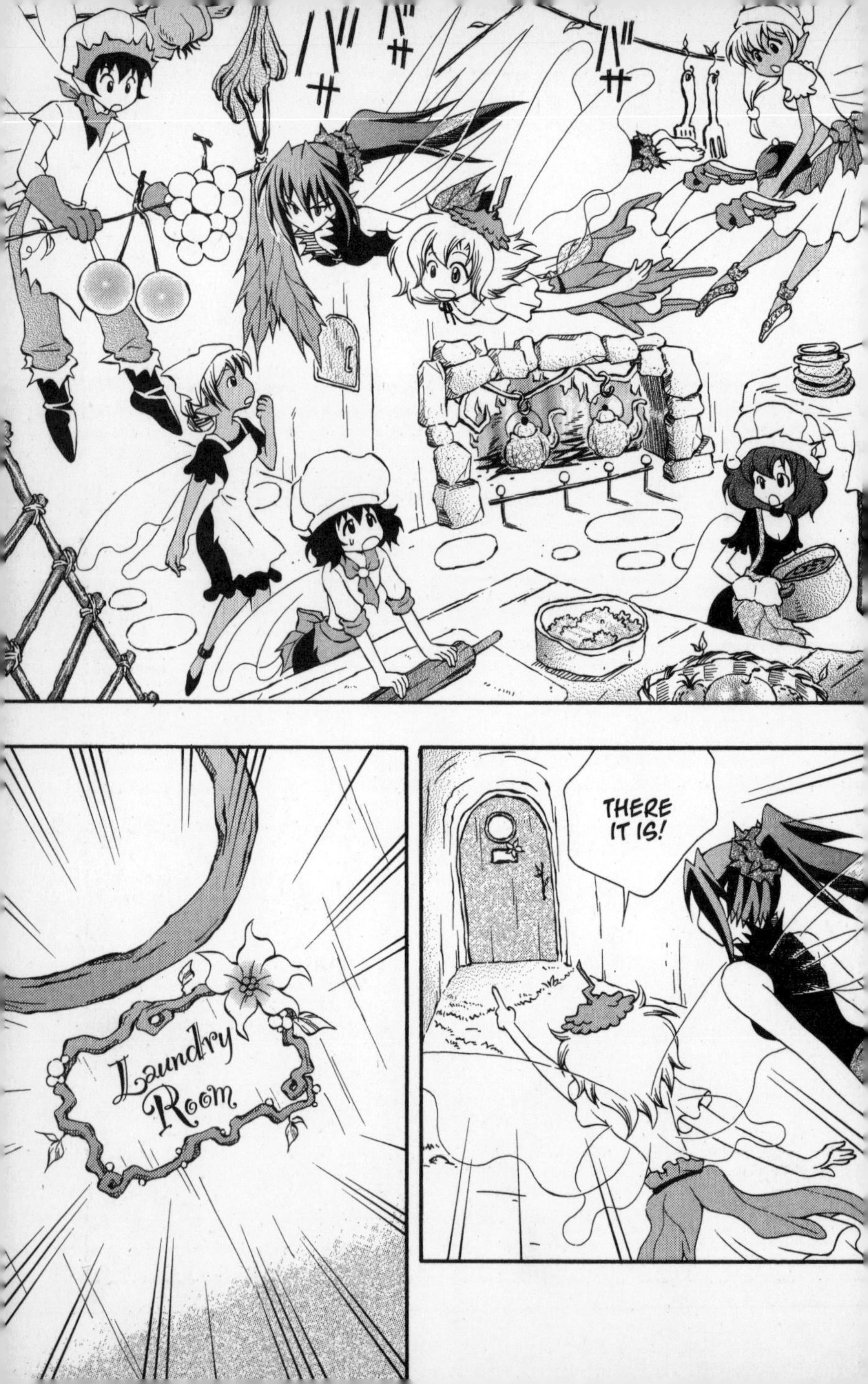
バサ
バサ
バサ
THERE IT IS!
Laundry Room

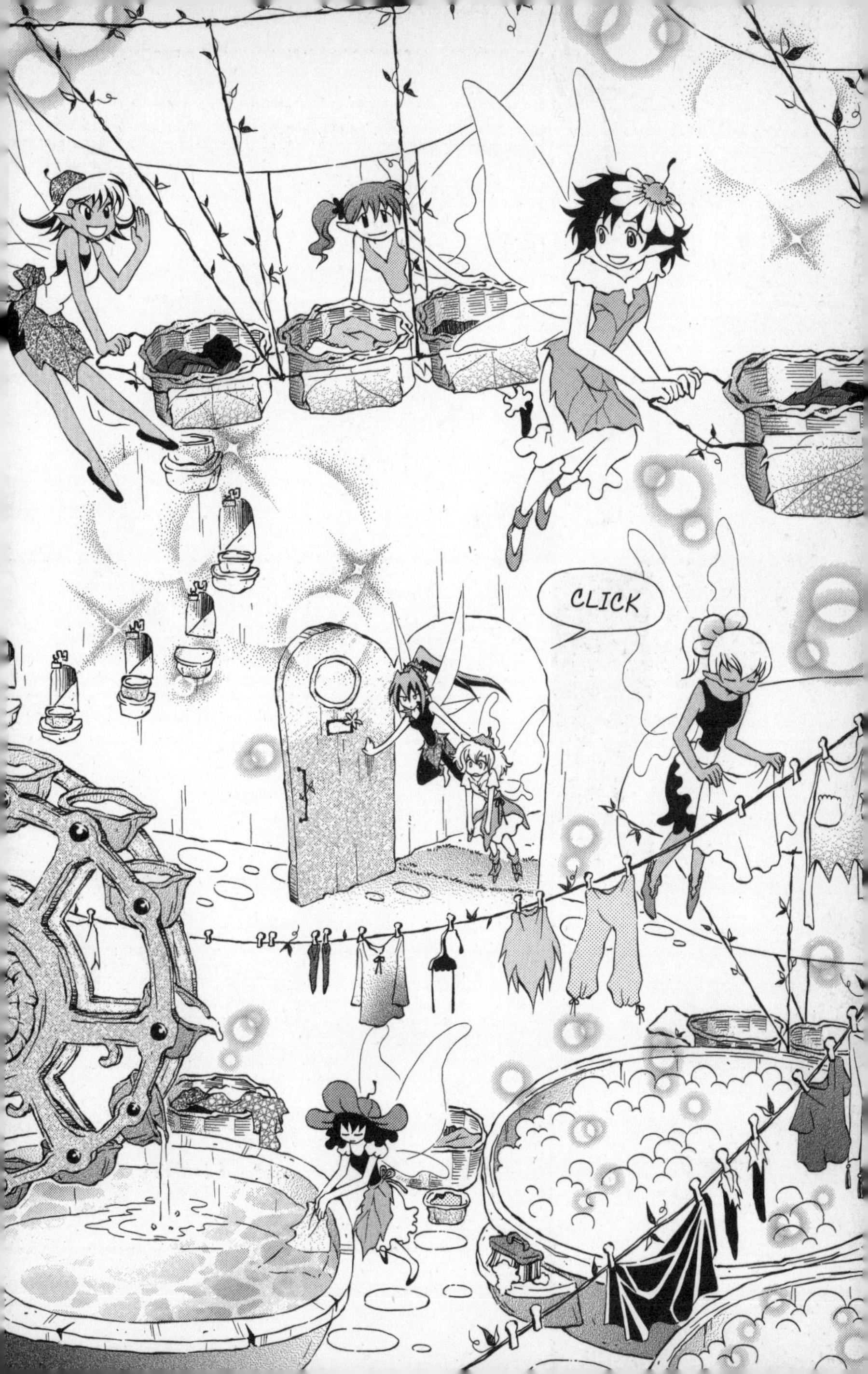
CLICK

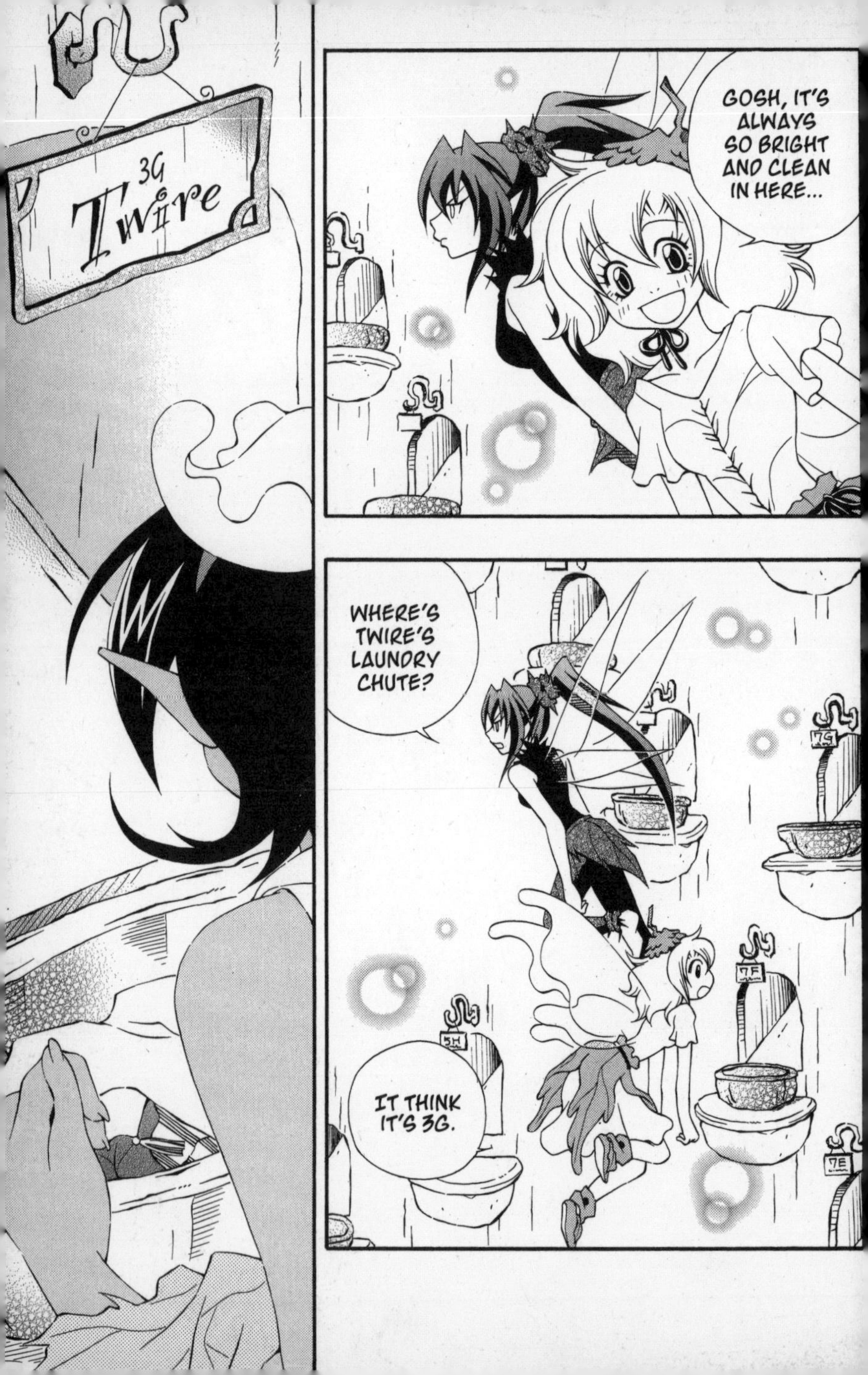
GOSH, IT'S ALWAYS SO BRIGHT AND CLEAN IN HERE...
WHERE'S TWIRE'S LAUNDRY CHUTE?
7G
7F
5H
IT THINK IT'S 3G.
7E
3G
Twire

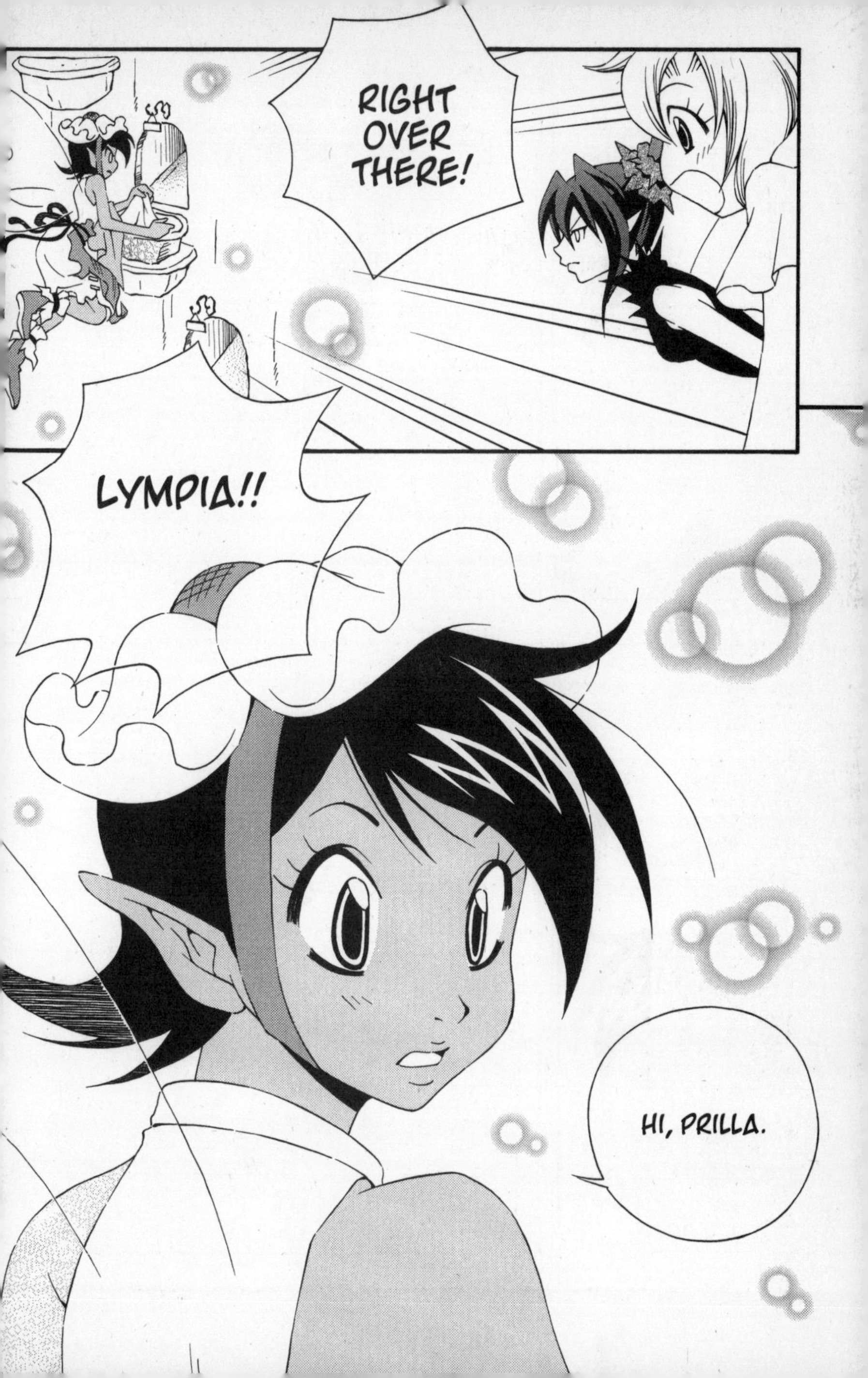
RIGHT OVER THERE!
LYMPIA!!
HI, PRILLA.

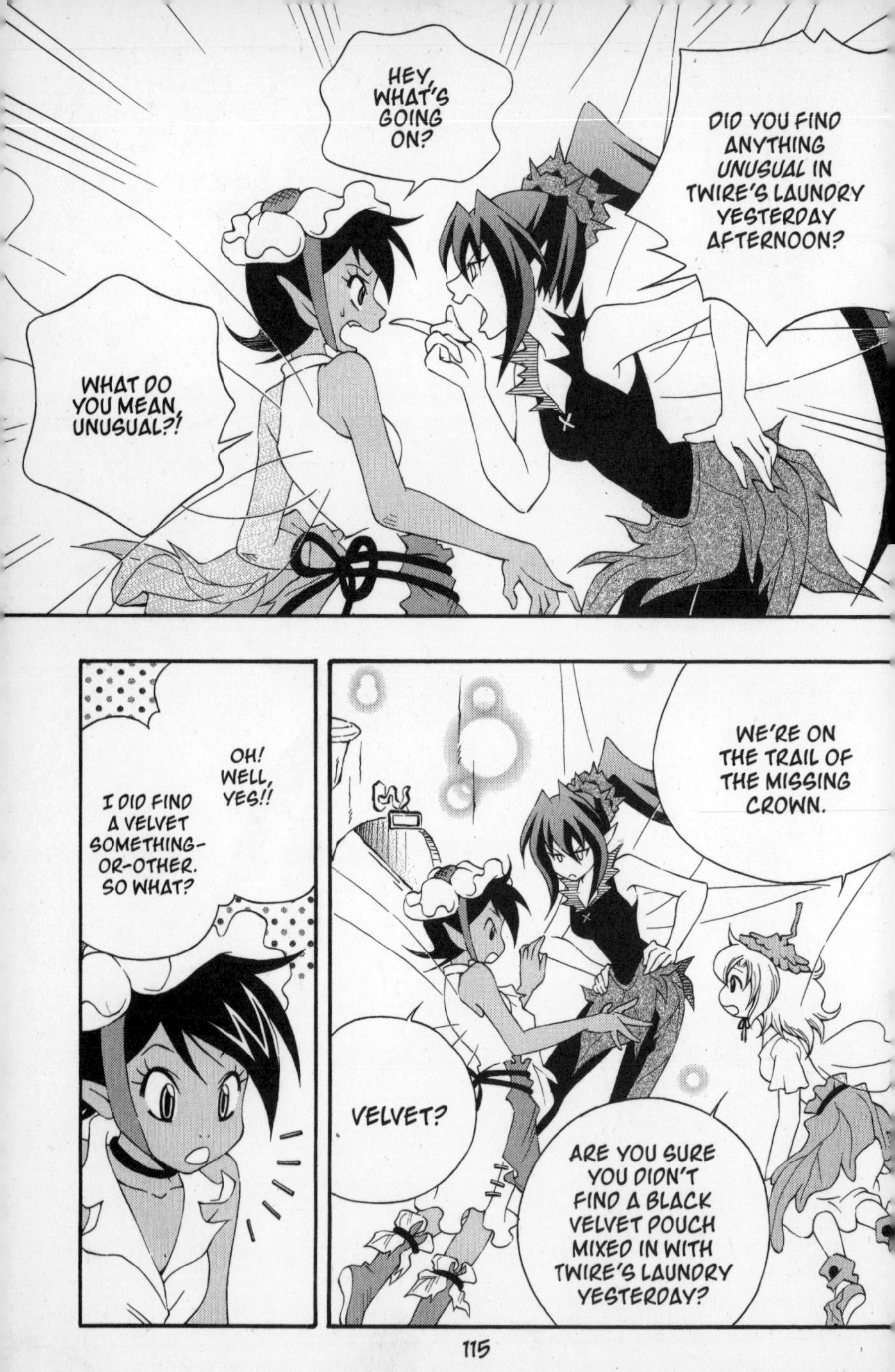
HEY, WHAT'S GOING ON?
DID YOU FIND ANYTHING UNUSUAL IN TWIRE'S LAUNDRY YESTERDAY AFTERNOON?
WHAT DO YOU MEAN, UNUSUAL?!
WE'RE ON THE TRAIL OF THE MISSING CROWN.
VELVET?
ARE YOU SURE YOU DIDN'T FIND A BLACK VELVET POUCH MIXED IN WITH TWIRE'S LAUNDRY YESTERDAY?
OH! WELL, YES!!
I DID FIND A VELVET SOMETHING-OR-OTHER. SO WHAT?

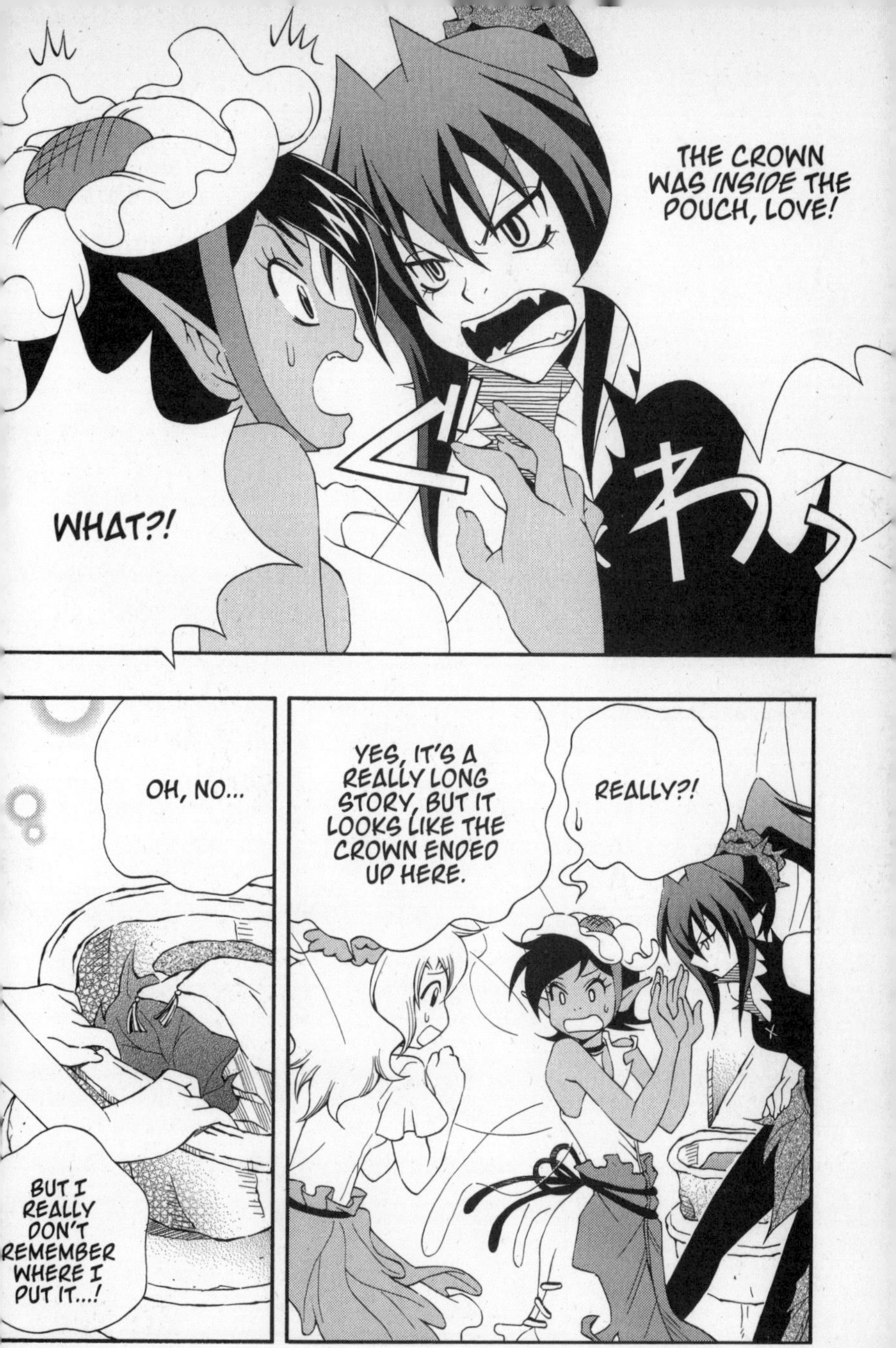
THE CROWN WAS INSIDE THE POUCH, LOVE!
くわっ
WHAT?!
REALLY?!
YES, IT'S A REALLY LONG STORY, BUT IT LOOKS LIKE THE CROWN ENDED UP HERE.
OH, NO...
BUT I REALLY DON'T REMEMBER WHERE I PUT IT...!

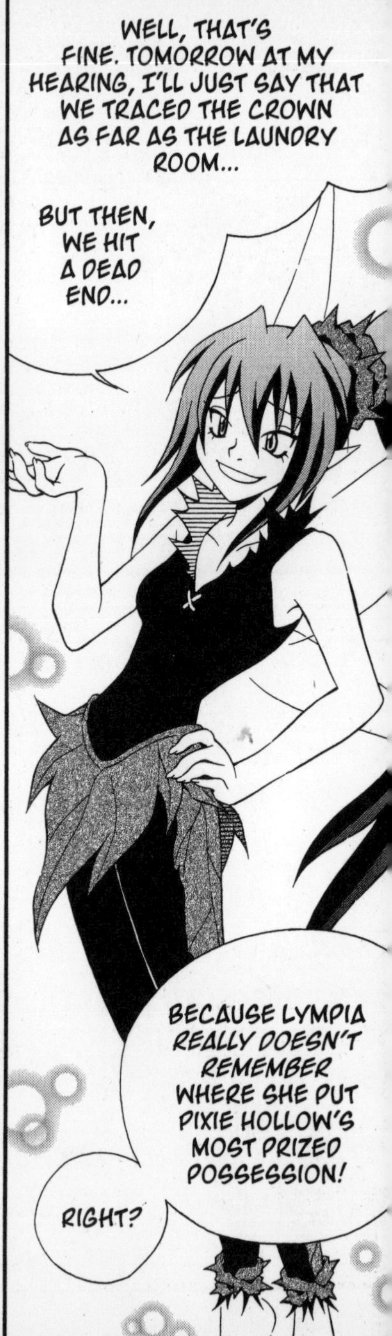
WELL, THAT'S FINE. TOMORROW AT MY HEARING, I'LL JUST SAY THAT WE TRACED THE CROWN AS FAR AS THE LAUNDRY ROOM...
BUT THEN, WE HIT A DEAD END...
BECAUSE LYMPIA REALLY DOESN'T REMEMBER WHERE SHE PUT PIXIE HOLLOW'S MOST PRIZED POSSESSION!
RIGHT?

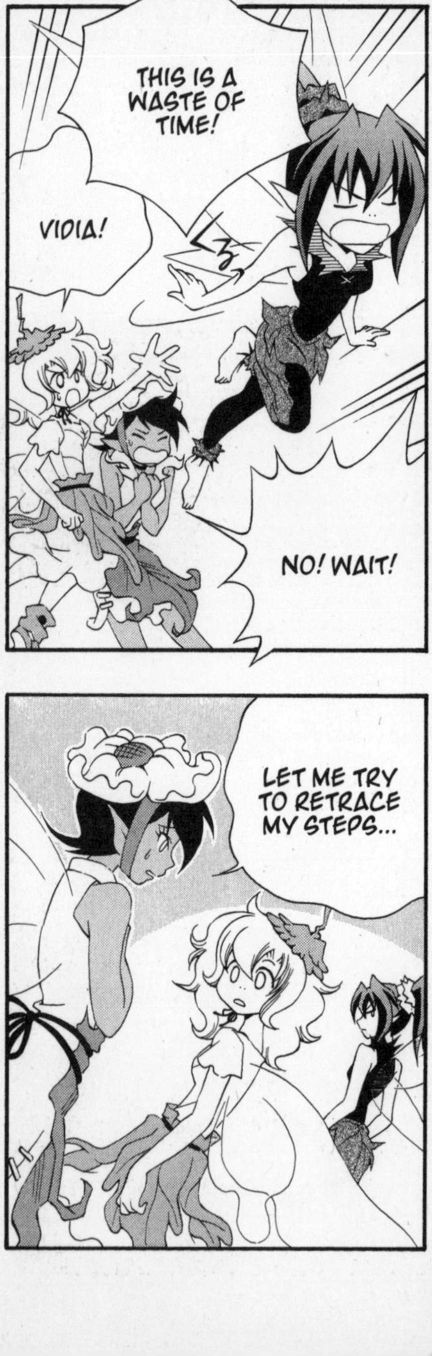
THIS IS A WASTE OF TIME!
VIDIA!
NO! WAIT!
LET ME TRY TO RETRACE MY STEPS...

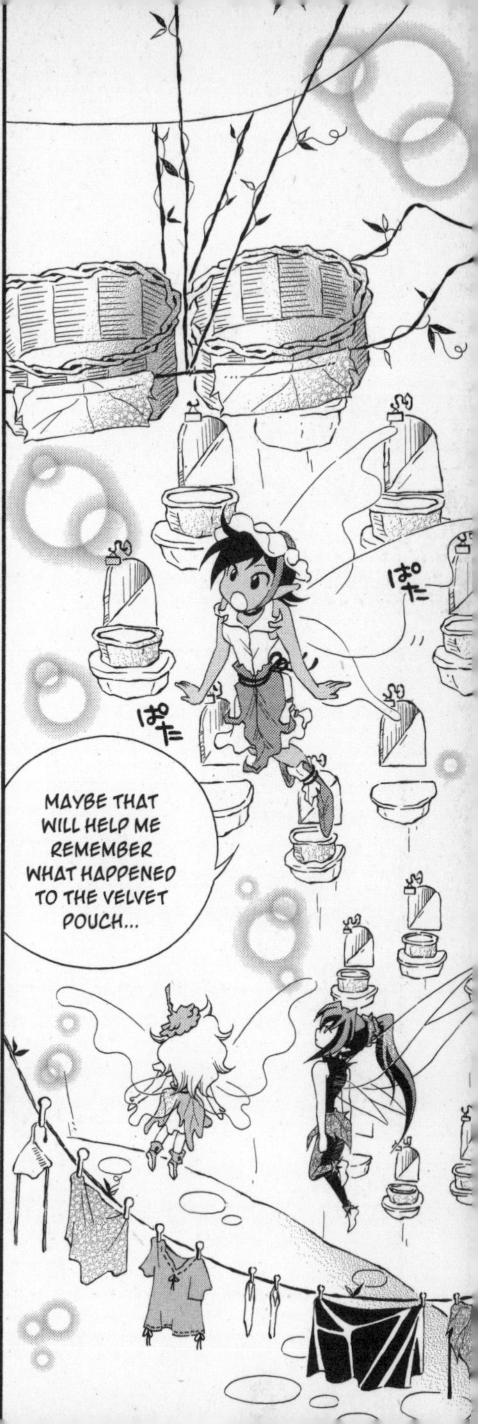
ぱた
ぱた
MAYBE THAT WILL HELP ME REMEMBER WHAT HAPPENED TO THE VELVET POUCH...
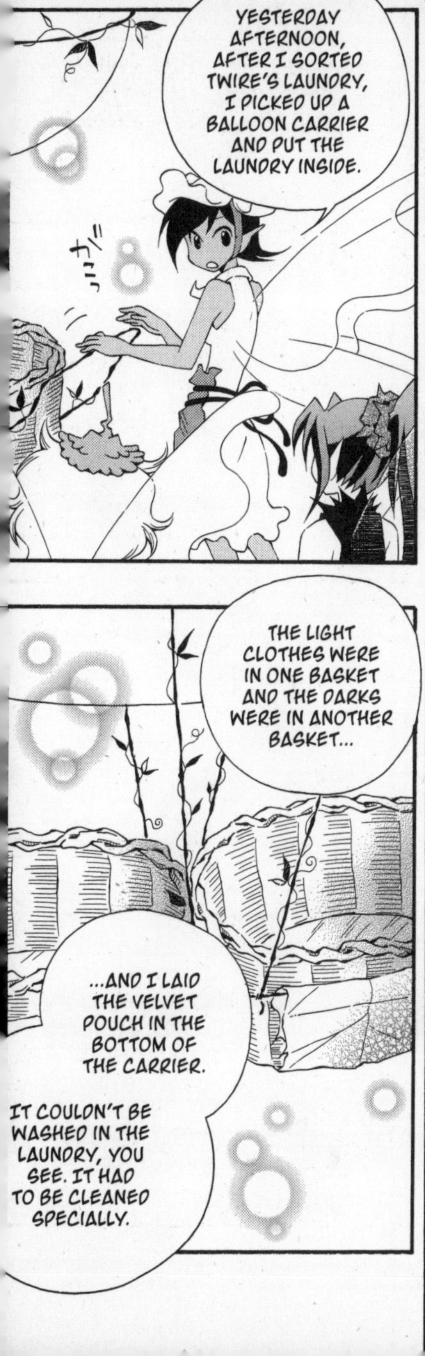
YESTERDAY AFTERNOON, AFTER I SORTED TWIRE'S LAUNDRY, I PICKED UP A BALLOON CARRIER AND PUT THE LAUNDRY INSIDE.
THE LIGHT CLOTHES WERE IN ONE BASKET AND THE DARKS WERE IN ANOTHER BASKET...
...AND I LAID THE VELVET POUCH IN THE BOTTOM OF THE CARRIER.
IT COULDN'T BE WASHED IN THE LAUNDRY, YOU SEE. IT HAD TO BE CLEANED SPECIALLY.

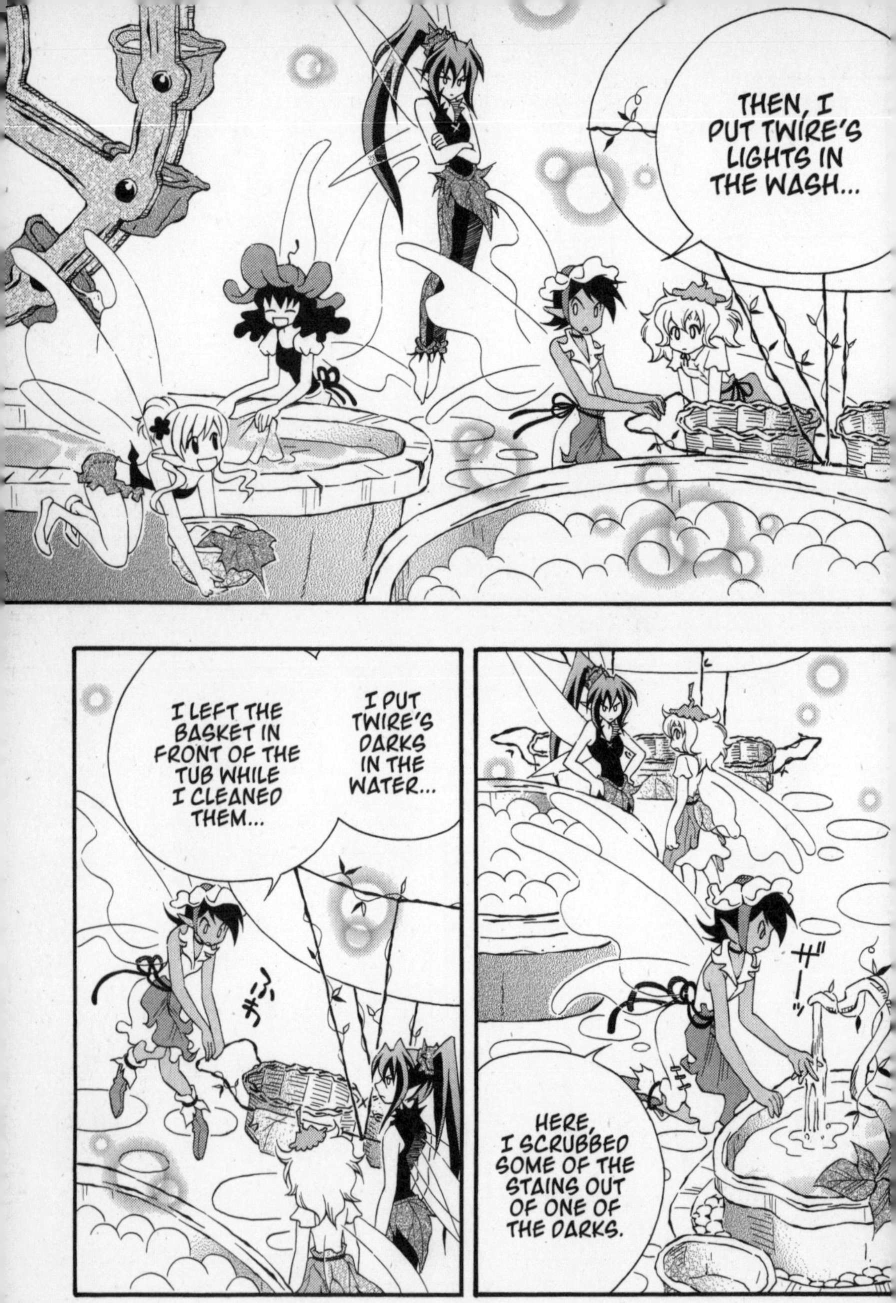
THEN, I PUT TWIRE'S LIGHTS IN THE WASH...
HERE, I SCRUBBED SOME OF THE STAINS OUT OF ONE OF THE DARKS.
I PUT TWIRE'S DARKS IN THE WATER...
I LEFT THE BASKET IN FRONT OF THE TUB WHILE I CLEANED THEM...

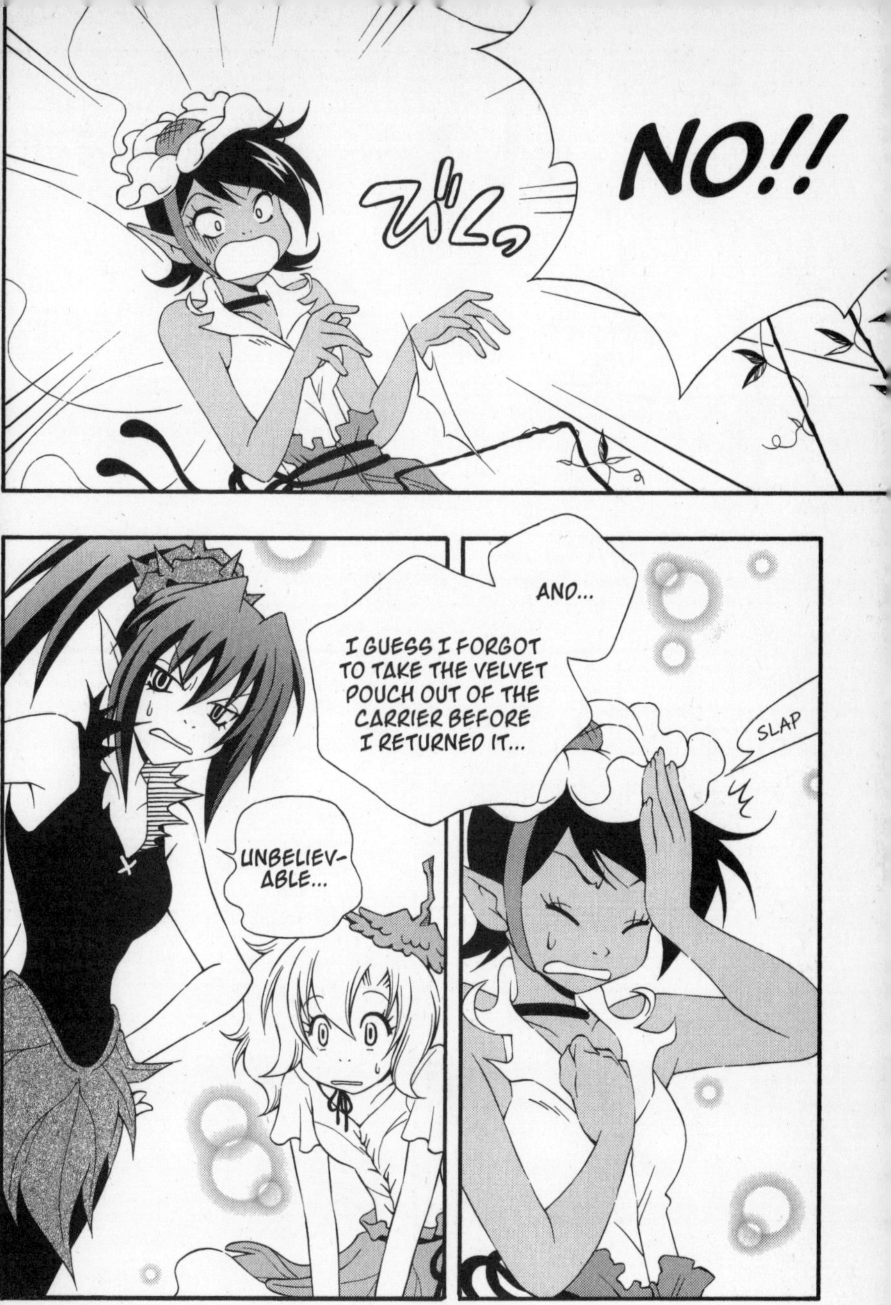
NO!!
びくっ
AND...
I GUESS I FORGOT TO TAKE THE VELVET POUCH OUT OF THE CARRIER BEFORE I RETURNED IT...
SLAP
UNBELIEV-ABLE...

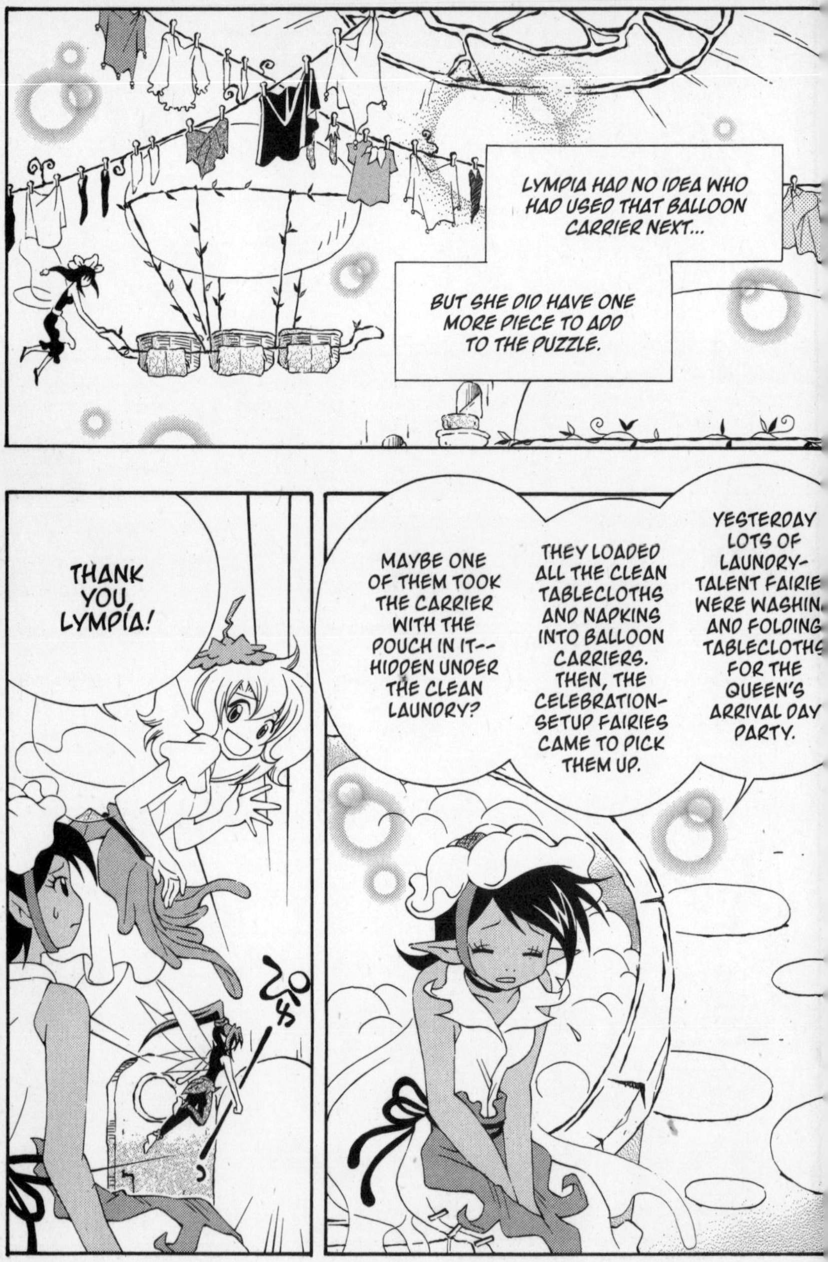
LYMPIA HAD NO IDEA WHO HAD USED THAT BALLOON CARRIER NEXT...
BUT SHE DID HAVE ONE MORE PIECE TO ADD TO THE PUZZLE.
YESTERDAY LOTS OF LAUNDRY-TALENT FAIRIE WERE WASHIN AND FOLDING TABLECLOTHS FOR THE QUEEN'S ARRIVAL DAY PARTY.
THEY LOADED ALL THE CLEAN TABLECLOTHS AND NAPKINS INTO BALLOON CARRIERS. THEN, THE CELEBRATION-SETUP FAIRIES CAME TO PICK THEM UP.
MAYBE ONE OF THEM TOOK THE CARRIER WITH THE POUCH IN IT--HIDDEN UNDER THE CLEAN LAUNDRY?
THANK YOU, LYMPIA!

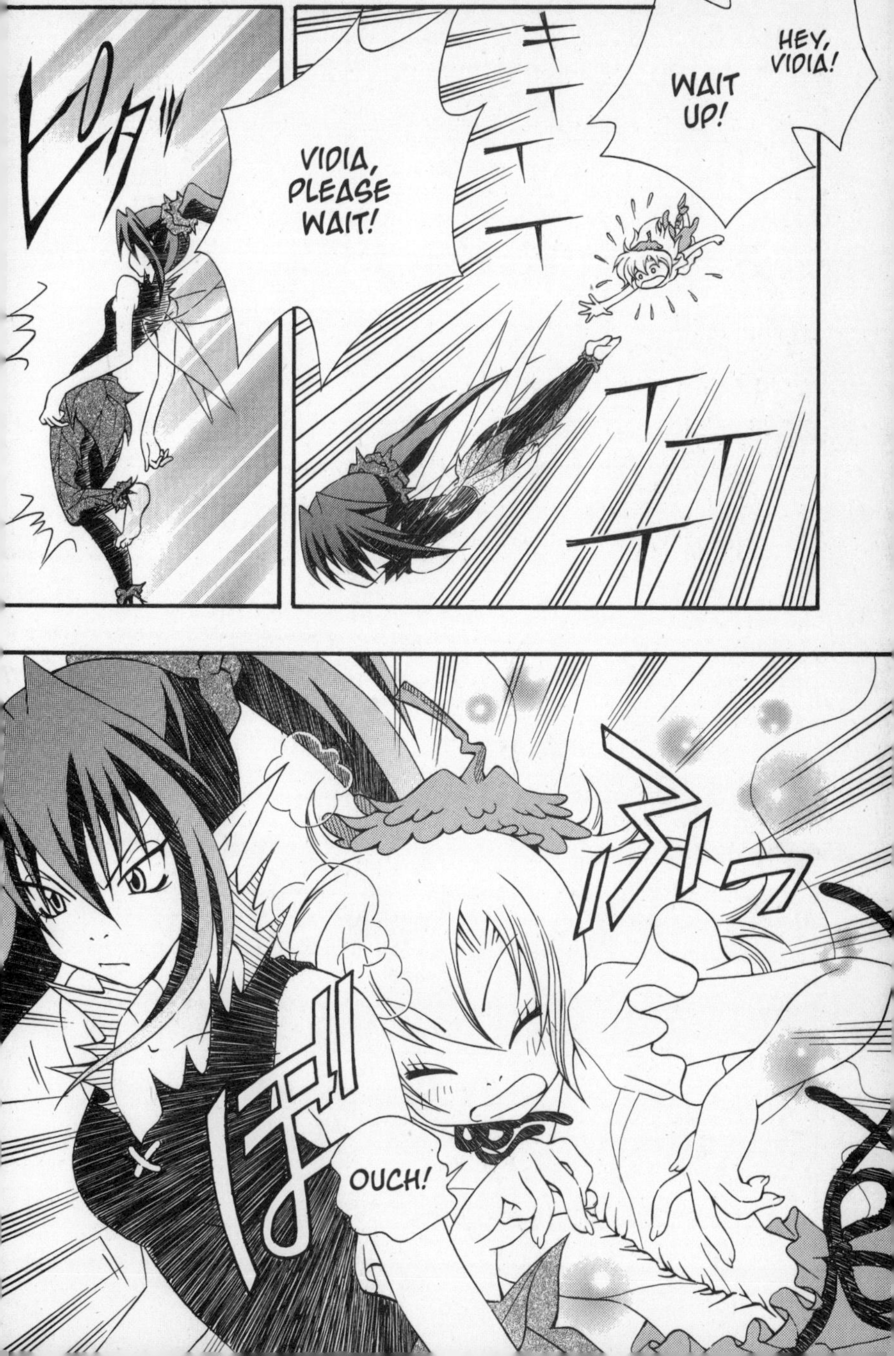
HEY, VIDIA!
WAIT UP!
VIDIA, PLEASE WAIT!
OUCH!

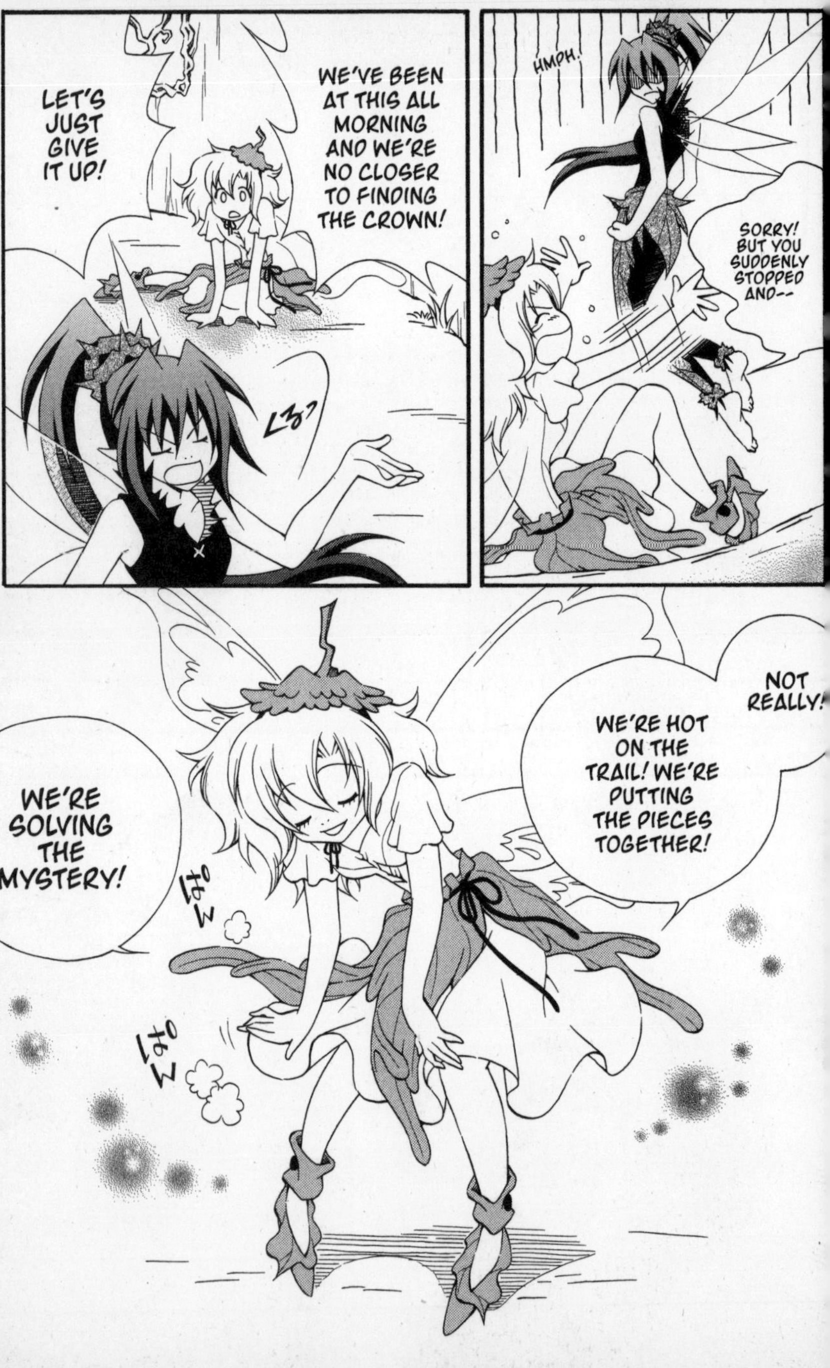
HMPH!
SORRY! BUT YOU SUDDENLY STOPPED AND--
WE'VE BEEN AT THIS ALL MORNING AND WE'RE NO CLOSER TO FINDING THE CROWN!
LET'S JUST GIVE IT UP!
NOT REALLY!
WE'RE HOT ON THE TRAIL! WE'RE PUTTING THE PIECES TOGETHER!
WE'RE SOLVING THE MYSTERY!

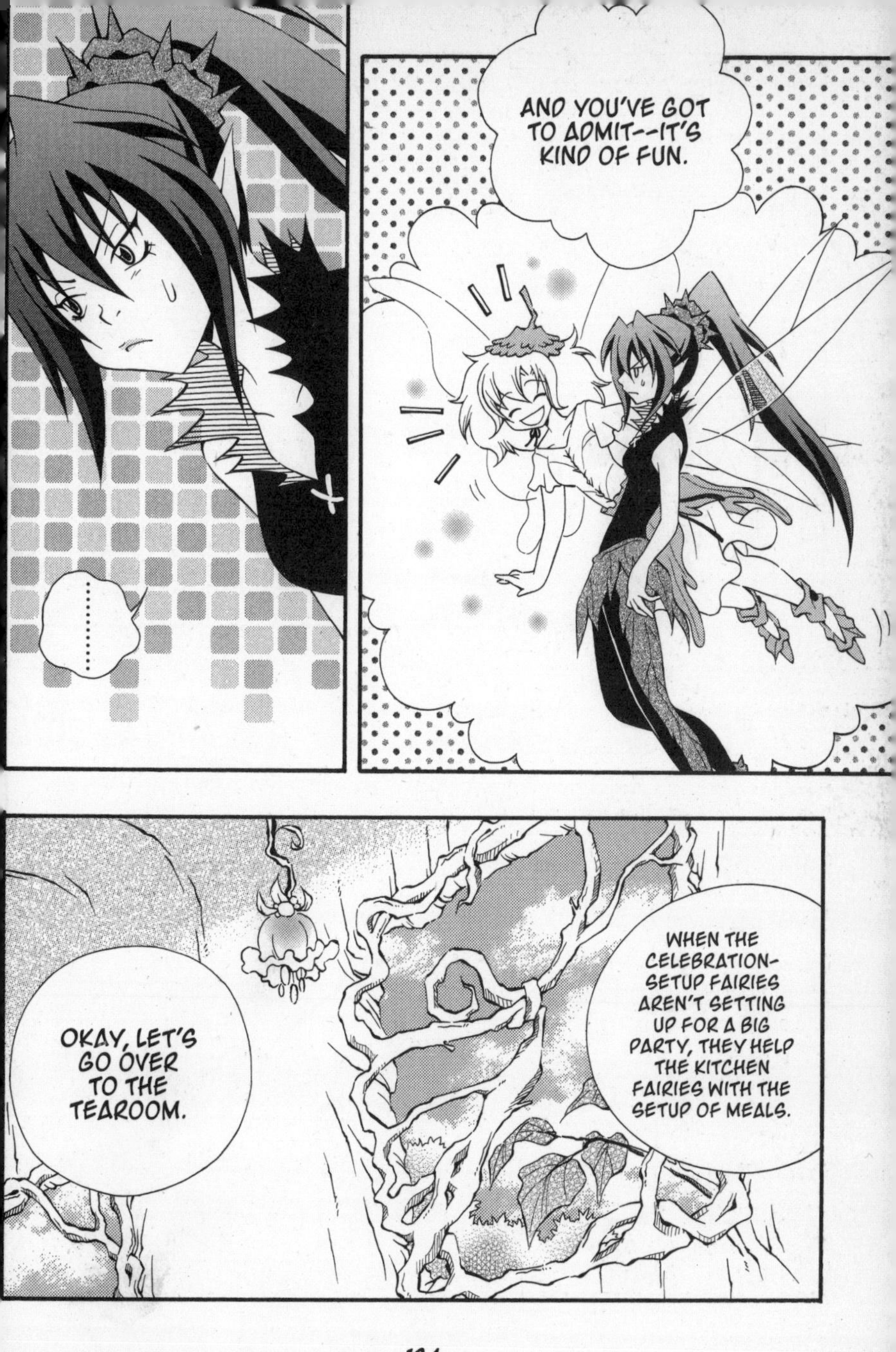
AND YOU'VE GOT TO ADMIT--IT'S KIND OF FUN.
......
WHEN THE CELEBRATION-SETUP FAIRIES AREN'T SETTING UP FOR A BIG PARTY, THEY HELP THE KITCHEN FAIRIES WITH THE SETUP OF MEALS.
OKAY, LET'S GO OVER TO THE TEAROOM.

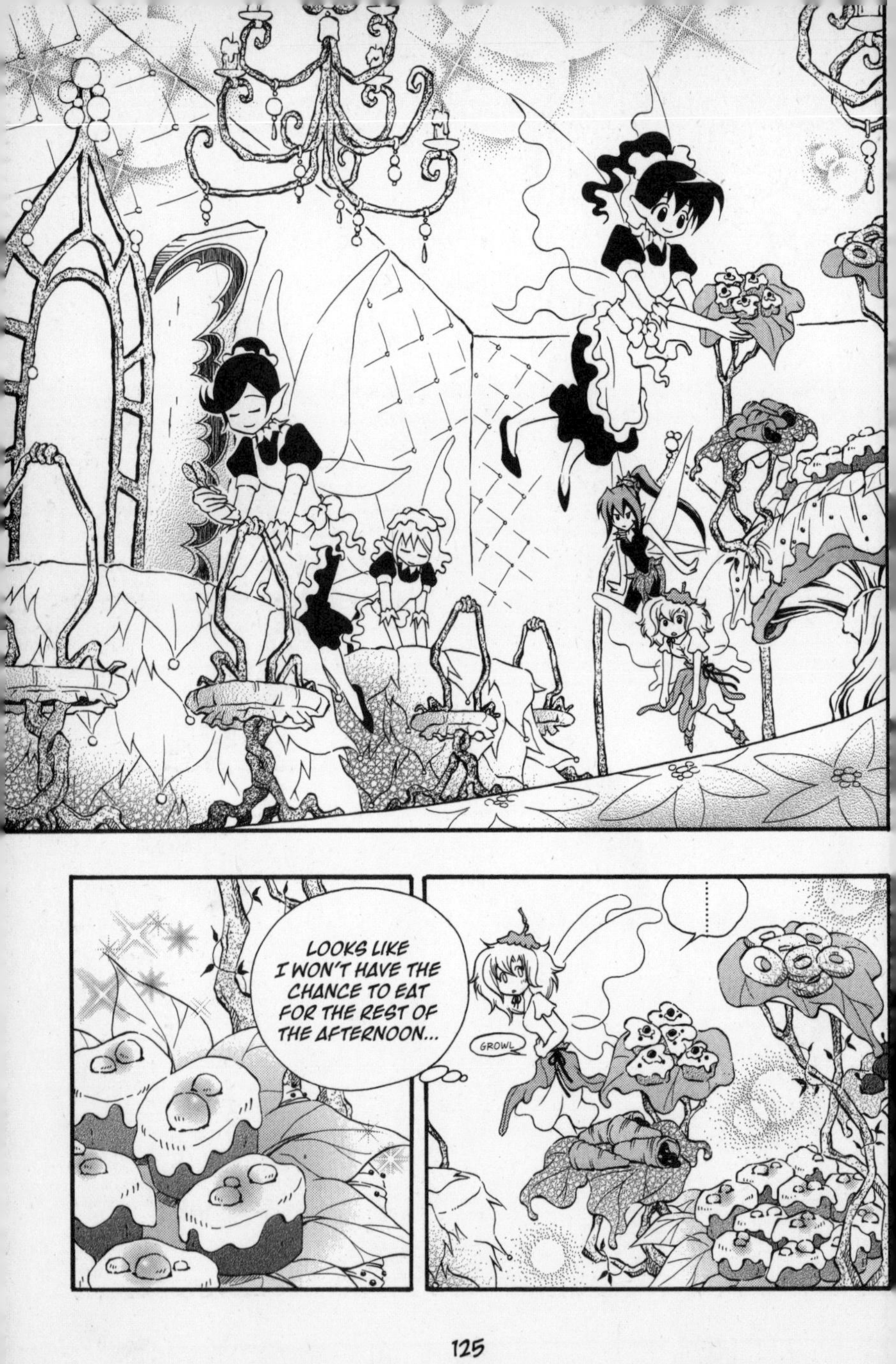
GROWL
LOOKS LIKE I WON'T HAVE THE CHANCE TO EAT FOR THE REST OF THE AFTERNOON...

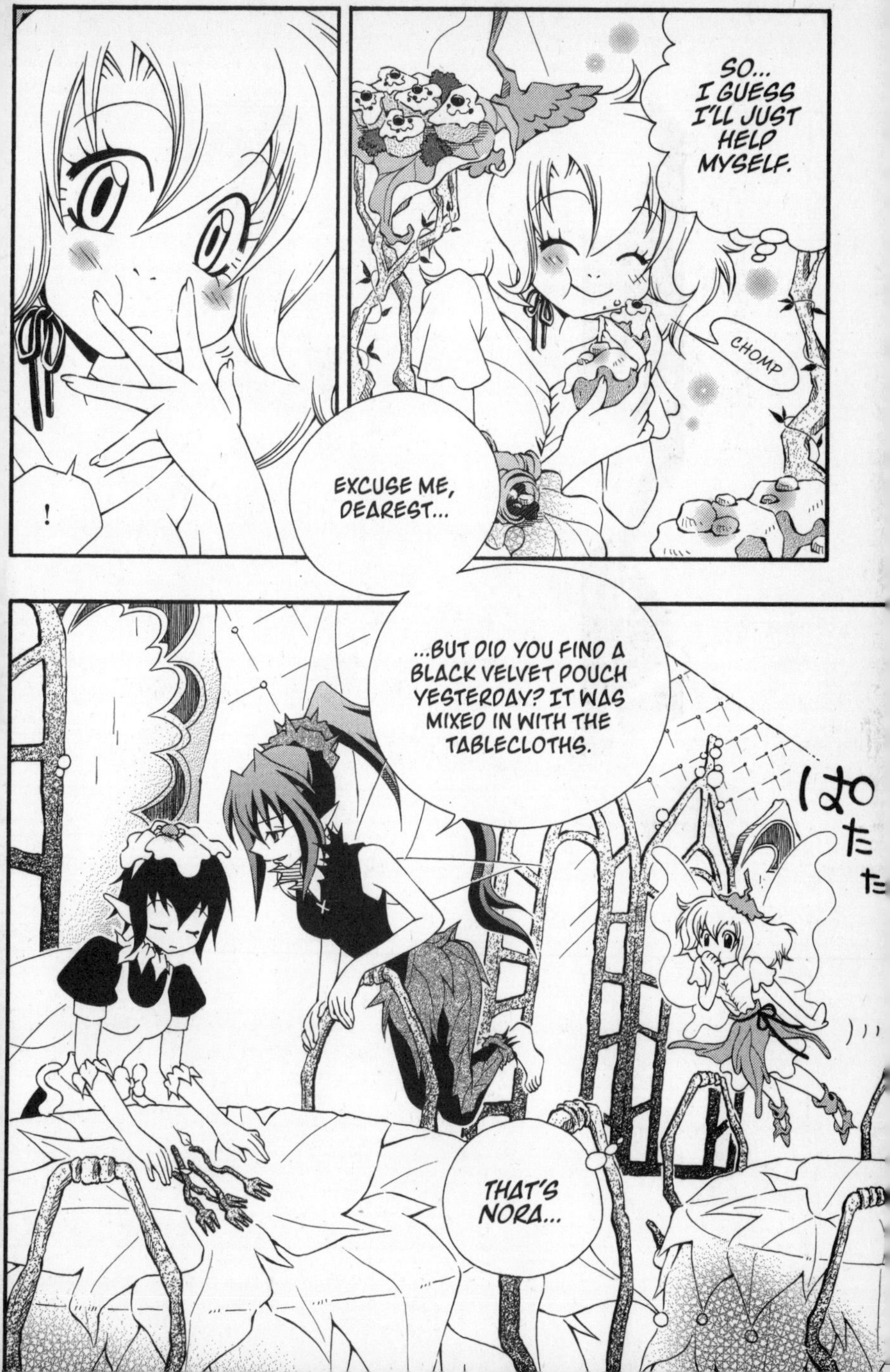
SO... I GUESS I'LL JUST HELP MYSELF.
CHOMP
!
ぱたた
EXCUSE ME, DEAREST...
...BUT DID YOU FIND A BLACK VELVET POUCH YESTERDAY? IT WAS MIXED IN WITH THE TABLECLOTHS.
THAT'S NORA...

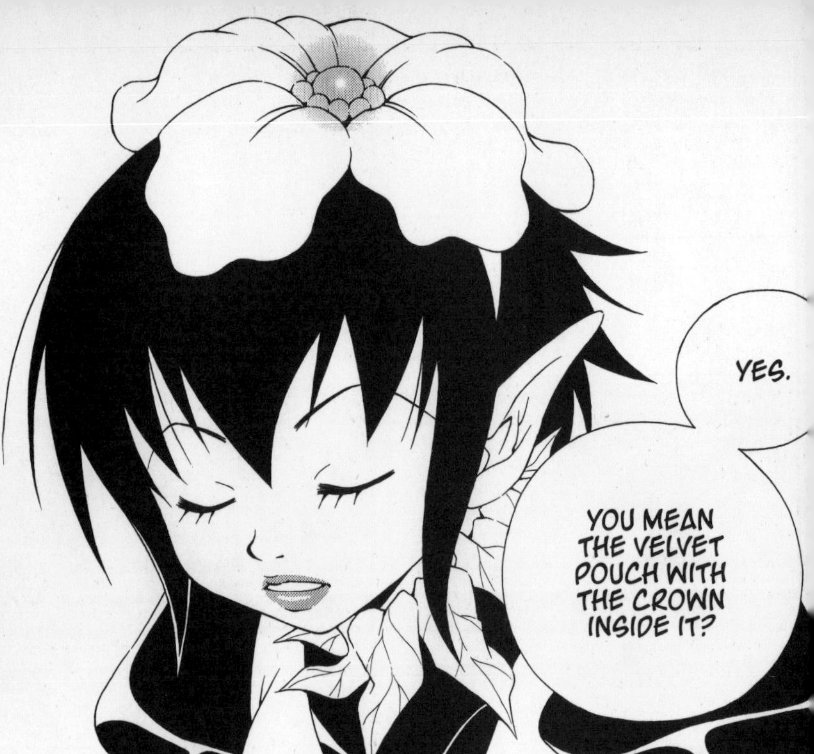
YES.
YOU MEAN THE VELVET POUCH WITH THE CROWN INSIDE IT?

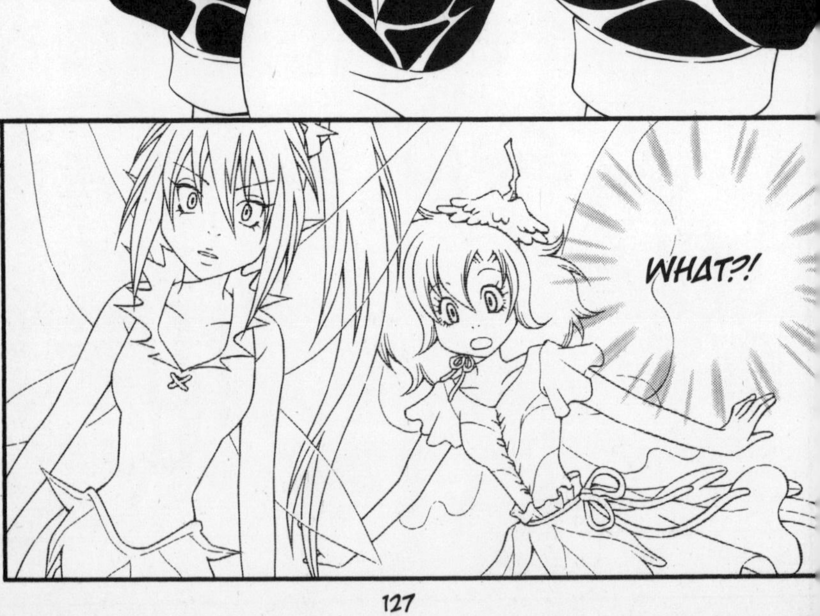
WHAT?!

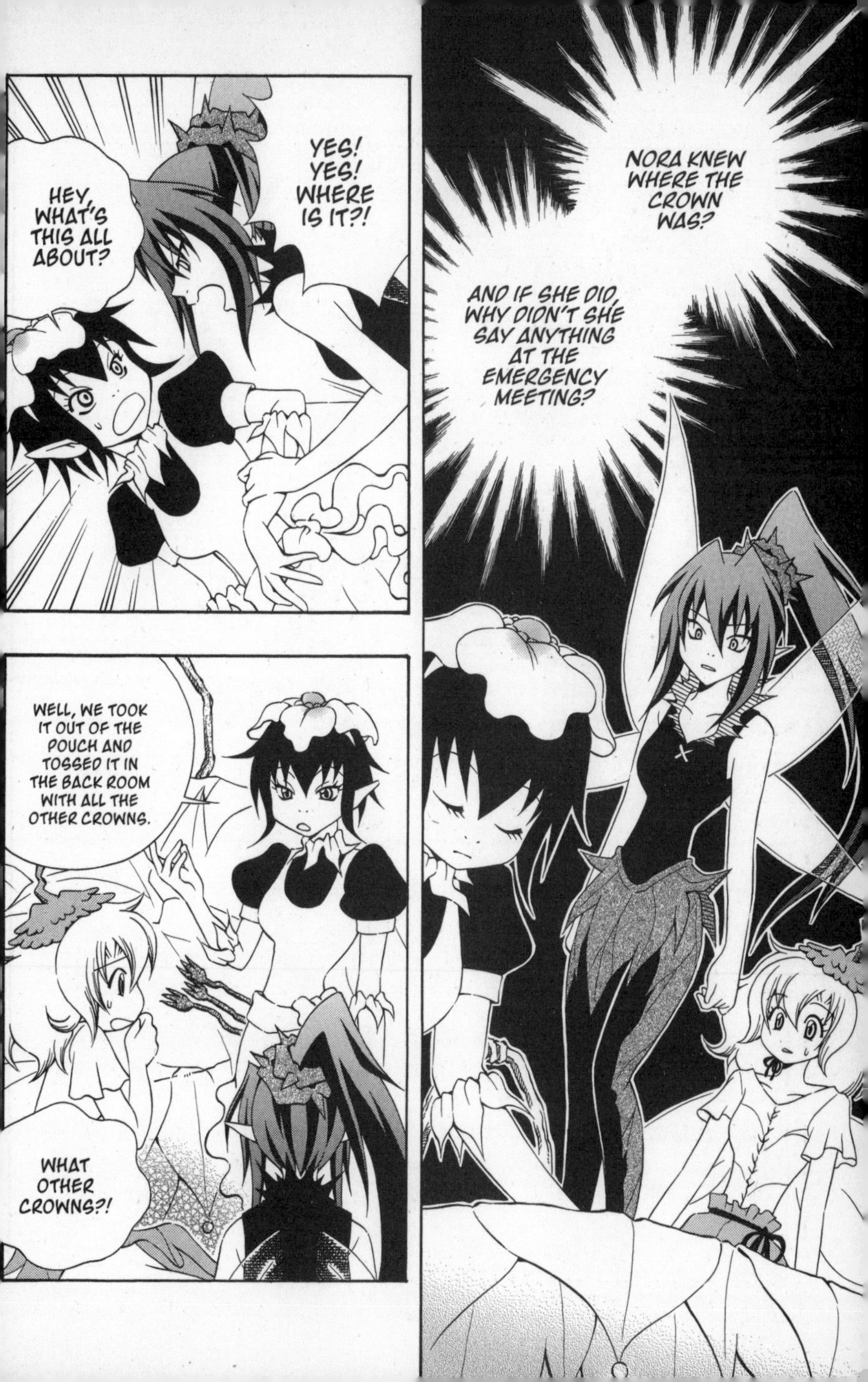
NORA KNEW WHERE THE CROWN WAS?
AND IF SHE DID, WHY DIDN'T SHE SAY ANYTHING AT THE EMERGENCY MEETING?
YES! YES! WHERE IS IT?!
HEY, WHAT'S THIS ALL ABOUT?
WELL, WE TOOK IT OUT OF THE POUCH AND TOSSED IT IN THE BACK ROOM WITH ALL THE OTHER CROWNS.
WHAT OTHER CROWNS?!

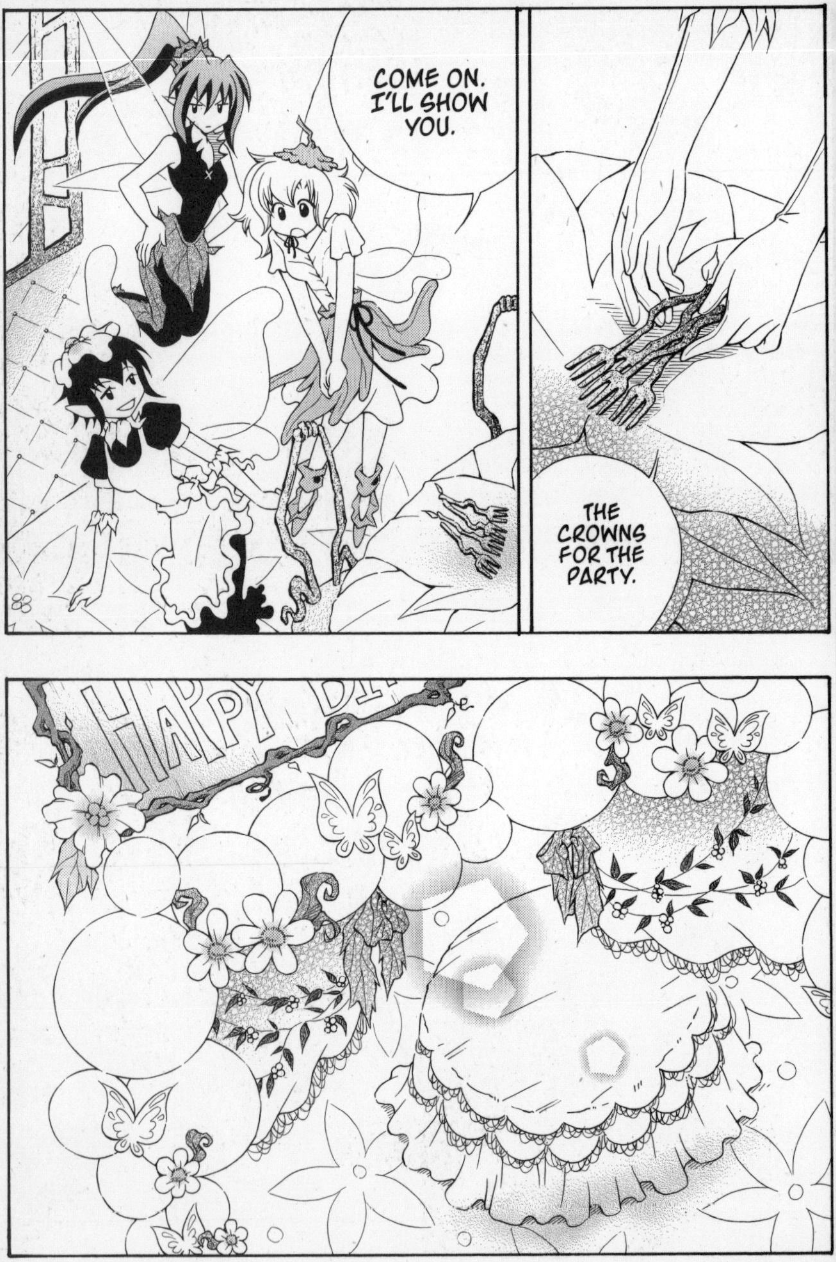
THE CROWNS FOR THE PARTY.
COME ON. I'LL SHOW YOU.
HAPPY

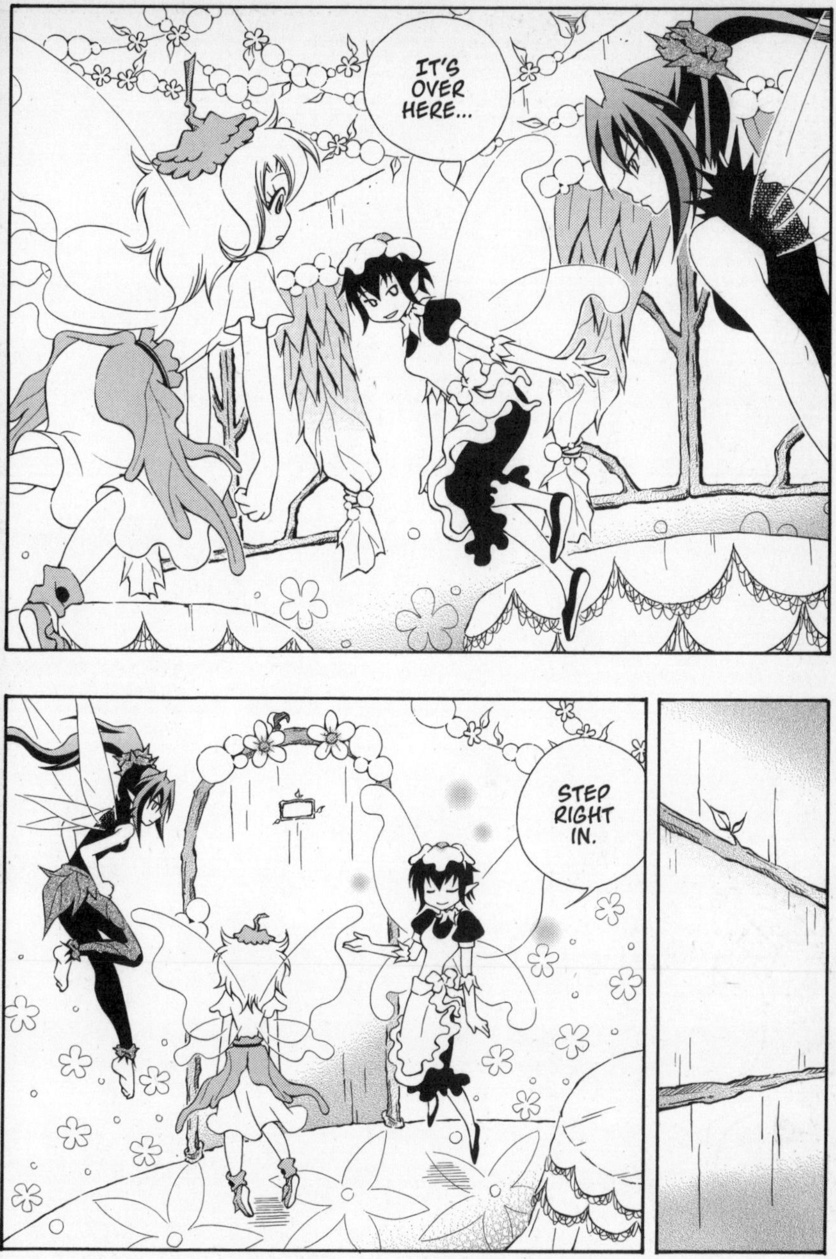
IT'S OVER HERE...
STEP RIGHT IN.

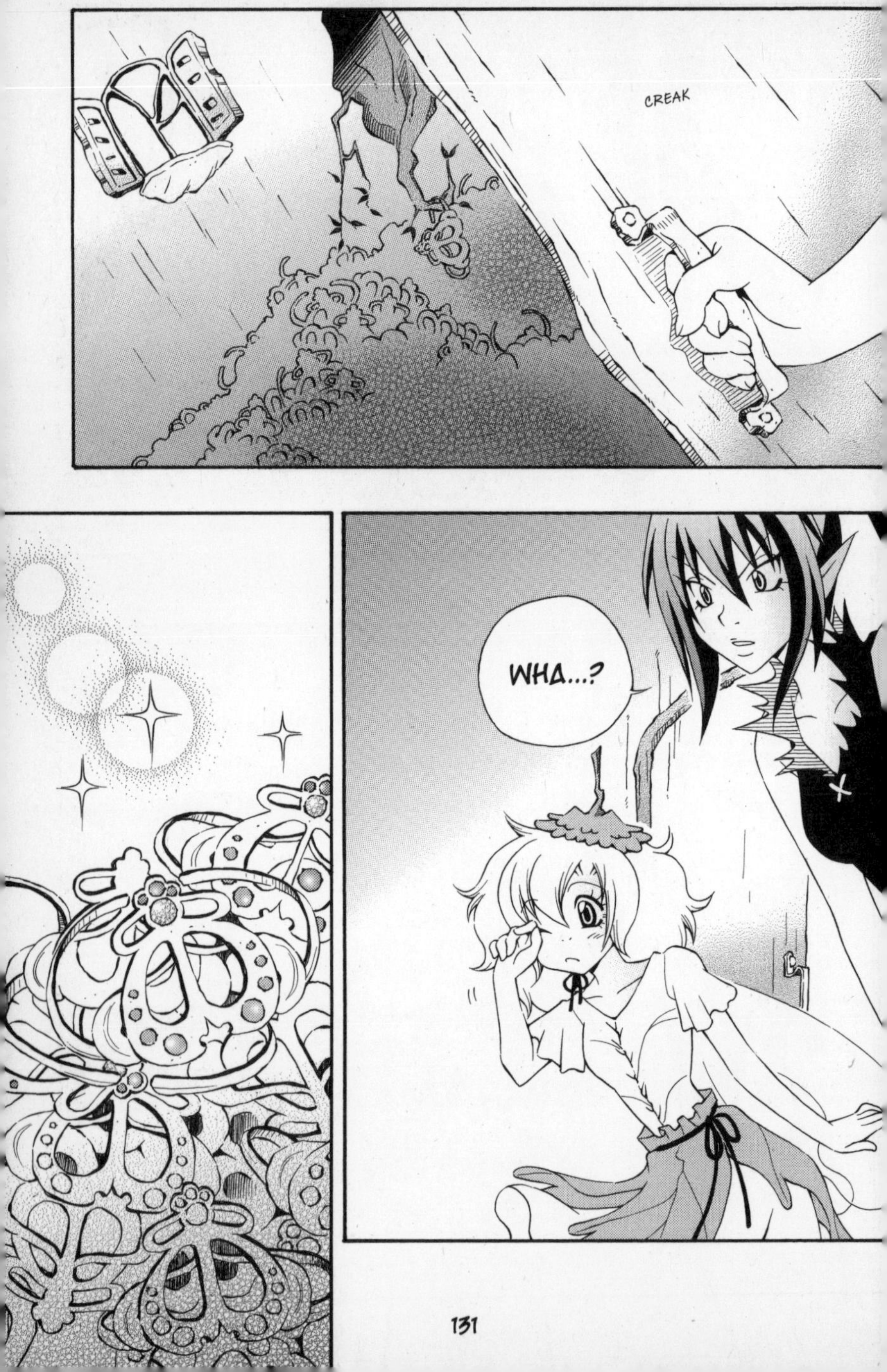
CREAK
WHA...?

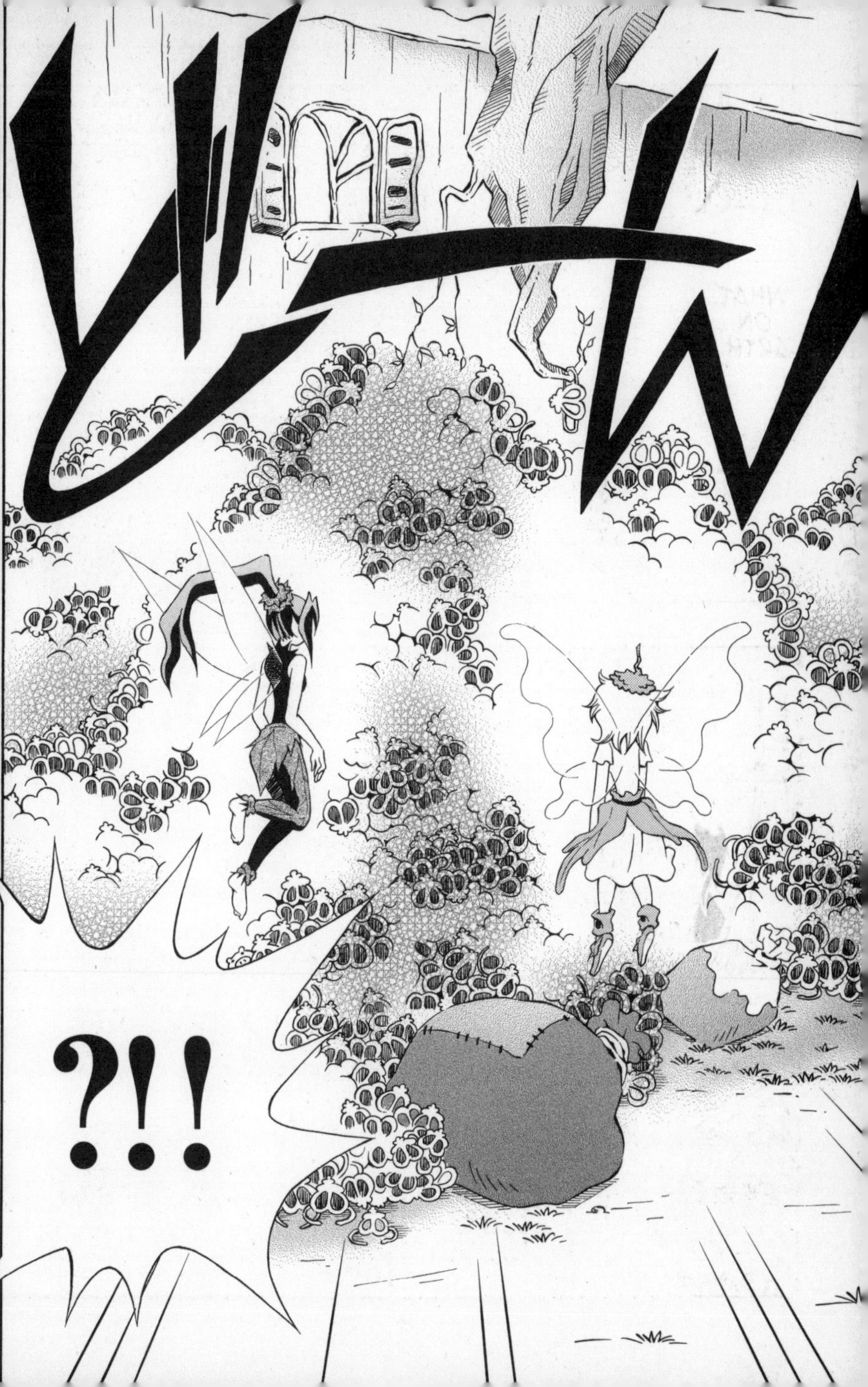
?!!

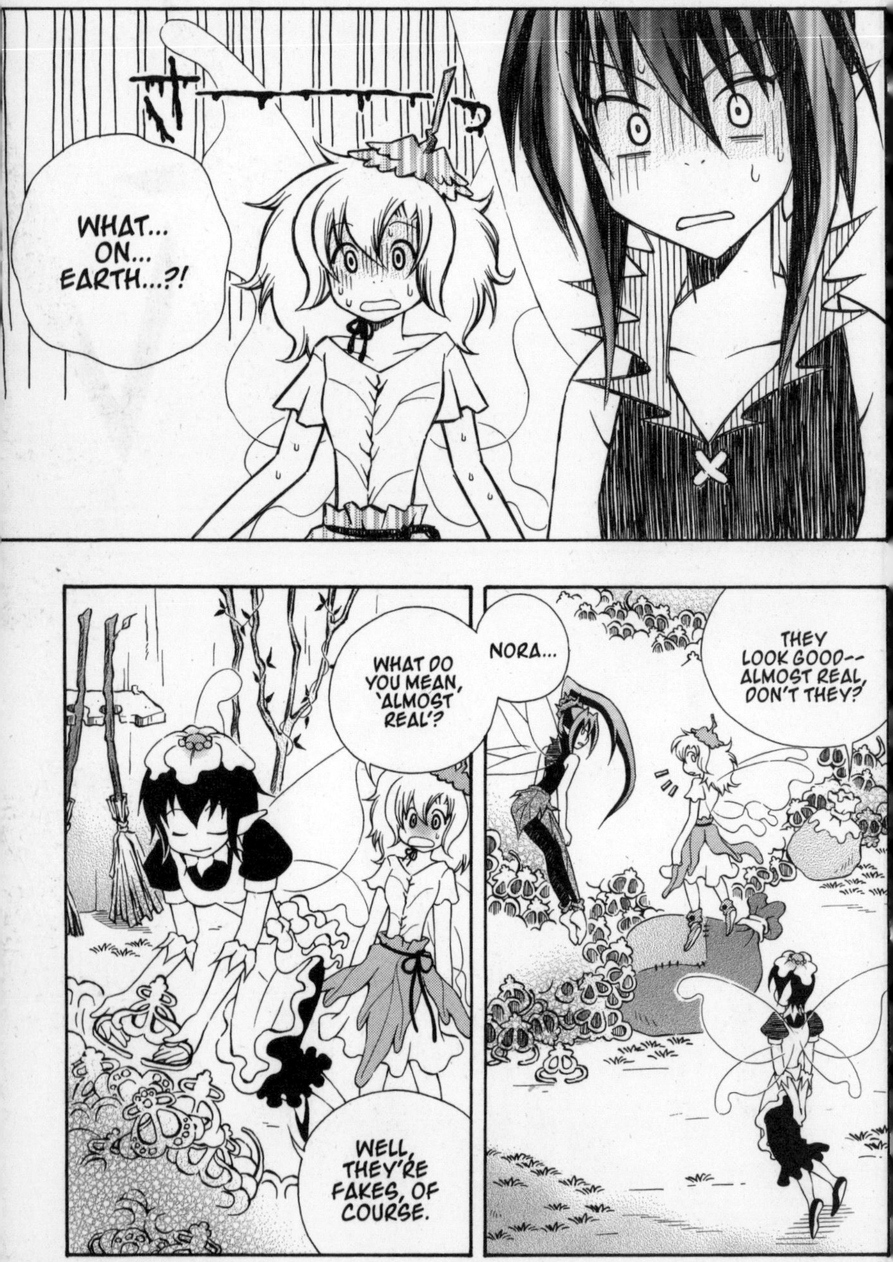
WHAT... ON... EARTH...?!
THEY LOOK GOOD-- ALMOST REAL, DON'T THEY?
NORA...
WHAT DO YOU MEAN, 'ALMOST REAL'?
WELL, THEY'RE FAKES, OF COURSE.

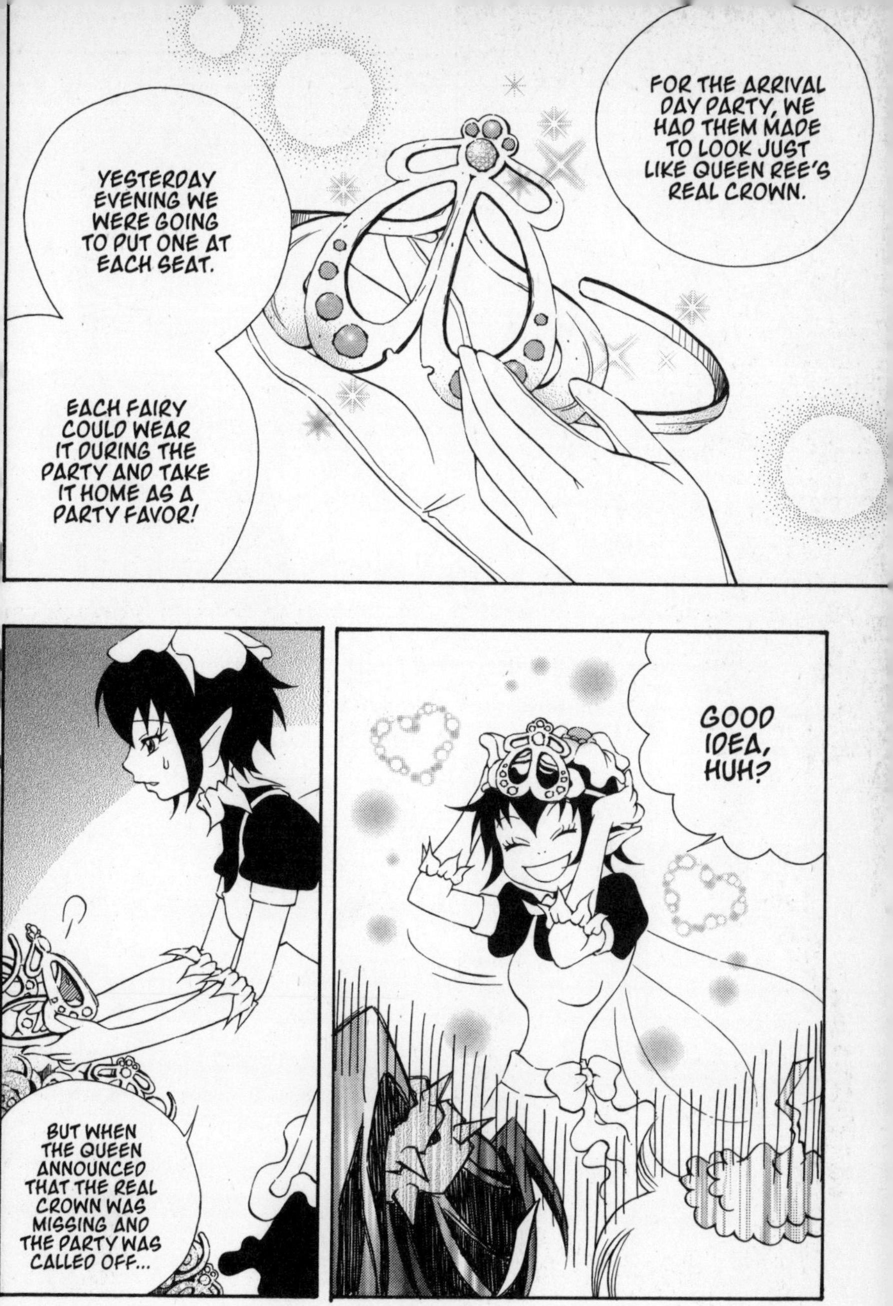
FOR THE ARRIVAL DAY PARTY, WE HAD THEM MADE TO LOOK JUST LIKE QUEEN REE'S REAL CROWN.
YESTERDAY EVENING WE WERE GOING TO PUT ONE AT EACH SEAT.
EACH FAIRY COULD WEAR IT DURING THE PARTY AND TAKE IT HOME AS A PARTY FAVOR!
GOOD IDEA, HUH?
BUT WHEN THE QUEEN ANNOUNCED THAT THE REAL CROWN WAS MISSING AND THE PARTY WAS CALLED OFF...

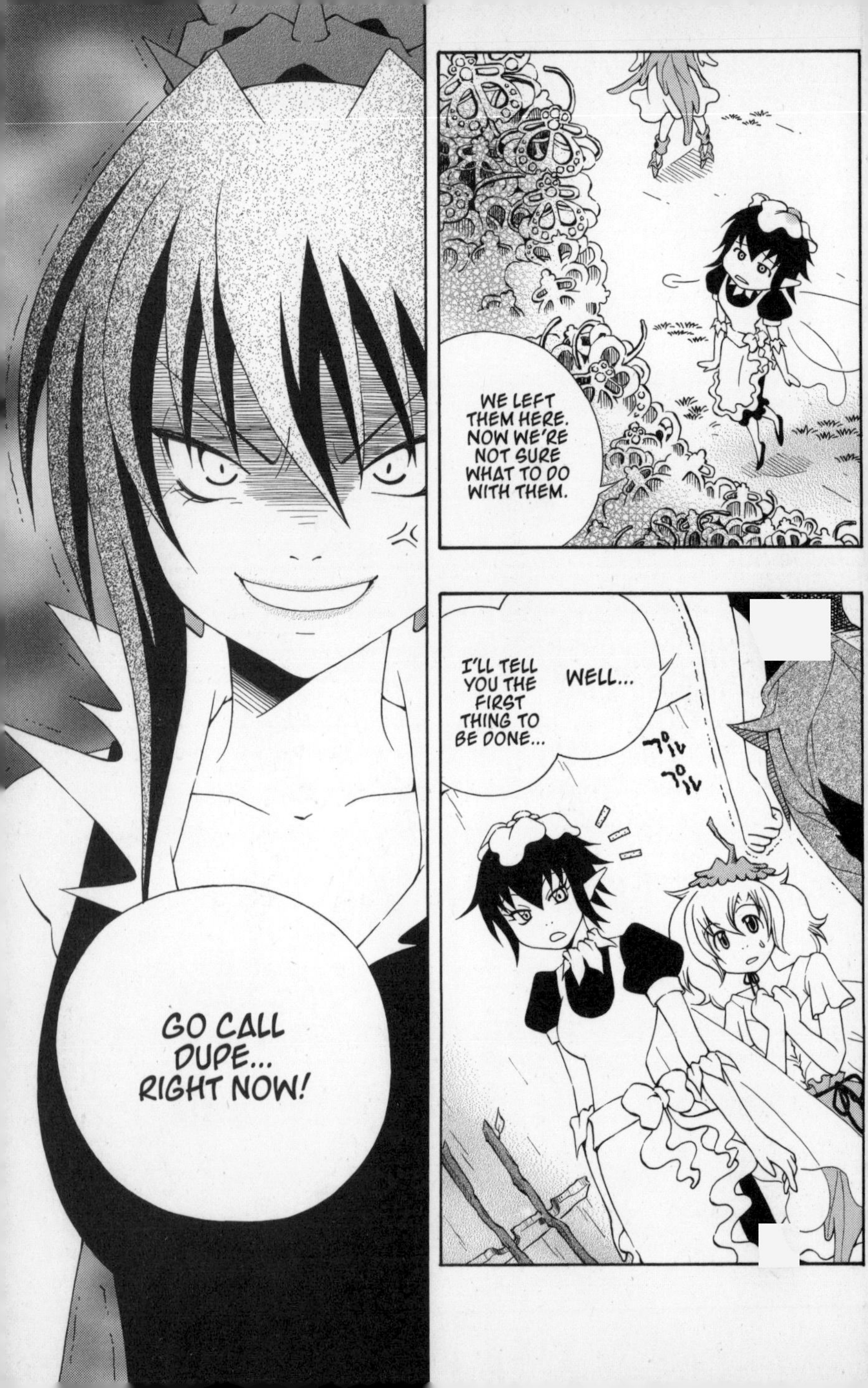
WE LEFT THEM HERE. NOW WE'RE NOT SURE WHAT TO DO WITH THEM.
WELL...
I'LL TELL YOU THE FIRST THING TO BE DONE...
プル
プル
GO CALL DUPE... RIGHT NOW!

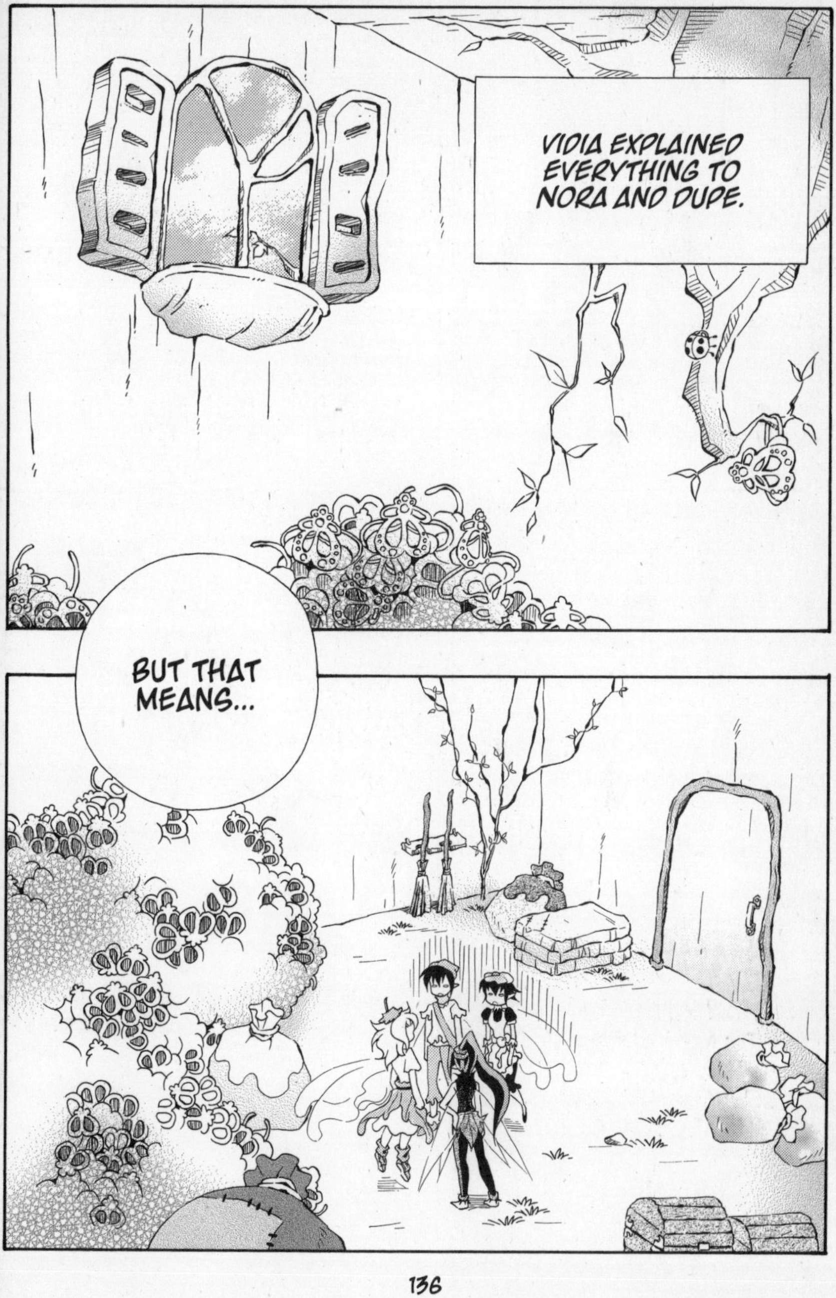
VIDIA EXPLAINED EVERYTHING TO NORA AND DUPE.
BUT THAT MEANS...

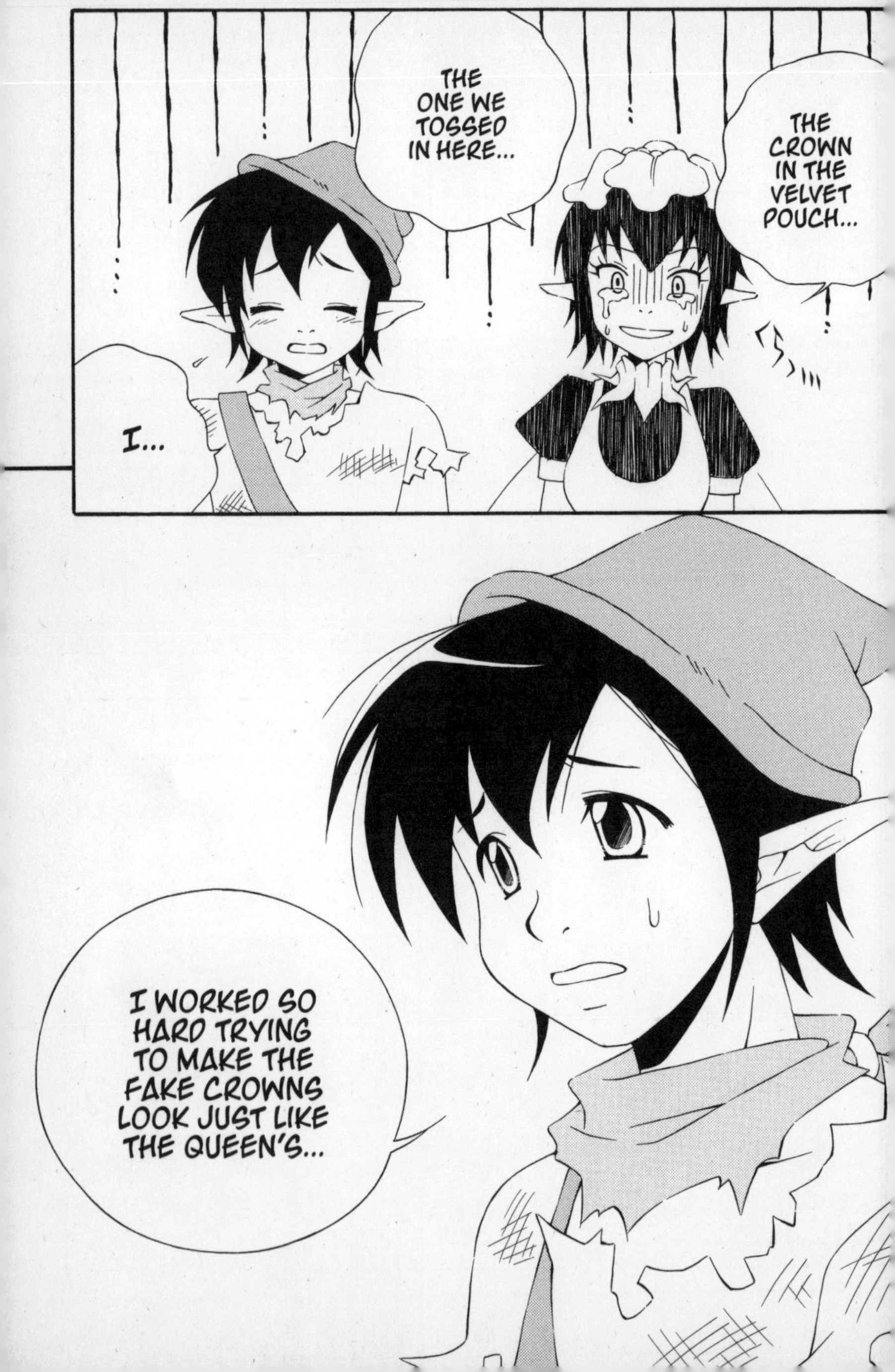
THE CROWN IN THE VELVET POUCH...
THE ONE WE TOSSED IN HERE...
I...
I WORKED SO HARD TRYING TO MAKE THE FAKE CROWNS LOOK JUST LIKE THE QUEEN'S...

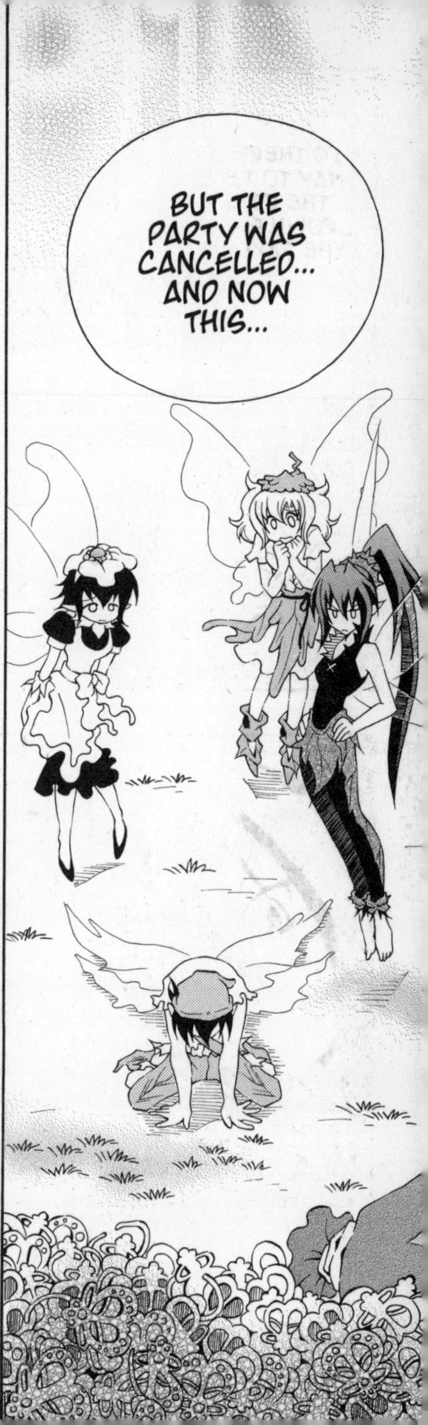
BUT THE PARTY WAS CANCELLED... AND NOW THIS...

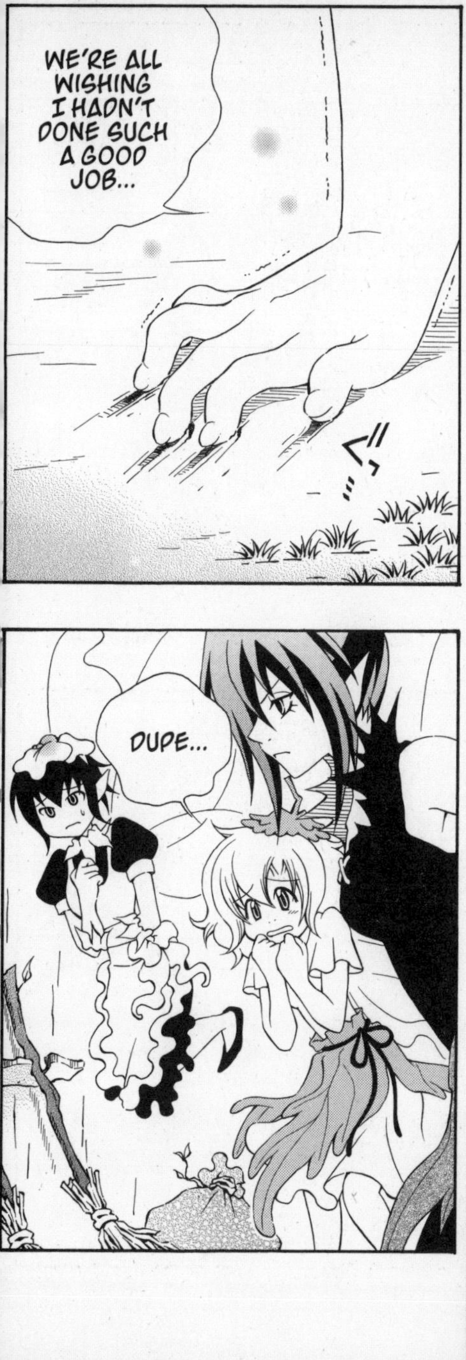
WE'RE ALL WISHING I HADN'T DONE SUCH A GOOD JOB...
DUPE...

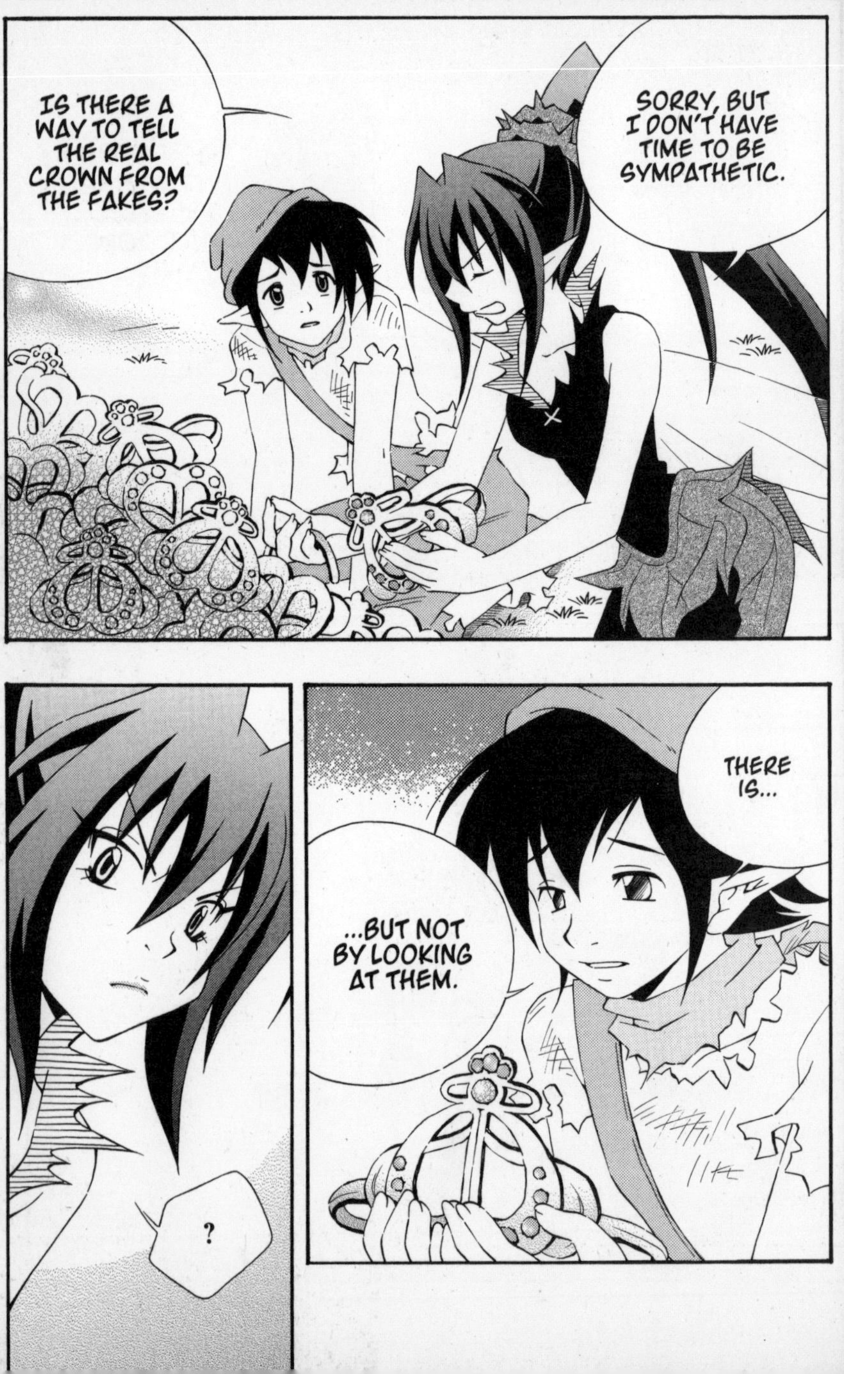
SORRY, BUT I DON'T HAVE TIME TO BE SYMPATHETIC.
IS THERE A WAY TO TELL THE REAL CROWN FROM THE FAKES?
THERE IS...
...BUT NOT BY LOOKING AT THEM.
?

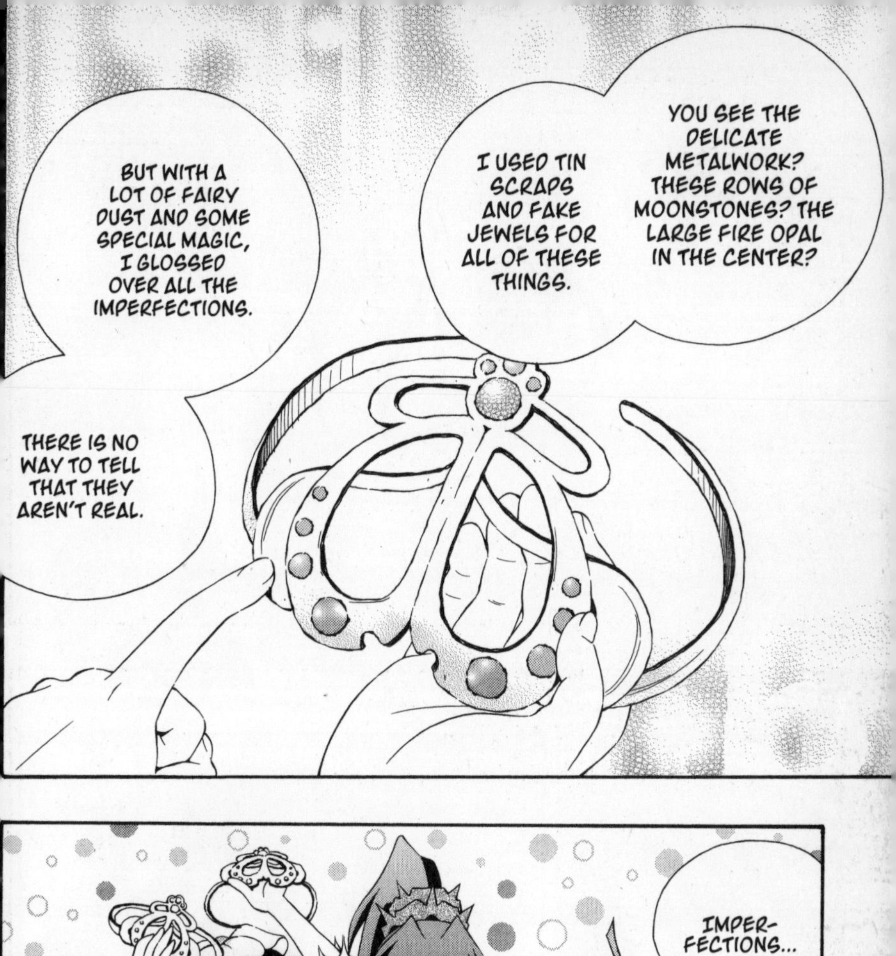
YOU SEE THE DELICATE METALWORK? THESE ROWS OF MOONSTONES? THE LARGE FIRE OPAL IN THE CENTER?
I USED TIN SCRAPS AND FAKE JEWELS FOR ALL OF THESE THINGS.
BUT WITH A LOT OF FAIRY DUST AND SOME SPECIAL MAGIC, I GLOSSED OVER ALL THE IMPERFECTIONS.
THERE IS NO WAY TO TELL THAT THEY AREN'T REAL.

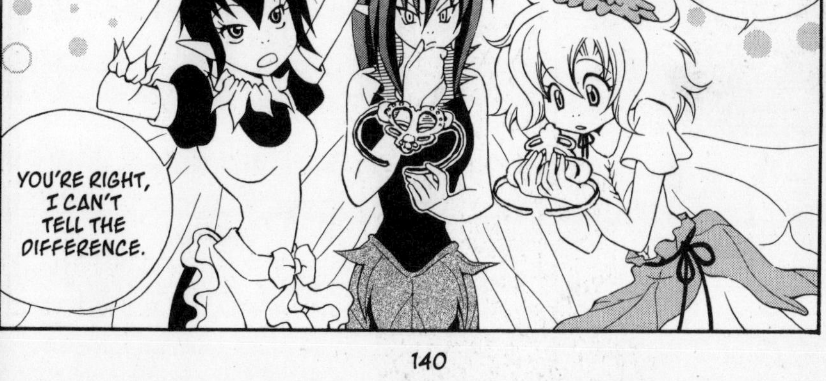
IMPER-FECTIONS...
YOU'RE RIGHT, I CAN'T TELL THE DIFFERENCE.

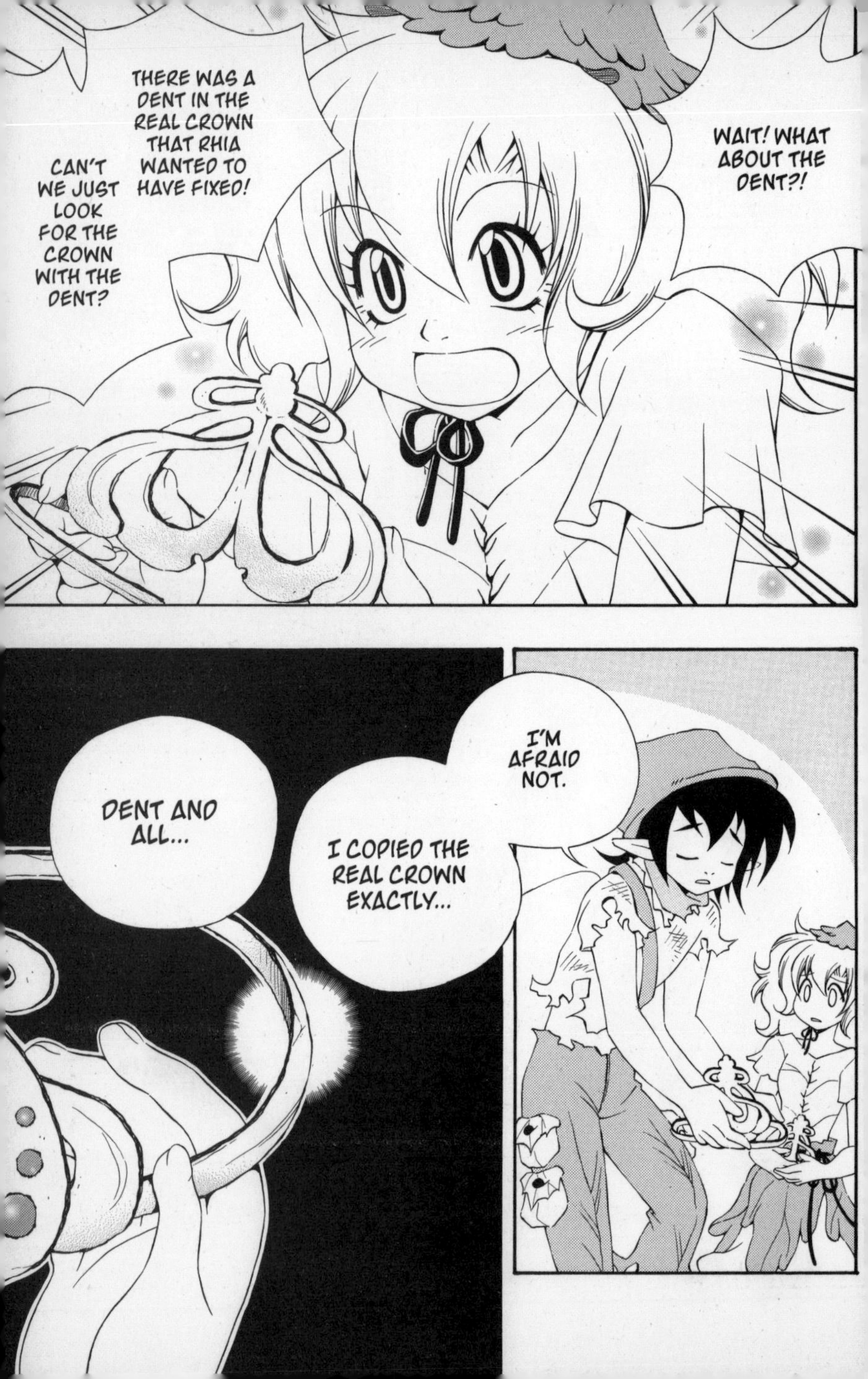
WAIT! WHAT ABOUT THE DENT?!
THERE WAS A DENT IN THE REAL CROWN THAT RHIA WANTED TO HAVE FIXED!
CAN'T WE JUST LOOK FOR THE CROWN WITH THE DENT?
I'M AFRAID NOT.
I COPIED THE REAL CROWN EXACTLY...
DENT AND ALL...

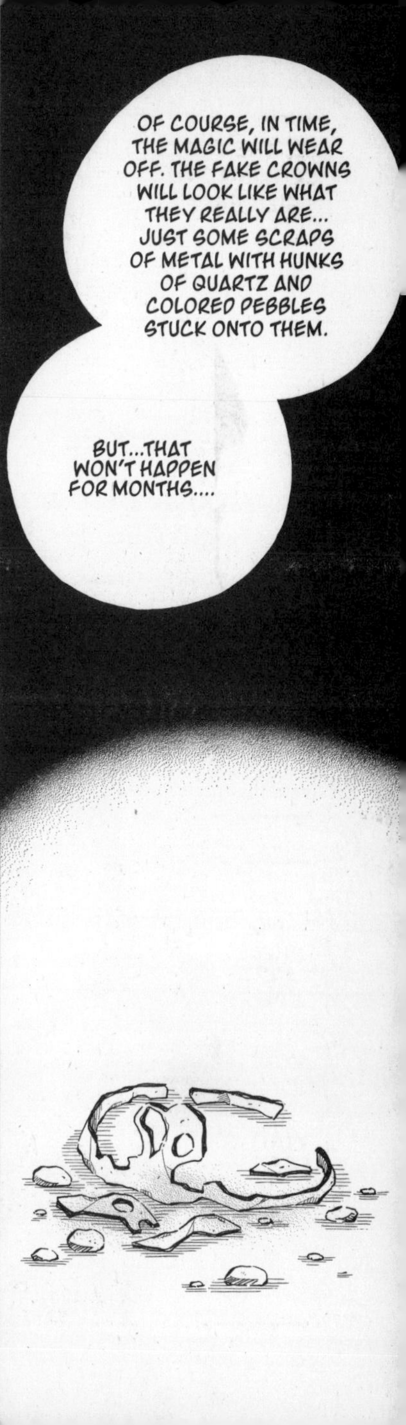
OF COURSE, IN TIME, THE MAGIC WILL WEAR OFF. THE FAKE CROWNS WILL LOOK LIKE WHAT THEY REALLY ARE... JUST SOME SCRAPS OF METAL WITH HUNKS OF QUARTZ AND COLORED PEBBLES STUCK ONTO THEM.
BUT...THAT WON'T HAPPEN FOR MONTHS....

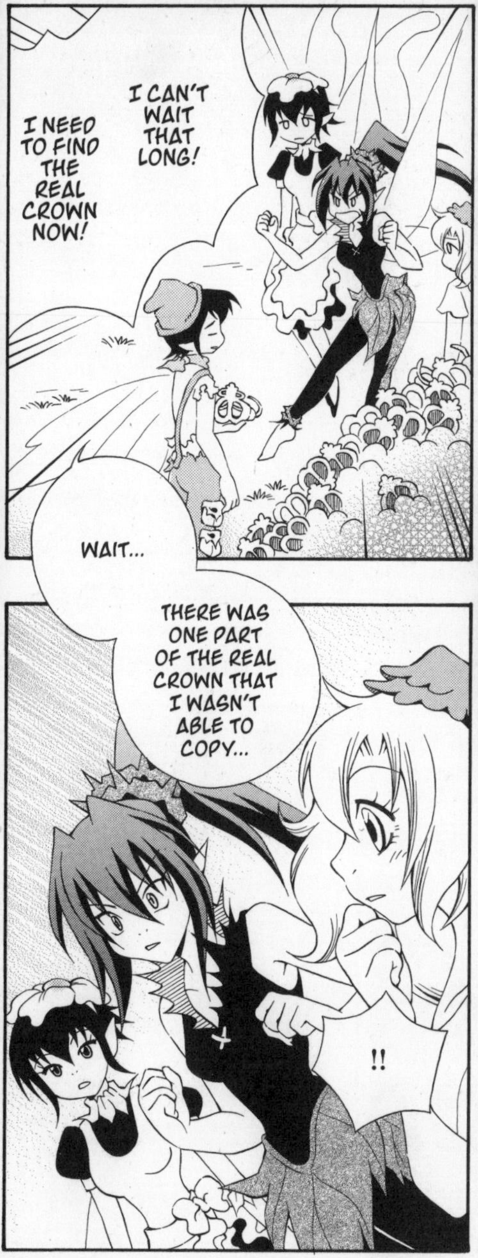
I CAN'T WAIT THAT LONG!
I NEED TO FIND THE REAL CROWN NOW!
WAIT...
THERE WAS ONE PART OF THE REAL CROWN THAT I WASN'T ABLE TO COPY...
!!

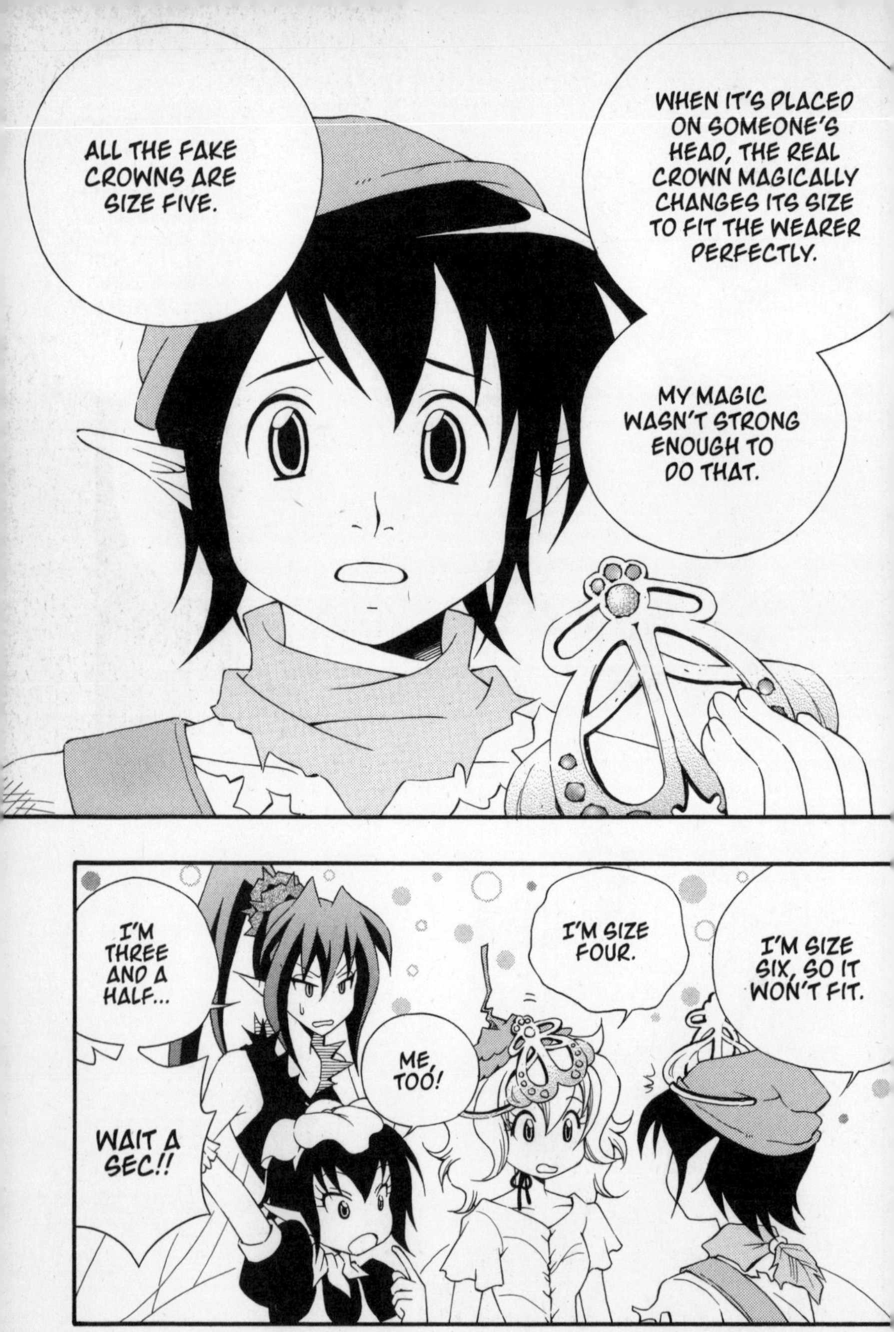
WHEN IT'S PLACED ON SOMEONE'S HEAD, THE REAL CROWN MAGICALLY CHANGES ITS SIZE TO FIT THE WEARER PERFECTLY.
MY MAGIC WASN'T STRONG ENOUGH TO DO THAT.
ALL THE FAKE CROWNS ARE SIZE FIVE.
I'M SIZE SIX, SO IT WON'T FIT.
I'M SIZE FOUR.
I'M THREE AND A HALF...
ME, TOO!
WAIT A SEC!!

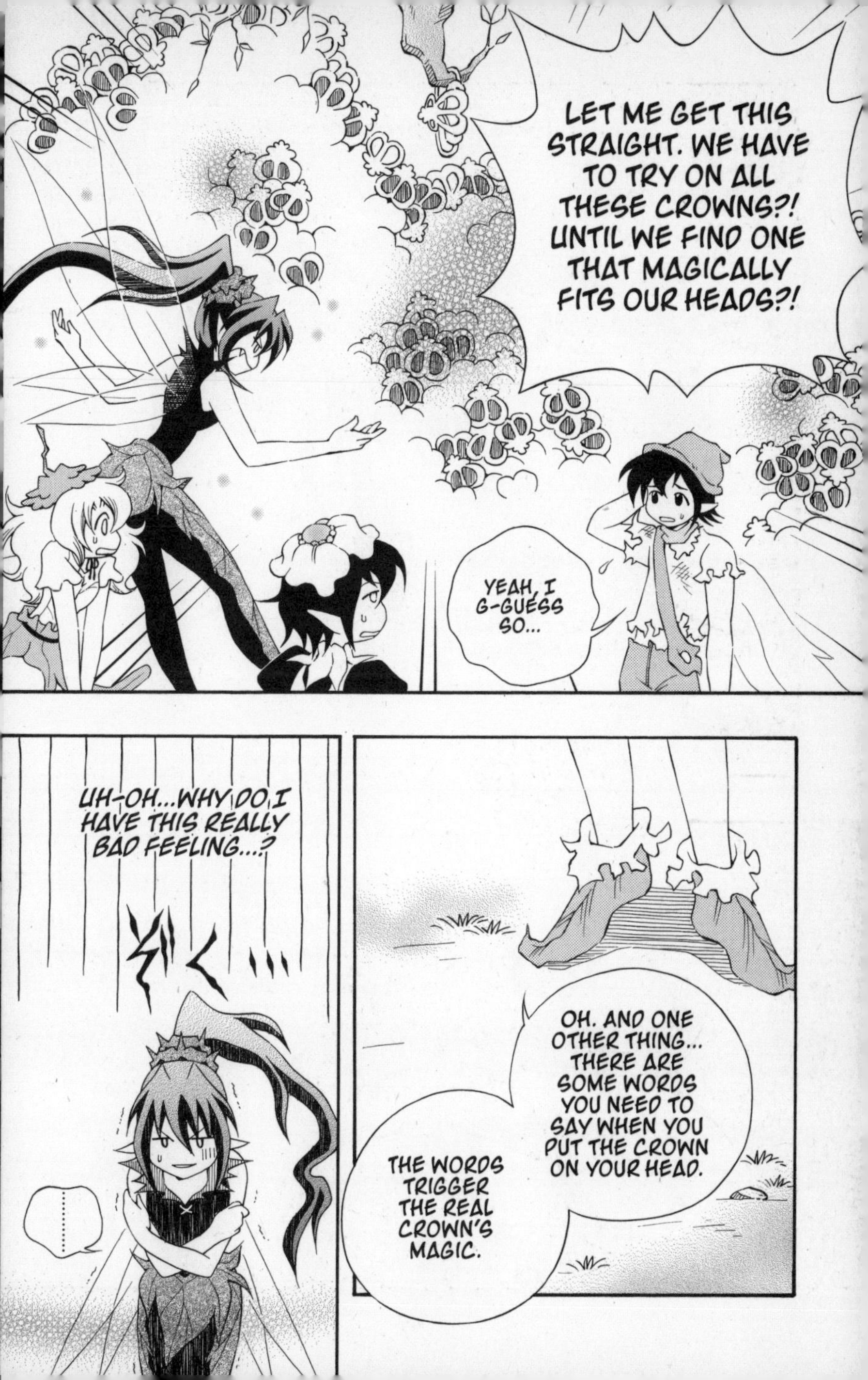
LET ME GET THIS STRAIGHT. WE HAVE TO TRY ON ALL THESE CROWNS?! UNTIL WE FIND ONE THAT MAGICALLY FITS OUR HEADS?!
YEAH, I G-GUESS SO...
OH. AND ONE OTHER THING... THERE ARE SOME WORDS YOU NEED TO SAY WHEN YOU PUT THE CROWN ON YOUR HEAD.
THE WORDS TRIGGER THE REAL CROWN'S MAGIC.
UH-OH...WHY DO I HAVE THIS REALLY BAD FEELING...?
......

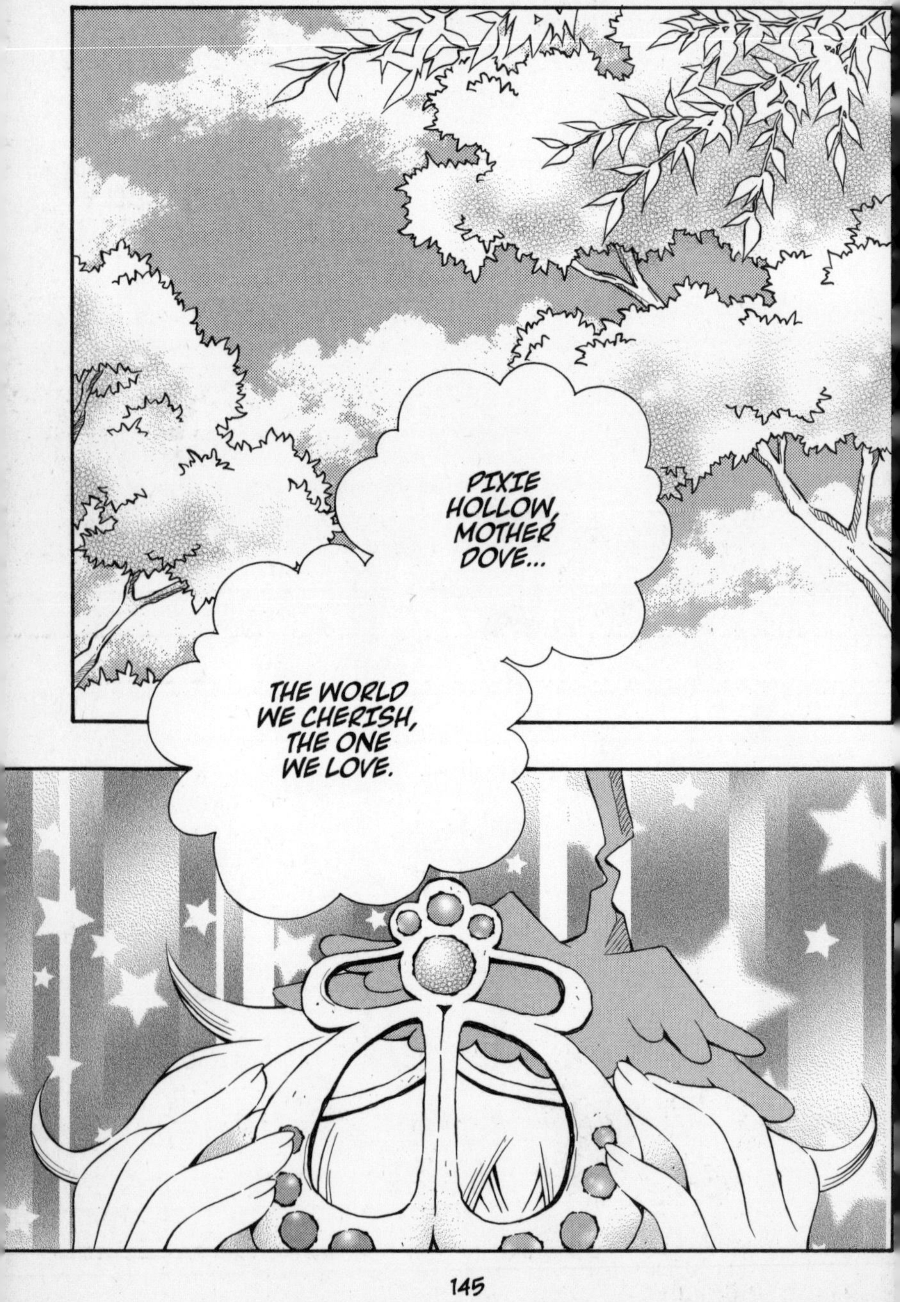
PIXIE HOLLOW, MOTHER DOVE...
THE WORLD WE CHERISH, THE ONE WE LOVE.

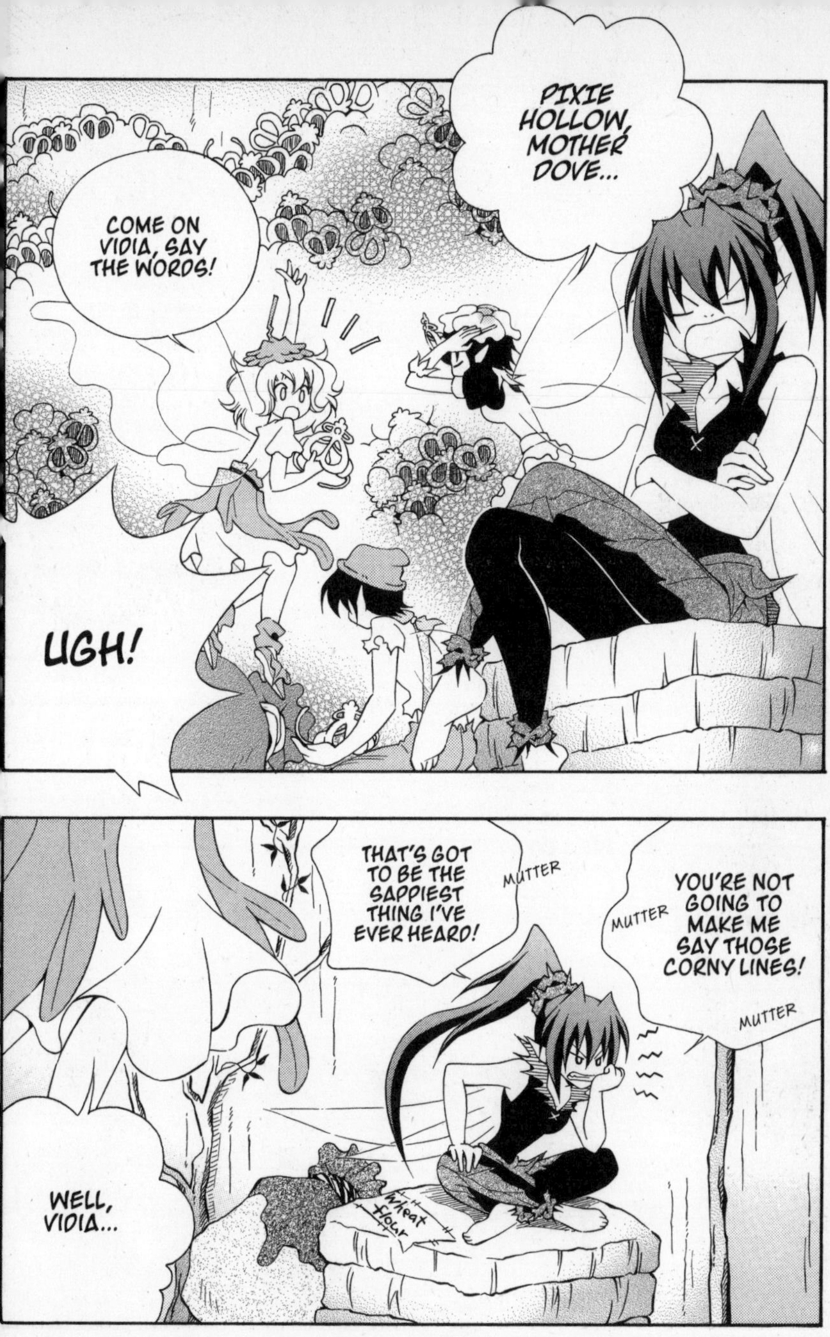
PIXIE HOLLOW, MOTHER DOVE...
COME ON VIDIA, SAY THE WORDS!
UGH!
MUTTER
YOU'RE NOT GOING TO MAKE ME SAY THOSE CORNY LINES!
MUTTER
THAT'S GOT TO BE THE SAPPIEST THING I'VE EVER HEARD!
MUTTER
wheat flour
WELL, VIDIA...

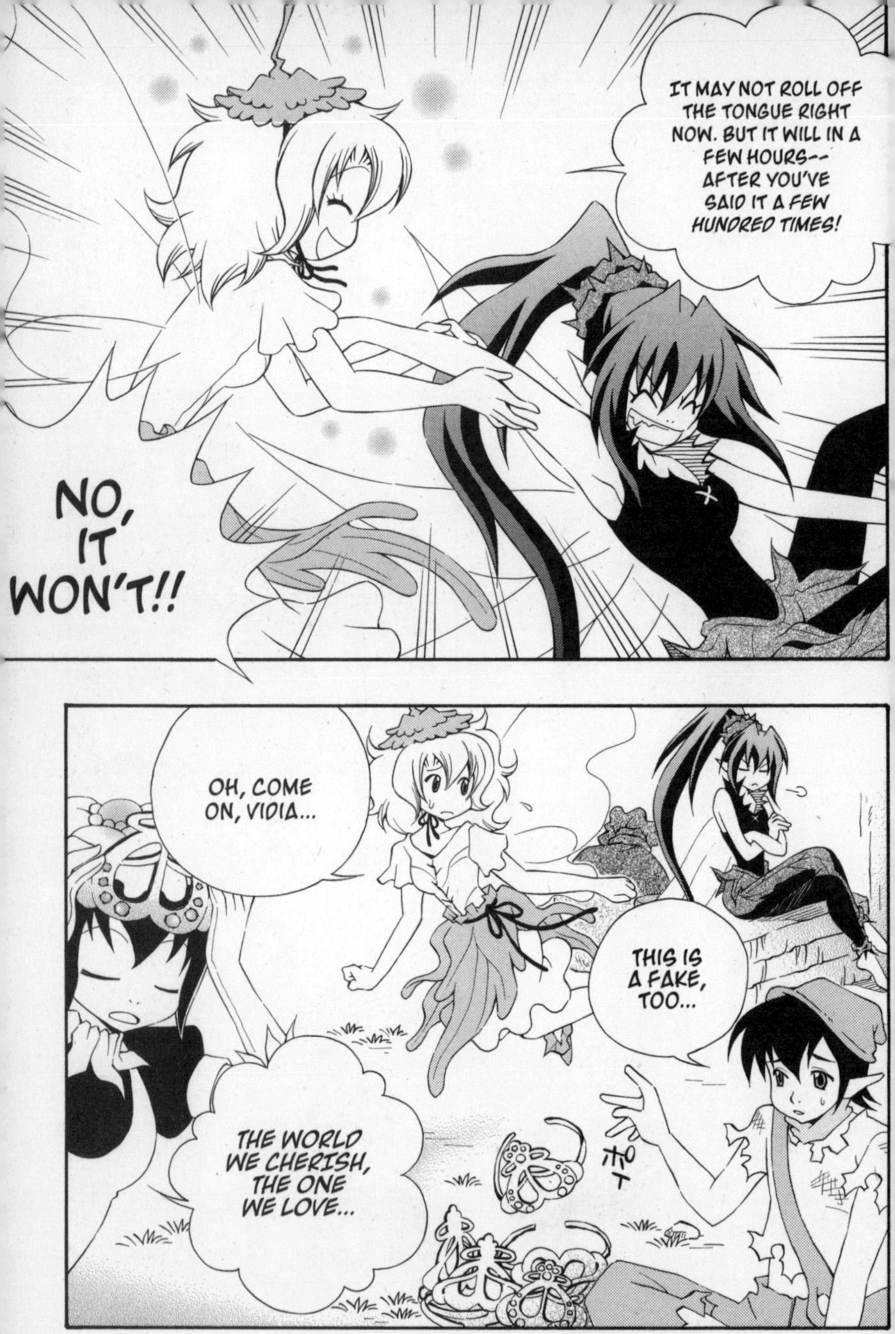
IT MAY NOT ROLL OFF THE TONGUE RIGHT NOW. BUT IT WILL IN A FEW HOURS-- AFTER YOU'VE SAID IT A FEW HUNDRED TIMES!
NO, IT WON'T!!
THIS IS A FAKE, TOO...
ポト
OH, COME ON, VIDIA...
THE WORLD WE CHERISH, THE ONE WE LOVE...

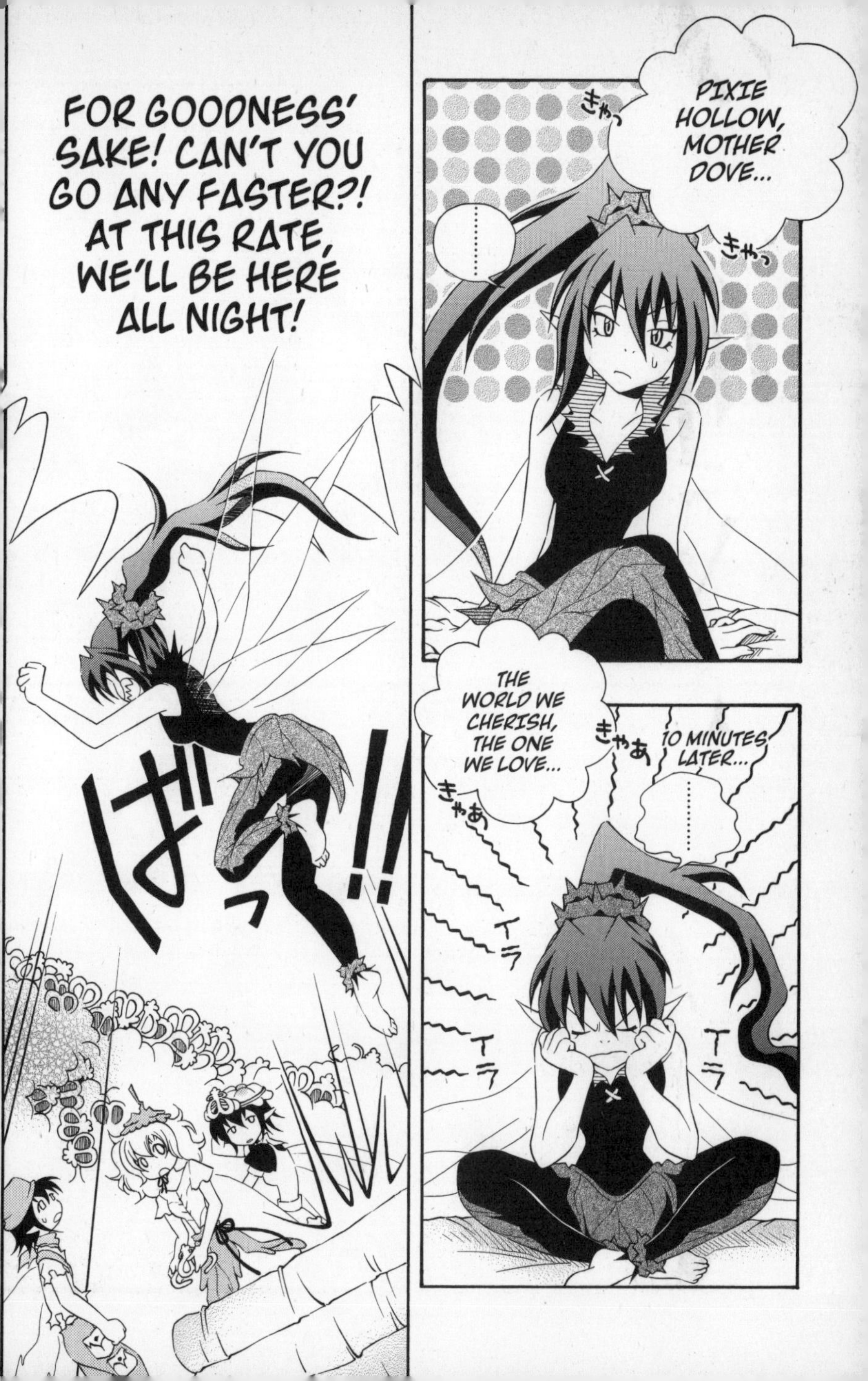

PIXIE HOLLOW, MOTHER DOVE...
きゃっ
きゃっ
......
THE WORLD WE CHERISH, THE ONE WE LOVE...
10 MINUTES LATER...
きゃあ
きゃあ
......
イラ
イラ
イラ
FOR GOODNESS' SAKE! CAN'T YOU GO ANY FASTER?! AT THIS RATE, WE'LL BE HERE ALL NIGHT!
ばっ!!

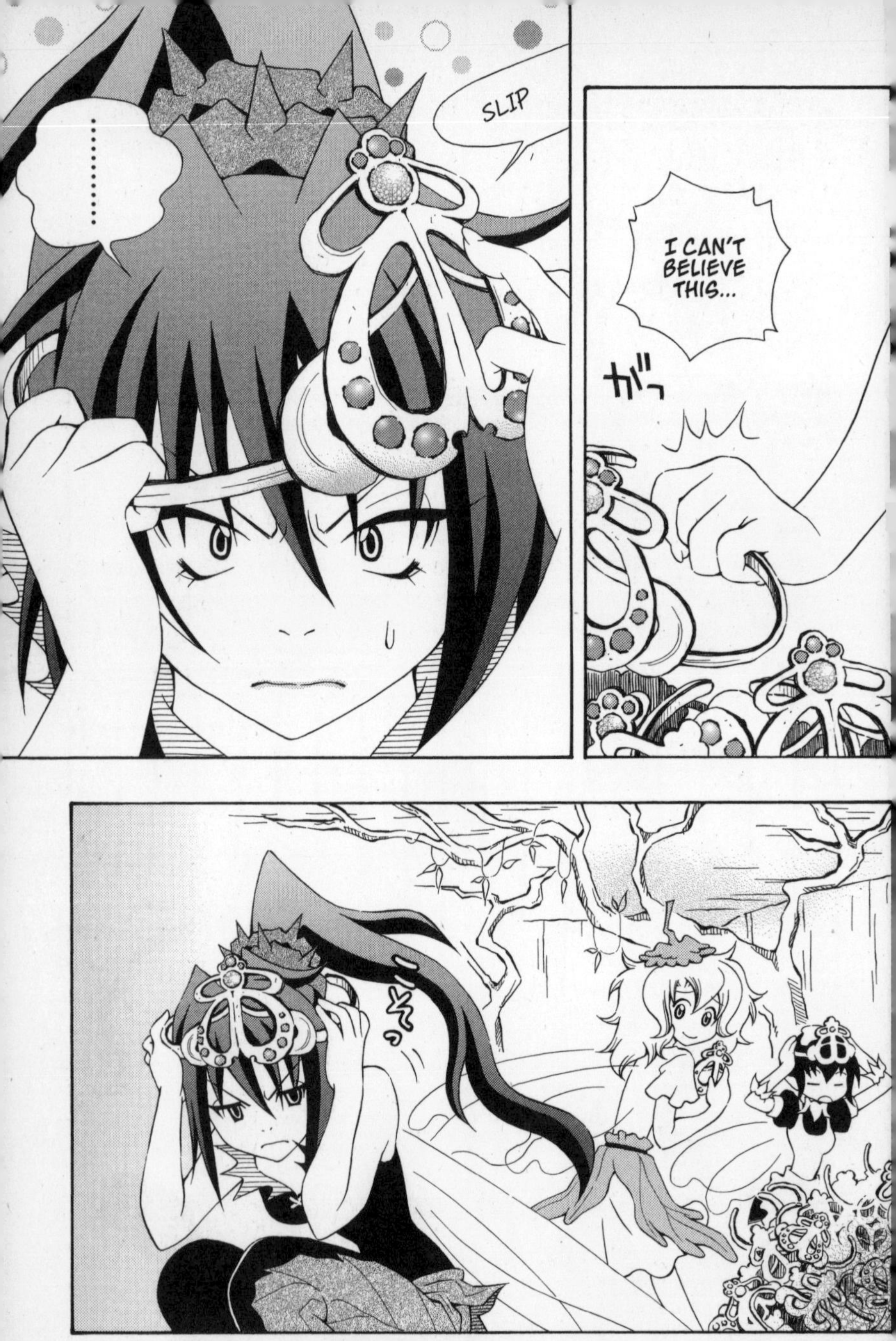
I CAN'T BELIEVE THIS...
ガッ
SLIP
......
こそっ

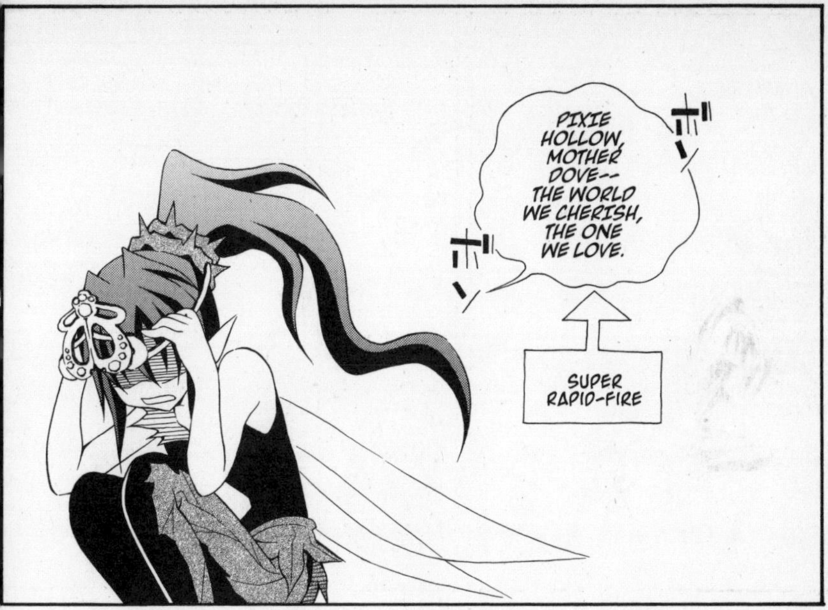
PIXIE HOLLOW, MOTHER DOVE-- THE WORLD WE CHERISH, THE ONE WE LOVE.
SUPER RAPID-FIRE

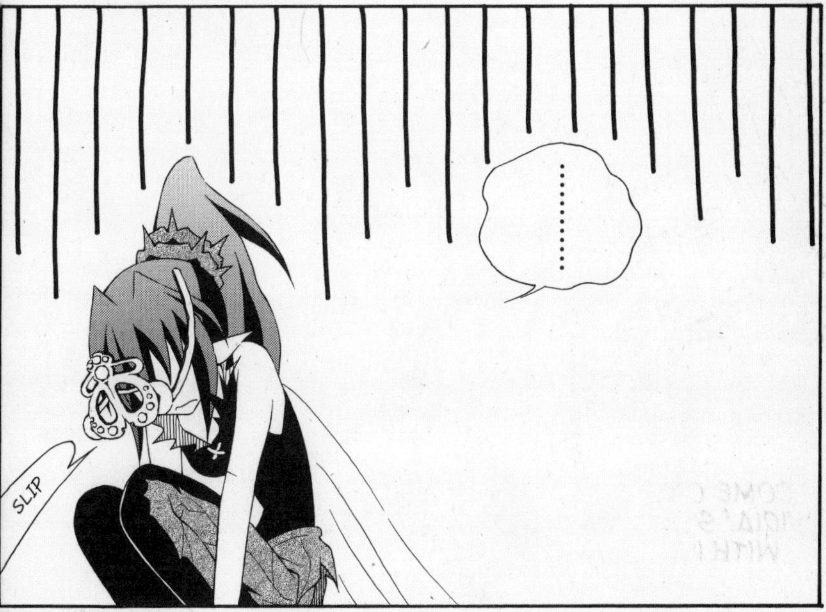
......
SLIP

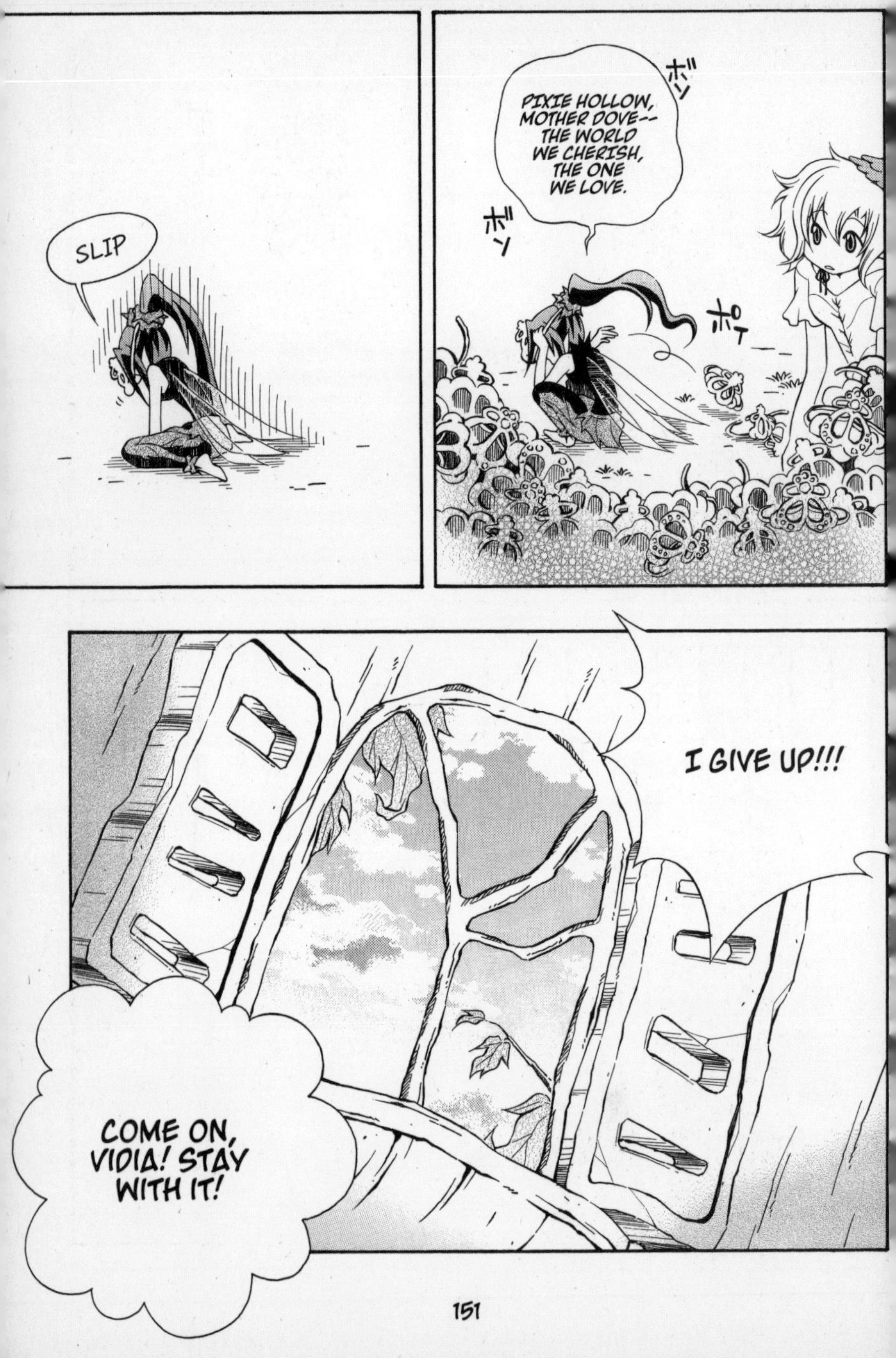
ボン
PIXIE HOLLOW, MOTHER DOVE-- THE WORLD WE CHERISH, THE ONE WE LOVE.
ボン
ポテ
SLIP
I GIVE UP!!!
COME ON, VIDIA! STAY WITH IT!

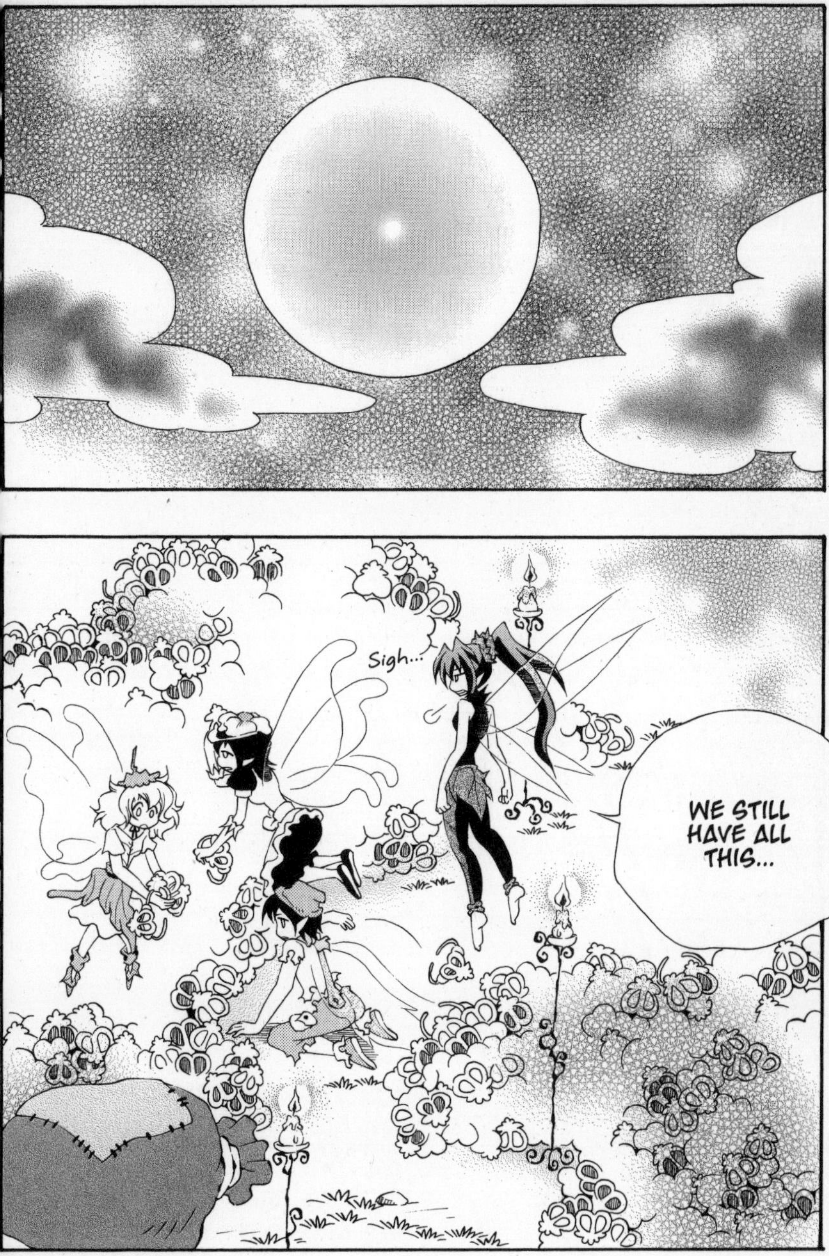
WE STILL HAVE ALL THIS...
Sigh...

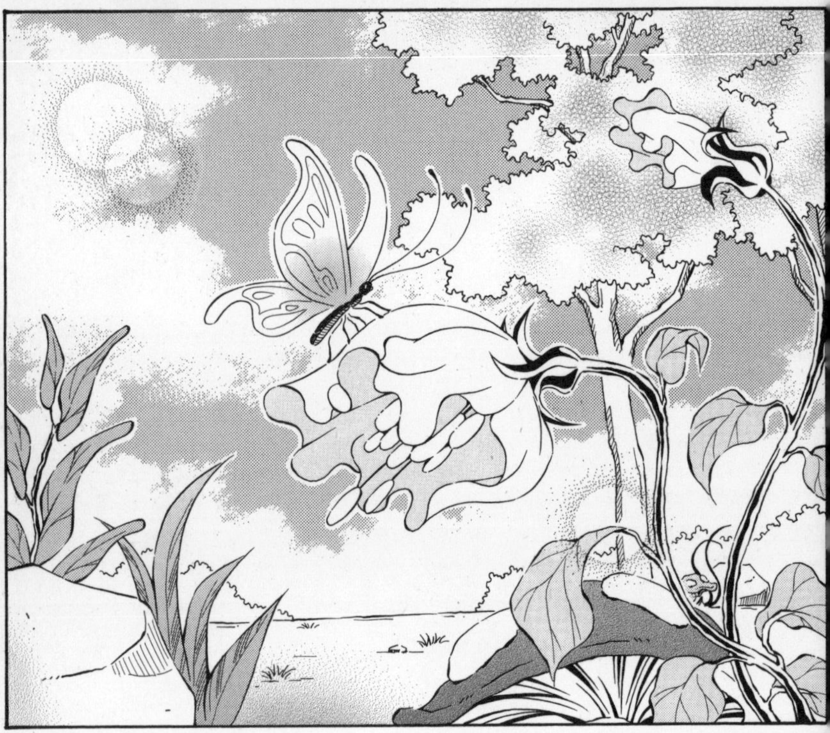

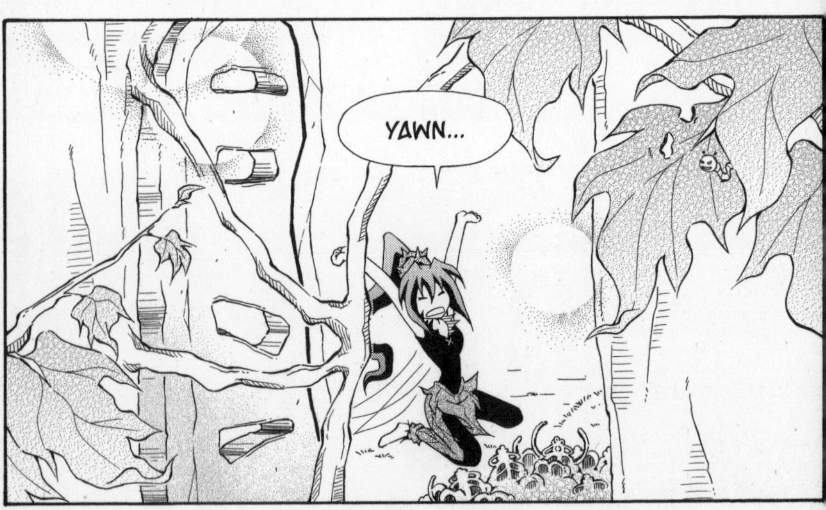
YAWN...

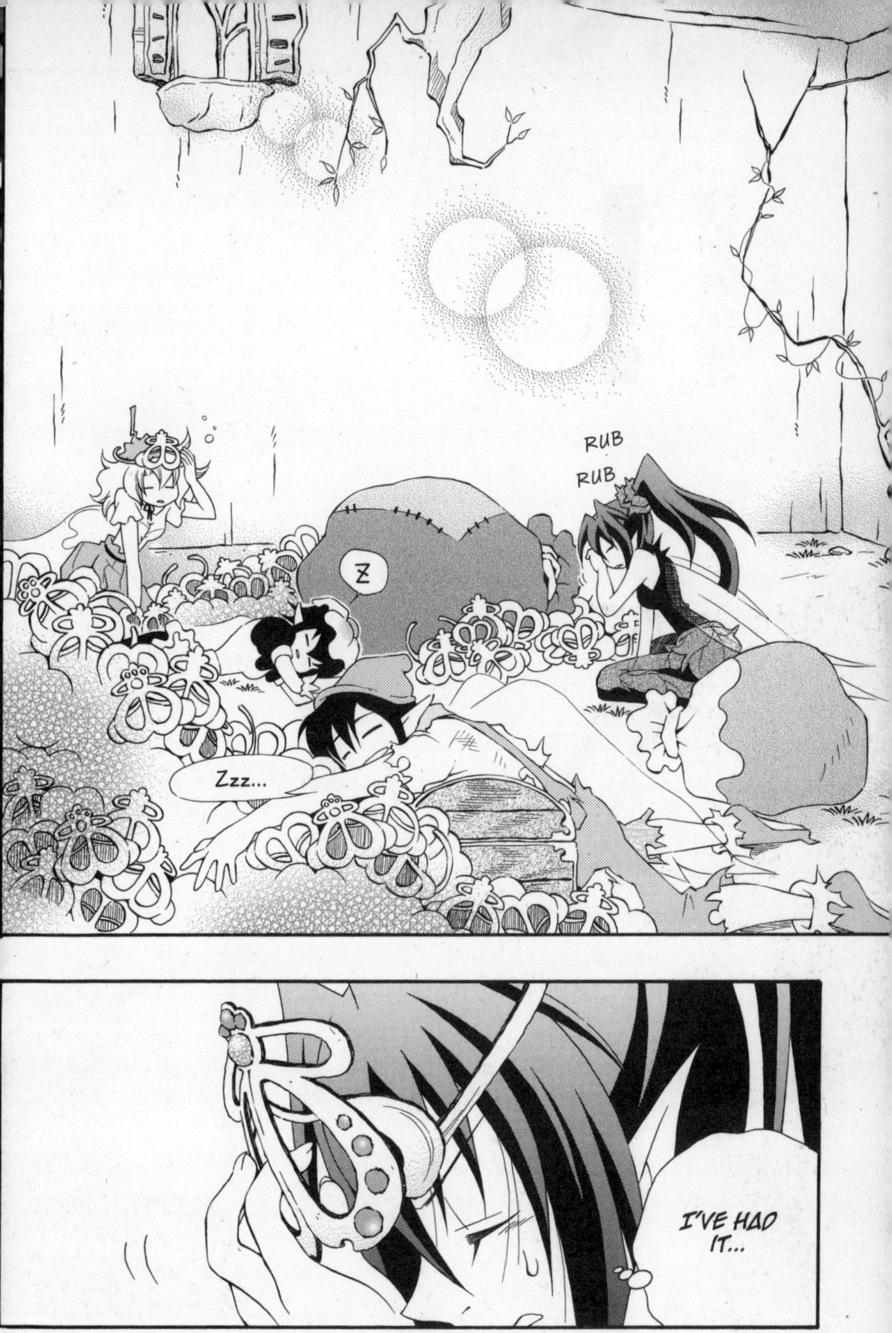
RUB
RUB
Z
Zzz...
I'VE HAD IT...

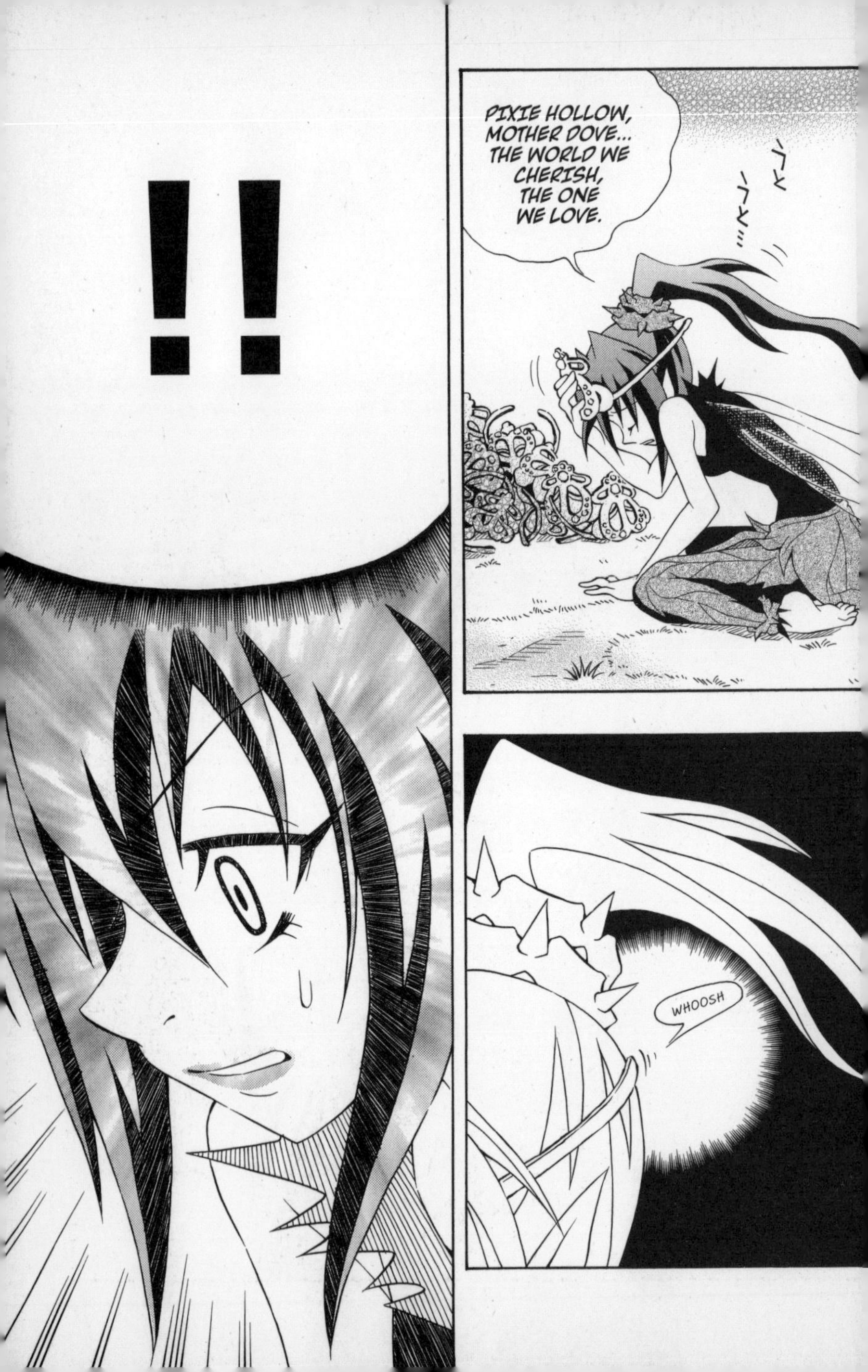
PIXIE HOLLOW, MOTHER DOVE... THE WORLD WE CHERISH, THE ONE WE LOVE.
WHOOSH
!!

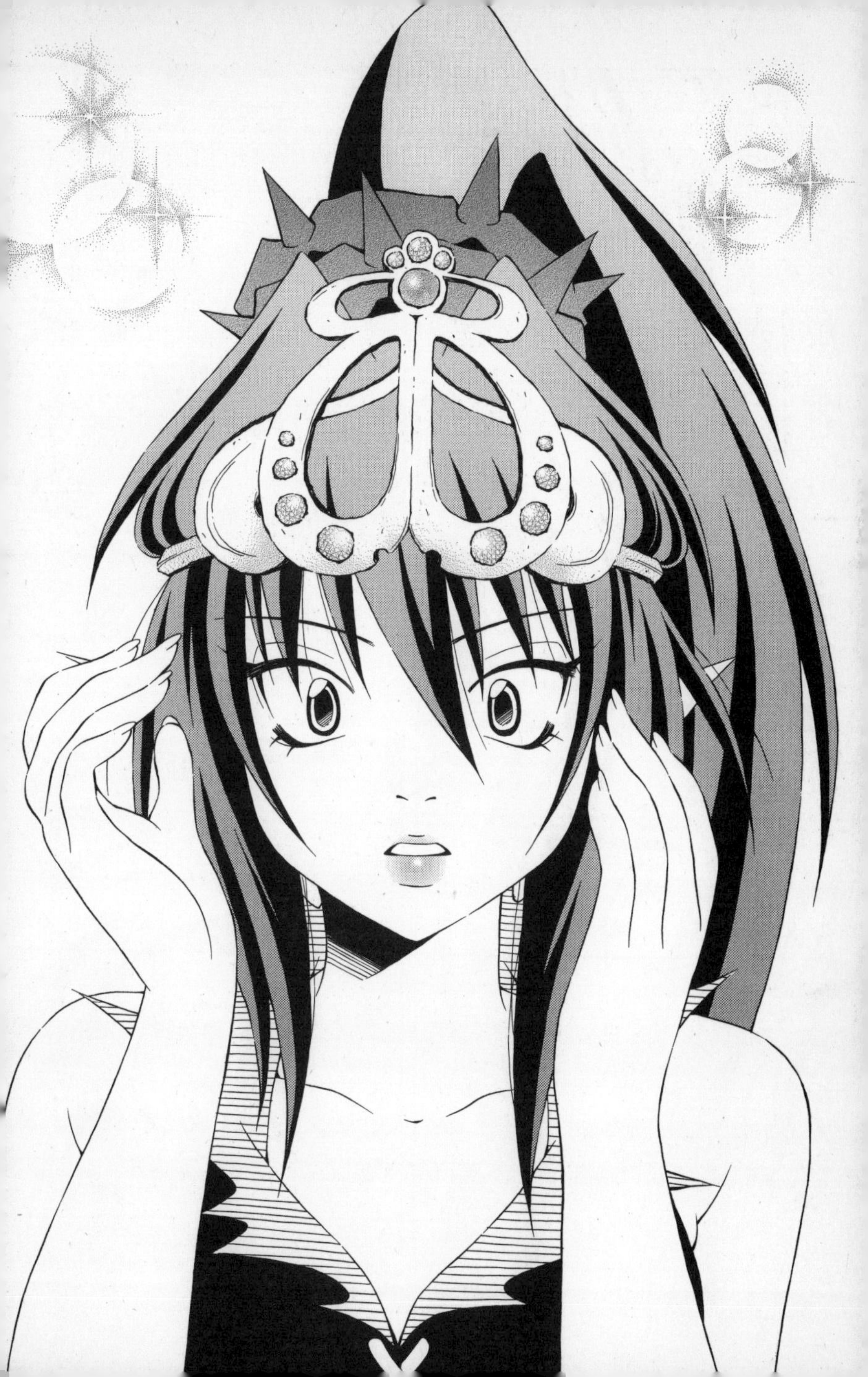

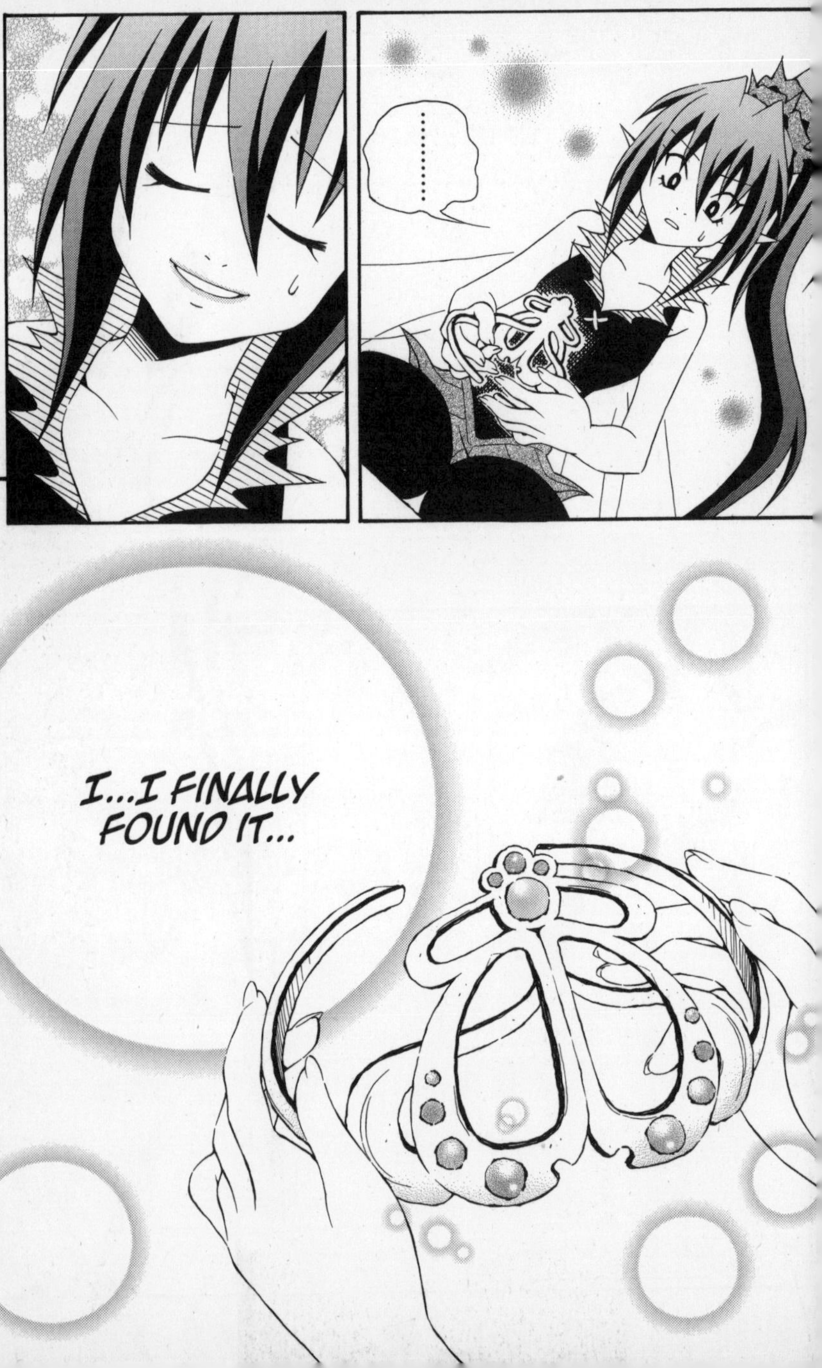
......
I...I FINALLY FOUND IT...

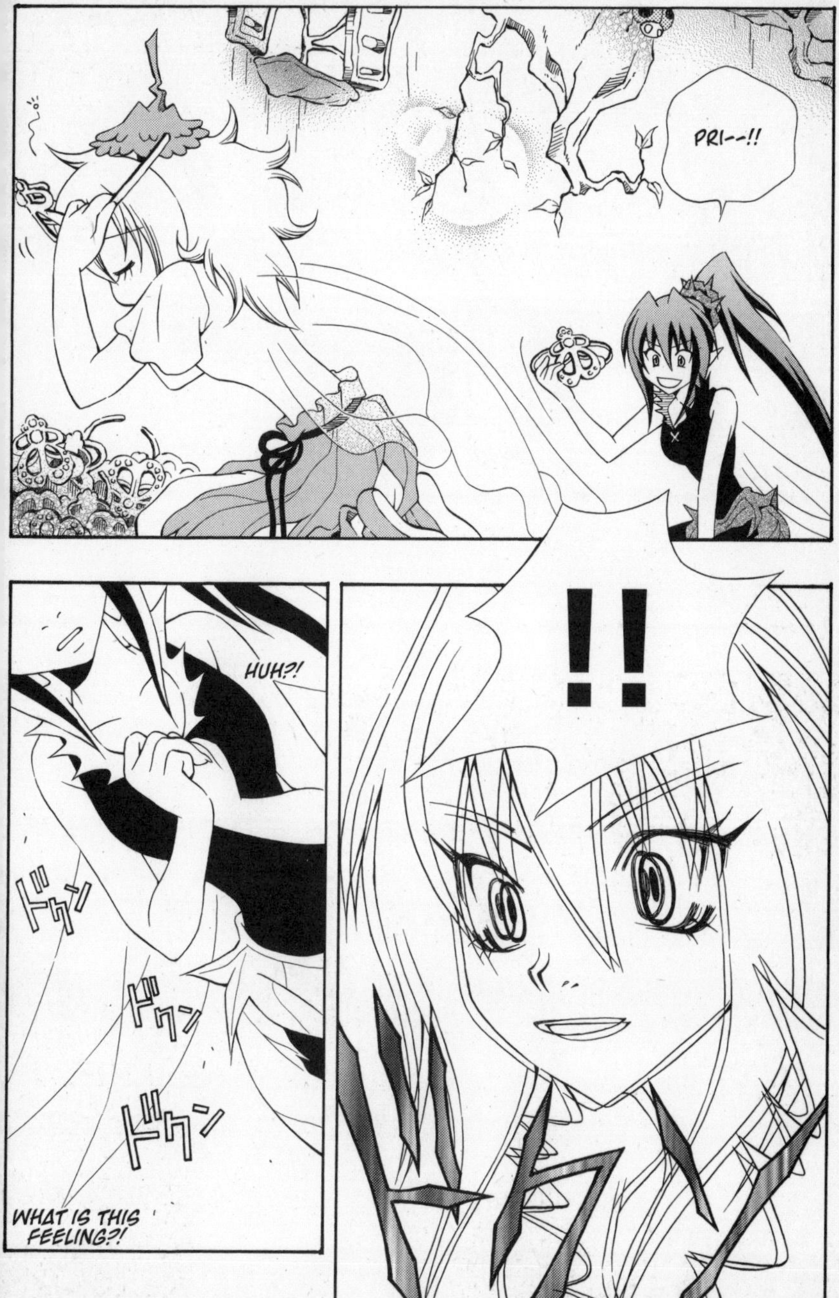
PRI--!!
!!
HUH?!
ドクン
ドクン
ドクン
WHAT IS THIS FEELING?!

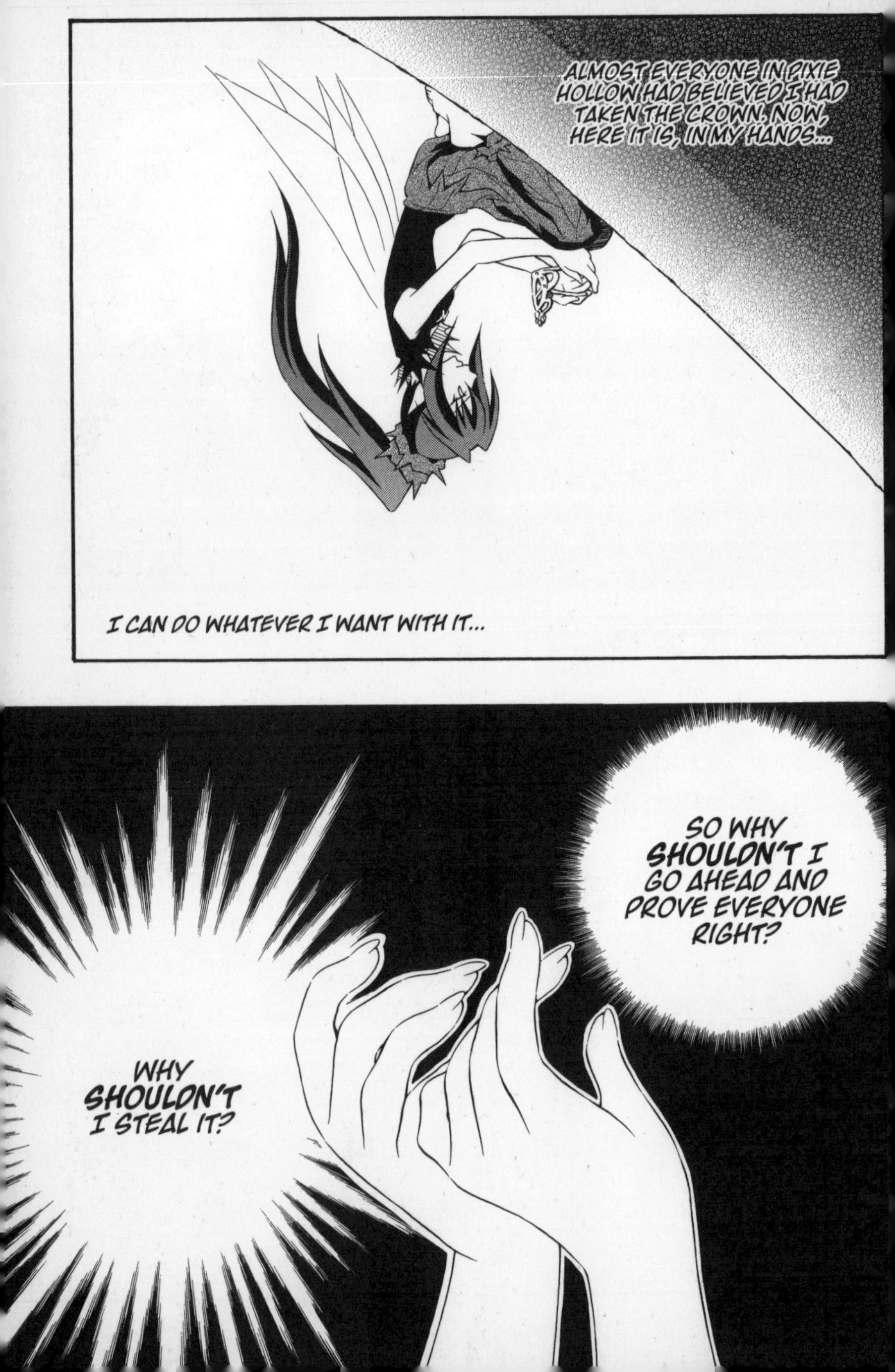
ALMOST EVERYONE IN PIXIE HOLLOW HAD BELIEVED I HAD TAKEN THE CROWN. NOW, HERE IT IS, IN MY HANDS...
I CAN DO WHATEVER I WANT WITH IT...
SO WHY SHOULDN'T I GO AHEAD AND PROVE EVERYONE RIGHT?
WHY SHOULDN'T I STEAL IT?

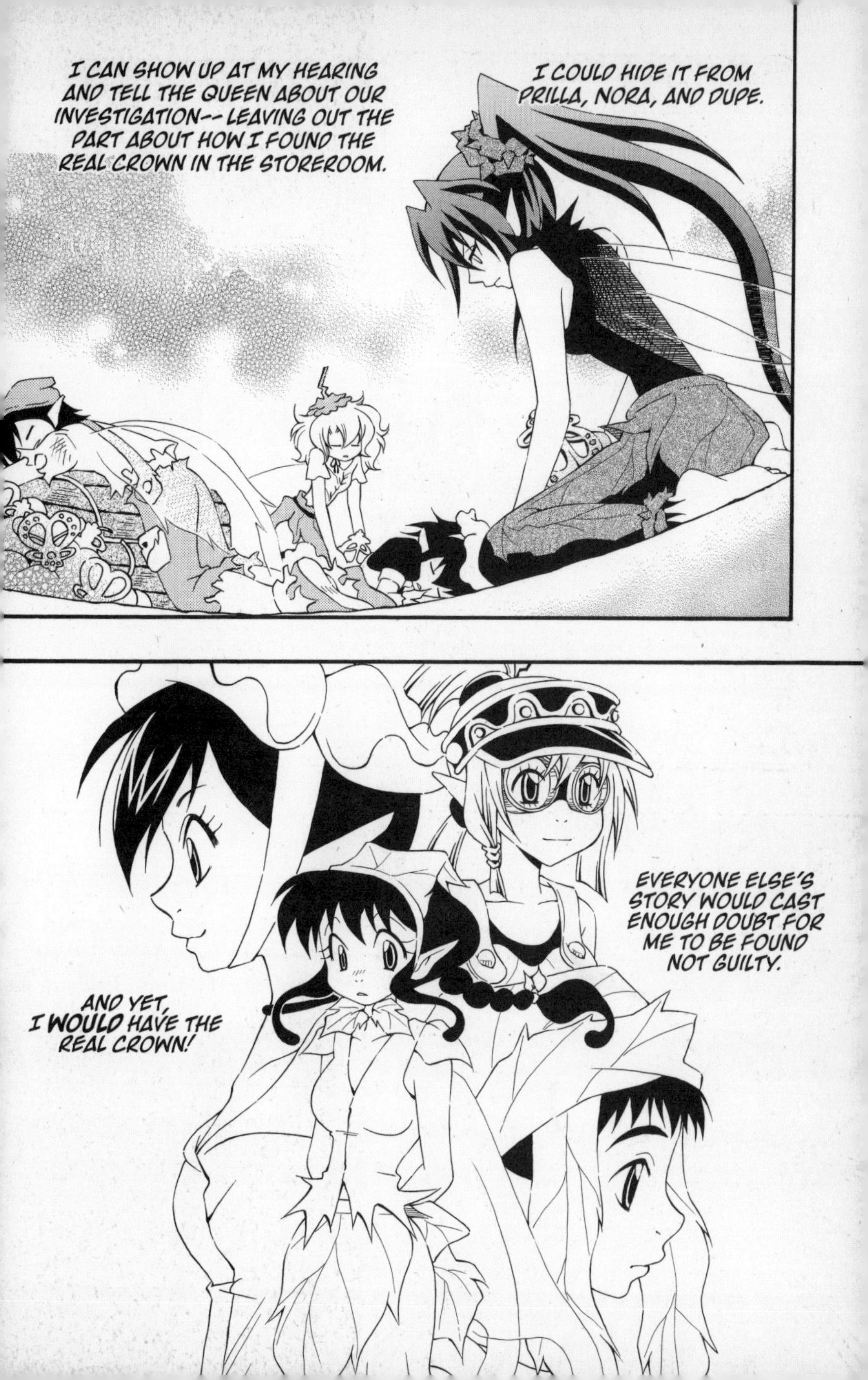
I COULD HIDE IT FROM PRILLA, NORA, AND DUPE.
I CAN SHOW UP AT MY HEARING AND TELL THE QUEEN ABOUT OUR INVESTIGATION-- LEAVING OUT THE PART ABOUT HOW I FOUND THE REAL CROWN IN THE STOREROOM.
EVERYONE ELSE'S STORY WOULD CAST ENOUGH DOUBT FOR ME TO BE FOUND NOT GUILTY.
AND YET, I **WOULD** HAVE THE REAL CROWN!

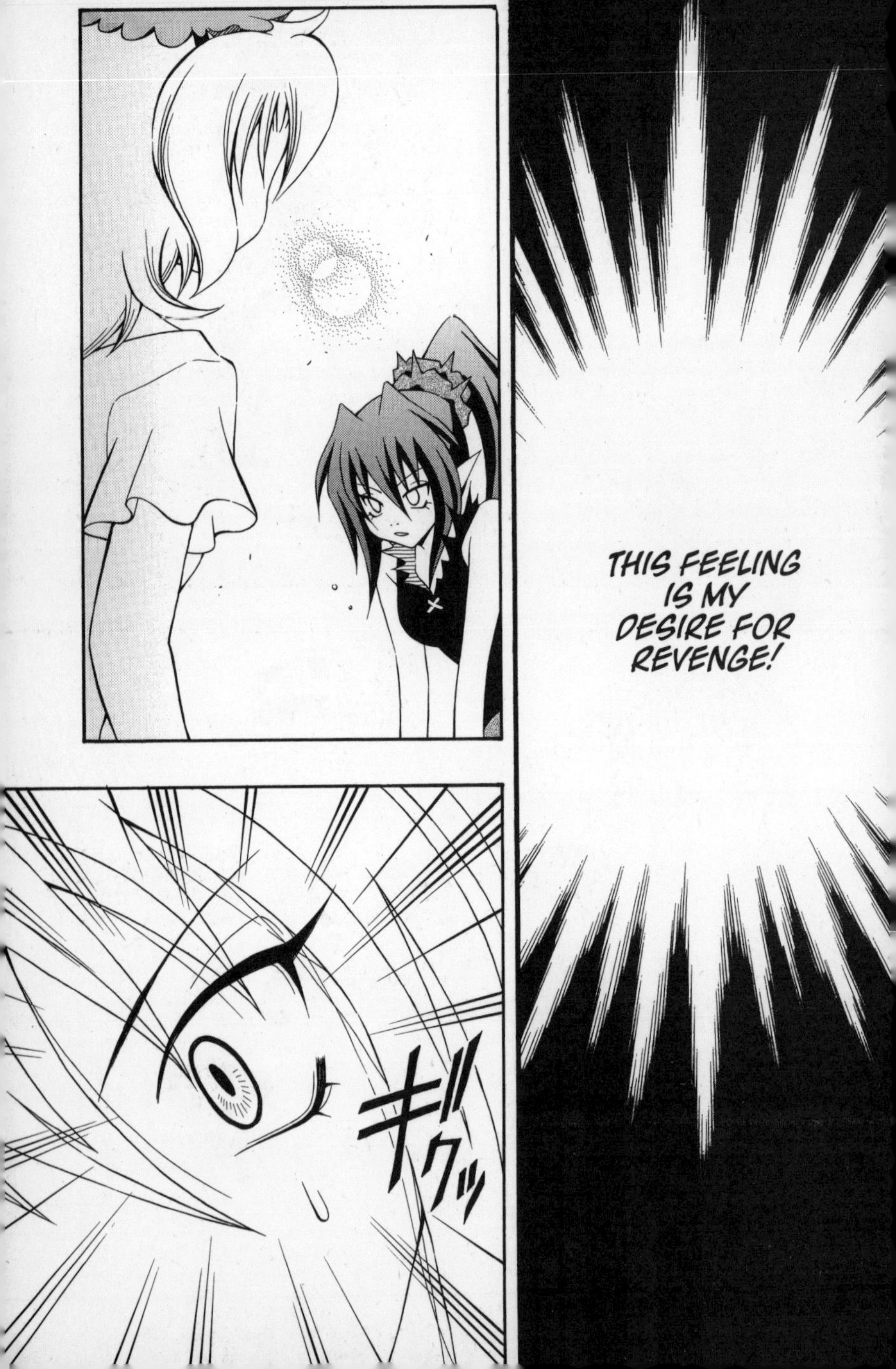
THIS FEELING IS MY DESIRE FOR REVENGE!
ギクッ

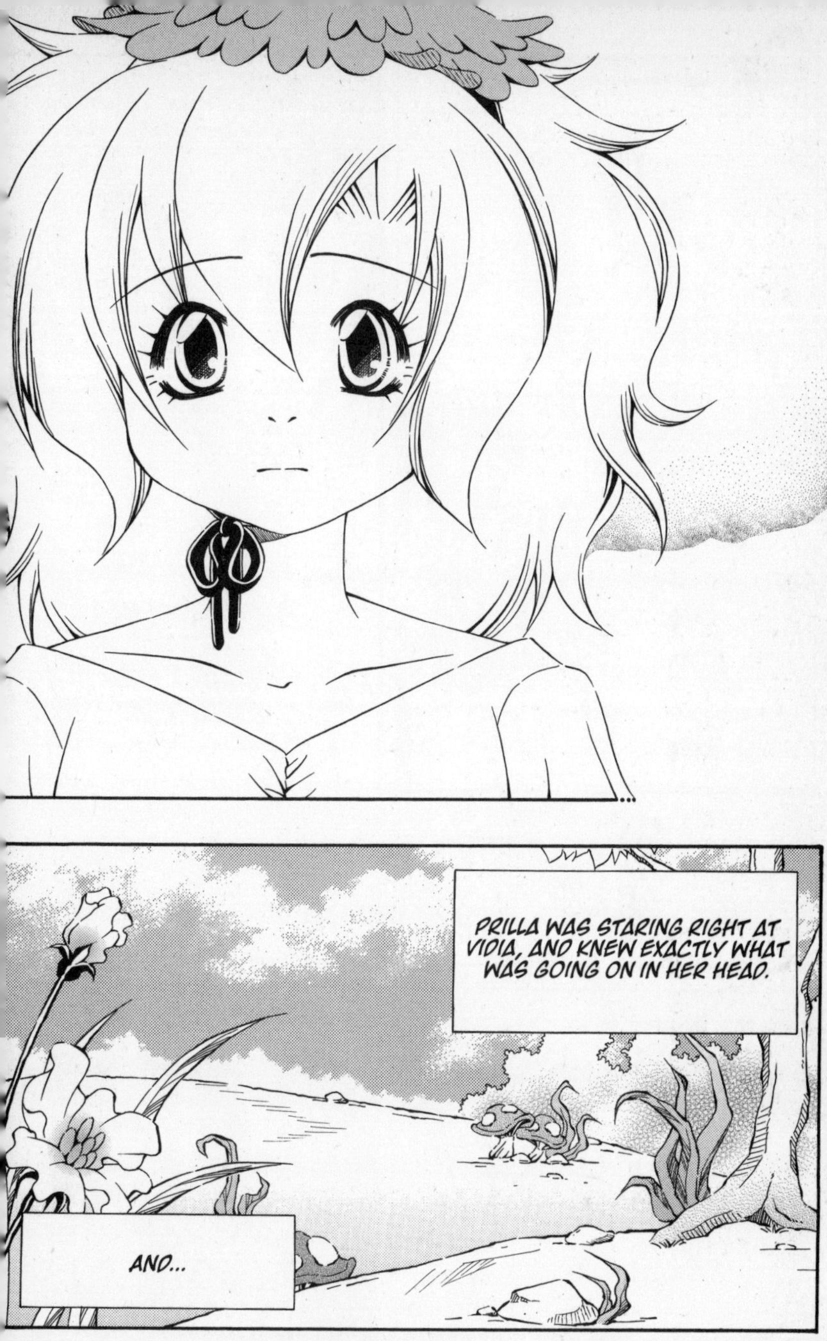
...
PRILLA WAS STARING RIGHT AT VIDIA, AND KNEW EXACTLY WHAT WAS GOING ON IN HER HEAD.
AND...

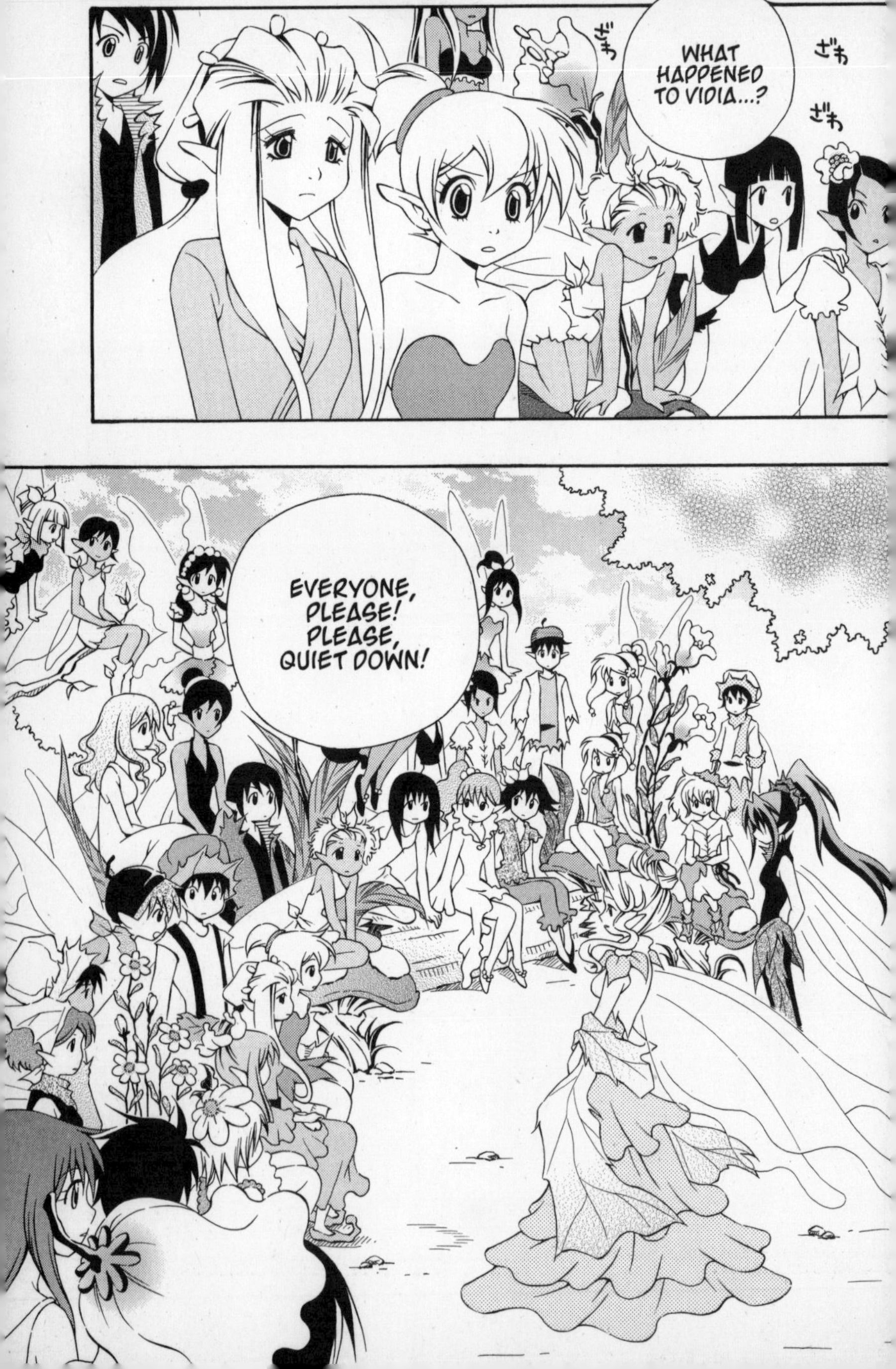
ざわ
ざわ
WHAT HAPPENED TO VIDIA...?
ざわ
EVERYONE, PLEASE! PLEASE, QUIET DOWN!

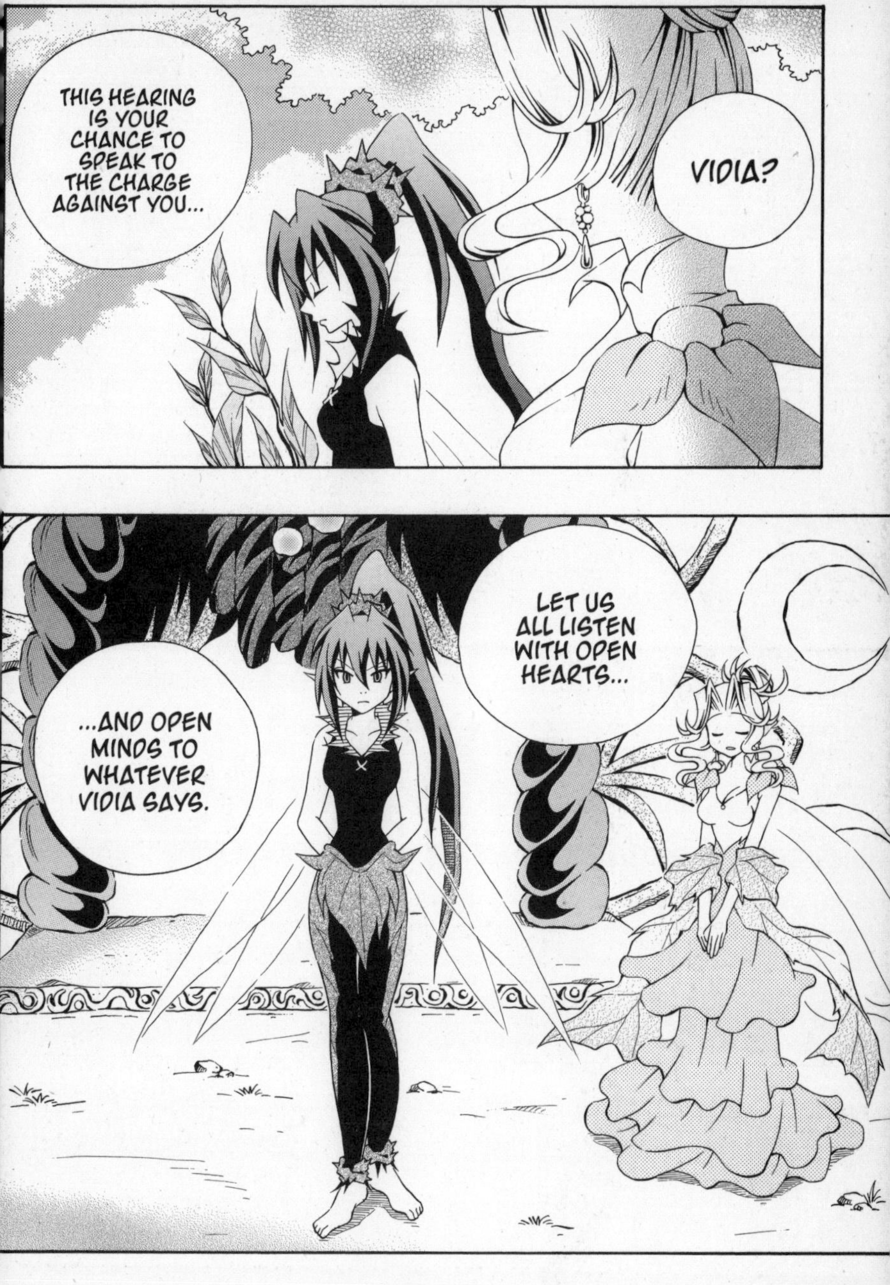
VIDIA?
THIS HEARING IS YOUR CHANCE TO SPEAK TO THE CHARGE AGAINST YOU...
LET US ALL LISTEN WITH OPEN HEARTS...
...AND OPEN MINDS TO WHATEVER VIDIA SAYS.

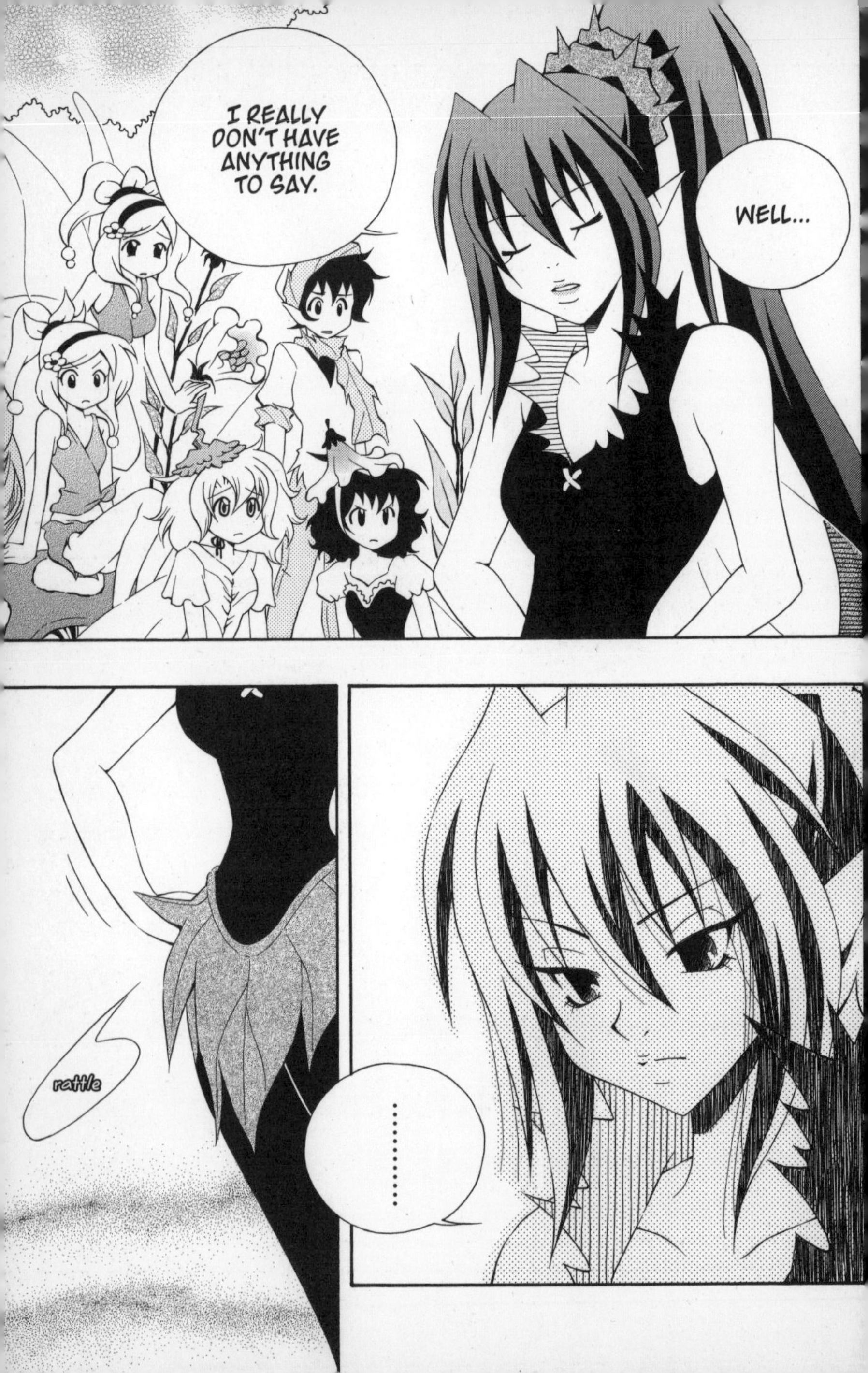
WELL...
I REALLY DON'T HAVE ANYTHING TO SAY.
……
rattle

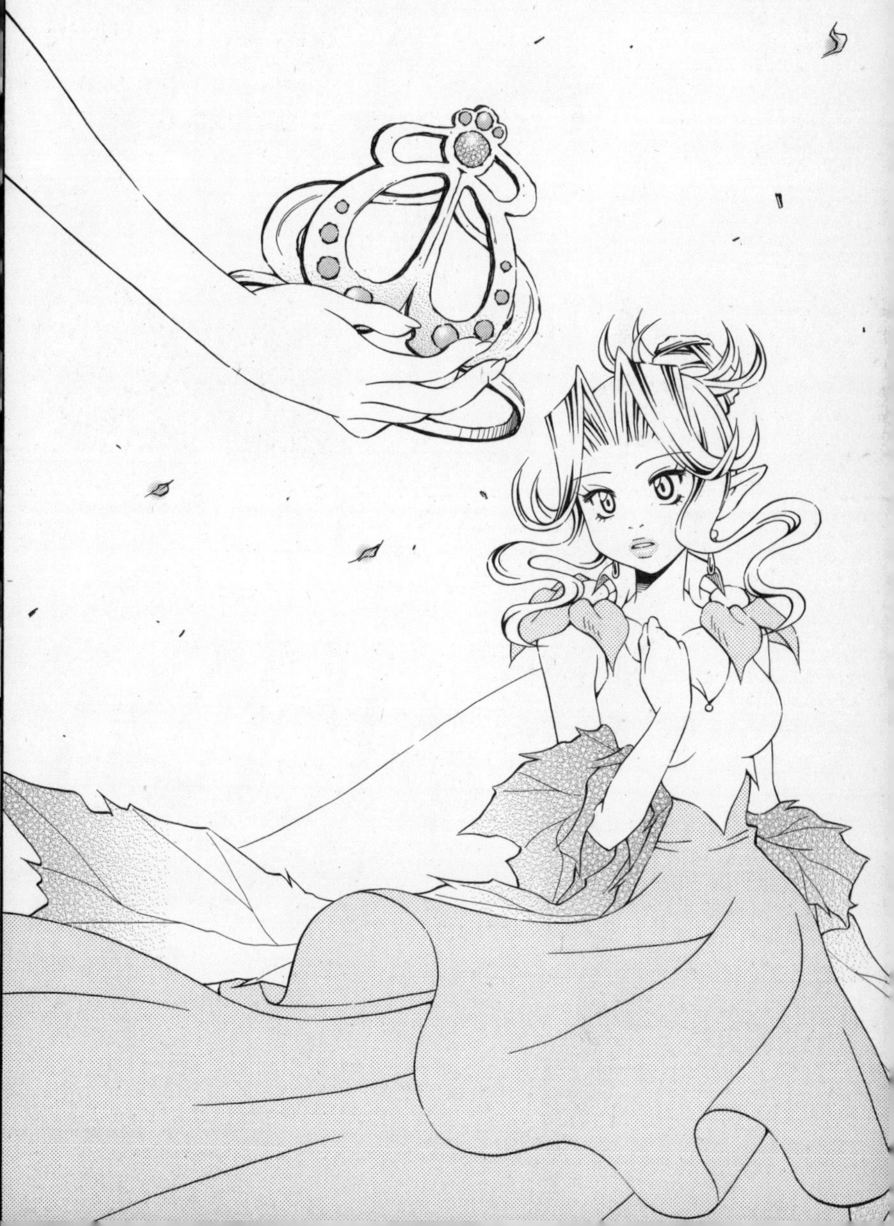

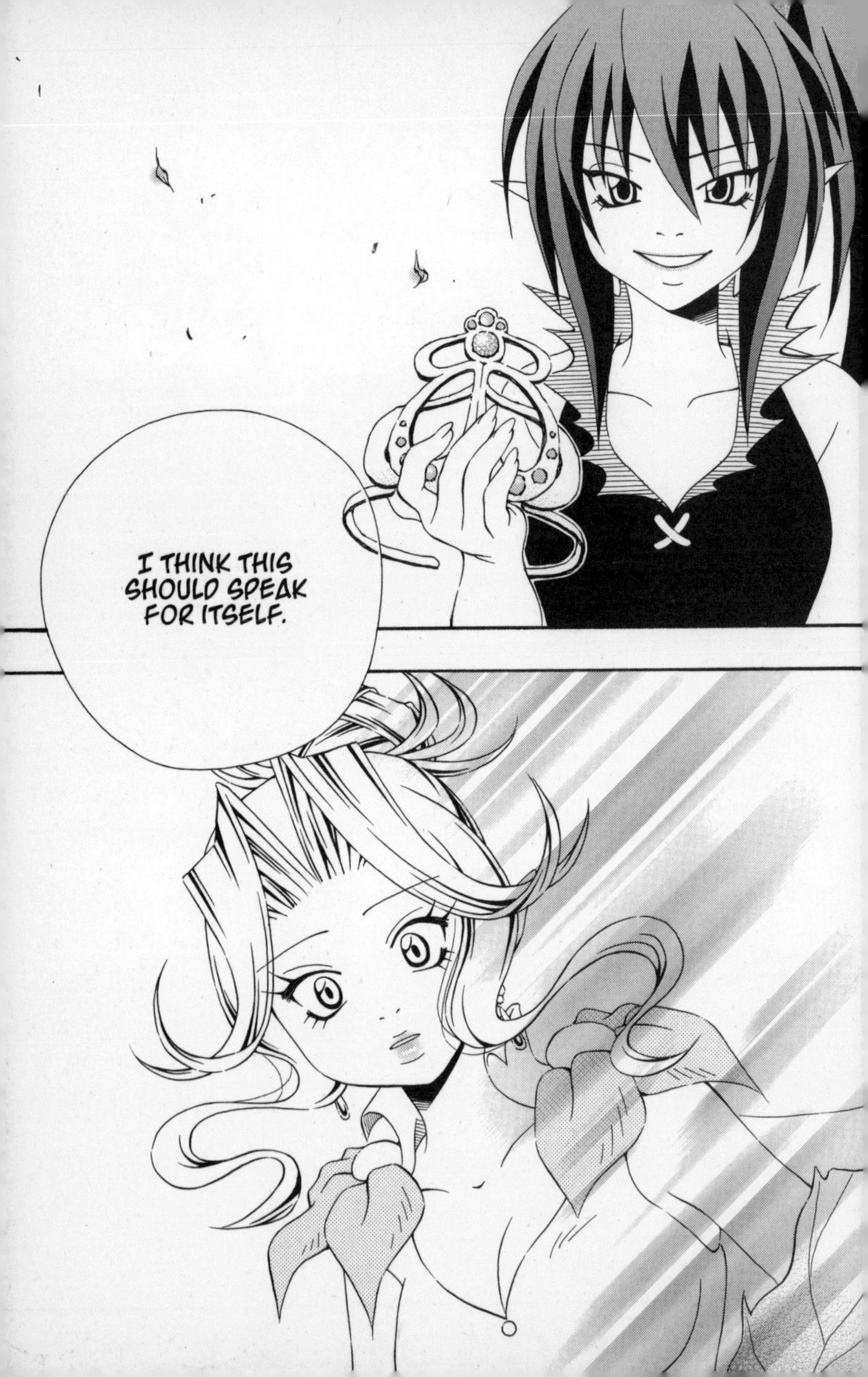
I THINK THIS SHOULD SPEAK FOR ITSELF.

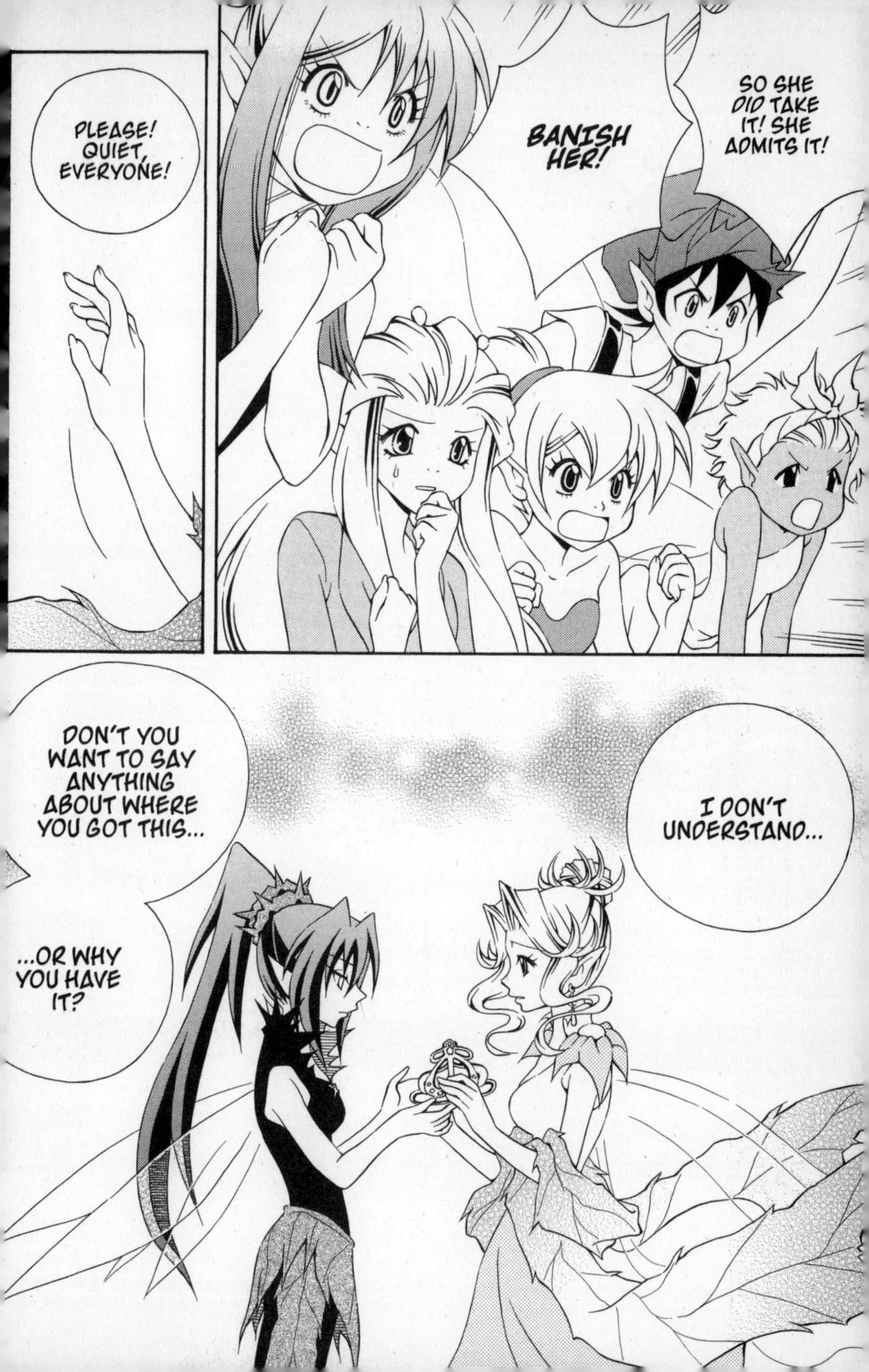
SO SHE DID TAKE IT! SHE ADMITS IT!
BANISH HER!
PLEASE! QUIET, EVERYONE!
DON'T YOU WANT TO SAY ANYTHING ABOUT WHERE YOU GOT THIS...
...OR WHY YOU HAVE IT?
I DON'T UNDERSTAND...

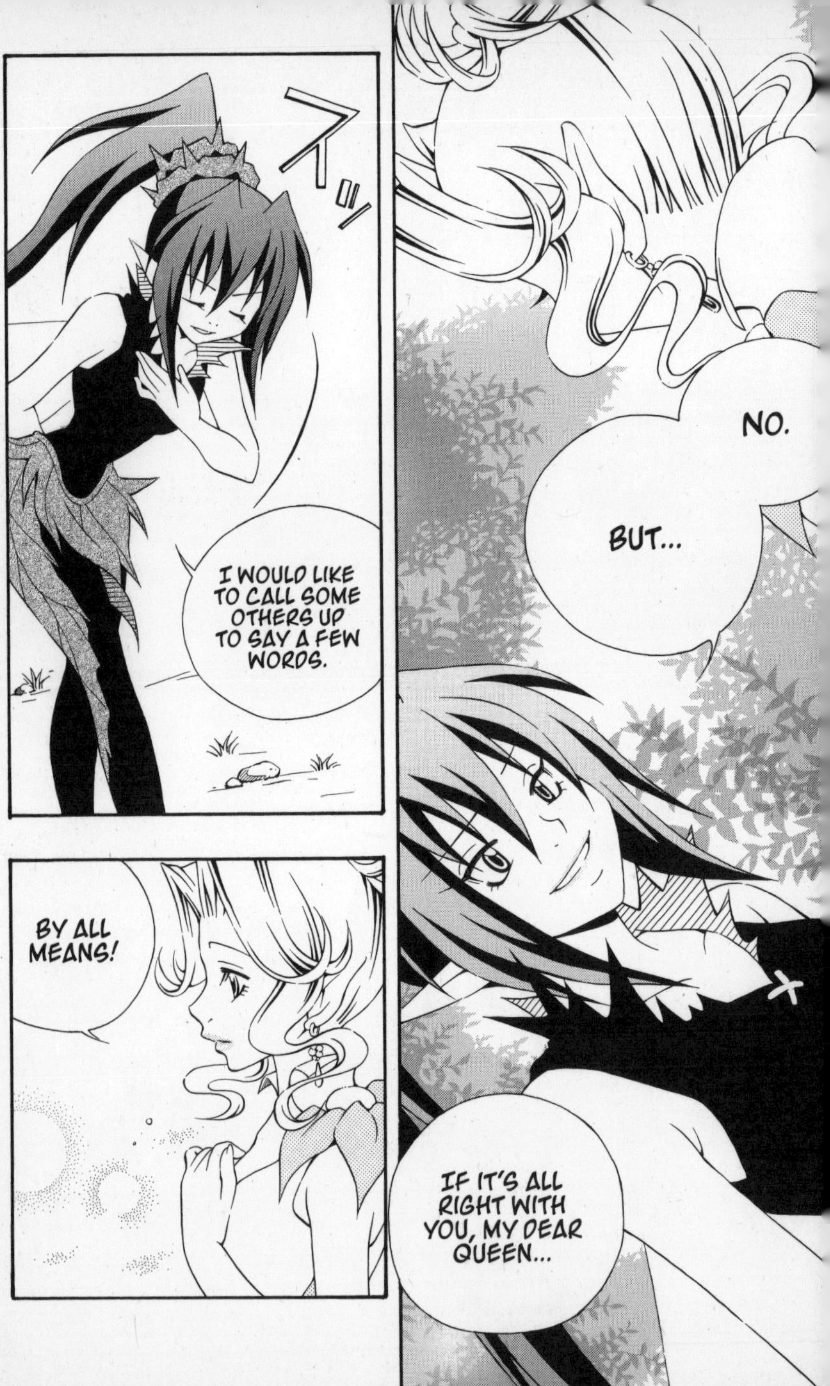
NO.
BUT...
IF IT'S ALL RIGHT WITH YOU, MY DEAR QUEEN...
I WOULD LIKE TO CALL SOME OTHERS UP TO SAY A FEW WORDS.
BY ALL MEANS!

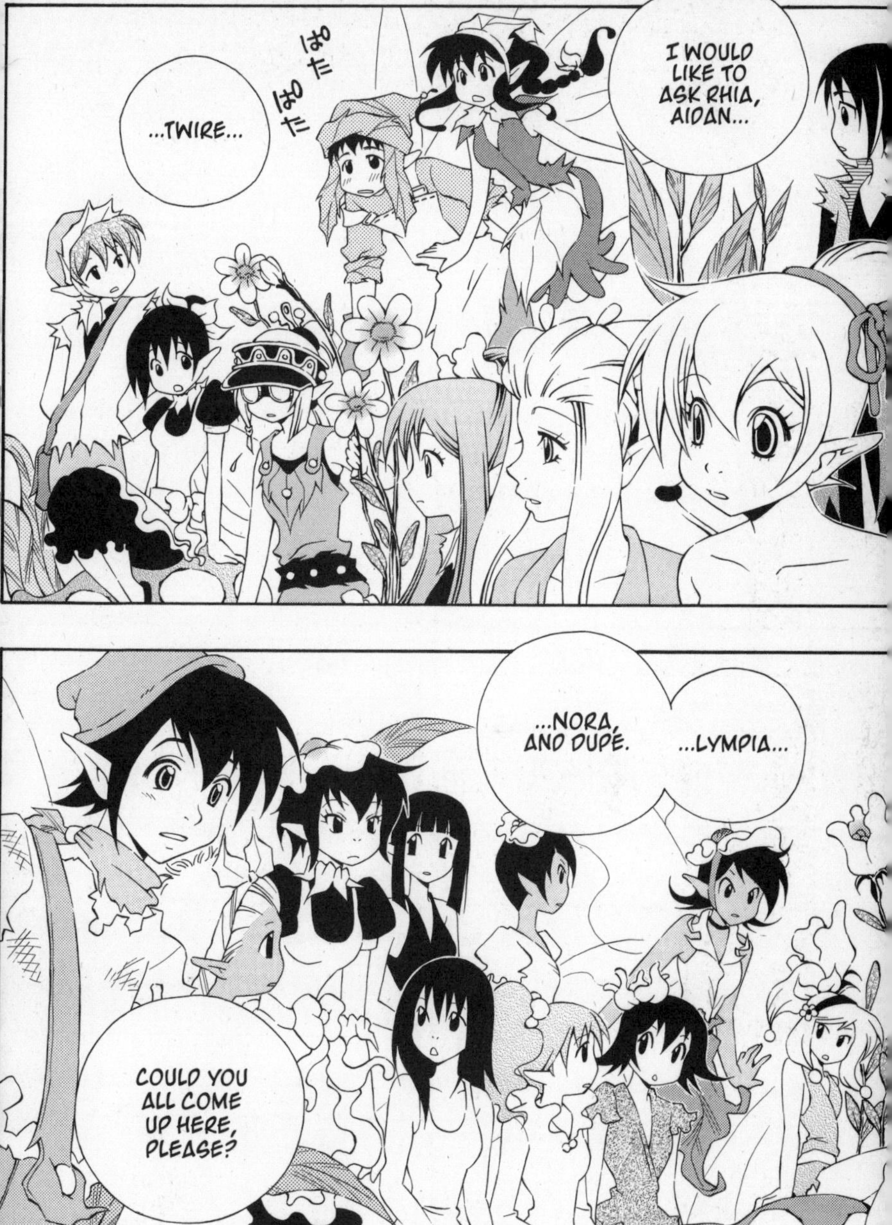
I WOULD LIKE TO ASK RHIA, AIDAN...
ぱたぱた
...TWIRE...
...LYMPIA...
...NORA, AND DUPE.
COULD YOU ALL COME UP HERE, PLEASE?

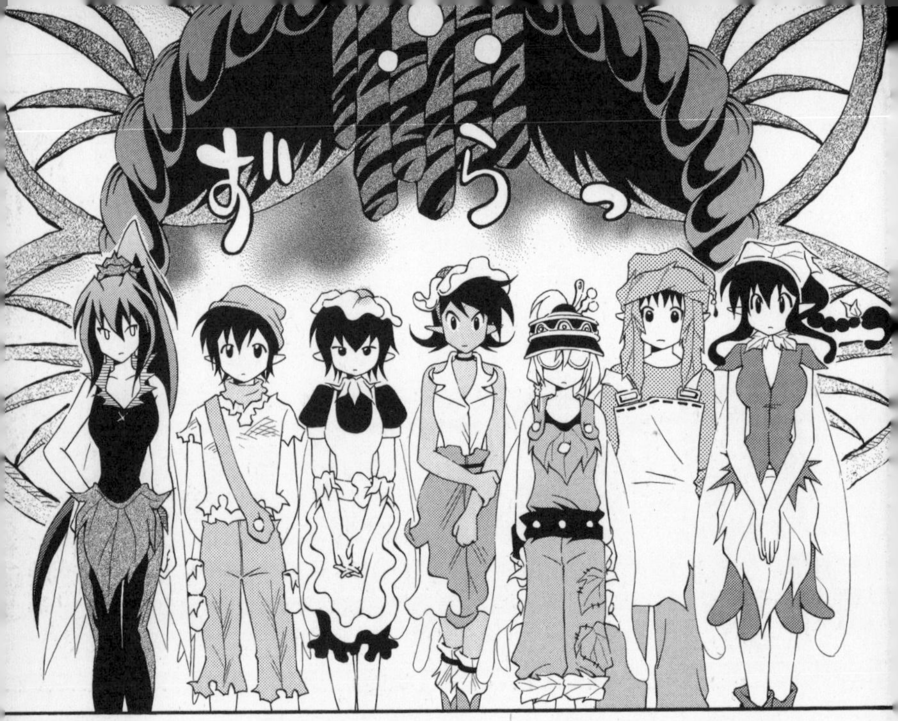
ずらっ
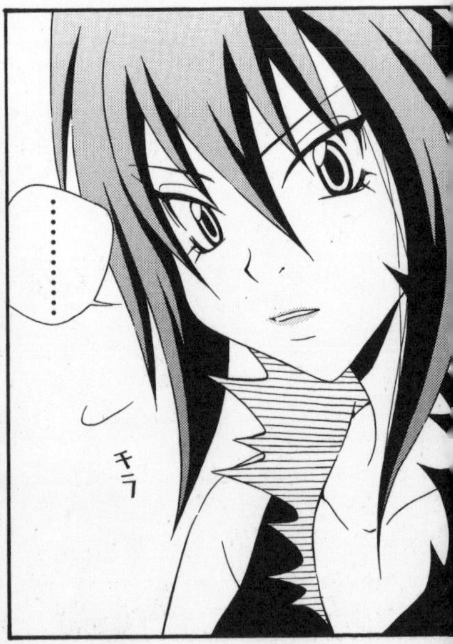
……
キラ
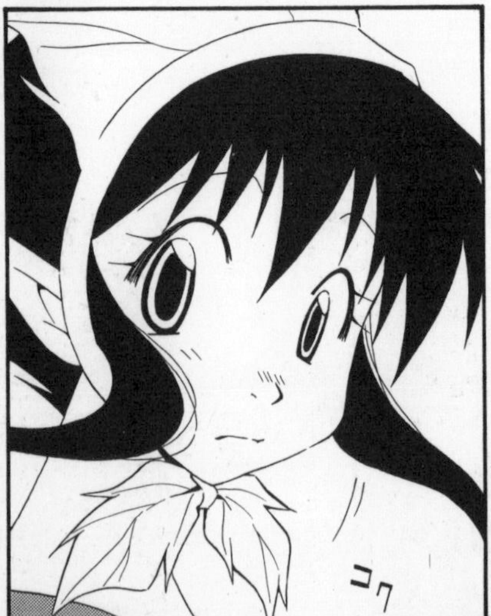
コク

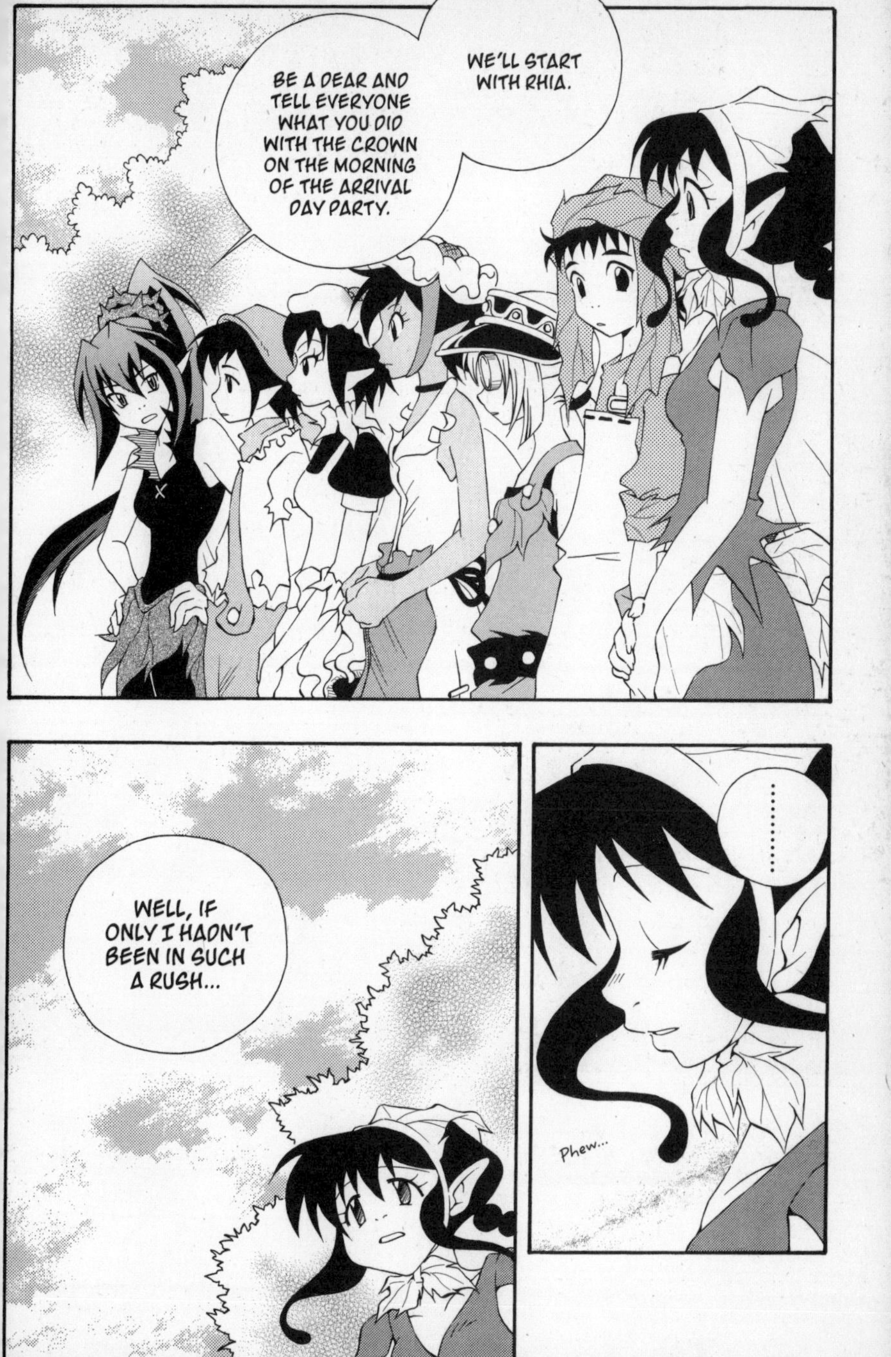
WE'LL START WITH RHIA.
BE A DEAR AND TELL EVERYONE WHAT YOU DID WITH THE CROWN ON THE MORNING OF THE ARRIVAL DAY PARTY.
....
Phew...
WELL, IF ONLY I HADN'T BEEN IN SUCH A RUSH...

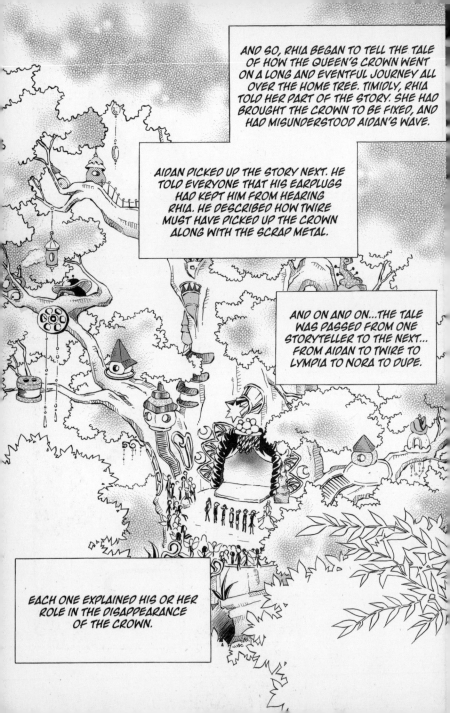

AND SO, RHIA BEGAN TO TELL THE TALE OF HOW THE QUEEN'S CROWN WENT ON A LONG AND EVENTFUL JOURNEY ALL OVER THE HOME TREE. TIMIDLY, RHIA TOLD HER PART OF THE STORY. SHE HAD BROUGHT THE CROWN TO BE FIXED, AND HAD MISUNDERSTOOD AIDAN'S WAVE.

AIDAN PICKED UP THE STORY NEXT. HE TOLD EVERYONE THAT HIS EARPLUGS HAD KEPT HIM FROM HEARING RHIA. HE DESCRIBED HOW TWIRE MUST HAVE PICKED UP THE CROWN ALONG WITH THE SCRAP METAL.

AND ON AND ON...THE TALE WAS PASSED FROM ONE STORYTELLER TO THE NEXT... FROM AIDAN TO TWIRE TO LYMPIA TO NORA TO DUPE.

EACH ONE EXPLAINED HIS OR HER ROLE IN THE DISAPPEARANCE OF THE CROWN.

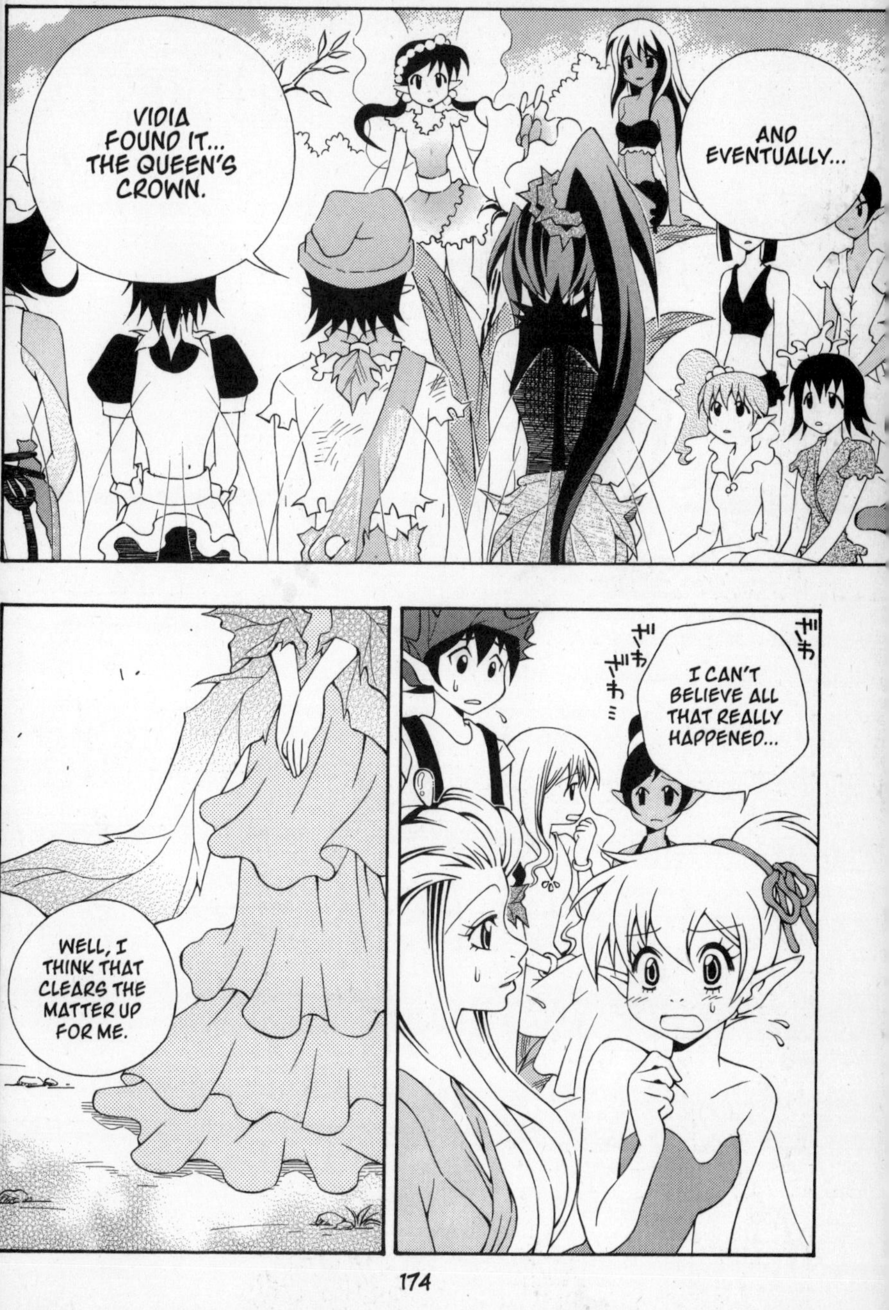
AND EVENTUALLY...
VIDIA FOUND IT... THE QUEEN'S CROWN.
ざわ
ざわ
ざわ
I CAN'T BELIEVE ALL THAT REALLY HAPPENED...
WELL, I THINK THAT CLEARS THE MATTER UP FOR ME.

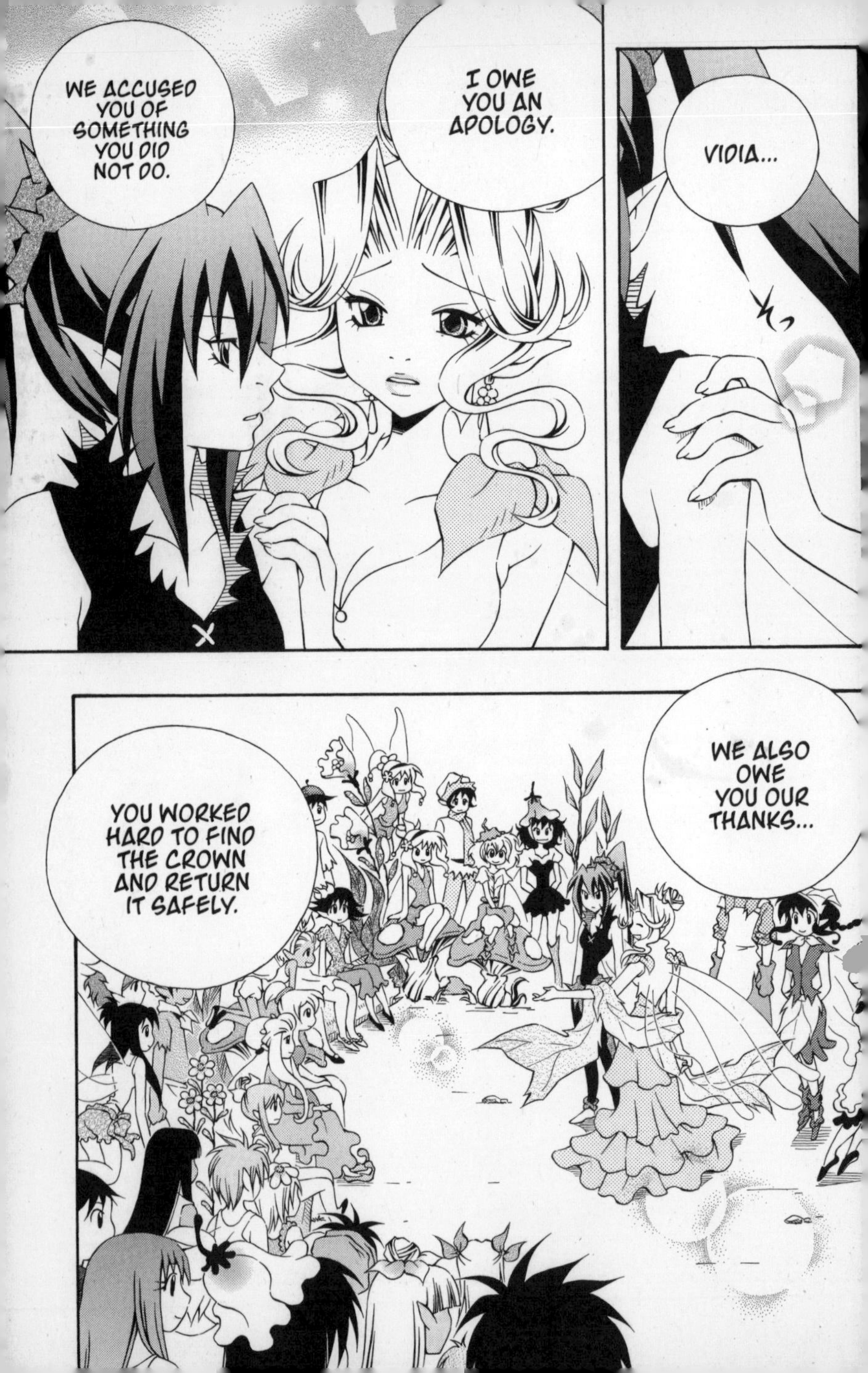
VIDIA...
I OWE YOU AN APOLOGY.
WE ACCUSED YOU OF SOMETHING YOU DID NOT DO.
WE ALSO OWE YOU OUR THANKS...
YOU WORKED HARD TO FIND THE CROWN AND RETURN IT SAFELY.

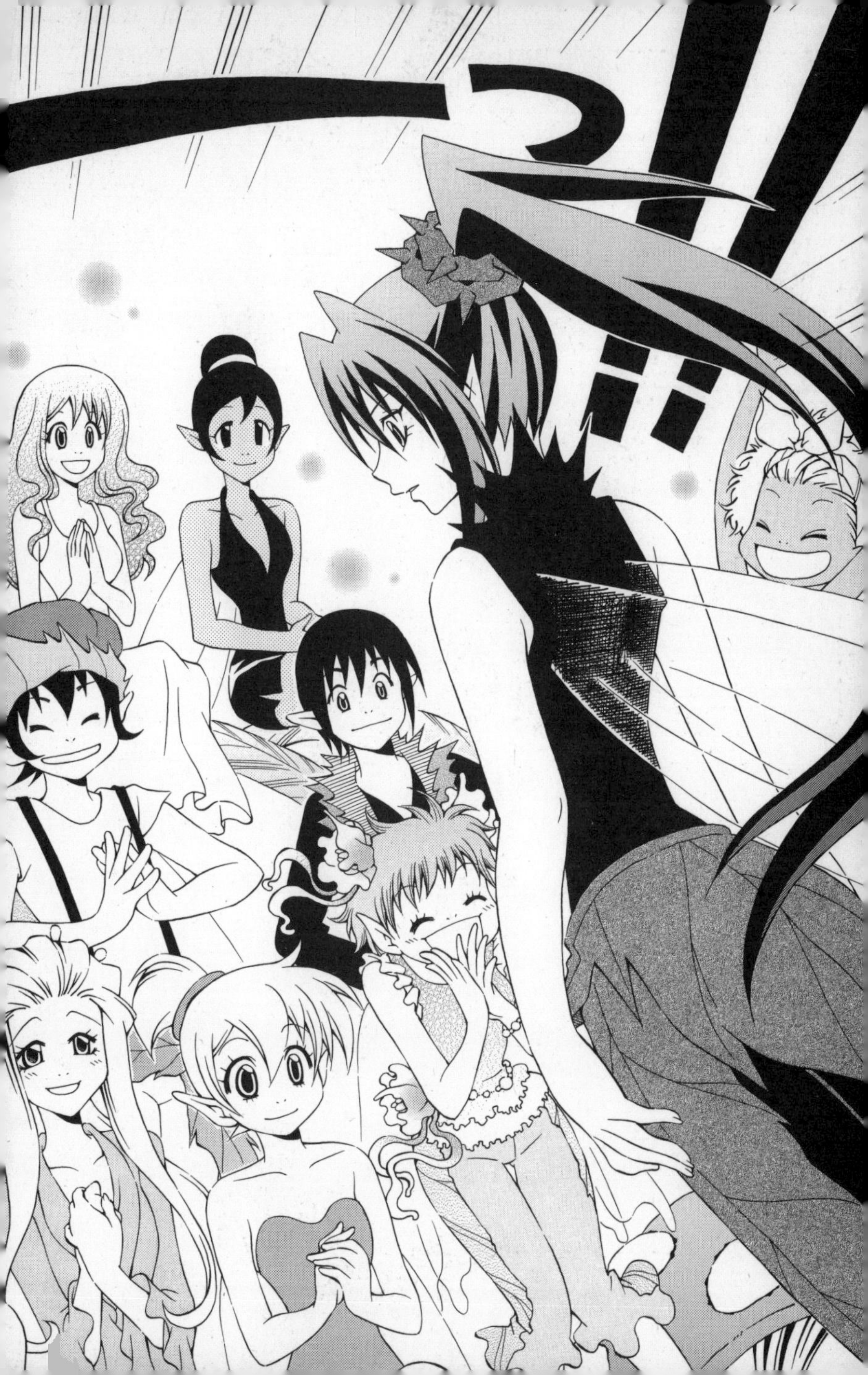
ーっ!!

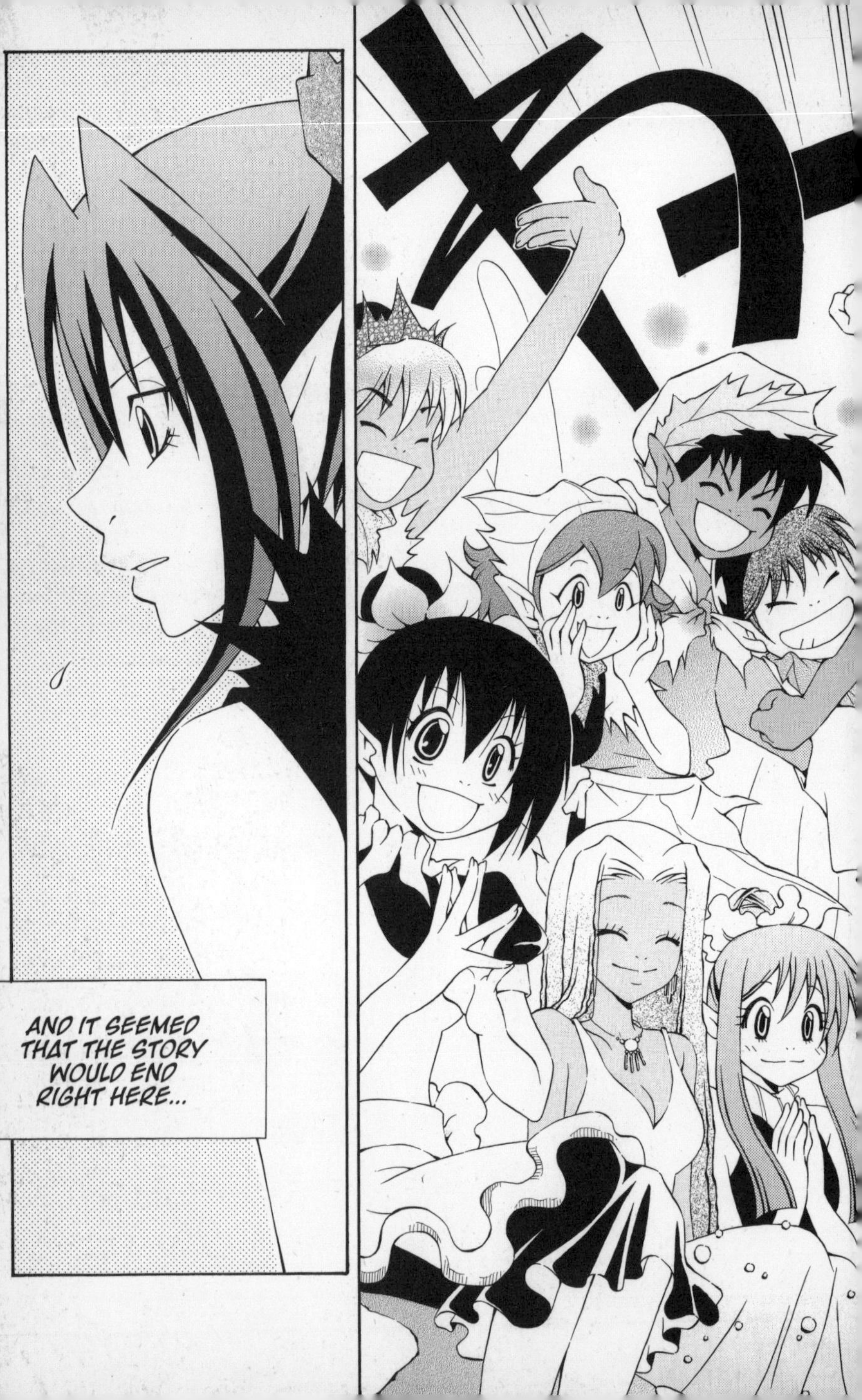
AND IT SEEMED THAT THE STORY WOULD END RIGHT HERE...

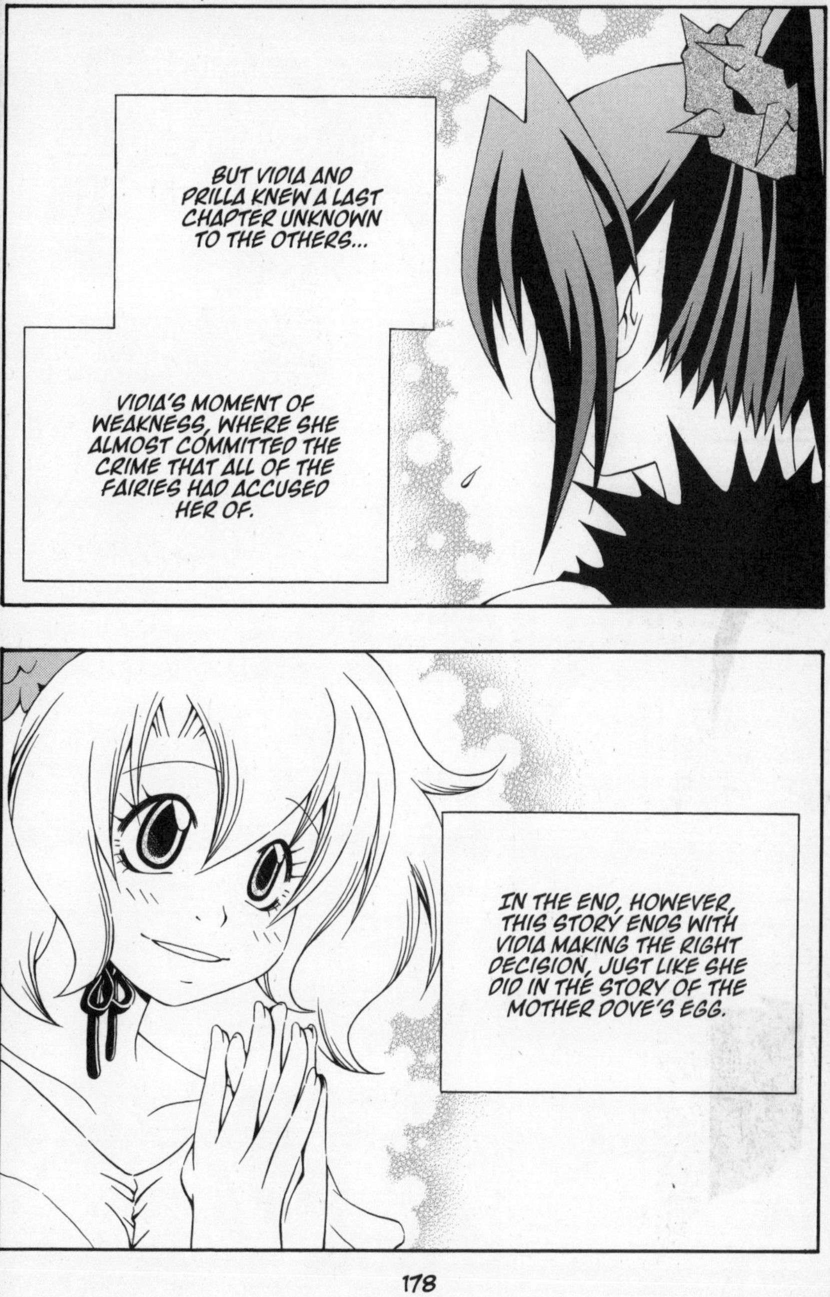
BUT VIDIA AND PRILLA KNEW A LAST CHAPTER UNKNOWN TO THE OTHERS...
VIDIA'S MOMENT OF WEAKNESS, WHERE SHE ALMOST COMMITTED THE CRIME THAT ALL OF THE FAIRIES HAD ACCUSED HER OF.
IN THE END, HOWEVER, THIS STORY ENDS WITH VIDIA MAKING THE RIGHT DECISION, JUST LIKE SHE DID IN THE STORY OF THE MOTHER DOVE'S EGG.

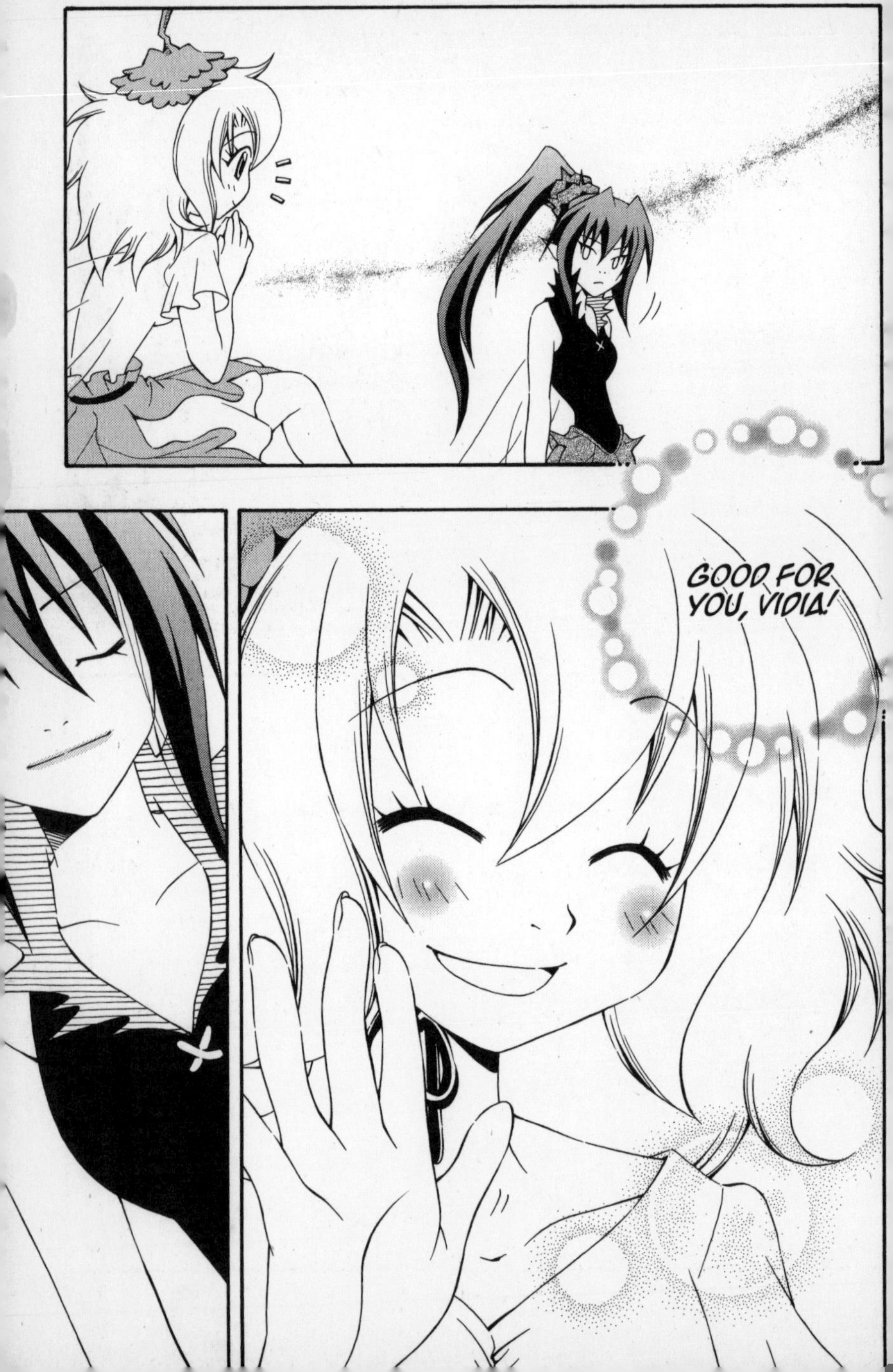
GOOD FOR YOU, VIDIA!

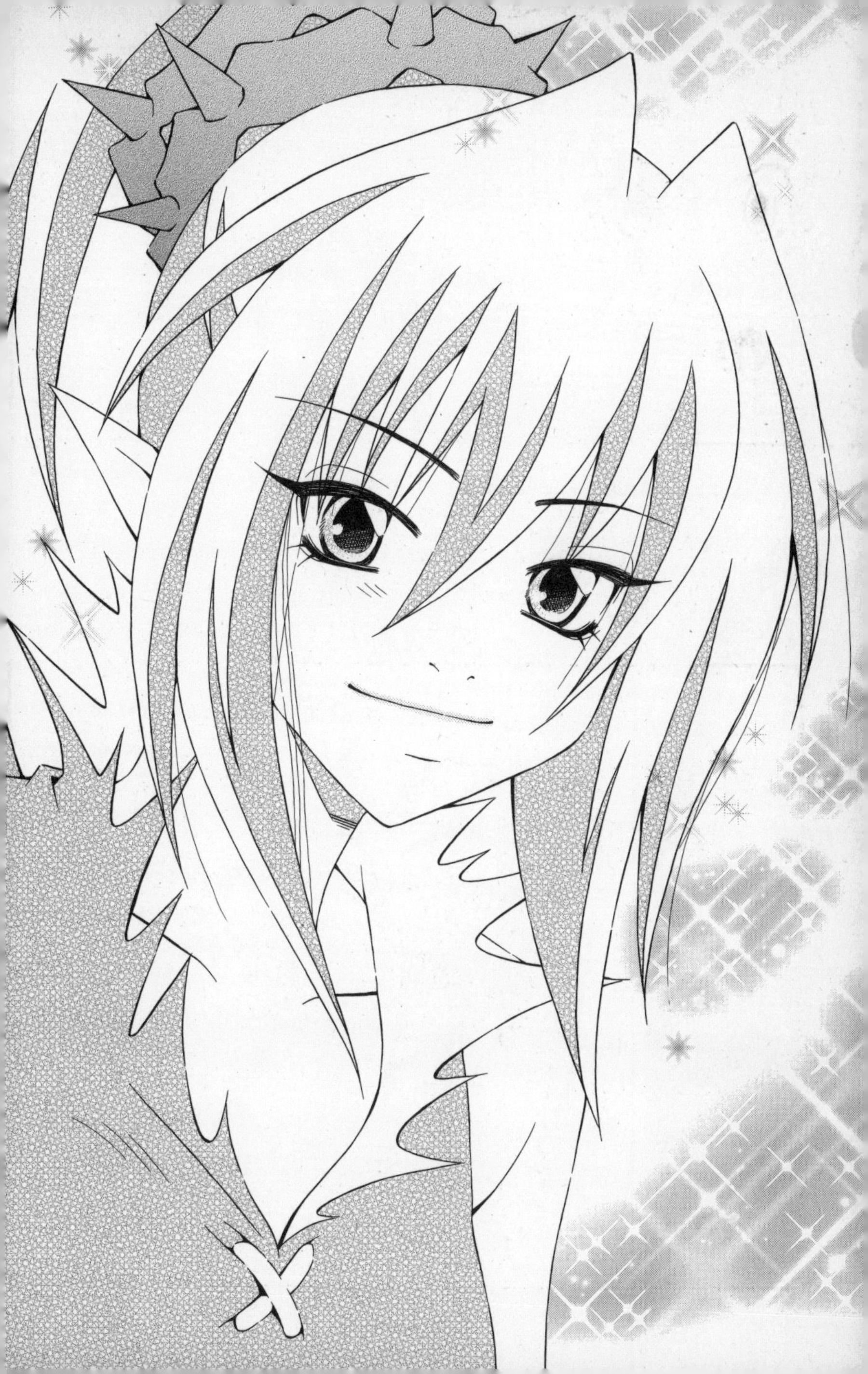

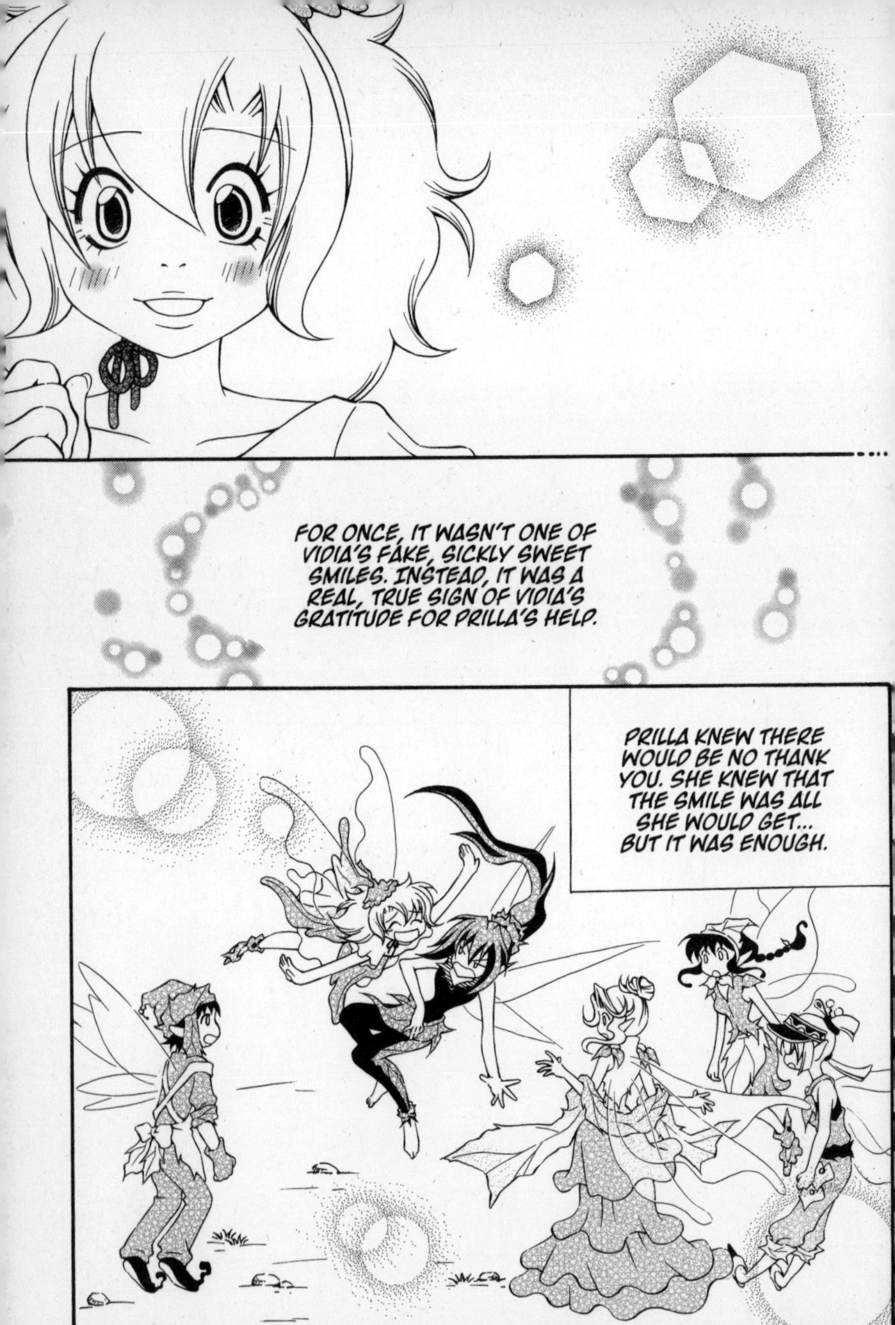
FOR ONCE, IT WASN'T ONE OF VIDIA'S FAKE, SICKLY SWEET SMILES. INSTEAD, IT WAS A REAL, TRUE SIGN OF VIDIA'S GRATITUDE FOR PRILLA'S HELP.
PRILLA KNEW THERE WOULD BE NO THANK YOU. SHE KNEW THAT THE SMILE WAS ALL SHE WOULD GET... BUT IT WAS ENOUGH.

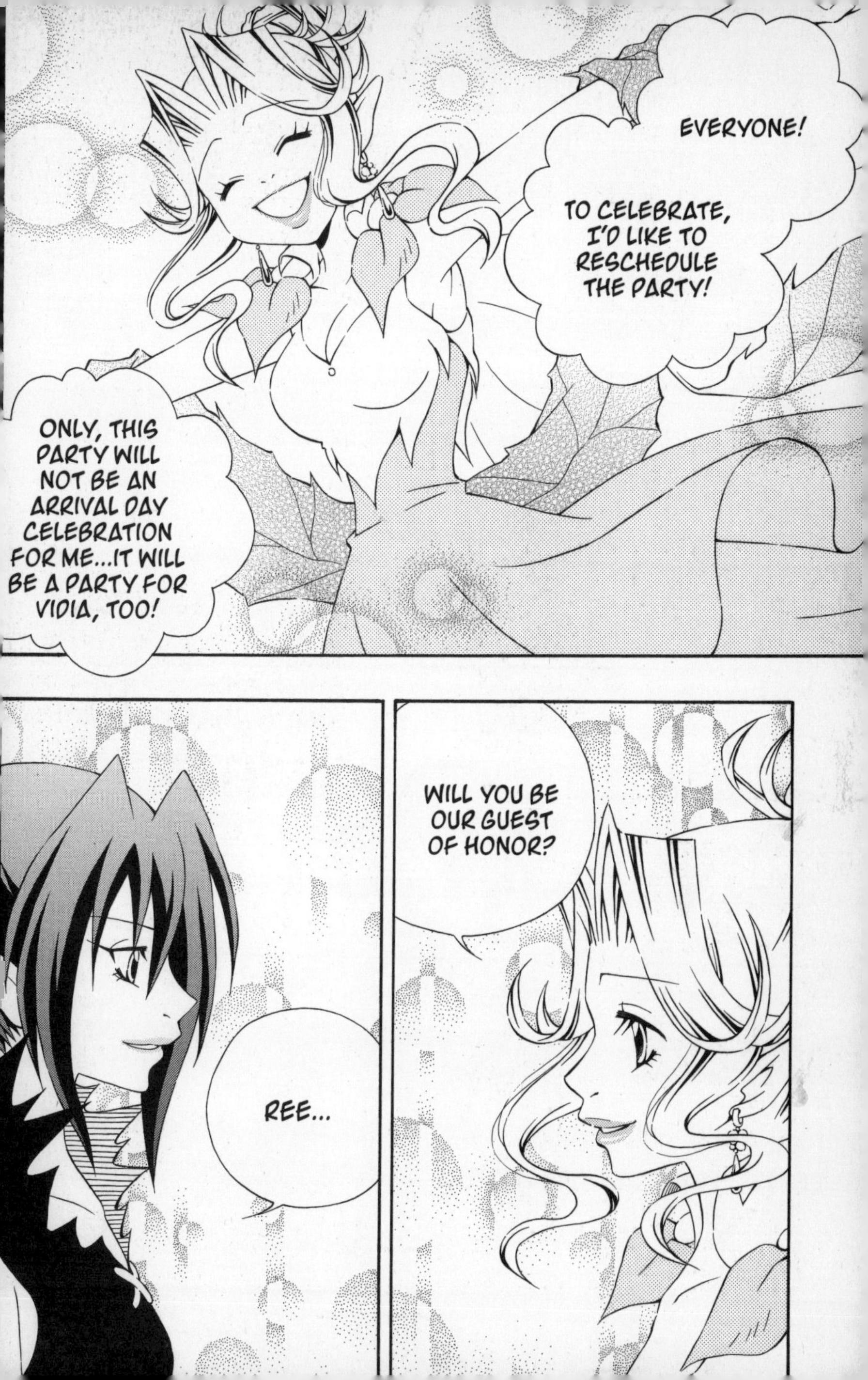
EVERYONE!
TO CELEBRATE, I'D LIKE TO RESCHEDULE THE PARTY!
ONLY, THIS PARTY WILL NOT BE AN ARRIVAL DAY CELEBRATION FOR ME...IT WILL BE A PARTY FOR VIDIA, TOO!
WILL YOU BE OUR GUEST OF HONOR?
REE...

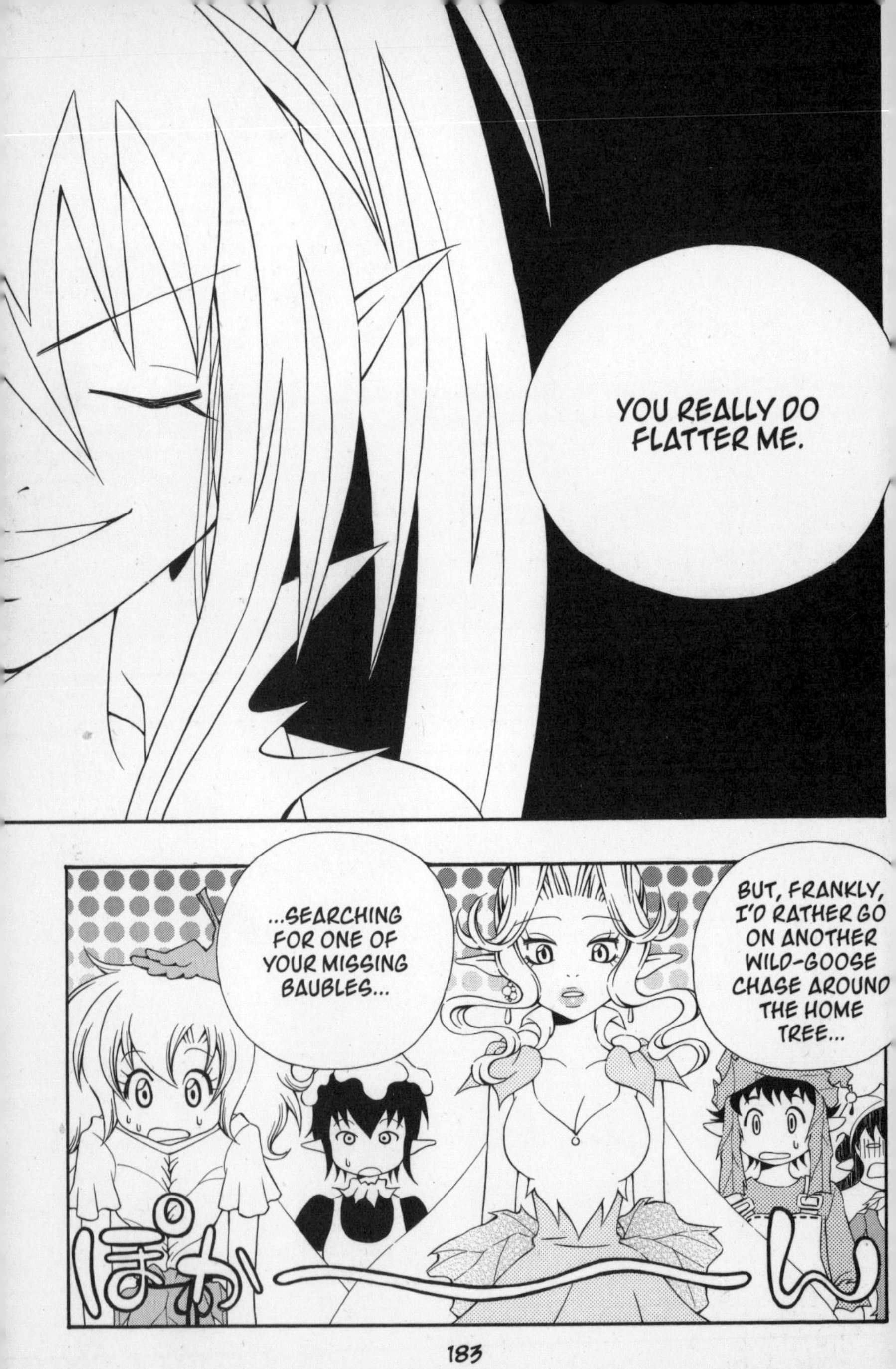
YOU REALLY DO FLATTER ME.
BUT, FRANKLY, I'D RATHER GO ON ANOTHER WILD-GOOSE CHASE AROUND THE HOME TREE...
...SEARCHING FOR ONE OF YOUR MISSING BAUBLES...
ぽわ〜ん

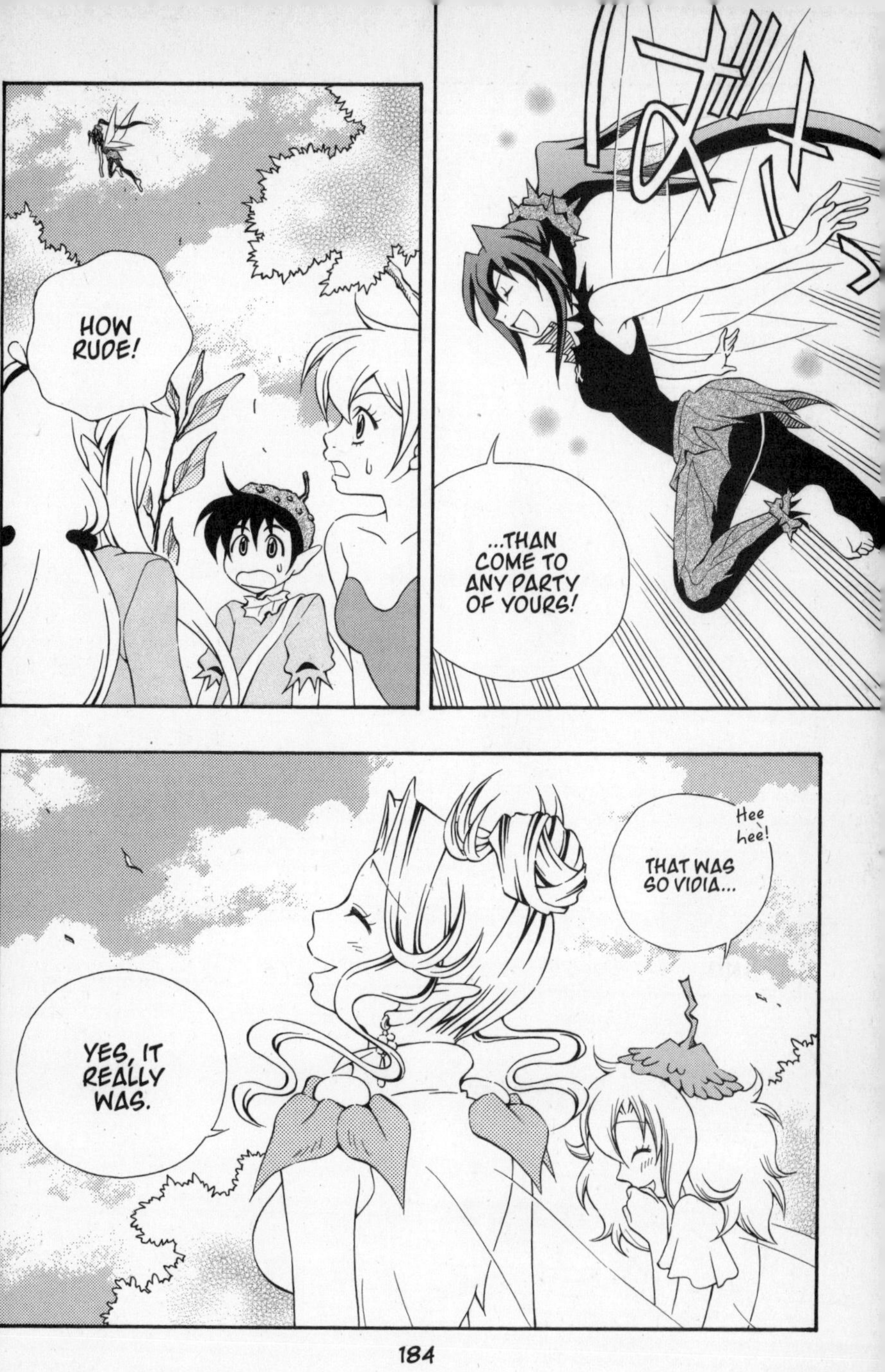
...THAN COME TO ANY PARTY OF YOURS!
HOW RUDE!
Hee hee!
THAT WAS SO VIDIA...
YES, IT REALLY WAS.

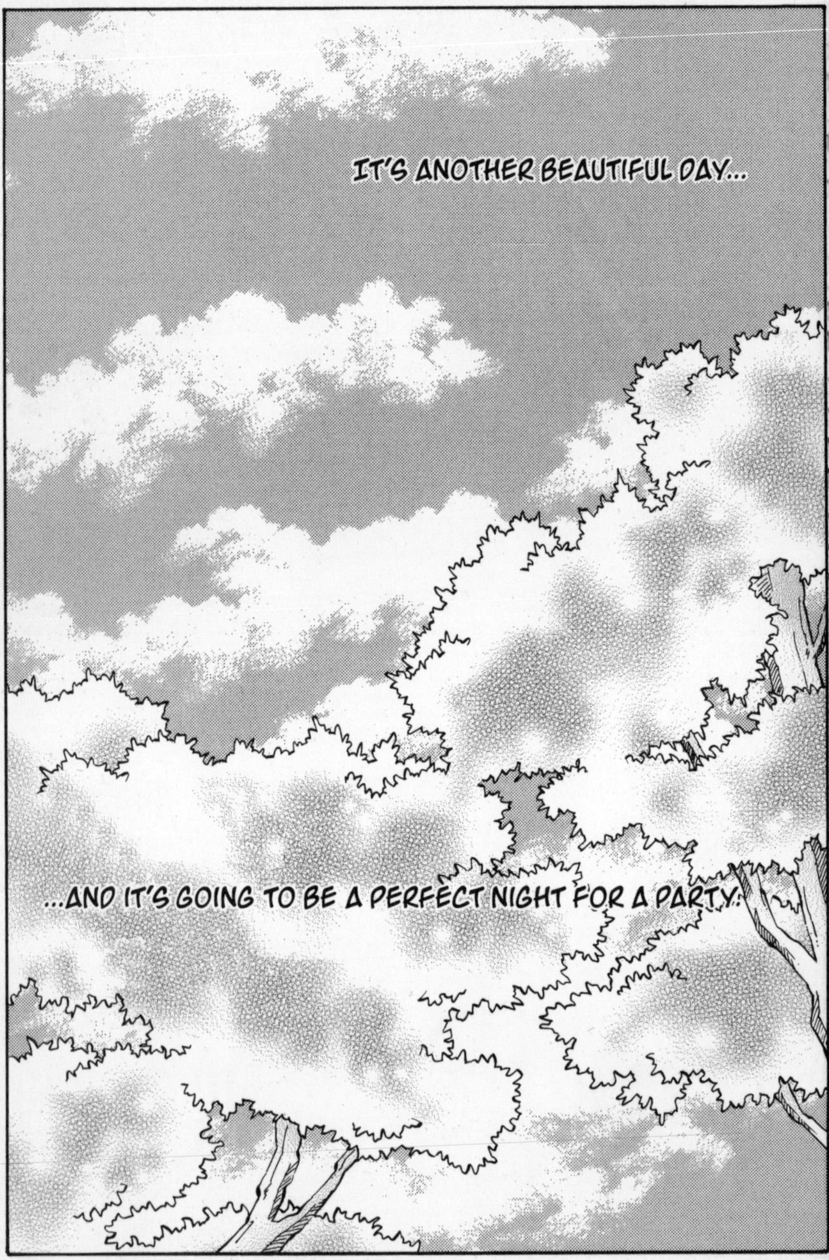
IT'S ANOTHER BEAUTIFUL DAY...
...AND IT'S GOING TO BE A PERFECT NIGHT FOR A PARTY.

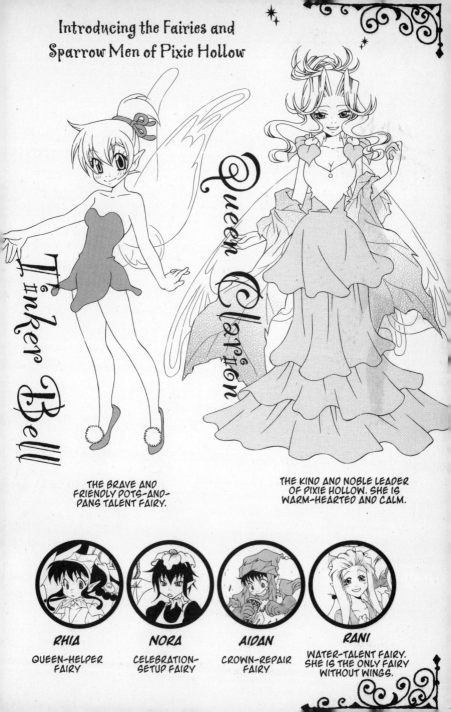

Introducing the Fairies and Sparrow Men of Pixie Hollow

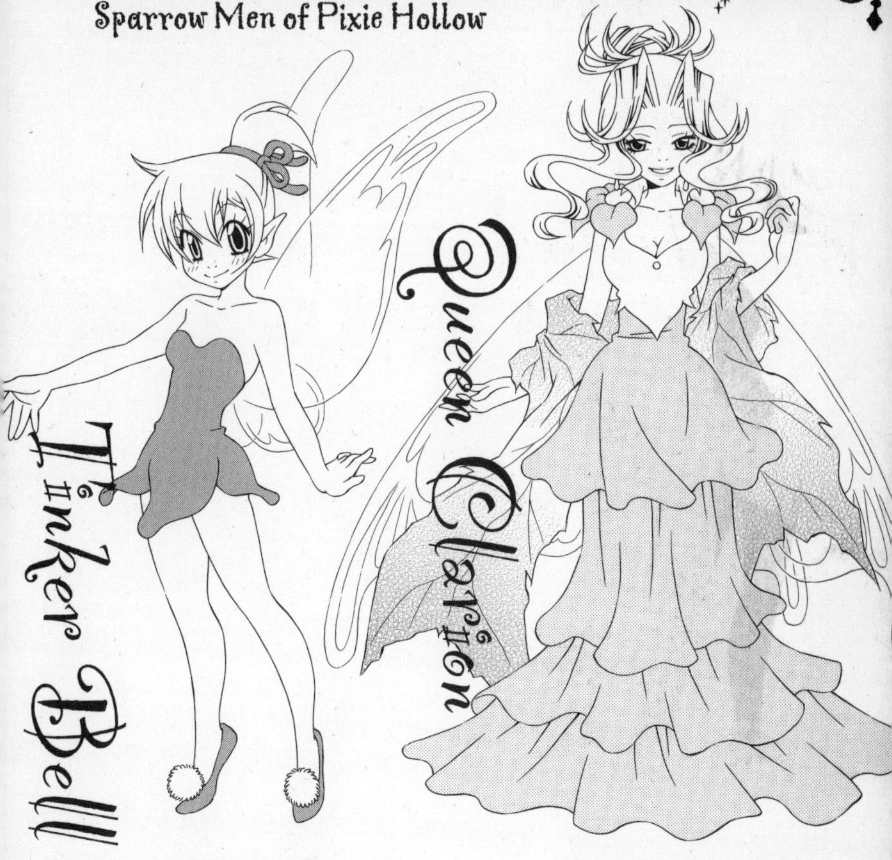

Tinker Bell
Queen Clarion

THE BRAVE AND FRIENDLY POTS-AND-PANS TALENT FAIRY.

THE KIND AND NOBLE LEADER OF PIXIE HOLLOW. SHE IS WARM-HEARTED AND CALM.

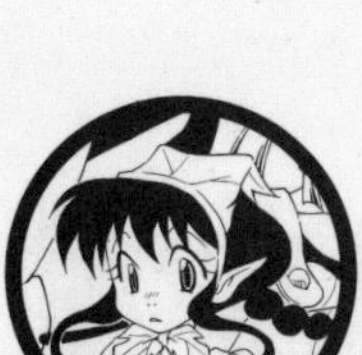

RHIA

QUEEN-HELPER FAIRY

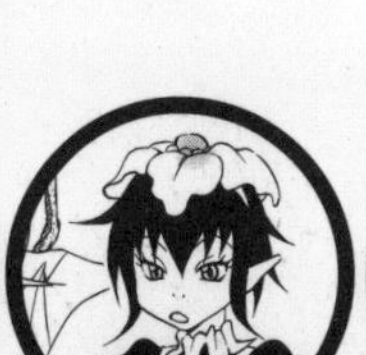

NORA

CELEBRATION-SETUP FAIRY

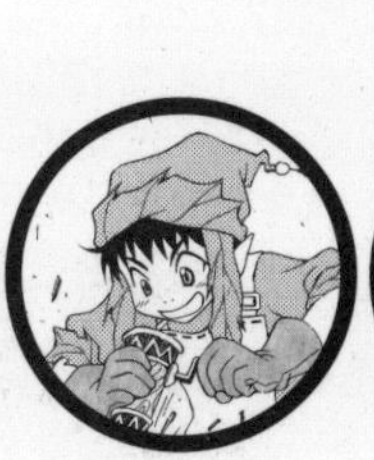

AIDAN

CROWN-REPAIR FAIRY

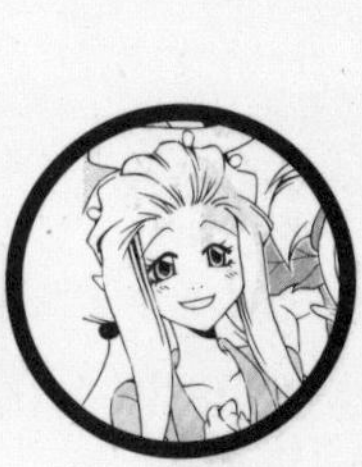

RANI

WATER-TALENT FAIRY. SHE IS THE ONLY FAIRY WITHOUT WINGS.

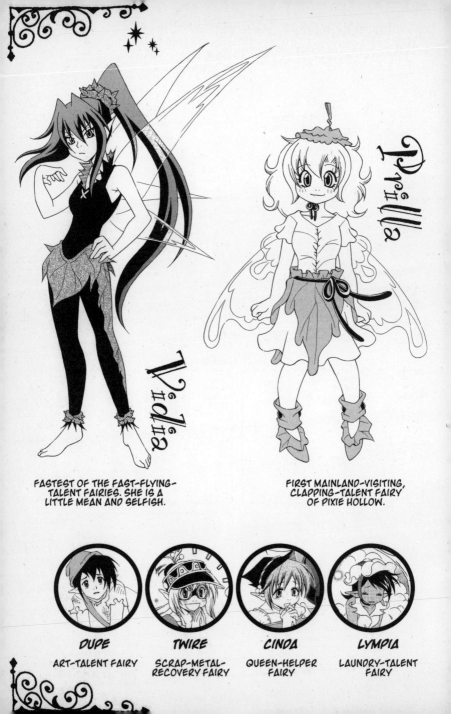

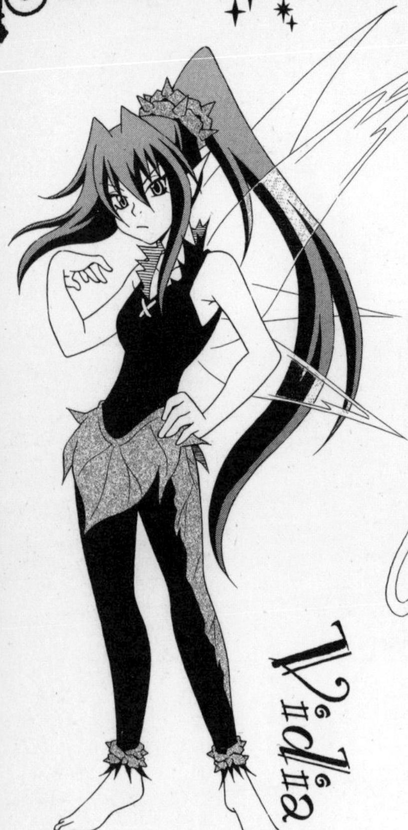
Vidia

FASTEST OF THE FAST-FLYING-TALENT FAIRIES. SHE IS A LITTLE MEAN AND SELFISH.

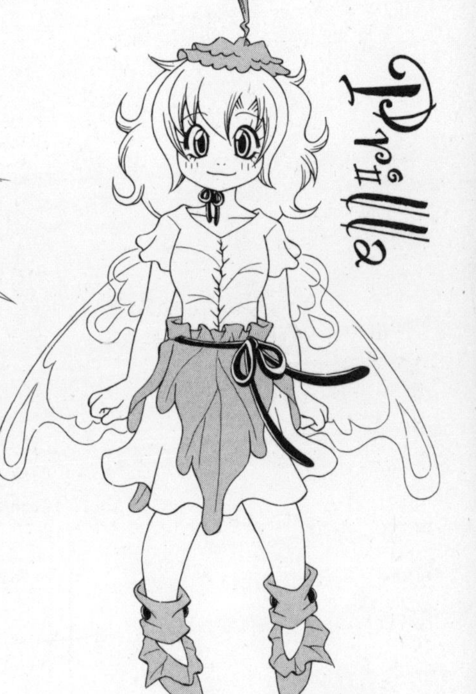
Prilla

FIRST MAINLAND-VISITING, CLAPPING-TALENT FAIRY OF PIXIE HOLLOW.

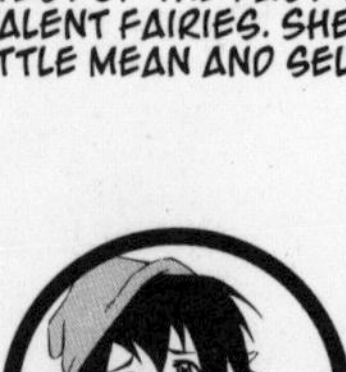

DUPE

ART-TALENT FAIRY

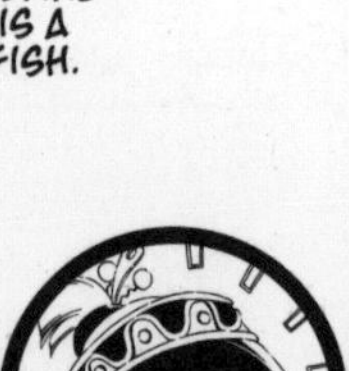

TWIRE

SCRAP-METAL-RECOVERY FAIRY

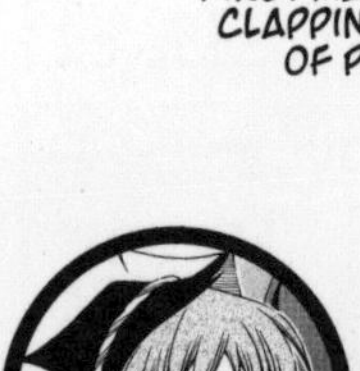

CINDA

QUEEN-HELPER FAIRY

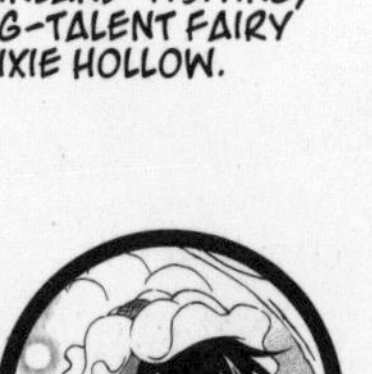

LYMPIA

LAUNDRY-TALENT FAIRY

日記ちっ… 妖精日記 chicchakute kawaii 妖精日記

Diary Of Cute Little Fairies

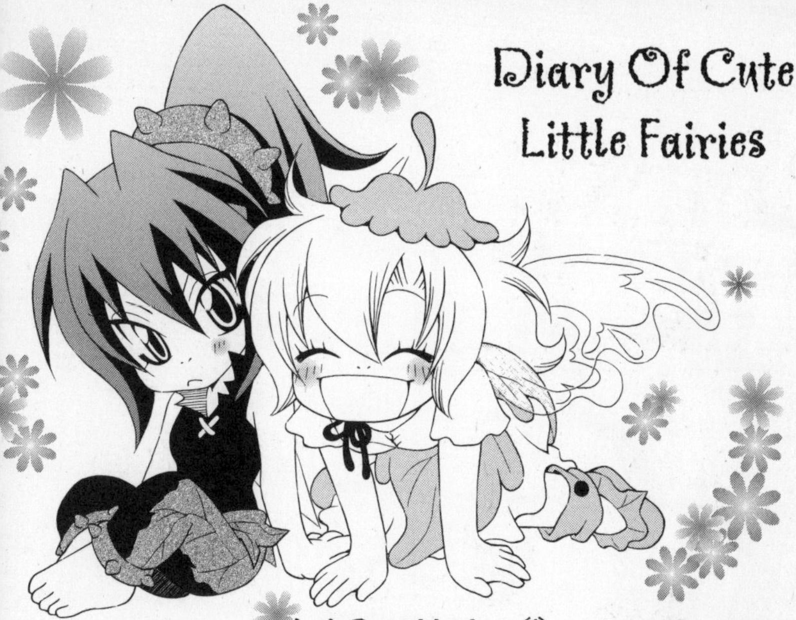

Let's Count Numbers (1)

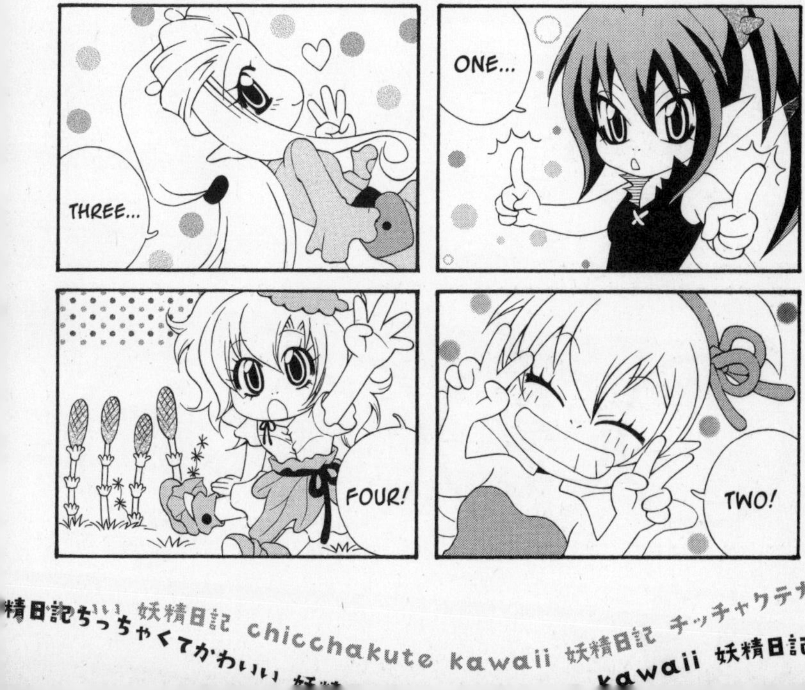
ONE...
TWO!
THREE...
FOUR!

精日記ちっちゃくてかわいい 妖精日記 chicchakute kawaii 妖精日記 チッチャクテカワイイ kawaii 妖精日記 チッチ

ちゃくてかわいい 妖精日記 chicchakute kawaii 妖精日記 チッチャクテカワ

Tink's Mood Swings

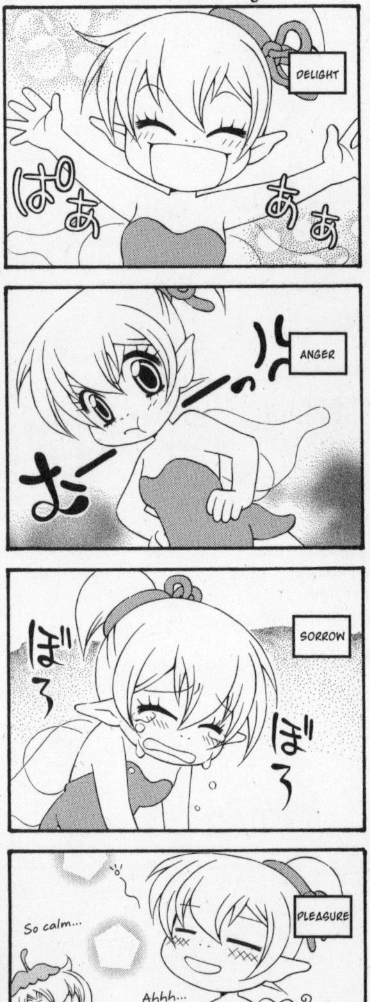
DELIGHT
ぱあ
ああ
ANGER
SORROW
ぽろ
ぽろ
PLEASURE
So calm...
Ahhh...
TOTALLY RELAXED... ♡

Vidia's Mood Swings

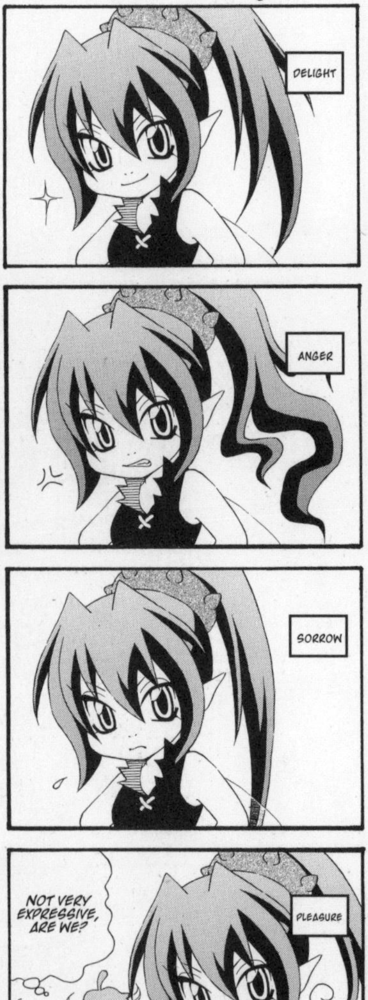
DELIGHT
ANGER
SORROW
PLEASURE
NOT VERY EXPRESSIVE, ARE WE?
Sheesh!

ちゃくてかわいい 妖精日記 chicchakute kawaii 妖精日記 チッチャクテカワ

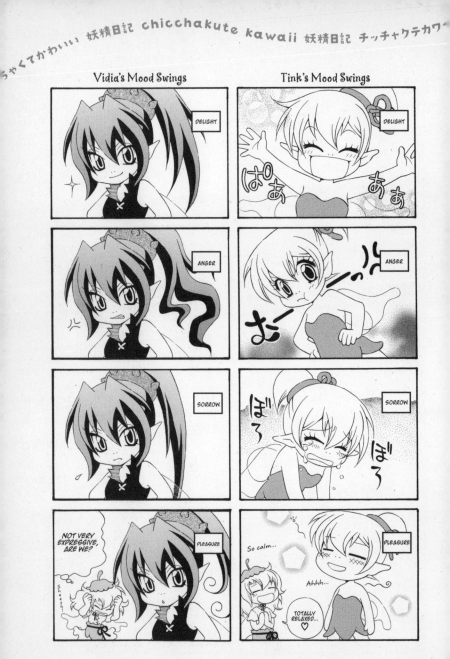

A Cup Of Tea

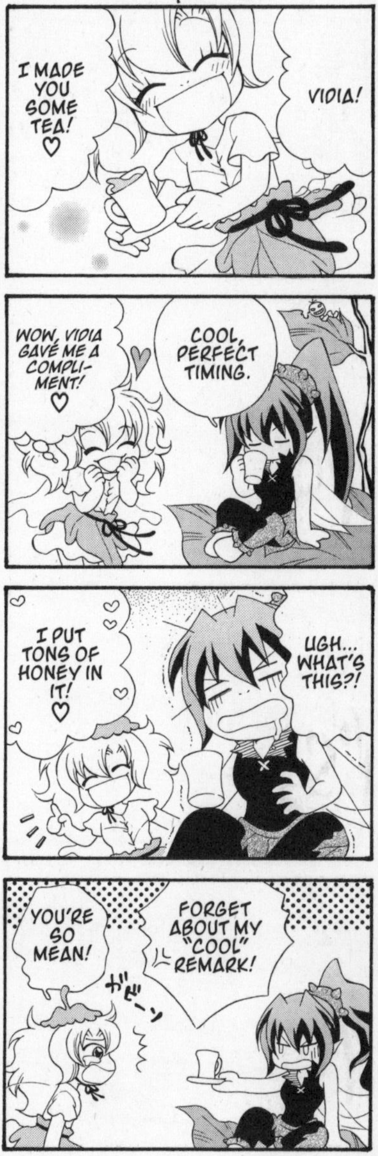
VIDIA!
I MADE YOU SOME TEA! ♡
COOL, PERFECT TIMING.
WOW, VIDIA GAVE ME A COMPLIMENT! ♡
UGH... WHAT'S THIS?!
I PUT TONS OF HONEY IN IT! ♡
FORGET ABOUT MY "COOL" REMARK!
ガビーン
YOU'RE SO MEAN!

Another Cup Of Tea

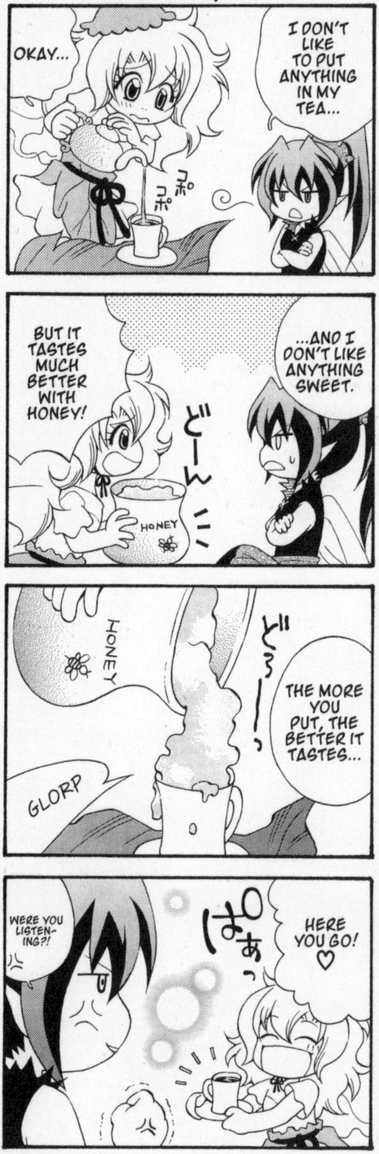
I DON'T LIKE TO PUT ANYTHING IN MY TEA...
コポコポ
OKAY...
...AND I DON'T LIKE ANYTHING SWEET.
どーん
BUT IT TASTES MUCH BETTER WITH HONEY!
どろーっ
THE MORE YOU PUT, THE BETTER IT TASTES...
HONEY
GLORP
HERE YOU GO! ♡
ぱあっ
WERE YOU LISTENING?!

ちゃくてかわいい 妖精日記 chicchakute kawaii 妖精日記 チッチャクテカワ

Let's Count Numbers (2)

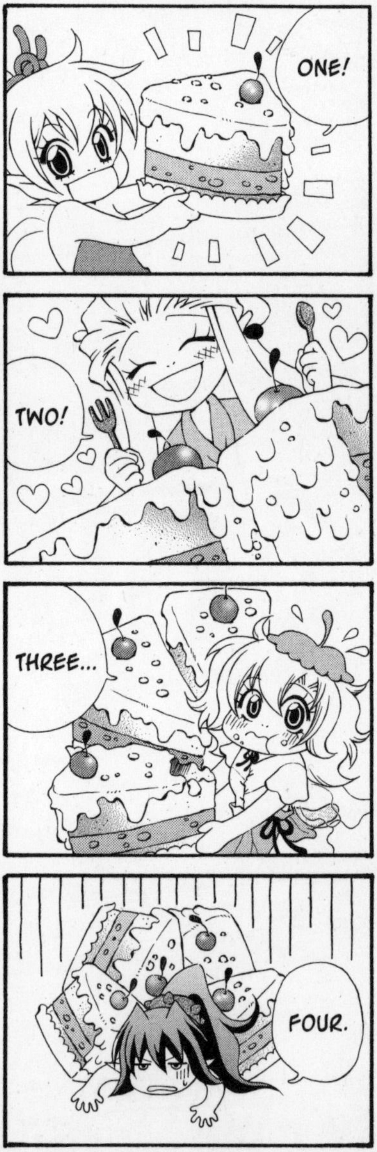
ONE!
TWO!
THREE...
FOUR.

Let's Nap Together

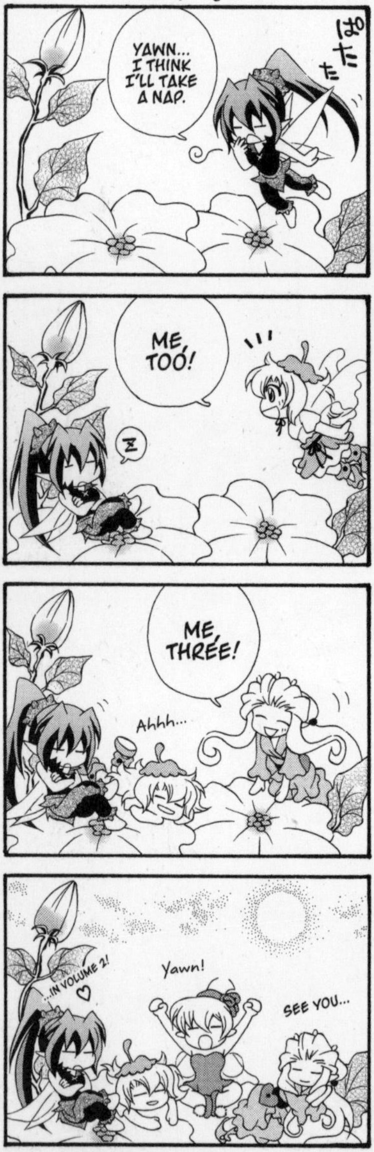
ぱたた
YAWN... I THINK I'LL TAKE A NAP.
ME, TOO!
z
ME, THREE!
Ahhh...
Yawn!
SEE YOU...
...IN VOLUME 2! ♡

To Be Continued In Volume 2 (Probably)

ちゃくてかわいい 妖精日記 chicchakute kawaii 妖精日記 チッチャクテカワ

妖精日記 chicchakute kawaii 妖精日記 チッチャクテカワイイ 妖精日記

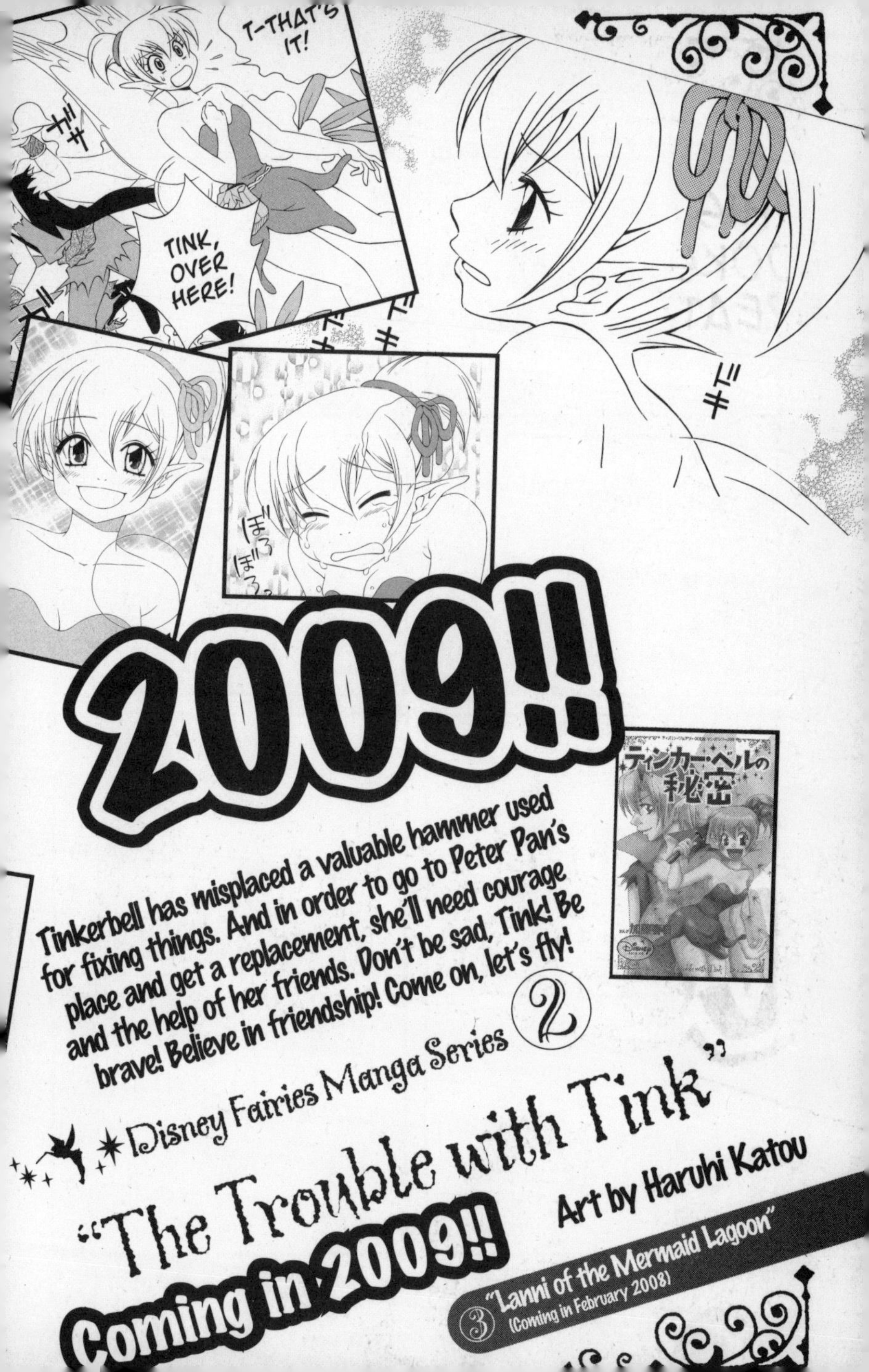

T-THAT'S IT!
TINK, OVER HERE!
2009!!
ティンカー・ベルの秘密
Tinkerbell has misplaced a valuable hammer used for fixing things. And in order to go to Peter Pan's place and get a replacement, she'll need courage and the help of her friends. Don't be sad, Tink! Be brave! Believe in friendship! Come on, let's fly!
Disney Fairies Manga Series 2
"The Trouble with Tink"
Art by Haruhi Katou
Coming in 2009!!
3 "Lanni of the Mermaid Lagoon" (Coming in February 2008)

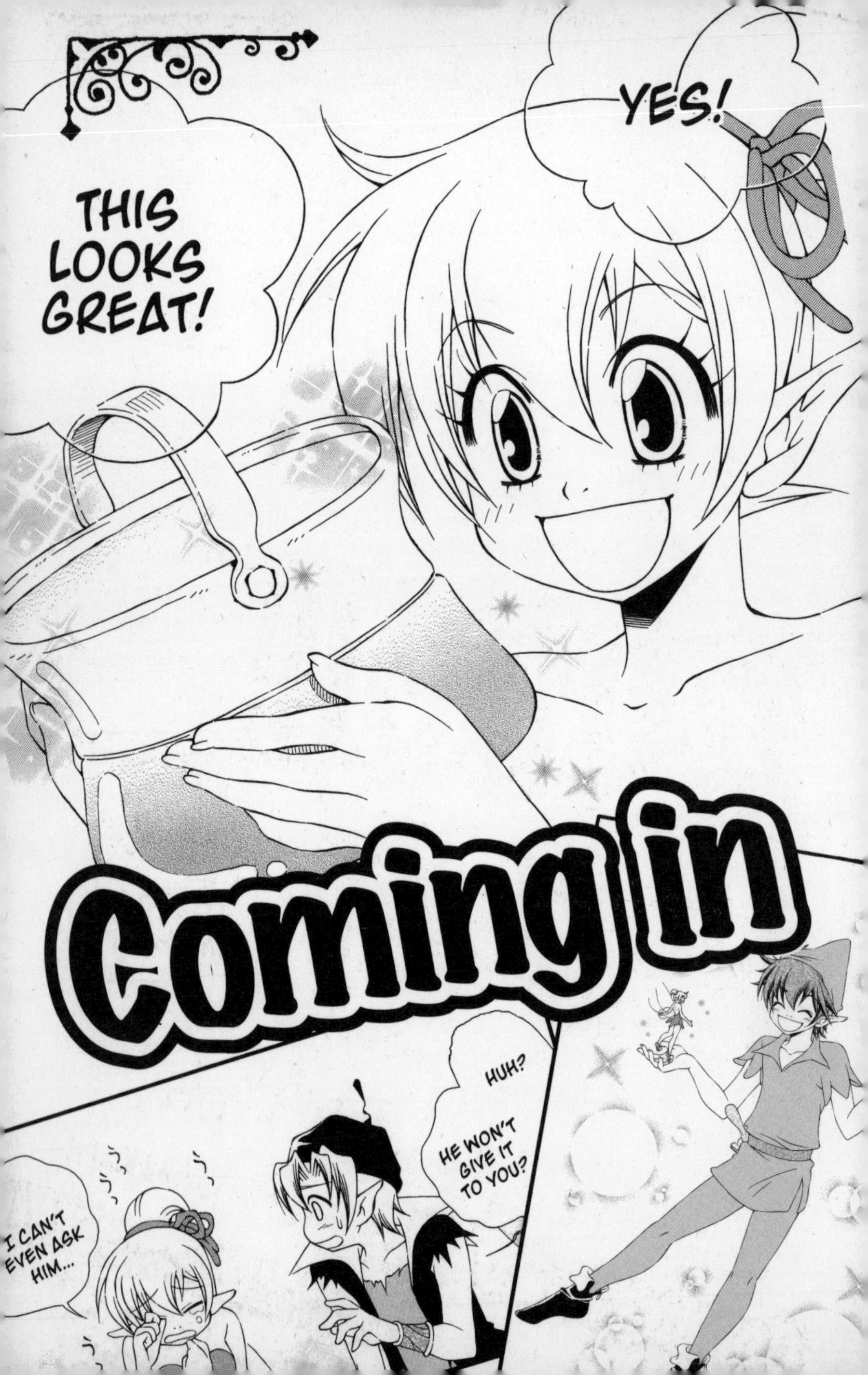
YES!
THIS LOOKS GREAT!
Coming in
HUH?
HE WON'T GIVE IT TO YOU?
I CAN'T EVEN ASK HIM...

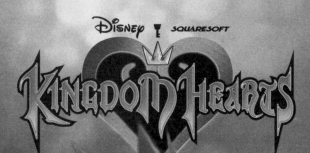

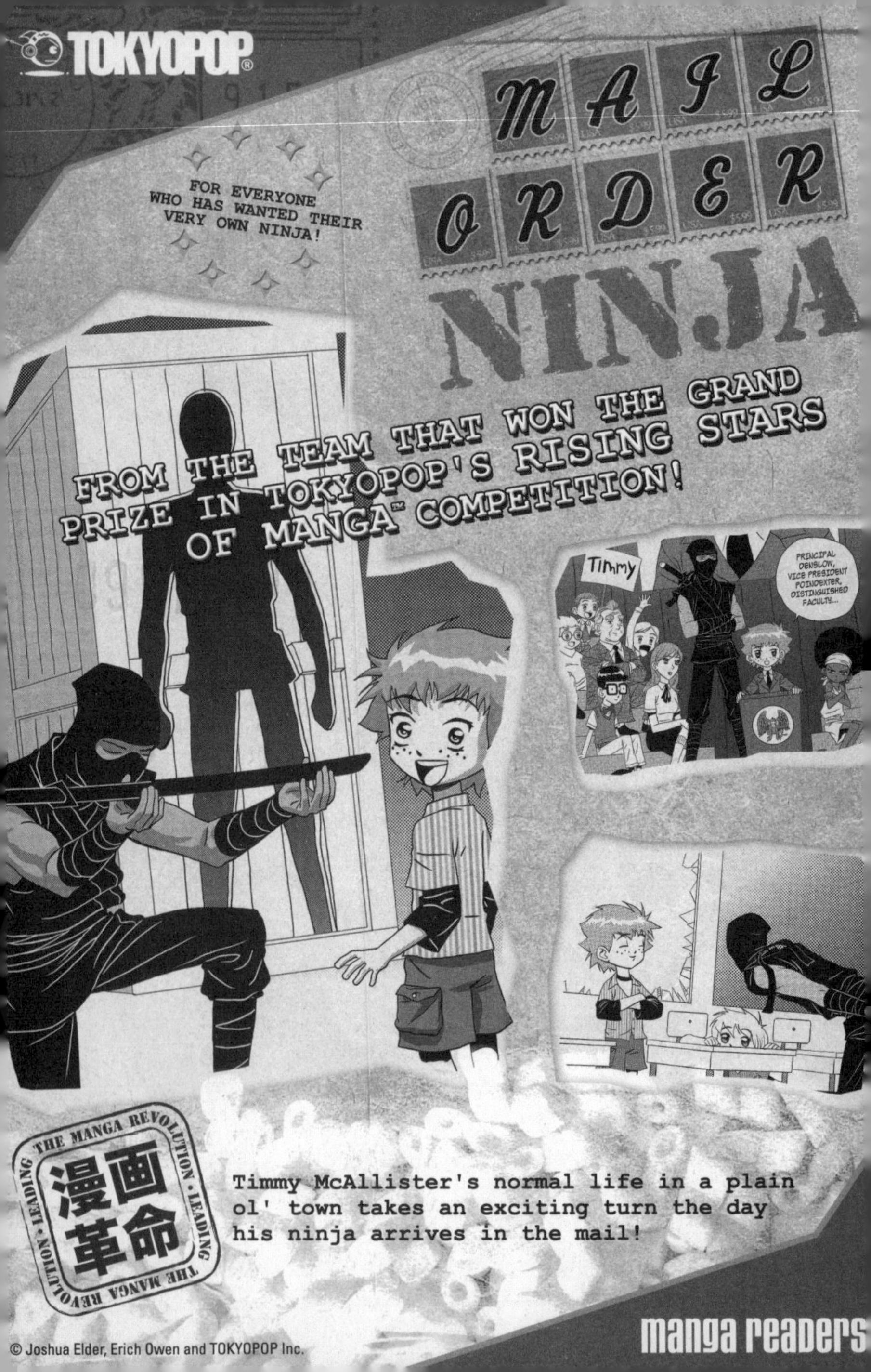
TOKYOPOP®
MAIL ORDER NINJA
FOR EVERYONE WHO HAS WANTED THEIR VERY OWN NINJA!
FROM THE TEAM THAT WON THE GRAND PRIZE IN TOKYOPOP'S RISING STARS OF MANGA™ COMPETITION!
Timmy
PRINCIPAL DENSLOW, VICE PRESIDENT POINDEXTER, DISTINGUISHED FACULTY...
THE MANGA REVOLUTION · LEADING THE MANGA REVOLUTION · LEADING
漫画革命
Timmy McAllister's normal life in a plain ol' town takes an exciting turn the day his ninja arrives in the mail!
manga readers
© Joshua Elder, Erich Owen and TOKYOPOP Inc.

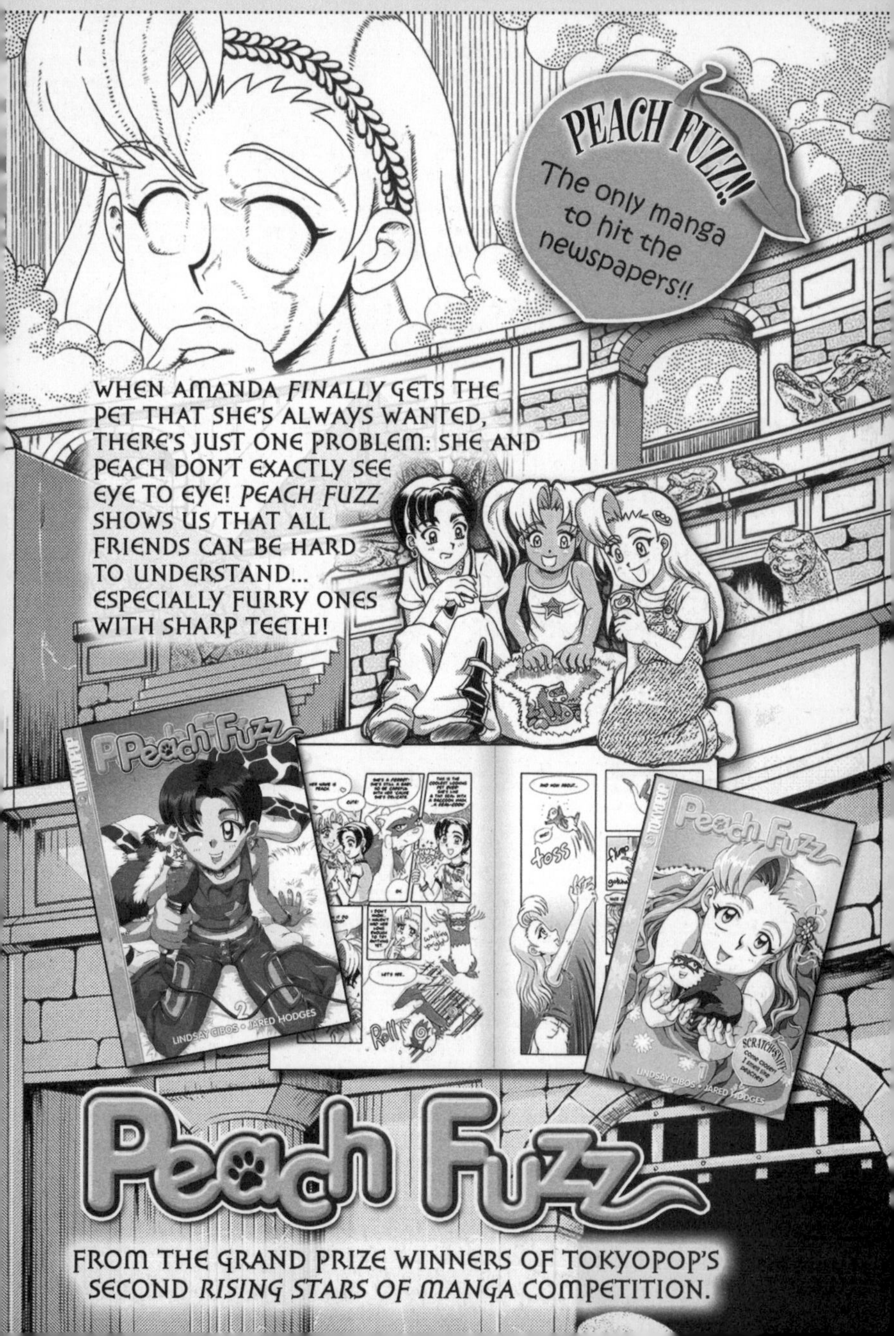
PEACH FUZZ!!
The only manga to hit the newspapers!!
WHEN AMANDA *FINALLY* GETS THE PET THAT SHE'S ALWAYS WANTED, THERE'S JUST ONE PROBLEM: SHE AND PEACH DON'T EXACTLY SEE EYE TO EYE! *PEACH FUZZ* SHOWS US THAT ALL FRIENDS CAN BE HARD TO UNDERSTAND... ESPECIALLY FURRY ONES WITH SHARP TEETH!
Peach Fuzz
TOKYOPOP
2
LINDSAY CIBOS • JARED HODGES
toss
Roll
Peach Fuzz
TOKYOPOP
1
LINDSAY CIBOS • JARED HODGES
Peach Fuzz
FROM THE GRAND PRIZE WINNERS OF TOKYOPOP'S SECOND *RISING STARS OF MANGA* COMPETITION.

THE EPIC STORY OF A FERRET WHO DEFIED HER CAGE.

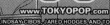

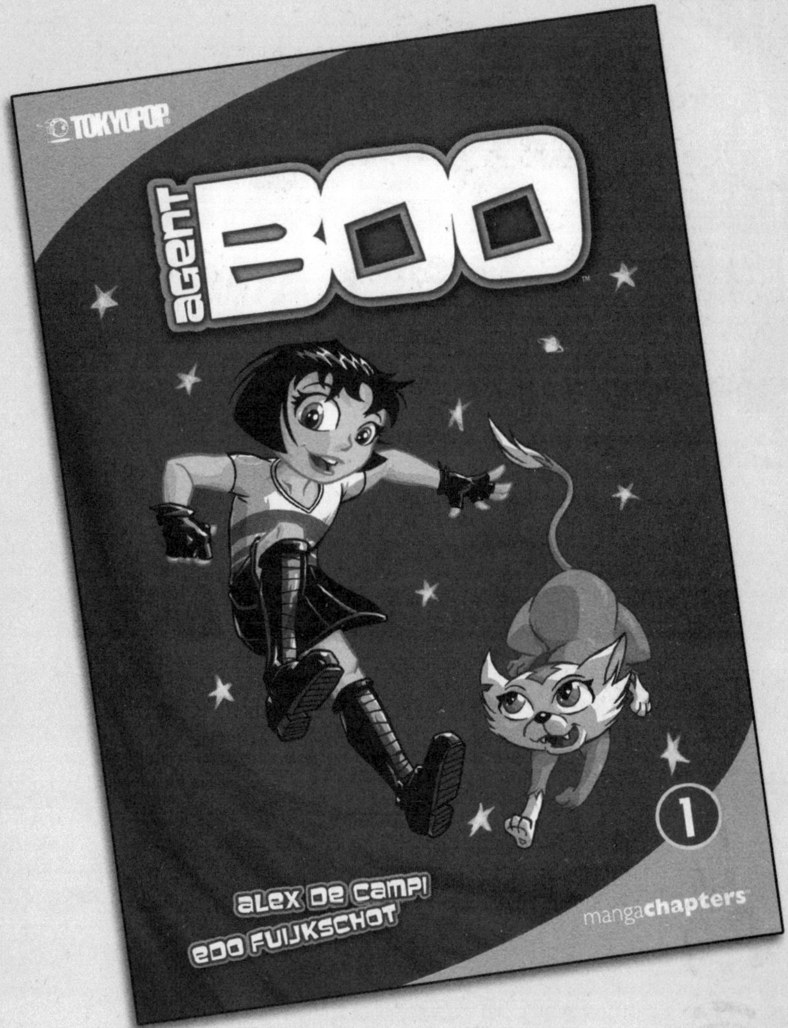
TOKYOPOP
agent BOO
1
alex de campi
edo fuijkschot
mangachapters

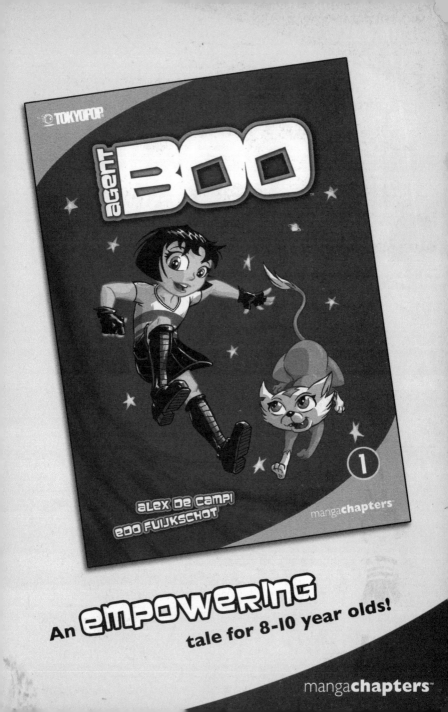

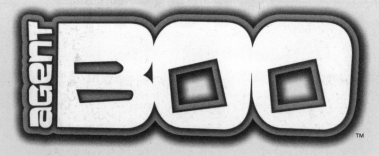
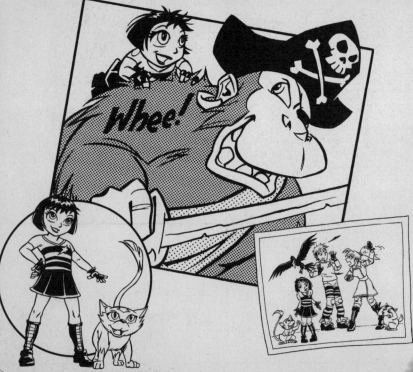

This is the back of the book.
You wouldn't want to spoil a great ending!

This book is printed "manga-style," in the authentic Japanese right-to-left format. Since none of the artwork has been flipped or altered, readers get to experience the story just as the creator intended. You've been asking for it, so TOKYOPOP® delivered: authentic, hot-off-the-press, and far more fun!

DIRECTIONS

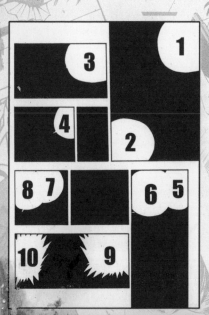

If this is your first time reading manga-style, here's a quick guide to help you understand how it works.

It's easy… just start in the top right panel and follow the numbers. Have fun, and look for more 100% authentic manga from TOKYOPOP®!

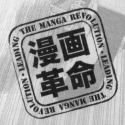